T0327509

GROWING PAINS

Eric G. **Flamholtz** and Yvonne **Randle**

GROWING PAINS

Building Sustainably Successful Organizations®

——————

5TH EDITION

WILEY

This book is printed on acid-free paper. ♾

Copyright © 2016 by Eric G. Flamholtz and Yvonne Randle. All rights reserved

Published by John Wiley & Sons, Inc., Hoboken, New Jersey
Published simultaneously in Canada

No part of this publication may be reproduced, stored in a retrieval system, or transmitted in any form or by any means, electronic, mechanical, photocopying, recording, scanning, or otherwise, except as permitted under Section 107 or 108 of the 1976 United States Copyright Act, without either the prior written permission of the Publisher, or authorization through payment of the appropriate per-copy fee to the Copyright Clearance Center, 222 Rosewood Drive, Danvers, MA 01923, (978) 750-8400, fax (978) 646-8600, or on the web at www.copyright.com. Requests to the Publisher for permission should be addressed to the Permissions Department, John Wiley & Sons, Inc., 111 River Street, Hoboken, NJ 07030, (201) 748-6011, fax (201) 748-6008, or online at www.wiley.com/go/permissions.

Limit of Liability/Disclaimer of Warranty: While the publisher and author have used their best efforts in preparing this book, they make no representations or warranties with respect to the accuracy or completeness of the contents of this book and specifically disclaim any implied warranties of merchantability or fitness for a particular purpose. No warranty may be created or extended by sales representatives or written sales materials. The advice and strategies contained herein may not be suitable for your situation. You should consult with a professional where appropriate. Neither the publisher nor the author shall be liable for damages arising herefrom.

For general information about our other products and services, please contact our Customer Care Department within the United States at (800) 762-2974, outside the United States at (317) 572-3993 or fax (317) 572-4002.

Wiley publishes in a variety of print and electronic formats and by print-on-demand. Some material included with standard print versions of this book may not be included in e-books or in print-on-demand. If this book refers to media such as a CD or DVD that is not included in the version you purchased, you may download this material at http://booksupport.wiley.com. For more information about Wiley products, visit www.wiley.com.

Library of Congress Cataloging-in-Publication Data:

Flamholtz, Eric G., author.
    Growing pains : Building Sustainably
Successful Organizations / Eric G. Flamholtz and Yvonne Randle. – Fifth edition.
        pages cm
    Includes index.
    ISBN 978-1-118-91640-7 (cloth)
    ISBN 978-1-118-91641-4 (ePDF)
    ISBN 978-1-118-91642-1 (ePub)
 1. New business enterprises–Management. 2. Organizational change. I. Randle, Yvonne, author. II. Title.
    HD62.5.F535 2016
    658.4′063–dc23
                                                                                        2015025337

Cover Design: Wiley
Cover Image: © iStock.com/Studio-Pro

Printed in the United States of America

10 9 8 7 6 5 4 3 2 1

CONTENTS

PREFACE

Growing Pains deals with the problems of building sustainably successful organizations® over the long term. The first edition of this book—published in 1986 and titled, *How to Make the Transition from Entrepreneurship to a Professionally Managed Firm*—was written after Eric Flamholtz became aware of the paucity of theory, research, and tools for the management of entrepreneurial organizations.

Prior to the first edition of this book, most if not virtually all of business education ignored entrepreneurship and focused instead on "business administration." This meant focusing on large established companies such as Bank of America, Boeing, Exxon, IBM, McDonald's, Procter & Gamble, and similar institutional "blue chip" companies that had already been in existence for many decades. There was very little literature or cases about starting entrepreneurial firms, or about what we like to think of as "organizational scale-up," the process of transitioning from a successful start-up to a much larger size and different stage of growth.

Now, three decades later, entrepreneurship is an established academic field. Entrepreneurs like Howard Schultz (Starbucks), Richard Branson (the Virgin Group), and the late Steve Jobs (Apple), and more recently Elon Musk (Tesla), Jack Ma (Alibaba), and Mark Zuckerberg (Facebook) are business icons and business heroes. However, there still remains a large gap in the published literature to explain the process of transitioning from the start-up phase of early entrepreneurship to the end-game phase of becoming a sustainably successful organization (or institution) like Starbucks, Apple, or Amgen. Filling this gap is and has been (for almost 40 years) our primary academic and practical focus.

During this period, we have developed one model to explain the determinants of organizational success, another to identify the stages in an organizational life cycle, and a third to explain the origin and underlying causes of growing pains (which occur when an organization has not developed the infrastructure required by its size and complexity at a given stage of growth). Initially, these models were developed to help explain the process of transition from the entrepreneurial stage to the professional management stage (see Chapter 3) in the life cycle of a business enterprise. Later we realized that what we had actually developed was an explanation or general theory of organizational success and failure at different stages of growth.

Purpose and Focus

The overall purpose of this book is to help readers understand what it takes to continue to grow an organization successfully after a new venture or entrepreneurship has been established. Specifically, it provides a lens or framework and related tools to help people understand how to manage organizational growth successfully at different stages from a start-up to a dominant world-class company like a Starbucks.

Unfortunately, too many entrepreneurial companies founder after promising or even brilliant beginnings. Companies such as Boston Market, People Express, Maxicare, and Osborne Computer were all once cited as great entrepreneurial successes, yet all have failed. In the face of these failures and difficulties, some cynical observers have even begun to define an entrepreneur as someone, such as Adam Osborne (who created the first portable computer) or Robert Campeau (a Canadian shopping center developer), who can start and build a company to a given level and then watch it fail.

Similarly, many established companies such as GM, Kodak, Sears, Reuters, and Xerox experience difficulties after decades of success. Some fail and others become no more than corporate zombies, with little life left in them. Xerox was once an icon of corporate success; people would say, "We want to be the next Xerox." Sadly, no one says that anymore. How did this happen? Can symbols of once-great corporate success be revitalized? How can this process be managed?

Our experience in doing research and consulting with many different types of companies in many different places in the world has led us to write this book to help present and potential entrepreneurs and CEOs of established companies (as well as their employees, advisers, bankers, and venture capitalists) understand the pitfalls typically faced by organizations at different stages of growth and to explain how to become sustainably successful over the long term. It is also intended to help governmental policymakers understand the causes of the premature demise of entrepreneurial companies that are so vital to our economy. Although this book will not solve all the problems faced by companies, our experience (as well as the positive feedback we received about the previous editions) indicates that if the ideas and methods described in this book are applied, organizations will have a significantly improved likelihood of sustainable success.

While earlier editions of this book focused almost exclusively on the transition from what we have termed an "entrepreneurship to an entrepreneurially oriented, professionally managed business" (organizations from start-up to approximately $100 million in annual revenues), this edition focuses on *all* stages of growth. We have also included new ideas and concepts (which we have developed over the past few years) as well as new examples and cases of companies—not just in the United States, but also in several other countries around the world. Stated differently, the strategic intent is to refresh the book and make it even more relevant to organizations through their entire life cycle from inception to decline and revitalization.

Intended Audience

This book is addressed to anyone interested in organizational success and failure. This includes the owners, managers, and employees of companies ranging from start-ups to global leaders to those in need of revitalization. The concepts, frameworks, and tools described in this book will also be of interest to investors, bankers, and venture capitalists, and to students and management scholars who are interested in answering the fundamental question, "Why, after successful or even brilliant beginnings, do companies often lose their way with many (if not most) even experiencing decline and bankruptcy?"

To answer this question, we identify the underlying factors that promote long-term success and describe what organizations must do to successfully manage the transitions they face as they grow. Case studies of companies at different stages of growth—drawn from a wide variety of industries—are included to illustrate different aspects of the transitions that must be made over the entire life cycle of organizations. The cases also show how the frameworks provided in this book can be used as conceptual maps of what needs to be done by an organization at each developmental stage. In addition, the book specifies the adjustments the founder or the CEO of an entrepreneurial company needs to make so that he or she can grow with the organization (as Howard Schultz did at Starbucks) and not be left behind.

Overview of the Contents

While this edition of *Growing Pains* focuses on the entire life cycle of an organization (versus exclusively on the transition from an entrepreneurship to a professionally managed organization) and what it takes to build a sustainably successful enterprise over the longer term, its title has remained unchanged. The title *Growing Pains* is still very relevant, even for the advanced stages of growth, and even when growth has ceased. For the absence of growth is, in a sense, a growing pain as well. Our research and practical experience in working with a wide variety of organizations over almost 40 years suggest that all organizations experience growing pains as a normal part of their development. Growing pains indicate that the company has outgrown its infrastructure and that it must develop new systems and processes, as well as a new structure, to support its size. When organizations ignore growing pains, significant problems and even failure can result.

The book's underlying framework and content are applicable to all organizations, from very small startups to very large companies, nonprofits, and even mega-companies such as IBM, Johnson & Johnson, and Walmart. In earlier editions, Starbucks was used as an example of a rapidly growing entrepreneurial company that had applied many of the concepts and methods in this book. Today, Starbucks has joined the elite group of world-class giants. The concepts, frameworks, methods and tools described in this book are still relevant to Starbucks and to other organizations of all sizes.

This book is divided into three parts. Part One begins with a chapter that provides an overview of the issues facing entrepreneurs and CEOs as they attempt to grow their organizations. It examines both the personal and the organizational issues and related transitions required. This is followed by four chapters that focus on frameworks for understanding organizational effectiveness and transitions: an organizational effectiveness model, an organizational life-cycle model, and a model to explain the origin and underlying causes of "growing pains" that occur when an organization has not developed the "infrastructure" required by its size and complexity at a given stage of growth. The organizational effectiveness model, termed the Pyramid of Organizational Development (discussed in Chapter 2) explains the variables that must be managed by companies to give them the optimal (most likely) chance of long-term success. The life-cycle model (discussed in Chapters 3 and 4) identifies seven stages of growth from a new venture (corporate birth) to an established organization in decline and requiring revitalization. Chapter 3 focuses on the first four stages of growth from a new venture to a mature organization, while Chapter 4 focuses on the advanced stages of growth in the organizational life cycle. The growing pains framework is discussed in Chapter 5.

Part Two presents the most significant managerial tools that can be used to build sustainably successful business enterprises: strategic planning, organizational structure, control/performance management systems, management and leadership development, and corporate culture management. Although the tools of planning, structural design, and the like may be, at least superficially, familiar to some readers, our approach to these key components of a management system differs in some very important respects from others; there is also an integrative aspect to the set of management systems components overall.

Part Three deals with some special issues and topics relating to organizational development and transitions. It includes a chapter dealing with the application of the concepts and frameworks to nonprofits. It also introduces the concept of a leadership molecule and deals with the key aspects of strategic and operational leadership. Finally, Chapter 13 presents several comprehensive case studies of companies that have used the concepts, methods, and tools described in this book to support their continued success.

Key Differences

This fifth edition of *Growing Pains* differs from the fourth edition in several important respects. Although the overall direction and thrust of the book have been retained, all chapters have been revised to include updated material, updated references to companies, and new case studies, as appropriate. However, in some instances we have kept certain examples because they are "classic," or prototypical, of the points we want to make, because there are no better current examples, or because of their historical significance.

Three new chapters have been added that focus upon: (1) how to use the frameworks, tools, and methods in nonprofits (Chapter 11); (2) specific leadership challenges and how to create a "leadership molecule" (Chapter 12); and (3) comprehensive case studies of the applications of our frameworks and tools and results of those applications in selected organizations worldwide (Chapter 13). In addition, we have cited new empirical research that has been published during the past several years that supports the framework and ideas presented in the book. Specifically, we present new data on "strategic organizational development" (in Chapter 2).

Throughout the book, several new cases, examples, or "mini-cases" of companies dealing successfully or unsuccessfully with growth management issues have been added. New mini-cases and international examples of entrepreneurship have been added because of the widespread flourishing of entrepreneurship around the globe, including examples from Europe, Australia, and Asia. A number of companies (including Starbucks) are used throughout the book to provide a consistent frame of reference for the perspective being developed. To a considerable extent, we have drawn on examples of companies where we have in-depth knowledge. In some cases, to protect the privacy of individuals and organizations, we have disguised the company's and individuals' names.

Conceptual Thinking

Our experience over the past 40 years in working with and coaching leaders of many companies throughout the world has shown that there is one key thing (not typically mentioned when discussing the requirement of leadership success) in addition to all of the standard things that leaders are supposed to be able to do. Specifically, this is to be able to think conceptually about their business. The ability of a leader or leadership group to step back from day-to-day operations and the concrete things that business involves is a critical ability that contributes to sustainable success of organizations.

This same cognitive ability is often the difference between great successes in virtually any activity, including sports that are very physical in nature such as American football. For example, National Football League (NFL) teams use the so-called "combine" to test for various abilities such as running speed, jumping ability, and cognitive ability. Specifically, they use the "Wonderlic Cognitive Ability Test." Because NFL football is one of the most physically demanding sports, the emphasis on cognitive ability might seem surprising. However, as coaches in the NFL undoubtedly know, there is also a conceptual aspect to the game. For example, in discussing the ability of his prized recruit at UCLA, quarterback Josh Rosen, Coach Jim Mora stated: "Josh is very intelligent. He is one of those kids that the game comes to more easily than some. He understands concepts."[1]

As the reader will see, some conceptual thinking is required by this book. However, the ability to do this type of thinking will pay great dividends.

Note

1. Chris Foster, "Rosen Is First Among QB Equals," *Los Angeles Times*, April 26, 2015, D9.

ACKNOWLEDGMENTS

This work is a product of nearly 40 years of action research and consultation with many different organizations. These range from new ventures to members of the *Fortune 500*. They were our research "laboratory." Simply stated, the most significant ideas that underlie this book were the products of observing, analyzing, and conceptualizing what actually happened in successful and unsuccessful organizations as they grew. The book could not have been written without having had access to those companies of various sizes, in different industries, with different degrees of success. Accordingly, we are greatly indebted to the CEOs, presidents, senior managers, and others who invited us to serve as researchers, consultants, or advisers for their organizations. (Many of these companies are not mentioned by name, to preserve their privacy. In some cases, fictitious names are used; in others, examples are cited without the company being named at all.)

The data presented in Chapters 2, 5, and 11 are drawn from the organizational effectiveness database compiled by Management Systems Consulting Corporation. They are derived from a survey developed by Eric Flamholtz. Omar Aguilera, Senior Consultant with our firm, Management Systems, assisted in the preparation and interpretation of some of the data (updated from the fourth edition) dealing with organizational growing pains and strategic organizational development.

We want to also acknowledge the help that Clara Penny, Management Systems' Vice President of Finance and Administration, provided in preparing the manuscript of this fifth edition. And, we would like to thank the other members of the Management Systems team—Leslie McKenna and Michael Tan—for their support.

Although we acknowledge with gratitude the contributions of all those cited, we remain responsible for the book and its imperfections.

Eric G. Flamholtz
Yvonne Randle
Los Angeles
April 2015

A Framework for Developing Successful Organizations

This first part of *Growing Pains* identifies the determinants of organizational success and provides a framework for understanding the key transitions that organizations and their leaders face as they grow. It also focuses on helping the entrepreneur or company leader understand and manage the personal transitions as well as organizational transitions that are required to support the enterprise's continued successful development.

The First Challenge for Entrepreneurs

The first challenge that entrepreneurs face is establishing a successful new venture. The basic skills necessary to meet this challenge are the ability to recognize a market need and the ability to develop (or to hire other people to develop) a product or service appropriate to satisfy that need.

If these two fundamental things are done well, a fledgling enterprise is likely to experience rapid growth. At this point, whether the entrepreneur recognizes it or not, the game begins to change. The organization's success creates its next set of problems and challenges to survival.

As a result of expanding sales, resources become stretched very thin. A seemingly perpetual and insatiable need arises for more inventory, space, equipment, people, funds, and so on. Day-to-day activities are greatly sped up and may even take on a frenzied quality.

The business's operational systems (those needed to facilitate day-to-day activities), such as marketing, production or service delivery, accounting, credit, collections, and personnel, typically are overwhelmed by the sudden surge of activity. There is little time to think, and little or no planning takes place because most plans quickly become obsolete. People become high on their own adrenaline and merely react to the rush of activity.

At this point the organization usually begins to experience some, perhaps all, of the following "organizational growing pains":

- People feel that there are not enough hours in the day.
- People spend too much time "putting out fires."
- Many people are not aware of what others are doing.
- People lack an understanding of the company's ultimate goals.
- There are not enough good managers.
- People feel that "I have to do it myself if I want to get it done correctly."
- Most people feel that the company's meetings are a waste of time.
- Plans are seldom made and even more seldom followed upon, so things often do not get done.
- Some people feel insecure about their place in the company.
- The company has continued to grow in sales but not to the same extent in profits.

These growing pains are not merely problems in and of themselves, they are a symptom of the underlying problem that there is an "organizational development gap" between the infrastructure required by the organization and the infrastructure it actually has. An organization's infrastructure consists of the resources, operational support systems and management systems, and culture required to enable the organization to function profitably on a short- and long-term basis. As described further in Chapter 2, a company's resources consist of the human capital, financial capital, and physical assets of an enterprise. Operational support systems consist of all the day-to-day systems required to produce a product or deliver a service and to function on a day-to-day basis. Management systems consist of the organization's planning system, organization structure, management development system, and performance management system. "Culture" refers to the values, beliefs, and norms that drive the behavior of people in the enterprise as well as the "system" for culture management (whatever that might be). These are the systems required to manage the overall enterprise on a long-term basis.

The Second Challenge for Entrepreneurs

Once an organization has identified a market and has begun to produce products or services to meet the needs of customers within that market, it will begin to grow. As the business grows, it will be faced with the need to make a fundamental transformation or metamorphosis from the spontaneous, ad hoc, free-spirited enterprise that it has been to a more formally planned, organized, and disciplined entity. The organization must move from a situation in which there are only informal plans and people simply react to events to one in which formal planning is a way of life; from one in which jobs and responsibilities are undefined to one in which there is some degree of definition of responsibilities and mutually exclusive roles; from one in which there is no accountability or control systems to one in which there are objectives, goals, measures, and related rewards specified in advance as well as formal performance appraisal systems; from one in which there is only on-the-job training to one in which there are formal management development programs; from one in which there is no budget to one in which there are budgets, reports, and variances; and, finally, from a situation in which profit simply happens to one in which there is an explicit profit goal to be achieved. In brief, the company must make the transition from an entrepreneurship to what we term "an entrepreneurially oriented, professionally managed organization."

As we will see in Chapter 1, this is a time when the very personality traits that initially made the founder-entrepreneur so successful can lead to organizational demise. Most entrepreneurs have either a sales or technical background, or they know a particular industry well. Entrepreneurs typically want things done in their own way. They may be more intelligent or have better intuition than their employees, who come to rely on their bosses' omnipotence. Typical entrepreneurs tend to be "doers" rather than managers, and most have not had formal management training, although they may have read the current management best-sellers. They like to be free of "corporate restraints." They reject meetings, written plans, detailed organization of time, and budgets as the trappings of bureaucracy. Most insidiously, they think, "We got here without these things, so why do we need them?" Unfortunately, the nature of the organization has changed—and so must its senior management.

There is no one pattern for a successful transition from an entrepreneurship to a professionally managed enterprise. Whatever path is followed, the key to a successful change is for the entrepreneur to recognize that a new stage in the organization's life cycle has been reached and that the former mode of operation will no longer be effective.

Making an Organizational Transition

As an organization grows, it will, in fact, face not just one but several significant transitions and transformations that need to be managed. A key question for senior leaders (whether they are the entrepreneur of a new company or the CEO of a billion-dollar-plus company), then, is, "What should we do to take the organization successfully to the next stage of growth?" To answer this question satisfactorily, it is necessary to understand that there are predictable stages of organizational growth, certain key developmental tasks that must be performed by the organization at each growth stage, and certain critical problems that organizations typically face as they grow. This understanding, in turn, requires a framework within which the determinants of successful organizational development may be placed.

Part One of this book focuses on identifying these determinants of success, on the identification of the predictable stages of organizational growth (each requiring transitions), and on the personal transitions that entrepreneurs and other leaders need to make to support the transitions from one stage of growth to the next.

Chapter 1 deals with the personal and organizational transitions that are necessary during the life cycle of a business enterprise. It examines a variety of personal and professional changes or transitions that must be made by the chief executive officer or "CEO" as a company grows. These individual transitions include the changing nature of the CEO's role, changes in managerial style, and the behavioral and attitudinal changes required to support successful organizational transitions. It also examines the strategic and "architectural design" changes required for healthy organizational development as a company grows over time.

Chapter 2 presents a holistic framework for successful organizational development. It deals with the issue of what makes an organization successful and profitable. Drawing on research and experience from consulting with organizations of all sizes and types over nearly 40 years, it presents a systematic approach to understanding the six critical variables that determine organizational effectiveness. It examines these six critical tasks of organizational development and describes what must be done to accomplish each. Chapter 2 presents a method for self-assessment of the strength of a business in terms of these variables, which we call the Pyramid of Organizational Development. A database is provided for the reader's comparison of their company's "strategic development scores" with that of other businesses.

Chapters 3 and 4 together identify and examine the seven different stages of organizational growth, from the inception of a new venture through the early maturity of an entrepreneurial organization, and to the ultimate decline and revitalization of a company. Chapter 3 focuses upon the first four stages of growth from a new venture to scale-up, and from scale-up to professionalization of the enterprise as well as consolidation. Taken together, the four stages described in Chapter 3 comprise the period or era from an entrepreneurial start-up through transformation to becoming an entrepreneurially oriented professionally managed enterprise. Chapter 4 examines the remaining three stages—diversification, integration, and decline-revitalization. These chapters also examine the relative emphasis that must be placed on each of the six critical developmental tasks at each stage of the organization's growth.

Chapter 5 identifies and describes the growing pains that all developing organizations experience. It provides a method for assessing these growing pains and determining their severity. Senior managers need to be able to recognize such growing pains as symptoms of the need to make changes in their organizations. Chapter 5 also presents a method for self-assessment of the "growing pains" being experienced by a business as well as for interpreting the degree of "risk" of problems (including ultimate failure) facing the company. A database is provided for the reader's comparison of their company's growing pains scores with that of other businesses.

Taken together, the ideas in Chapters 1 through 5 provide a conceptual map of the "tasks" that must be focused upon to build a sustainably successful business. Part One also provides a guide for analyzing and planning the transitions that must be made in moving a company from one developmental stage to the next.

CHAPTER 1

Transitions Required to Build Sustainably Successful Organizations®

It is well established that approximately 50% of all new ventures will fail within five years. For every Southwest Airlines that succeeds, there is a People Express that goes bankrupt. For every Facebook, there is a Myspace that was once popular, but that is now an afterthought. For every Starbucks, there is a Diedrich Coffee that failed. For every Dell, there is an Osborne Computer (who very few people even remember—even though it reached $100 million in sales revenue in three years before going bankrupt, and was a leader in personal computers prior to the founding of Dell).

It is a great achievement to create a successful start-up, given their 50% failure rate. It is an even greater challenge to create a company that is sustainably successful over "the long run." As we view it, the long run relates to sustainable success over several *decades*. At a minimum, it involves success over at least two generations of company leaders. In sports such as baseball, basketball, or football, it is possible to have sustained success with a specific group of players and a single coach; but true "sustainable success over the long run" exists only when leadership has passed from generation to generation with sustained success. One company that has achieved this is General Electric (GE). Founded in 1878, GE continues to be a global leader. Another is Heineken, the Netherlands-based beer company. Heineken was founded in 1864, and also continues to be a world leader in its space. A third is Toyota. Toyota, focused on the production of automobiles, was founded in 1933 as a department of Toyoda Automatic Loom Works, which itself traces its history to 1926. Toyota Motors was created as a spinoff from the parent company as Toyota Motor Company in 1937.

Sustainable success for a long period is very challenging, but possible, as shown by GE, Heineken, and Toyota. It is difficult even over a relatively shorter period such as 15 years. A comparison of companies listed on the Nasdaq stock exchange from 2000 to 2015 shows that there were significant changes in the composition of the top listed companies by "market cap" (market capitalization, the standard measure of a public company's value).[1] Only three companies were in the top 10 on both dates: Microsoft, Intel, and Cisco. Several companies that were listed as among the top 10 in 2000 were no longer on the list in 2015, including Dell, Sun Microsystems (purchased by Oracle), JDS Uniphase, and Yahoo!.

Organizational Success, Decline, and Failure

Why are some companies able to continue to manage growth successfully over the longer term (at least 10 years) while others are not? Why are some company founders and leaders like Howard Schultz at Starbucks and Richard Branson of Virgin Group able to continue to grow with their companies, while other founders and leaders such as Donald Burr, who founded People Express (and who had an MBA from Harvard!) or Adam Osborne, who founded Osborne Computer, fail to make the required transitions as their businesses increase in size and complexity? What do successful companies and their leaders do differently compared with those that are less successful or even those that have failed? Is it simply chance or something that can be learned and managed?

Through rigorous research and analysis of organizations and their leaders over the past four decades,[2] we have answered these questions and have developed practical tools that can help leaders of companies at all sizes increase their probability of long-term success. Why, for example, did Starbucks Coffee (originally founded as a local roaster with stores in 1971 and later reconceived in 1986–1987 as a "specialty retail/café" hybrid) become a global brand and industry leader,[3] while Diedrich Coffee (which was similarly founded in 1972 and later redefined like Starbucks as a cafe in 1983) has been broken into pieces (company stores and franchised stores) and sold to competitors including Starbucks?[4] How did Starbucks become the global leader in its space even though other companies like Coffee Bean and Tea Leaf (founded 1963) and Peet's (founded 1966) existed before Starbucks was ever purchased and refocused? As we will see in the next chapter, Starbucks' success is not an accident, nor is it unique. The keys to Starbucks' success were some critical transitions made both by its founder and CEO, Howard Schultz, and by the organization itself. Starbucks developed and followed a plan, not just a classic strategic plan but one that focused upon organizational development as well.

We shall describe this in some detail and distill the lessons for other company founders and their organizations.

Lessons like these are not only important for the founders of entrepreneurial companies like Howard Schultz, Steve Jobs (Apple Computer), or John Paul DeJoria (Paul Mitchell hair products and Patron Spirits Company), they are important for venture capital and private equity investors, boards of directors, banks that lend to such companies, managers of such companies, and students of management who aspire to either start their own business or work in a company going through such transitions over time. They are also of importance to society as a whole. Companies create jobs. Successful companies create more and more jobs, while failing companies destroy jobs. For example, successful companies such as Starbucks, Google, and Apple are job-creating machines! However, when companies like Borders (retailer of books), Woolworths (specialty department store), People Express (airline) and Osborne Computer (computer manufacturer) fail, they destroy jobs and people's livelihood, and negatively impact lives.

Government programs to stimulate companies' growth have been established in countries such as Canada and Poland for just this reason. Canada created the Build in Canada Innovation Program (BCIP) to kick-start businesses and get their innovative products from the lab to the marketplace. The government of Poland has created the Polish Agency for Enterprise Development. It is a tragedy when a company fails after a promising entrepreneurial start because the entrepreneurs do not understand how to build the organization.

Building Sustainably Successful Organizations®

The purpose of our research and really, what we might describe as our life's work, is to help entrepreneurs and others understand what must be done to build sustainably successful organizations®. We have been helping organizational leaders plan for and implement the transitions required to promote long-term success for almost 40 years. This book will summarize our methods, tools, and insights in a practical and systematic way.

Two Types of Transitions Required for Sustainable Success

Our research and experience have shown that there are two different but related types of transitions that must be made at different stages of growth in order for an organization to continue to flourish and grow successfully.

One type of transition concerns the founder or ultimate leader of an organization—which is typically the chief executive officer or CEO. This person must make a variety of personal and professional changes or transitions as their company grows. These include understanding and embracing the changes in the CEO role that need to occur to effectively manage an increasingly larger and more complex organization, developing new skills, adopting a new mindset (that supports, among other things, having increasingly less direct control over results), and changing one's managerial style. For simplicity, we term these the "personal transitions."

The second type of transition relates to the organization's strategic and "architectural design." These organizational development transitions can include changes in the organization's systems, processes, or structure, as well as changes to what the company actually does (who its target customers are and what it offers them).

If these two types of transitions are not made effectively, they will have a significant impact on organizational effectiveness, efficiency, and success. In fact, the inability to make effective and appropriate personal and organizational transitions is a key underlying reason why organizations experience problems and, in some cases, fail. This chapter will focus on both types of transitions.

The Personal Transitions Facing Founders and CEOs

As organizations grow and change, those in management and leadership roles also need to grow—in their skills and capabilities—and change how they approach their roles. For example, the CEO of a start-up needs to spend his or her time very differently from that of a $1 billion enterprise. We will discuss tools and techniques for making these changes in Chapter 9. In this chapter, we focus on the very specific challenges facing the founder or the entrepreneur as his or her business grows.

Unlike the CEOs of large, *Fortune 500*–type organizations, who are typically promoted through the ranks over a period of many years, the CEO of an entrepreneurial company is typically someone who either was the founder of a company, was part of a founding group, or is the spouse or child of the founder. Examples are legion and include not only those cited above but also some other very familiar names such as Mark Zuckerberg (Facebook), Larry Ellison (Oracle), Jack Ma (Alibaba, China), Anita Roddick (The Body Shop), Martha Stewart (Martha Stewart), as well as some currently less familiar but equally significant names, including Ren Zhengfei (Huawei), Li Ning (Li-Ning, China), Isaac Larian (MGA Entertainment), and Yerkin Tatishev (Kusto Holdings, Singapore). To understand transitions that founders/entrepreneurs must make as their companies grow, it is useful to first consider who they are as people and how they got to be CEOs.

Characteristics of Entrepreneurs

Although there are no precise demographic and psychological profiles available, our experience has shown that CEOs of entrepreneurial companies tend to have certain things in common. About 90% of these people have one of three types of background: (1) a marketing background, (2) a background in some technical area, such as engineering or computers, or (3) a background in a particular industry. For example, an individual may have sold computer-related devices for a large company before deciding to start his or her own company focused on developing and producing similar products. Alternatively, a person may have been an engineer or other technical specialist and become skilled at product development before deciding to establish a new business. Finally, someone may have worked in a particular industry such as travel, executive search, construction, real estate, garment manufacturing, or a variety of technology areas including software development, computer chips, or telecommunications.

Most CEOs of entrepreneurial companies are enthusiastic about markets and products but are not very interested in management or the "nuts and bolts" of day-to-day operations. Many of them find accounting boring. They have no more interest in their own accounting system than the typical homeowner has in the household's plumbing: They want it to work, but they do not care to understand how it works. Many tend to look at financial statements only to determine "the bottom line."

Entrepreneurs are typically above average in intelligence, willing to take risks, uncomfortable in environments in which they are told what to do, want things done quickly, and are fond of seeing things done their way. Most, but not all, do not have good listening skills and many seem to have ADD (attention deficit disorder). They are like butterflies flitting from one thing to the next, or like Tennessee Williams's proverbial "cat on a hot tin roof."[5] Anyone who has spent serious time with many entrepreneurs will recognize the behavior that includes an inability to focus on one thing for very long, an ingrained impatience, and an expectation of virtually instant results. One colleague estimates that 90% of entrepreneurs have the ADD syndrome.

Most of these CEOs have made open-ended commitments to their business, which means that business does not merely consume a great deal of their life; in most instances, their business is their life. The pejorative term *workaholic*, however, would be a misleading description of such people; rather, they view the business as a very complex, infinitely interesting game. It is a source of profound personal pleasure.

Entrepreneurs are accustomed to being the dominant person in business situations. Above all, entrepreneurs possess a strong desire to be independent of others' ability to control their behavior. They like to feel in control. The typical CEO of an entrepreneurial company either consciously or unconsciously values control both as an end in itself and as a means to other ends. This personal preference has most likely been reinforced in a variety of ways for a relatively long time.

The Impact of the Need for Control on Continued Successful Growth

In the early stages of organizational growth, the typical attributes of an entrepreneurial CEO are beneficial and necessary for the company. Fledgling enterprises need strong direction and open-ended commitment to make everything work properly. At this time, a compulsive CEO who knows about everything that is going on and who pays attention to the smallest detail will have a tremendous positive impact on operations.

As the organization increases in size, however, an entrepreneurial CEO's typical way of doing things (and personality) can begin to adversely affect success. Specifically, everyone in the company (including the CEO) may have become used to the idea that almost every issue—whether major or not—will be brought to the CEO's attention for decision or final approval. In other words, the CEO may have become an unwitting bottleneck in the organization. More insidiously, if the CEO has not been extremely careful, an entire organization inadvertently may have been built on people weaker than the CEO. Even though the business has grown in size and added many managers and professional specialists, the CEO may remain the most skilled person in the company in most, if not all, areas. This means that the CEO has not been able to increase the company's capabilities beyond his or her own admittedly considerable personal skills. Such a situation puts limits on the organization's capacity to grow and develop.

The CEO's desire for personal control over everything done in the organization, which was a considerable strength during the start-up stage, thus becomes a limitation or bind on the company during later stages of growth. The CEO's need to control everything can lead to an unintended dysfunctional consequence of slowing an organization down to a bureaucratic pace.

Also, some CEOs consciously want to retain control at all costs and therefore do not want to hire people who are better than they are at any particular task. Others are afraid that if they hire someone to perform a task that they cannot do themselves, they will become too dependent on that person. For example, the CEO of one service firm with $5 million in annual revenues was doing most of the company's computer programming work himself. When asked why he was spending his time in this way, he replied, "If I had someone else do it, I would be vulnerable if he left me."

Some CEOs are able to recognize their own limitations relative to their companies' changing needs. As one founder and CEO of an entrepreneurial company aptly stated, "I'm an entrepreneur.

I'm very good at controlling things—making a decision and seeing it accomplished by sheer willpower alone, if necessary. But our company has grown beyond that style. I'm not uncomfortable with the company, but I'm not as effective." Such CEOs realize that, for the good of the enterprise, they need to make the transition from a manager who is used to controlling everything and being the center of all that happens to someone who is still important but is not an omnipresent, omnipotent figure.

Even when the need for it is recognized, however, this type of change can be stressful. For some CEOs, whose identities are closely bound up with their companies, it represents a threat—a potential loss of perceived potency. Many CEOs are simply not able to give up control to any significant degree and end up strangling their organizations.

Some CEOs go through the motions of giving up some degree of control because intellectually they know that this is essential; but emotionally they cannot really bring themselves to do it. For example, one entrepreneur built an organization that achieved a billion dollars in revenues in less than one decade. Recognizing that the size of the enterprise now made it impossible for him to manage in the old way, he brought in two heavyweights—experienced professional managers whom he had to pay high salaries to attract. One was a marketing manager, and the other was a finance-oriented manager who would be responsible for day-to-day operations. The entrepreneur himself moved up to chairperson. Unfortunately, he then proceeded to turn the professional managers into managerial eunuchs. When the organization began to do poorly, he announced that he had experimented with professional managers but, reluctantly, he had to reassume personal control himself. Similarly, this was the root cause of Steve Jobs' battles with John Sculley during his first term at Apple (which ended in 1985). Steve Jobs was, in common parlance, a control freak.

The Tendency to Stick to a Success Formula

Another barrier to continued successful growth relates to the understandable human tendency to repeat what has worked in the past. If a success formula has worked in the past, it is reinforced by success, and tends to be repeated—even after the conditions that enabled it to be successful have changed. For the founder and CEO, many factors reinforce the set of behaviors that has been successful, including conventional wisdom that says, "If it ain't broke, don't fix it." The problem is that organizational success leads to changes in the key underlying determinant of future success—that is, size. Size matters in business as well as in other areas of life. The greater the size of an organization, the greater its complexity. This, in turn, means that managing and leading the business will also be more complex. Like a rubber band that is stretched to its ultimate breaking point, an organization will inevitably grow to a size where the success formula that created its success (including the way that the CEO has managed and led the business and its development) will no longer function as well and will require change.

The Core Dilemma Facing the CEO or Founder

All of the critical characteristics of a founder or CEO of an entrepreneurial company combine to create what can be characterized as the core dilemma that must be resolved if an organization is going to continue to grow successfully over time: *The mindset, skills, and capabilities of entrepreneurial leadership that led to initial success are no longer sufficient or appropriate for future success once an organization reaches a certain critical size.* Specifically, at some point, the significant or possibly total focus on markets and products, and the lack of interest in and subsequent neglect of management of the nuts and bolts of day-to-day operations will turn strength into a limitation. Similarly, the willingness and desire to personally "do whatever is necessary" (and, in turn, control everything) will also turn from strength to a limitation. Taken together, this means that the entrepreneurial success formula must inevitably change, if success is to continue.

Aligning the Entrepreneur's Mindset to Support Continued Successful Growth

There are three key ideas that must be embraced by company leaders as their organizations grow. First, a key notion that must be embraced is that *past success is not a guarantee of future success.* This means that both the mode of operation and the way that a company is operated must inevitably change. This also typically means that the founder or CEO and his or her team will need to develop new skills and change the way that they execute their roles.

The second key idea that must be embraced is that *infrastructure matters.* When a company is founded and begins to grow, the most important questions are: "Do we have market?" "Do we have a product or service that is desired by the market?" and "Can we make a profit providing that product or service to the market?" If these questions are answered in the affirmative, the company will be successful and grow—at least for a while. At a certain point in this growth, however, significant attention needs to be devoted to developing the infrastructure required to continue to grow and operate successfully. As used here, "infrastructure" relates to the resources, systems, processes, structure, and organizational culture required to support effective and efficient day-to-day operations and continued growth. Just as a city or nation requires an infrastructure to facilitate growth, so does an economic organization like a company require an infrastructure.

The problem with focusing upon and developing organizational infrastructure is twofold. Although it is not typically an objective that excites or energizes an entrepreneurial leader, infrastructure is as critical to a business as to a house. In a house, when you turn on the lights or the water tap, you want it to work flawlessly, but you might not really care about whether or not you have certain types of wiring or copper pipes. You might well be much more concerned about the decorations and furnishings of the house. You *know* that wiring and pipes are important, but the details are not inherently interesting. With organizational infrastructure, the entrepreneur might know that it is important, but not find it inherently interesting.

The third key notion that must be changed or managed is that developing infrastructure (systems, processes, etc.) means creating bureaucracy. Infrastructure implies process and systems; and processes and systems (to many entrepreneurs) imply bureaucracy. Since bureaucracy is the mortal enemy of innovation and entrepreneurship, an entrepreneurial leader might recoil at the thought of embracing what seems to be tantamount to bureaucracy—just as he or she might not want to embrace a poisonous snake! Another challenge for the entrepreneurial leader, then, is to understand that not only is infrastructure important, but that it does not necessarily mean creating bureaucracy.

The construct we use as the basis for the vision of the required transformation is *making the transition from an early stage entrepreneurship to an entrepreneurially oriented, professionally managed organization.* This means that the organization must develop the processes, systems, and capabilities to manage the large, more complex enterprise it has (or will soon) become. Many entrepreneurs also equate professional management with bureaucracy, and reject that as an aspiration. For example, Steve Jobs once referred to professional managers as "bozos," and once said: "Why would anyone respect professional managers? They can't *do anything*." This is a misunderstanding of the role and function of professional management. It also explains why Jobs was once fired by his own firm. When Jobs returned to Apple, he changed his perspective and approach and hired Tim Cook, a quintessential professional manager, who became the company's CEO in 2011.[6]

Alternatives for the CEO as the Organization Grows

Faced with the difficulties described above, what can a founder or entrepreneurial CEO do?

Four basic alternatives are available to the CEO who recognizes that the organization can no longer be run in the old way. As described below, they are: (1) do nothing and hope for the best, (2) sell the business and start over, (3) move up to chairperson and bring in a professional manager to run the organization, or (4) make a systematic effort to change personal behavior to fit the needs of the company at its new stage of development. Let us look more closely at each of these alternatives.

Business as Usual. First, the CEO can do nothing—or, rather, do "business as usual"—and hope for the best. This could be called the "ostrich strategy." The strongest argument for this course of action is that the company has been successful with its current style to date, and "If it's not broken, don't fix it." Unfortunately, corporate graveyards are littered with companies that had promising starts but, because of this strategy, did not continue to develop.

Sell the Business and Start Over Again. A second strategy is for the entrepreneurial CEO to sell the company when it gets too big to continue with an entrepreneurial style, and then set about building a new company. A variation on this theme is merging with another company to bring in new senior managers. This was the strategy of Steve Jobs, who began to develop a new company, "Next," after leaving Apple. This means the founder must become a serial entrepreneur. Some founders are capable of doing this, while for others their business was a one-idea opportunity that cannot be repeated.

Bring in a Professional Manager. The third strategy is for the CEO to become chairperson and bring in a professional manager to run the business. When a founder has sufficient self-insight to realize that he or she is really an entrepreneur or "creative person" and not really an executive, this can be an attractive option. The founder can become the Chief Creative Officer (or whatever other title seems appropriate) and turn over operation to others more capable of running an organization. A great example of this is Mark Zuckerberg, founder of Facebook. As Zuckerberg has stated, "I'm not an operator."[7] Some of our clients have also pursued this alternative—including a package delivery business, where the founder realized he was "not CEO material" and hired a CEO to whom he reported (as COO) on an operational level. The founder was, of course, the owner of the company and had to approve the CEO's recommended strategic plan and capital expenditure budgets. He was also disciplined enough not to throw his weight around and overrule the CEO's managerial decisions and actions, even when long-term employees came complaining about something. As a result, he did not undermine his CEO.

A variation on this theme is for the entrepreneur to turn over the CEO position to another individual in the business who is better suited to handle the CEO position. This was done reasonably successfully by Howard Schultz at Starbucks who turned the business over to Orin Smith. However, after Smith retired from Starbucks, the next successor, Jim Donald, came from outside the organization and was later fired, with Schultz returning to the position of CEO. Schultz later stated that Starbucks would never again hire someone in that position from outside the organization who did not deeply understand the company's distinctive culture.

Change Behavior, Skills, and Role. Finally, a CEO may choose to make the personal and managerial style changes necessary to be able to take the organization to its next growth stage successfully. This can also involve a redefinition of the CEO's role. We will provide more detail on the specifics of leadership transitions in the context of leadership development—the subject of Chapter 9.

As described earlier in this chapter, a critical ingredient in the success of such an attempt is the CEO's willingness to live with less control over the organization and its activities. Our experience in coaching CEOs through this transition is that it is possible, but it is not easy.

Cultural factors can play a role in a CEO's willingness to give up a degree of control. In many Asian counties, founders and CEOs (both men and women) are expected to be "strong" individuals, as they typically are. The cultural expectation can lead to a situation where the CEO makes all of the major (and probably many, if not most, of the minor) decisions. This can result in the CEO being the only strong individual in the company, surrounded by "helpers" or people capable of executing tasks and decisions, but not making them. This makes the company totally dependent on the CEO and results in a self-fulfilling situation where the CEO does not expect others to be capable of making decisions and therefore makes them himself or herself. Similar expectations and behavior are also found in various Latin American countries, including Mexico.

Such a situation does not exist only in Asian and Latin American countries; there are many examples of this behavior in the United States and Europe as well. For example, in one medium-sized bank in which we worked as consultants, the founder was an exceptionally strong and dominating individual, and had "trained" other managers not to challenge him. They simply waited for him to make decisions, which they executed. After his retirement, when the next president took over, he had different expectations, and wanted a true managerial team. It took about two years to change this "obedience culture" in which people simply followed orders.

Still another factor that might limit a CEO's willingness to reduce the degree of control exercised over operations is personal experience. Some CEOs have tried to reduce their level of control, but the results have been disappointing. Other CEOs have not tried to do it themselves, but have observed others try with unsuccessful results. These are powerful barriers to changing leadership practices. For example, one CEO, who headed a residential real-estate development company we worked with for many years, had observed only negative results in decentralization of operations. He was therefore very reluctant to follow the same organizational strategy in his firm. He ultimately became convinced that a variation on this was a necessity for his company to facilitate further growth, which, in turn led to positive results.

The CEO's Existential Dilemma: What Do I Do Now?

The CEO who elects to stay with the company and delegate authority to managers now faces another problem. As more than one CEO has asked us, "What do I do now? What is my role?" It is likely to be more than a little discomforting for a person who has been hyperactive and involved in virtually all phases of an organization's activities to find that all tangible roles have been delegated and the only thing left is to be responsible for intangibles. These intangibles include ultimate responsibility for the company's vision, organizational development, and culture management.

The entrepreneurial CEO has become accustomed to being the most versatile person in the orchestra: the individual who could play violin, bass, trombone, drums, or harp. He or she could even be a one-person band. Now, however, the CEO's job is more like that of an orchestra leader. The CEO may not be at all sure that he or she likes or values this new and unfamiliar role. It does not seem to be productive in a concrete way.

In fact, this new or redefined role is indispensable. The CEO needs to focus on ensuring that the company has a clear and well-communicated vision. People need to know where the company is going and, in this sense, the CEO is the person who is responsible for charting and then working with his or her team of senior executives to keep the organization on course. The CEO is responsible for championing a holistic view of the development of the entity to ensure that there is a focus on creating strengths, overcoming limitations, and identifying areas for improvement. This function is known as "strategic organizational development." Again the CEO is not responsible for the specific organizational development initiatives; he or she is responsible for orchestrating the process. Finally, the CEO needs to focus on ensuring that there is a clear definition of the corporate culture, as well as a method for managing it. In all of these areas, the CEO is responsible for articulating the "what" (is done), but not the "how" (it is being done).

A CEO may not be equipped to handle this new role because he or she does not adequately understand this new role or have the skills required to effectively perform it, or both. Moreover, many CEOs cannot admit weakness by letting anyone guess that they know neither what to do next nor how to do it. Some try to bluff their way through by acting in an executive manner and issuing peremptory edicts. Others try to cope by becoming hyperactive, burying themselves in their work. Often, however, this is merely make-work or busy work, an attempt to fool themselves into believing that they are still doing something valuable. A CEO who does not know what to do next but is afraid to admit it and seek help is setting the stage for future organizational crises.

At this stage of the company's development, the CEO's role involves becoming a strategic leader. The focus needs to be on the future direction of the enterprise and its long-term objectives, versus doing work or managing day-to-day operations. There needs to be a focus on managing the organization's culture and on serving as a role model for others. Each of these aspects of the CEO's new role requires the ability to think abstractly or conceptually about the business rather than merely in terms of concrete products.

The Need for Organizational Transition

In addition to making personal changes, CEOs and other senior managers must face the challenge of managing organizational transitions. It is obvious that a company with $100 million in annual revenues is fundamentally different from one with annual sales of $1 million. It follows, then, that as an organization grows, it needs to develop new systems, processes, structures, and ways of managing the business (that is, it needs a different infrastructure). Through our work and research, we have identified a specific progression of infrastructure development that needs to occur to support organizational success. This progression is embedded in a "stages of organizational growth" framework that will be the subject of Chapter 3 and Chapter 4.

Building a sustainably successful business, then, involves understanding and effectively managing these stages of growth. The remainder of this book is intended to provide CEOs and their leadership teams with the information that they need to effectively develop and manage their company's infrastructure.

Transitions Required for Continuing Success: An Overview Case Example

As an introduction to the remainder of this book and to illustrate the personal and organizational transitions that typically occur as a company grows, this section presents a case study of an entrepreneur, Robert Mason and his company, Medco. Although the case selected is that of a medical products company, the issues faced by the entrepreneur and the company cited here are similar to those faced by CEOs in diverse organizations with revenue ranging from $1 million to substantially more than $1 billion. In brief, it has been selected as a prototype of a widespread phenomenon, not one that is limited to certain companies or industries.

Medco's Early History

Bob Mason, the founder of Medco, began his career as a salesman for a major medical products manufacturing and marketing firm. He worked hard to learn all he could about the industry, and discovered that the company for which he was working was not adequately meeting all of its customers' needs, and that there was an untapped market for medical products. So he decided to start his own company, a medical products business.[8]

Apparently Bob's belief about the demand for his products was accurate, because within a few years, his business began to experience rapid growth. Within five years, the company had reached more than $20 million in annual revenues, and it was estimated that within four more it would achieve $50 million in yearly sales.

The Onset of "Growing Pains"

When Medco reached $20 million in sales, and Bob Mason was feeling good about that, he also became aware that the business was beginning to experience certain organizational problems, which are what we term "growing pains," as described below:

Many People Were Not Aware of What Others Were Doing. A significant number of people did not understand what their jobs were, what others' jobs were, or what the relationships were between their jobs and the jobs of others. This problem resulted, in part, from a tendency to add personnel without developing formal descriptions of roles and responsibilities. Since employees were added on an ad hoc basis whenever a staff shortage seemed imminent, there was often little time to orient them to the organization's operations or to train them adequately in what their own responsibilities would be. Indeed, there was no formal training program.

Some people were given job descriptions, but did not adhere to their specified roles. Others were given a title, but no explicit responsibilities. Surprisingly, many individuals often did not know to whom they were to report, and managers did not know for which employees and activities they would be held accountable. People learned what they were supposed to do on a daily basis; long-range planning was nonexistent.

Interactions between Departments Was Also a Problem. Managers often did not understand what their responsibilities were and how what they were doing fit in with the firm's overall operations. New departments were created to meet Medco's product and marketing needs, but many managers were not aware of how these departments fit in with the rest of the organization. One manager complained, "People sit outside my door, but I don't even know what they do." Another new manager described his introduction to Medco as follows: "I was walked to an area and was told: 'It's your department. Run it.'"

This lack of formal roles and responsibilities made it easy for personnel to avoid responsibility whenever a task was not completed or was completed unsatisfactorily. This also led to duplication of effort between departments. Since no one knew precisely whose responsibility a particular task was, two or more departments or people often would complete a task, only to find that it had already been accomplished by someone else.

People Felt There Were Not Enough Hours in the Day. Most employees felt overloaded. They commonly stayed after hours to complete their work. Department managers, in particular, felt that their workload was too great and that deadlines were unrealistic.

This situation resulted, in part, from the lack of adequately developed day-to-day systems to support Medco employees' work. The accounting, operational planning, and communication systems were adequate for a small company, but quite inadequate for one as large as Medco had become. Systems for purchasing, inventory control, and even distribution were either poorly developed or nonexistent.

People Spent Too Much Time Putting Out Fires. Perhaps the best indication that Medco was beginning to choke on its growth was that employees spent an increasing amount of time dealing with short-term problems resulting from the lack of long-range planning. This was particularly evident in the constant lack of space within the company's headquarters. It appeared to most employees that as soon as the company increased its office space, the space already was filled, and it was time to begin planning for another move. It seemed that there was never enough space or equipment to support the company's staff adequately. When they worked at the firm's headquarters, salespeople usually arrived early to ensure they would be able to find a vacant desk from which to make their calls. Employees who did not go out into the field attempted to handle the cramped space by creating "schedules" for using phones, computers, and even desks.

Employees Began to Feel That Medco Never Planned, It Simply Reacted. A joke around the company was: "At Medco, long-range planning means what I am going to do after lunch." This was caused partly by the changes in the marketplace and the new demands placed upon the company. It also resulted from the tendency of entrepreneurial companies like Medco to spend most of their time simply staying afloat without keeping an eye on the future.

Employees began to think that, simply because crisis is the norm at the company, that is the way they should operate. They began to call themselves "the fire fighters," and even took pride in their ability to deal with crises.

There Were Not Enough Good Managers. Most managers at Medco were promoted to their positions in recognition of service. Some were good managers, but most were described by their direct reports as "good technicians who lack people skills." Further, they were seen as clones: Many employees believed that management had one and only one way of doing things, and that to deviate from the norm would result in adverse consequences.

Plenty of people had the title "manager," but relatively few really behaved as managers. After promotion, many people simply kept doing the things they had done in their former roles. They were poor delegators, often doing the work themselves rather than assigning it to others. As a result, employees came to believe that their managers did not trust them.

Bob Mason was a strong individual who wanted things done his way, and he wanted to control almost everything. He recognized this, referring to himself as "someone who sticks his nose into everything." Few decisions were made without Bob's approval or review. As a consequence, one of two things tended to happen concerning managers: (1) the stronger managers tended to butt heads with Bob and ultimately left; and (2) the remaining managers were slowly marginalized. Those managers who decided not to leave Medco tended not to take Bob on, at least directly, and they had little real authority and certainly no power. Inadvertently, Bob had created an organization of "managerial pygmies." In effect, Bob was a victim of his own need for control. This phenomenon is part of what we have previously termed the *entrepreneur's syndrome*."[9]

When Business Plans Were Made, There Was Very Little Follow-Up, and Things Did Not Get Done. As is true of many small and growing firms, Medco had traditionally operated on an ad hoc basis. No formal strategic planning system was needed, since Bob had provided all of the organization's direction. Further, the informal structure had allowed Medco's employees the freedom to generate new product and marketing ideas.

As the company grew, however, Bob and his senior management team began to realize that they needed to monitor its operations. Unfortunately, Medco had not developed the systems necessary to have accountability.

There Was a Lack of Understanding About Where the Firm Was Going. Many Medco employees complained that not only did they not know what was expected of them; they could not understand where the company was headed in the long term. This resulted from the inability of Medco's management to communicate its vision for the future to the company's personnel. Employees were aware that changes were being made, but were not always sure how these changes would affect them or their departments. Consequently, employees experienced high levels of anxiety. When this anxiety became too great, many left the firm.

Most People Felt Meetings Were a Waste of Time. Employees complained that too many meetings were held among top managers and not enough among the lower levels of the organization. In addition, those meetings that were held were often inefficient and did not result in resolutions to problems. It was because few meetings had written agendas or minutes—many of those attending described them as "free-for-alls." They were at best discussions, and at worst fights between departments or individuals. Worst of all, they went on interminably.

Moreover, people complained that most meetings were called on an ad hoc basis. Since these meetings were unscheduled, people typically came to them without any sense of their purpose and certainly with no preparation. Thus, they tended to have the atmosphere of bull sessions in which people shot from the hip. In addition, people felt that they could not plan their work because they were constantly interrupted for "crisis" meetings.

Some People Began to Feel Insecure About Their Places at the Firm. This problem grew out of the many changes taking place and the large number of problems the firm was encountering as it grew. Some original founding members were terminated and replaced. This caused people to wonder who was next. Although many recognized that some employees had not grown as the company grew, they worried about their jobs and their places within the firm. This, in turn, led people to spend an increasing amount of their time covering their vested interests.

The Company Grew in Sales but Not in Profits. Medco, like many entrepreneurial firms, traditionally had been most concerned with increasing sales. It adopted the philosophy of many growing firms: "If we're selling more, we must be making more profits." Unfortunately, this is not often the case. The other side of the profit equation, costs, often increases along with sales, and if costs are not contained, the firm soon may find itself in a position of losing, rather than making, money. Thus, although Medco sales were increasing at a rapid rate, profits were remaining relatively constant.

Medco's problems certainly are not unique. Indeed, these are the classic symptoms of what we have termed "growing pains," as will be described in detail in Chapter 5. It should be noted that while these "symptoms" represent problems in and of themselves, they also suggest a deeper, more systemic organizational problem. Specifically, they signal that the organization is coming precariously close to choking on its own growth. This, in turn, indicates that the organization must change its very nature; it must make a transition to a different kind of organization, a more professionally managed firm with processes and systems to facilitate growth.

The Need for Transitions

Bob Mason recognized that his business was experiencing problems. He realized that the organization had outgrown the current way it was being managed, and that both he and the organization needed to make some serious changes in the way things were being done.

His first step was to get deeper insight into the kinds of problems he was facing at Medco. He did a search for books that would help, and obtained a copy of an earlier edition of *Growing Pains*. After reading the book, he initiated action to help his company overcome the problems associated with growth. Specifically, he began a program of organizational development for Medco. The four specific steps in the program were as follows:

STEP I: Conduct an organizational assessment.

STEP II: Formulate an organizational development plan.

STEP III: Implement the organizational development plan.

STEP IV: Monitor progress.

Step I: Conduct an Organizational Assessment

An organizational assessment was performed to evaluate Medco's current state of development and future needs. The assessment involved collecting information from employees about their perceptions of Medco and its operations. One tool used in this process was the Growing Pains Survey©, which will be presented and described in Chapter 5. This survey measures the extent to which an organization is experiencing the 10 classic symptoms of growing pains.

At Medco, the scores on this survey ranged from 30 to 34, with an average score of 32. As explained further in Chapter 5, this indicated that the company was experiencing some "very significant problems," which required immediate attention. Specifically, the assessment revealed that the company needed to:

- Better define organizational roles and responsibilities and linkages between roles.
- Help employees plan and budget their time.
- Develop a long-range business plan and a system for monitoring it.
- Increase the number of qualified present and potential managers.
- Identify the direction the company should take in the future.
- Reduce employee and departmental feelings that they always "needed to do it themselves" if a job was to get done correctly.
- Make meetings more efficient by developing written agendas and taking and distributing meeting minutes.
- Become profit oriented rather than strictly sales oriented.

Steps II–IV: Formulate and Implement an Organizational Development Plan and Monitor Progress

Having identified its organizational problems and developmental needs, Medco proceeded to the next step: designing and implementing a program that would resolve problems and help the company develop the infrastructure necessary to accommodate its rapid growth. Management met at a retreat to design a plan for the firm. The plan included specific action steps to overcome its problems.

Some of these steps were (1) acquisition of human resources and development of operational systems needed to support current operations and continued growth; (2) implementation of a strategic plan that clearly defined where the company was going, and how it was going to get there; (3) implementation of performance management systems to motivate people to achieve the company's goals; (4) design of a management and leadership development program to help people become better managers and overcome the "doer syndrome"; (5) development of a system to explicitly manage the corporate culture. In addition, Bob began to focus on making some important changes in his own role, behavior, and attitudes.

Acquisition of Resources and Development of Operational Systems. As the company grew, so did its need for greater skills and sophistication in certain functional areas. A controller was recruited to replace the firm's bookkeeper. A national sales manager was appointed. Medco also hired a personnel director and a marketing manager. Moreover, Medco engaged a consultant to serve as its adjunct management and organizational development adviser. In brief, the firm made a significant investment in its human resources. These people, in turn, were responsible for developing the day-to-day operational systems required to manage growth in various areas.

Implementing Strategic Planning. One of the first steps Medco took to manage its growth was to develop a strategic plan and begin implementing a formal strategic planning process. The major goal of this process was to motivate the company's managers to begin to take a longer-range view than "what's happening after lunch." A related goal was to affect the corporate culture at Medco and make planning a way of life.

The process began with a two-day strategic planning retreat that focused on some fundamental issues necessary to guide the future development of the company, including:

1. What business is Medco in?
2. What are our competitive strengths and limitations?
3. Do we have a market niche?
4. What do we want to become in the long term?
5. What are the key factors responsible for our past success, and to what extent will they contribute to our future success?
6. What should our objectives and goals be for developing Medco as an organization?
7. What should our action plans be, and who is responsible for each action plan?

In addition to these generic strategic planning issues, which are relevant to all organizations, the company also examined certain company-specific strategic issues.

After the strategic planning retreat, a draft of a corporate strategic plan was prepared. This plan clearly identified the business that the company was in, its long-term goals, and its competitive strategy. The plan also included specific, measurable, time-dated, short-term goals—with each goal being assigned to a specific member of the senior leadership team. The plan was circulated among the firm's senior managers for their comments and input. It was revised and approved by Bob, and then distributed to all senior managers. The plan provided a "blueprint" for future development, including specific goals focused upon eliminating the problems leading to the company's growing pains.

Medco then held quarterly meetings to review the company's results, compare them with the plan, and make required adjustments. This signaled that the plan was more than merely a "paper plan"—it was a real management tool.

A key decision made by management during this retreat was to be more selective in accepting new business until the firm had digested its present growth by building the required infrastructure.

Performance Management Systems. Medco developed and implemented a more formal performance management system. A first step in this process was to develop a measurement system for tracking progress against each goal in the firm's strategic plan. These measurements were developed as part of an organizational development team meeting in which all of Medco's senior management participated. Once the measurements had been decided upon, the next step was for Medco to revise its information system so that the data required could be obtained. Some of the data came directly from the firm's accounting information system. For example, information about sales, gross margins, and net profitability came from this source. Other information had to be obtained separately. The firm's management team felt that one of the vital aspects of the business concerned the percentage of merchandise that was being shipped to dealers as opposed to end users. This information began to be monitored on a regular basis.

Management and Leadership Development. Bob and Medco's other senior managers realized that people were Medco's true asset. The firm's technology, products, and equipment were really not proprietary; the true differentiating factor was the motivation and skills of its people.

Recognizing this, Medco believed the company had to make an investment in building its management and leadership capabilities for two reasons. First, there simply was not a sufficient number of effective managers. Although many people had managerial titles and could recite the right buzzwords, relatively few were really behaving as managers. They were spending too much time as doers rather than managers. There was little true delegation, and insufficient effort was given to planning, organizing people, performance appraisal, and team training. Another need for management development was more symbolic. Bob recognized that some of the people who had helped build Medco to its current size were in jeopardy of becoming victims of the Peter Principle: They had been promoted to their level of incompetence. Bob felt that the company owed its people a chance to grow with it and he saw management development as a chance to provide them that opportunity. Quite frankly, he felt that if people had this opportunity and failed to grow, the organization could feel it had met its responsibilities to them.

To deal with these issues, Medco asked a consultant to design a management development program for its personnel. Two programs were developed: one for top managers and one for middle managers.

Corporate Culture. Although Bob Mason had been aware that his firm had a culture, he had never taken any serious steps to manage it. He had always wanted the firm to be sales oriented, aggressive, and profit oriented. He hadn't realized that there were also a great many other facets to the firm's culture, which had been embedded since the earliest days of its operation.

As the firm began to change, Bob became increasingly aware that he needed to manage the firm's corporate culture in order to reinforce the change. One of the unintended aspects of the firm's culture that had developed was that people felt that if they worked hard they should be rewarded regardless of the results. Bob felt that people needed to learn that hard work was simply not enough and that they had to be oriented toward bottom line results.

A second aspect of the firm's culture had been that decisions would be pushed up to Bob. Since Bob was acknowledged to be an entrepreneurial genius and since his personality had tended to lead to nuclear explosions whenever someone made a mistake, people naturally pushed decisions to his desk. Bob now wanted to reverse the culture, and push the decisions down to the lowest level of responsibility in the firm where they could be meaningfully made. The firm also tried to emphasize that under the new culture, mistakes would be examined, and corrected, but that people would not feel the brunt of a nuclear explosion if a mistake was made.

A third aspect of the Medco culture had been that "we're good crisis managers." This meant that Medco managers had to learn to turn on a dime and solve whatever crises came up. Mason now wanted Medco to revise its culture to emphasize the importance of long-range planning. He wanted the culture to become one of "planning is a way of life at Medco." A fourth aspect of the Medco culture had been "we're hands-on managers." This needed to be revised so that managers stayed in touch with operations, but delegated responsibility to the lowest level capable of performing the required tasks.

One of the most important aspects of this change was that Bob, together with the senior managers, now realized that the management of the corporate culture was an important part of the strategic leadership function that they had to perform.

Changes in the CEO. Bob Mason realized that just as Medco had to change, so did he. His basic skills were as a salesman and as an entrepreneur. He had worked hard, and he had built a successful company. He had the title of president, but he realized he was not acting like a president.

In spite of the fact that he was the CEO of the company, Bob continued to spend too much time dealing with the technical and marketing aspects of the business. This is what he knew how to do, and this is what he enjoyed. He knew he was not devoting a sufficient amount of time to the broader aspects of organizational development.

Bob also understood that there were certain other problems with his management style and capabilities. In spite of the fact that his organization had grown substantially, he still wanted to control too many details of the business. He knew he still poked his nose into too many areas of the business. He began to understand that this was not only a problem that he was facing, but his behavior was seen as a role model by other managers in the organization who, in turn, were doing the same things at their level of responsibility.

The first change that Bob made was to decide to change. He then proceeded to redefine his concept of his role. He decided to spend more time on the planning and organizational development aspects of the business and less time in many of the technical areas. He made a decision to give up control over the marketing area by delegating more responsibility than he had in the past. He decided to change his leadership style from "making all decisions" to "involving the senior leadership team" in many of the decisions that needed to be made. There were always going to be decisions where he would, in effect, have to decide what was best for the company and then announce it to the organization. However, he decided to significantly increase the extent to which his senior managers were involved in planning overall organizational changes and in making day-to-day operational decisions.

Another aspect of Bob's behavior that needed to be changed was the way he was dealing with stress. Bob, like most entrepreneurs, was constantly under a great deal of pressure. Periodically he would "explode" or as one of his managers put it, "go nuclear." When Bob went nuclear, everybody headed for the hills. If something went wrong, Bob might "nuke 'em" in a meeting. This had led, over time, to people avoiding bringing Bob bad news. In turn, this had created serious problems for the business because Bob was, at times, simply not in touch with information he and other senior managers needed to have to make effective decisions. As people began to see Bob dealing with conflict but not exploding, they became more open in discussing problems, and even disagreeing with the direction that Bob was proposing. His management team began to be a team in the true sense of the word.

Bob sent another signal to the organization about his willingness to change by participating in the organization's new management development program. As he stated: "If I want people to change, I've got to lead by example as well as by word."

Program Results

For 18 months, Medco implemented its new program of organizational development. After this period, the organizational growing pains score decreased from an average score of 32, which put the company in a red-flag danger zone, to a score of 21, which indicated some problems but nothing of major concern. This improvement occurred despite the fact that the firm continued to grow. Moreover, the firm's profitability increased significantly during this period, as a wide variety of operational inefficiencies were eliminated.

In brief, Medco had made a fundamental transformation. It had gone from a firm about to choke on its own growth to one that was able to absorb growth and operate profitably and effectively. In addition, Bob Mason had made the transition from an entrepreneur to a true CEO.

Summary

This chapter has examined the issues of success and failure typically facing organizations and their leaders after promising entrepreneurial starts. We have identified the need for continued success, and described the personal and organizational transitions to promote that continued success. We have identified and discussed the changes that the CEO needs to make as his or her organization grows, and we have examined the alternatives available to CEOs who face such transitions.

The chapter presents a comprehensive case example of the transitions required by Medco, which faced classic growing pains and developed strategies for addressing them. The steps that Medco took to identify its challenges and work to address them illustrate how an organization can build the infrastructure needed to promote sustainably successful growth. The personal challenges faced by Bob Mason, Medco's CEO, and how he addressed them provide a good example of how to make the personal transitions required to support an organization's continued successful development.

There is no one way to make a successful transition from an early-stage entrepreneurship to a future stage of growth. However, the key to making this change is for the entrepreneur to recognize that the company's former mode of operation will no longer be effective.

All change is accompanied by risk, and many of us feel uncomfortable during the process of change. Unfortunately, the need for organizational transitions and their accompanying personal changes is inevitable. Those who do not believe this are likely to increase the risk that their organizations will experience significant difficulties. However, if knowledge is truly power, then entrepreneurs and others who understand the need for the kind of transitions described in this book will be set up for the possibility of continuing success.

The remainder of this book deals with how to make these required personal and organizational transitions—beginning with the next chapter, which presents a framework (based upon research and experience) that identifies the key factors that must be focused upon in building a sustainably successful organization.

Notes

1. Dean Starkman and Russ Mitchell, "Nasdaq: Déjà vu 15 Years Later," *Los Angeles Times*, March 3, 2015, B4.
2. We have published many articles presenting our models, testing them empirically. We have also published case application articles showing how our frameworks and tools have actually been used.
3. Starbucks was originally founded by a three-man group in Seattle as a "local roaster," not a café. Howard Schultz who had worked at Starbucks left to found Il Giornale Coffee in 1986, and then purchased Starbucks and rebranded his company as Starbucks in 1987.
4. Diedrich Coffee was founded in 1983 by Martin Diedrich. It was an outgrowth of an earlier family business begun as a coffee plantation and then a local roasting store that opened in 1972. Diedrich Coffee went public in 1996. In September 2006, Diedrich Coffee announced its plans to close its company-owned retail stores, 40 of which were sold to Starbucks and reopened under that brand. Diedrich's franchisee-owned stores remained unchanged. The company continued as a roaster and wholesaler of coffee beans, with a few independently owned and operated Diedrich stores that remained open in California and Texas. On November 3, 2009, Peet's announced that it was buying Diedrich, but its offer was exceeded by Green Mountain Roasters, Inc., which currently owns the company.
5. *Cat on a Hot Tin Roof* is a play by Tennessee Williams. It was winner of the Pulitzer Prize for Drama in 1955. The use of this phrase here is not intended literally, but to suggest the motivation "to movement" by the entrepreneur.
6. Timothy "Tim" Cook spent 12 years at IBM in its personal computer business. He ultimately became the director of North American Fulfillment. Later, he served as COO of the computer reseller division of Intelligent Electronics. Finally, before joining Apple, in 1998 he was Vice President for Corporate Materials at Compaq for six months.
7. Ryan Knutson and Sam Schectner, "Zuckerberg Seeks Calm with Telecom Carriers," *Wall Street Journal*, March 4, 2015, B4.
8. This case is based upon an actual situation, but details have been changed and the company has been disguised.
9. Eric Flamholtz and Yvonne Randle, *The Inner Game of Management* (New York: AMACOM, 1987).

Building Sustainably Successful Organizations®

The Pyramid of Organizational Development

As a new venture begins to grow, the CEO and other members of senior management must simultaneously cope with endless day-to-day problems and keep an eye on the future. Making this even more difficult is that many managers of growing entrepreneurships are going through the process of building an organization for the first time. This is about as easy as navigating uncharted waters in a leaky rowboat with an inexperienced crew while surrounded by a school of sharks. The sea is unfamiliar, the boat is clumsy, the skills needed are not readily apparent or not fully developed, and there is a constant reminder of the high costs of an error in judgment.

Just as the crew of such a boat might wish urgently for a guide to help them with navigation, training, and ship repair, the senior managers of a growing enterprise may frequently wish for a guide to help them build their organization. The crew might also be glad to know that others before them have made the voyage successfully and to hear some of the lessons that the other voyagers learned in the process.

This chapter attempts to provide a guide for senior managers who are faced with the special challenge of building a sustainably successful company. It gives a framework or "lens" for understanding and managing the critical tasks that an organization must perform at each stage of its growth. The framework for organizational development that is presented in this chapter is an outgrowth of nearly four decades of research and consulting experience with organizations who have faced and dealt with the need to make a transition from one stage of growth to the next.

The Nature of Organizational Development

Organizational development is the process of planning and implementing changes in the overall capabilities of an enterprise in order to increase its operating effectiveness and profitability. It involves thinking about a business organization (or any organization, for that matter) as a whole and planning necessary changes in certain key areas in order to help it progress successfully from one stage of growth to the next. Based upon our empirical research and experience, the key areas that require focus include the organization's business foundation (the conceptual foundation on which the rest of the company's systems and processes are built), as well as six key organizational development tasks.

The Business Foundation

All business or economic organizations (including nonprofits) are based upon a conceptual foundation, which is either explicitly defined or implicitly understood. The foundation consists of three related concepts: (1) the business concept or definition, (2) the strategic mission, and (3) the core strategy.

The Business Concept. A business concept is a statement of what the organization is in business to do. It defines an organization's identity and gives it strategic focus. It provides the raison d'etre of the business. For example, Coca-Cola is in the beverage business, Federal Express is in the package transportation business, and Disney is in the entertainment business.

The overriding key problem or challenge of creating a business concept is that it must be valid or validated by customers in the marketplace. This means that the business must provide something (tangible or intangible) that the market wants or will accept. Validation occurs when there are customers who purchase the enterprise's product or service, thereby enabling it to continue to operate and survive as a business entity. When a new business concept fails to achieve this, or an existing business concept no longer works in the market, the organization will suffer and ultimately fail or die. For example, many of the first dot-coms (such as Webvan, eToys, Pets.com, and many more) did not succeed in creating valid business concepts and ultimately perished. Similarly, RadioShack was once a successful enterprise, serving several generations of electronics hobbyists; but its business concept became outdated and muddled, leading to a long period of irrelevance in the market and decline that suggests its ultimate disappearance from the retail market space.[1]

Another key strategic problem or challenge of creating a business concept is to strike a balance between one that is too narrow to facilitate future growth and one that is so broad as to be strategically meaningless. We shall deal with the development of a business concept in Chapter 6, when we address strategic planning. At this point, our primary concern is with the purpose or function of a business concept in the context of building a successful organization over the long term.

In brief, the identification and clear definition of a business concept provide the foundation on which all other aspects of the business are and should be built. The customers to be served, products offered, and the company's day-to-day systems are all built upon the foundation of the business concept, as explained below.

The Strategic Mission. While the business concept defines what an organization is, the strategic mission identifies what the enterprise wants to achieve or become. It is a statement of the strategic intent of the enterprise. It answers the question "What do we want to achieve or become?" over a defined time period. For example, in its early days (1994) Starbucks Coffee Company (now Starbucks) established the strategic mission of becoming "the leading brand of specialty coffee in North America by the year 2000." It was an aspirational statement. Similarly, in 2014, Techcombank (then the eighth largest bank in Vietnam) established the strategic mission of becoming the leading bank in Vietnam. We will discuss the nature and development of strategic missions further in Chapter 6.

The Core Strategy. While a strategic mission identifies what the enterprise wants to achieve or become, a core strategy is a statement of how the organization will compete and achieve its strategic mission. Most organizations have several strategies, but relatively few have core strategies. Core strategies depend upon the type of business. For example, the core strategy for a commodity type of business (such as Walmart, a retailer, or Rio Tinto, a mining company) is to be the low-cost provider. The *core* strategy is the central theme around which all other strategies are created. We will discuss the nature and development of core strategies further in Chapter 6. However, it must be noted here that many companies do not have core strategies. They can have lots of strategies without a true core strategy that ties all strategies together.

Six Key Organizational Development Tasks

Once a company has identified its business foundation (either implicitly or explicitly), it begins the process of developing the organization that will support this foundation. Our research[2] and consulting experience suggests that there are six organizational development areas or tasks that are critical in determining whether an organization will be successful at any particular stage of growth. Taken together, these six key tasks make up the "Pyramid of Organizational Development," shown in Figure 2.1. As can be seen in this figure, this pyramid is built upon the organization's business foundation. We will first identify and describe each key organizational development task individually and then examine the Pyramid of Organizational Development as a whole.

Identify and Define a Market and, if Possible, Create a Niche. The most fundamental prerequisite for developing a successful organization is the identification and definition of a market and, if feasible, the creation of a market niche. A market is made up of the present and potential buyers of the goods and/or services that a company intends to produce and sell. A market segment is simply a place in the market differentiated by products offered (e.g., luxury, mid-sized, compact, and used automobiles) or customers served (e.g., businesses, schools, homes, etc.). As used here, a market niche is a place within a market where a company has developed a sufficient number of sustainable competitive advantages so that it controls a market segment. Although this distinction will be discussed more fully in Chapter 6, which deals with strategic planning, it should be noted that, in contrast to popular usage and its implicit connotation, a market niche does not have to be small. A true market niche can be very large, as illustrated by Microsoft and its control over most of the operating system software in the PC market. Similarly, Amgen, a leading biotechnology-based pharmaceutical company, has a niche in the market for kidney dialysis with its product Epogen, which historically controlled about 95% of the market for this type of product. In both Microsoft's and Amgen's case, part of their niche is derived from patent protection. Another and more important contributing factor to the creation of the niche for both of these companies, however, is the focus they have placed on understanding and meeting their customers' needs.

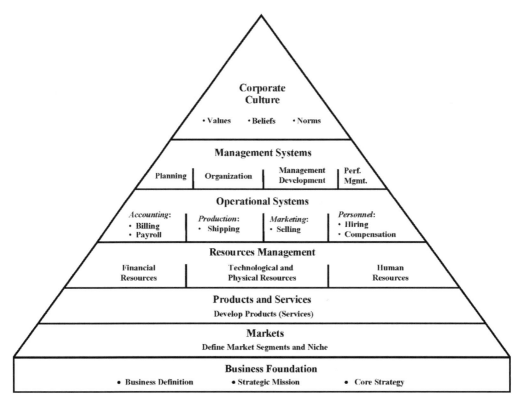

Figure 2.1   The Pyramid of Organizational Development

The first challenge to organizational survival or success, then, is identifying a market need for a product or service to which the company will seek to respond. This can be either a need that has not yet been recognized or that is not currently being satisfied by other companies. The chances for organizational success are enhanced if an organization identifies a need that is not being adequately fulfilled or that has little competition for its fulfillment. This challenge is faced by all new ventures; indeed, it is the challenge for a new venture to overcome. It has also been the critical test of growing concerns and has even brought many once proud and great companies to near ruin or total demise.

Many businesses have achieved great success merely because they were one of the first in a new market. For example, Apple Computer grew from a small entrepreneurship in a garage to a $1 billion firm in a few years because its founders identified the market for a personal computer. Dreyer's, a manufacturer of ice cream (which is a relatively undifferentiated product), went from sales of $14.4 million to sales of $55.8 million in just five years because the company saw and cultivated a market segment between the super-premium ice creams such as Häagen-Dazs and the generic (commodity) ice cream sold in most supermarkets. Many Internet companies (like Amazon.com, eBay, and Alibaba) have also experienced rapid growth as a result of developing ways to sell products leveraging this transformational technology.

The reverse side of this happy picture is seen in businesses that have experienced difficulties and even failed either because they did not clearly define their market or because they mistakenly abandoned their historical market for another. For example, a medium-sized national firm that manufactured and sold specialty clothing wished to upgrade its image and products and become a high-fashion boutique. However, it failed to recognize that its historical market was the medium market, and its efforts to rise out of this market were unsuccessful. Similarly, Custom Printing Corporation with more than $10 million in annual revenues found itself in difficulty after trying to upgrade its position in the medium-priced printing market. Attracted by the market segment where the highest-quality work was done (with accompanying high profit margins), the company purchased the best equipment available. It also hired a high-priced sales manager to recruit a sales force that could compete in the new market segment. However, the company had underestimated the strength of existing companies in that market segment, and it found itself unable to break into this higher-priced market as easily as managers had hoped. Moreover, the additional investments it had made and the related increases in its overhead made the company's cost structure higher than that of its former competitors, so it began losing business from its historical market. Thus, the company found itself in a cost-price squeeze.

The first task in developing a successful organization, then, is the definition of the market in which a business intends to compete and the development of a strategy to create a potential niche. This process involves the use of strategic market planning to identify potential customers, their needs, and so on. It also involves laying out the strategy through which the company plans to compete with others for its share of the intended market. The nature and methods of strategic planning will be described in Chapter 6.

Develop Products and Services. The second task of an entrepreneurial organization is "productization." This is the process of analyzing the needs of present and potential customers in order to design products and/or services that will satisfy their needs. For example, the founders of Google, Larry Page and Sergey Brin, met in 1995 while they were PhD students at Stanford University. They saw the need for an Internet search engine "to organize a seemingly infinite amount of information on the web."[3] By 1996, they had built a search engine (initially called BackRub) that used links to determine the importance of individual webpages.

Although many organizations are able to correctly perceive a market need, they are not necessarily able to develop a product that is capable of *sustainably* satisfying that need adequately. For example, Myspace (an online social networking service) was one of the first of its kind. It was launched in July 2003 and by April 2004 it had 1 million unique U.S. visitors. It was later acquired by News Corporation; but over time it lost its cool image and was abandoned by users. Myspace was overtaken by Facebook in the number of unique U.S. and worldwide visitors in May 2009.

Similarly, there were many companies that developed coffee bars or cafes such as Peet's Coffee, Coffee Bean and Tea Leaf, Gloria Jeans, and others; but Starbucks has grown to dominate this market. Thus, being the first to recognize a need and the so-called "first mover advantage" can be useful but is not necessarily sufficient for sustainable success.

The productization process involves not only the ability to design a "product" (defined here to include services as well) but also the ability to produce it. For a service firm, the ability to "produce" a product involves the service delivery system, the mechanism through which services are provided to customers. For example, although coffee is nominally the core product of Starbucks, the real product is the coffee experience provided by Starbucks' cafés. The company called EAS (Experimental and Applied Sciences), founded by entrepreneur Bill Phillips, markets and sells performance nutrition products. However, the company is also committed to providing education and information (provided through articles that appear in their magazine *Muscle Media* and *The Sports Supplement Review*) on what people can do to become more physically fit.

The development of successful products depends to a great extent on effective innovation *and* strategic market planning. This involves understanding potential customers, their needs, how they buy, and what they perceive to be value in a product or service.

The success of productization depends, to a very great extent, on success in defining the company's market (i.e., its customers and their needs). The greater the degree to which a company understands the market's needs, the more likely that its productization process will be effective in satisfying those needs. Productization is the second key development task in building a successful organization.

These first two tasks of organizational development can be thought of as the entrepreneurial building blocks of the enterprise. They are required for proof of concept of the business; that is, whether the business has a valid market and product. Once they are established, the next tasks relate to organizational scale-up, which involves acquiring the resources required for growth and developing the operational systems needed for day-to-day functioning of the enterprise.

Acquire Resources. The third major task of developing an organization is acquiring and developing the additional resources it needs for its present and anticipated future growth. A company may have identified a market and created products but may not have sufficient resources to grow. For example, once Starbucks established proof of concept of its retail/café, it required resources to grow. Stated differently, "No bucks—no Starbucks!"

An enterprise's success in identifying a market and in productization creates increased demand for its products and/or services. This, in turn, stretches the organization's resources very thin. The organization may suddenly find that it requires additional physical resources (space, equipment, and so on), financial resources, and human resources. The need for human resources, especially in management, will become particularly acute. At this stage of development, the organization's very success ironically creates a new set of problems. These are the problems of organizational growth and scale-up.

The company must now not only acquire additional resources, but also become more adept at resource management, including the management of cash, inventories (if a manufacturing company), personnel, and so forth. It is at this stage that an entrepreneur must begin to think longer term about the company's future needs. Failure to do this can be costly. For example, one entrepreneur told how he kept purchasing equipment that became obsolete within six months because of the firm's rapid growth. Instead of purchasing a photocopying machine that would be adequate for the company's needs as it grew but was more than currently required, for example, he purchased a machine that was able to meet only current needs. The result was that he spent much more on equipment than he would have if he had purchased machinery that was adequate for potential future needs. Similarly, another entrepreneur found himself with insufficient space six months after moving into new offices that he had thought would be adequate for five years, because the company grew more rapidly than he had anticipated. Another entrepreneur described how he had had to unexpectedly move his offices every five years because, after five years it always seemed that he had run out of space.

Another resource-related dilemma facing entrepreneurial companies involves the people that they can hire. Often, entrepreneurs facing the need to hire people believe that they cannot afford to hire those with long-range potential to help them build their businesses and settle for those with lesser skills and abilities. Unfortunately, this may be a false economy. A few entrepreneurial firms do invest for the future and hire people who can grow with them. For example, one of the secrets to Starbucks' success was that they hired people who could help them build a billion-dollar-plus business from a very early stage. Starbucks' CEO, Howard Schultz, realized that human resources would be as much a key to Starbucks' long-term success as its now famous coffee. This insight helped Starbucks grow during a 10-year period from a small entrepreneurial company in Seattle with two retail stores to an institution with more than $1.4 billion in revenue and more than 1,400 stores. By 2014, Starbucks had become the largest café company in the world with more than 21,000 retail outlets/cafes in 63 countries and more than $15 billion in revenues.[4]

Develop Operational Systems. To function effectively, an organization must not only produce a product or service but also administer basic day-to-day operations reasonably well. These operations include accounting, billing, collections, advertising, personnel recruiting and training, sales, production (or service delivery), information systems, transportation, and related systems. The fourth task in building a successful organization is the development of the systems needed to facilitate these day-to-day operations—that is, operational systems. It is useful to think of a company's operational systems as part of its "organizational plumbing." Just as plumbing is necessary for a house or building to function effectively, organizational plumbing is necessary for a business to function well. Thus, operational systems comprise part of an organization's infrastructure, and are necessary to facilitate growth.

Typically, businesses that are busy focusing upon their markets and products tend to neglect the development of their operational systems. As an organization increases in size, however, an increasing amount of strain is put on such systems because the company tends to outgrow the organizational plumbing or infrastructure available to operate it. For example, in one electrical components distribution firm with more than $200 million in annual revenues, salespeople were continually infuriated when they found deliveries of products they had sold could not be made because the company's inventory records were hopelessly incorrect. Similarly, a medium-sized residential real estate firm with annual revenues of about $10 million found that it required almost one year of effort and embarrassment to correct its accounting records after the firm's bookkeeper retired. A $100 million consumer products manufacturer had to return certain materials to vendors because it had insufficient warehouse space to house the purchases (a fact no one noticed until the deliveries were at the door). A $15 million industrial abrasives distributor found itself facing constant problems in keeping track of customer orders and in knowing what was in its inventory. The firm's inventory control system, which was fine when annual sales were $3 to $5 million, had simply become overloaded at the higher sales volume. One manager remarked that "nothing is ever stored around here where any intelligent person could reasonably expect to find it." A $10 million professional service firm had no way of knowing if the services it provided to customers were, in fact, profitable. Their financial management system did not provide this type of data, so they continued to offer their package of services and to hope for the best. A $100 million distributor of consumer products had a computer system that was so antiquated that few, if any, important reports were prepared accurately or on time. Whatever information was available had to be collected and analyzed manually.

These are just a few of the types of problems that organizations encounter when they have not developed effective operational systems. A key reason for this neglect is that entrepreneurs are more interested in growth and deals than in the infrastructure needed to manage their companies.

The bottom line is that if these systems continue to remain underdeveloped, they can literally bring a business to a standstill. What is not well recognized by most entrepreneurs is that their companies are competing not just in products and markets, but in operational infrastructure as well. To illustrate this we will use an important historical example—Walmart versus Kmart and Sears. Walmart is the classic example of how a small entrepreneurial company grew larger and more successful than its giant competitors, and in turn became the dominant giant of its space. In the 1960s, Sears was the number one retailer in the United States and Kmart was the number two retailer overall but the number one discount retailer. Walmart was a small company headquartered in Bentonville, Arkansas. By analyzing his competition, Sam Walton understood that he could not compete head-to-head with Sears and Kmart but he could create some strengths for Walmart (which might even become competitive advantages) by developing his company's logistics and information systems. Today, Walmart has surpassed Sears and Kmart, and has developed unsurpassed logistics and information systems, because Sam Walton understood that he was competing not just in products but in operational systems as well. These infrastructure advantages led to a cost advantage in the operations of Walmart vis-à-vis Kmart and Sears. Since all sell the same products, the winner of the competition between Walmart, Sears, and Kmart is the company that has the lowest cost of operations. Since Walmart has the lowest cost of operations, it is the ultimate winner in the competition with Sears and Kmart. In 2015, Walmart had more than $500 billion in revenues, while Sears and Kmart continued to struggle.

Develop Management Systems. The fifth task required to build a successful organization is developing the management systems required for its long-term growth and development. There are four management systems: (1) planning, (2) organization structure, (3) management development, and (4) performance management systems. Management systems are another component of an organization's infrastructure, or organizational plumbing.

The planning system consists of how the company develops and implements its long-term plans for organizational development. It also includes operational planning, scheduling, budgeting, and contingency planning. An organization can create a plan and have a strategy, but still lack a planning system. The basic concepts and methods of strategic planning are presented in Chapter 6.

The organization structure of the business determines how people are organized, who reports to whom, and how activities are coordinated. All enterprises have some organizational structure (formal or informal), but they do not necessarily have the correct structure for their needs. The concepts and methods for design and evaluation of organization structure required at different stages of growth are presented in Chapter 7.

Performance management systems encompass the set of processes (budgeting, leadership, and goal setting) and mechanisms (performance appraisal) used to motivate employees to achieve organizational objectives. These systems include both formal control mechanisms, such as responsibility accounting, and informal processes, such as organizational leadership. Chapter 8 provides tools and techniques for designing and implementing effective performance management systems.

The management development system helps facilitate the planned development of the people needed to run the organization as it grows. Chapter 9 presents strategies for designing and delivering management and leadership development programs.

Until an organization reaches a certain critical size (which tends to differ for each organization), it typically can operate without formal management systems. Planning tends to be done in the head of the entrepreneur, frequently on an ad hoc basis. The organizational structure tends to be informal, with ill-defined roles and responsibilities for people that sometimes overlap. Management development tends to consist of "on-the-job training," which basically means "You're on your own." When performance management systems are used in such organizations, they tend to involve only the accounting system rather than a broader concept of management control.

The basic organizational growing pain (which is a symptom of the need for more developed management systems) is the decreasing ability of the original entrepreneur or senior executive to manage or control all that is happening. The organization simply becomes too large for senior managers to be personally involved in every aspect of it, and there is the gnawing feeling that things are out of control. This marks the need for the development or upgrading of the organization's management systems.

Manage the Corporate Culture. Just as all people have personalities, all organizations have a corporate personality or culture: a set of shared values, beliefs, and norms that govern the way people are expected to behave on a day-to-day basis. Values are what the organization believes are important with respect to product quality, customer service, treatment of people, and so on. Beliefs are assumptions that people in the corporation hold about themselves as individuals and about the firm as an entity. Norms are the unwritten rules that guide day-to-day interactions and behavior—including language, dress, and humor.

Organizational culture can have a profound impact on the behavior of people for better or for worse. Many companies, such as Starbucks, Johnson & Johnson, IBM, GE, Toyota, Southwest Airlines, Walmart, and Huawei have achieved greatness at least in part because of a strong corporate culture. Culture, then, is a critical factor in an enterprise's successful development and performance. It functions as an informal "control system," because it prescribes how people are supposed to behave. It must be noted, however, that even companies with what can be generally characterized as a "great" culture (which we define as a strong "functional culture," as explained in Chapter 10) can have cultural problems. IBM, Toyota, and Walmart all have generally strong functional cultures, but each has experienced cultural problems.[5] On the contrary, other companies have experienced difficulties and even failure because of a dysfunctional culture, including once great companies such as GM, AIG, and Reuters.[6]

Some managers believe that what is espoused (stated) as their corporate culture is actually the culture that affects people's behavior. Unfortunately, this is often an illusion. For example, one rapidly growing entrepreneurship in a high-technology industry stated that its culture involved the production of high-quality products, concern for the quality of the working life of its employees, and encouragement of innovation. In reality, the firm's culture was less positive. Its true concerns were to avoid conflict among its managers, set unrealistic performance expectations, avoid accountability, and overestimate its performance capabilities. Moreover, the company saw itself as hard-driving and profit-oriented, but its real culture was sales-oriented regardless of profitability.

Sophisticated managers understand that their companies compete as much with culture as with specific products and services. The CEO of a major New York Stock Exchange company once said that he could predict a division's organizational problems as soon as he had identified its culture. The sixth and final challenge in building a successful organization, then, is to manage corporate culture so that it supports the achievement of its long-term goals. The nature and management of corporate culture are examined in Chapter 10.

The Pyramid of Organizational Development

The six tasks of organizational development just described are critical to any business's successful functioning, not only individually but as an integrated system. They must harmonize and reinforce rather than conflict with one another. An enterprise's markets, products, resources, operational systems, management systems, and corporate culture must be an integrated whole. Further, the Pyramid of Organizational Development must support and be supported by the organization's business concept—the foundation on which the business is built. Stated differently, each variable in the Pyramid of Organizational Development affects and, in turn, is affected by each of the other variables (including the organization's business concept). Thus, although the foundation of the Pyramid of Organizational Development is the market, the market is affected by and affects the company's culture. The management of an organization must learn to visualize this pyramid and evaluate their organization in terms of the extent to which its pyramid has been successfully designed and built.

Implications of the Pyramid of Organizational Development

There are several important implications of the Pyramid of Organizational Development for management. First, the business foundation and the six key organizational development tasks comprise different phases of the business game. Just as the American game of football (the "business concept"—which is part of the business foundation) is comprised of six key phases (rushing offense, passing offense, rushing defense, passing defense, and kicking and receiving), there are six key phases of the "game" of business—markets, products, resources, operational systems, management systems, and culture management. If an organization is weak in any phase of its game, it will experience a variety of growth-related problems (discussed in Chapter 5).

Another implication is that all organizations compete with other enterprises at all levels of the pyramid. For example, Walmart and Kmart do not compete only with products, but with their operational and management systems and culture, as well. Walmart's logistics and information systems are a clear source of competitive advantage vis-à-vis Kmart and other discount retailers.

A third important implication is that, in the long term, the most sustainable competitive advantages are typically found *at the top three levels* of the pyramid (operational systems, management systems, and culture) rather than in products and markets. All markets can be entered by competitors, and all products can be copied or improved upon over time (even pharmaceuticals can have generic versions), but the top three levels of the pyramid take time and money to develop and are difficult to copy. Even if an attempt is made by a competitor to copy an enterprise's operational systems, management systems, and culture, their effort can be fruitless because of the unique aspects of each organization. In this sense, an organization's culture can be viewed as its ultimate strategic asset because it cannot be copied.[7] We shall examine the strategic implications of the Pyramid of Organizational Development further in Chapter 6.

Winning with Infrastructure. The bottom line is that our research and experience indicate that an organization ultimately wins with infrastructure. It might superficially look as though a company is winning with products, but products (with the possible exception of an initial product at the start-up phase) are created by infrastructure. This is clear in certain types of industries such as pharmaceuticals, where research and development is the lifeblood of the industry. However, a closer look at virtually all industries will show that infrastructure is the "secret sauce" or secret weapon of companies.

Assessing the Degree of Strategic Organizational Development

The Pyramid of Organizational Development can and should be used as a template for assessing the degree or strength of an organization's strategic development both qualitatively and quantitatively. Strategic development refers to the extent to which an organization has successfully developed each of the six key strategic building blocks comprising the Pyramid of Organizational Development. Qualitative assessment involves identifying and describing a company's specific strengths and limitations (or "opportunities to improve") of a business in qualitative terms. We will illustrate this in our discussion of strategic planning in Chapter 6.

Quantitative assessment involves using numerical ratings to assess the degree of strategic development—overall and at each level in the Pyramid of Organizational Development. We have developed and validated a 65-item survey, The Organizational Effectiveness Survey©, that can be used to provide this quantitative assessment. While this proprietary instrument is not included in this book (but is commercially available for readers' use),[8] we have also created a "short-cut method" to get an approximation of an organization's strategic development scores that is provided here. This can be done by "rating" the strength of each key strategic building block using numbers from 1 to 5, where 5 is the highest number (greatest strength) and 1 is the lowest number (greatest opportunity to improve). This method provides a quick approximation of the actual situation of an organization. Readers can use the short-cut method to get an approximation of their strategic development score. This short survey can be administered to any number of managers and/or employees and a mean (average) score can be calculated for each pyramid level and for the overall pyramid. An example of an organization's mean strategic development scores is shown in Table 2.1.

Our use of the Organizational Effectiveness Survey© has led to the development of a set of standards for strategic development scores, as shown in Table 2.2. The higher its strategic development score, the greater is the likelihood that the organization will be successful over the long run. As seen in Table 2.2, a score of 4.5 or greater is required for a company to be a "Global Leader"; 4.0 or greater to be a "Superior" organization; and 3.5 or greater to be a "Sustainably Successful" organization. An

Table 2.1   **Example of an Organization's Strategic Development Scores**

Pyramid Level	Sample Mean
Markets	3.2
Products/Services	2.9
Resources	2.8
Operational Systems	2.7
Management Systems	3.0
Culture	3.0
Overall Strategic Development Score	**2.9**

Table 2.2   **Strategic Development Scores Required for Different Levels of Success over the Long Run**

Level	Success	Required Overall Strategic Development Score
I	Global Leader	4.50+
II	Superior	4.00+
III	Sustainably Successful	3.50+
IV	Marginally Successful	3.00+
V	At Risk/Unsuccessful	<3.00
VI	Likely to Be in Crisis	<2.50

organization with a score of 3.0 to 3.4 is classified as "Marginally Successful," meaning that its success is not likely to be sustainable over the long term. An organization with a score of less than 3.0 is considered "At Risk/Unsuccessful." An organization with a score of less than 2.5 is very likely to be in crisis.

As seen in Table 2.2, our research and experience indicate that organizations need to have a strategic development score above 3.5 to have the greatest chance of sustainable success over the long run. Research and experience also indicate that a company with a score of less than 3.0 has a 33% chance of great difficulties or even failure within two years.

Table 2.3 presents examples of well-known companies with our judgmental best guesses of the category into which each would fit, based upon the "Scores Required for Different Levels of Success" as shown previously in Table 2.2. We do not necessarily have empirical data for this classification.

Our use of the Organizational Effectiveness Survey© has also led to the development of a database that can be used as the basis for identifying the percentage of companies that fall into each level of strategic development.[9] This set of percentile scores is shown in Table 2.4.

As seen in Table 2.4, fewer than 1% of the organizations in our database (which includes both for-profit businesses and nonprofits) have achieved scores greater than 4.5. Similarly, 3% of

Table 2.3   **Examples of Companies with Different Levels of Strategic Development**

Level	Success	Examples
I	Global Leaders	Starbucks, Microsoft, IBM, Caterpillar
II	Superior	Amgen, Nike, Walmart
III	Successful	Mövenpick, Komatsu, Li Ning
IV	Marginally Successful	Nokia, Ford, Sony
V	At Risk/Unsuccessful	Sears, Radio Shack, Kmart

Table 2.4   **Distribution of Overall Strategic Development Scores per Management Systems' Database**

Mean Score	Percent of Companies with Mean Scores
4.5–5.0	Less than 1%
4.0–4.4	3%
3.5–3.9	26%
3.0–3.4	50%
<3.0	20%

companies have achieved scores between 4.0 and 4.4. Most companies (about 76%) have scores in the range of 3.0 to 3.9, and about 20% have scores less than 3.0.

Readers can use the short-cut method described earlier to get an approximation of their strategic development score. They can then compare that score with both the Scores Required for Different Levels of Success shown in Table 2.2 and the database of percentiles of companies with each level of scores shown in Table 2.4 in order to self-assess their overall strength. Our data suggest that organizations with scores less than 3.0 are at serious risk of difficulties and possible failure.

The Pyramid and Financial Performance

During the past few years, a growing body of research has provided empirical support for the validity of the Pyramid of Organizational Development framework.[10] This research has consistently indicated that there is a statistically significant relationship between the variables contained in the pyramid and the financial performance of companies. The six variables are hypothesized to account for as much as 90% of financial performance, with the remaining 10% attributable to exogenous factors. See Figure 2.2 for a graphic representation of these variables as drivers of financial results. Empirical research to date has, in fact, indicated that as much as 80% of gross margin and 55% of EBIT (earnings before interest and taxes) is explained by the variables in the model. Additional research has indicated that the pyramid has a statistically significant relationship to ROI (return on investment).

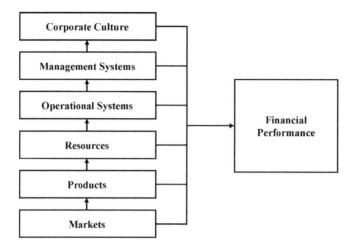

Figure 2.2   Six Key Drivers of Financial Results

The Pyramid as a Lens to Build and Evaluate Organizations

The pyramid framework can be used as a template for planning to build an organization and as a strategic lens through which to evaluate the strengths and limitations (or areas for improvement) of an existing enterprise. As such, it becomes the guide for planning to build a new business or to strengthen an existing business. This topic is addressed more fully in Chapter 6, which deals with strategic planning and organizational development.

Although an organization should focus on the six levels in the pyramid, the emphasis on the components or subsystems of the pyramid must be somewhat different at different stages of organizational growth. Before we can explore this idea further, we must examine the different stages of growth through which all organizations develop. This topic is the focus of Chapters 3 and 4. First, however, we illustrate how the pyramid can be used to build and/or improve a successful enterprise by describing the examples of Guangzhou Construction (the disguised name of an actual company) and Starbucks Coffee Company. Guangzhou Construction is an example of how the pyramid can be used to improve an enterprise, while Starbucks is an example of how it can be used to build a successful or even a dominant company.

Improving Strategic Organizational Development at Guangzhou Construction, China

Guangzhou Construction was established in 1983 in the city of Guangzhou, China. Guangzhou's services include general contracting, project management, design, permitting, construction, procurement, decoration, final inspection, and acceptance. Guangzhou Construction is qualified as a Class I Design Institute and Class I General Contractor (highest level of construction licenses) to do a wide range of design and construction through three regional branch companies in South China, East China, and North China. The company also provides complete design-and-build.

Table 2.5   Revenue and Employees at Guangzhou Construction

	2006	2007	2008	2009
Revenue (in millions of RMB)	570	1080	960	880
Number of employees	290	442	442	470

Over a 30-year period, the company grew rapidly and successfully, providing services to over 220 major projects. The company's revenue and employee growth from 2006 to 2009 is shown in Table 2.5.[11]

Origins of the Organizational Development Initiative

In 2009, Guangzhou Construction's CEO, George Li, attended the CEO Leadership Program offered by Cheung Kong Graduate School of Business (CKGSB). Eric Flamholtz, one of the instructors for this program, was engaged by CKGSB to coach approximately 40 CEOs in China and to help them enhance their leadership and organizational effectiveness during a nine-month program. As part of his sessions, Dr. Flamholtz had the program's participants (along with their senior management teams) complete two proprietary organizational effectiveness surveys: (1) "The Growing Pains Survey" (to be described in Chapter 5) and (2) the "Organizational Effectiveness Survey," described earlier in this chapter. Both surveys have been validated and have demonstrated predictive validity to financial performance.[12]

The surveys were administered twice—first in 2009 and again in 2010. This was done to measure the progress made after an organizational development program had been implemented. The strategic development scores for Guangzhou Construction are shown in Table 2.6. (Guangzhou Construction's Growing Pains Scores are shown and discussed in Chapter 5.)

Table 2.6   Guangzhou Construction Organizational Effectiveness Survey Results 2009 versus 2010

Pyramid Level Plus Financial Results	Mean		Change (+, −, 0)
	2009	2010	
Markets	3.5	3.8	+
Products/Services	3.1	3.6	+
Resources	3.2	3.8	+
Operational Systems	3.2	3.8	+
Management Systems	3.3	3.8	+
Culture	3.5	3.8	+
Financial Results Management	3.3	4.0	+
Overall	3.3	3.8	+

Implementing a Program of Organizational Development

The results of these two surveys—with the Organizational Effectiveness Survey indicating that the company was only "marginally successful" and the Growing Pains Survey indicating that the company had a high level of growth-related problems—served as the catalyst for Guangzhou Construction's CEO to embark on a program of organizational development. George Li planned on a one-year timeframe in which he would do the following:

- Initiate a process to create a new vision for the business
- Initiate a culture management program to emphasize new values for the organization

As an initial step, the CEO articulated a mission for the company: "Guangzhou Construction's mission is to improve human beings' living and working environment." However, workers at Guangzhou found that to be too abstract and not directly relevant to their work, so the CEO took steps to explain the company's mission in terms that could be understood by all workers. As he stated: "First line managers thought it was too intangible and far from their current work. As a result, I spent time with them in illustrating what we meant by this and how it was relevant to their daily work. I explained to them that even trivial things like 'spit' or leaving trash in workplace are against our mission of improving people's living and working environment and that this should be prevented. Those are all very tangible."

The next step for George Li was to redefine the mission into a strategic mission for Guangzhou Construction. As he stated: "We set our strategic mission as 'to be the most reliable construction company in China.'"

The next step was to articulate a set of core values for Guangzhou Construction: integrity, passion, initiative, good quality, teamwork, and continued improvement. In order to make these values real and operational in the company, George Li spent a great deal of time communicating with people. As he stated, "I spent much time in communicating and getting mid-level and senior management aligned with our mission, vision, and core values."

He worked hard to translate those values into specific norms of behavior that could be understood by all employees. He wanted to emphasize integrity, but realized that people might be unwilling to be criticized for mistakes. His solution was clever: "We emphasize 'forgiveness for honest mistakes' in order to promote taking initiative while retaining a high level of integrity. We have demonstrated to our employees that we actually did not punish people if they made mistakes with good intention; at the same time, some people were fired for being dishonest and doing harm to the company's integrity." George Li went on to explain the difference between an honest mistake, which can be forgiven, and a dishonest mistake, for which there can be no forgiveness: For example, if someone takes or gives a bribe, they will be fired. However, honest mistakes are forgiven. As George Li explains, "One day my secretary forgot to bring me something I had asked for. I said it was 'no problem.' Everyone makes mistakes."

Program Results and Impact

As seen in Table 2.6, the strategic development scores for Guangzhou Construction improved very significantly from 2009 to 2010—a very short timeframe for such dramatic change. The overall score improved from 3.3 (indicating a marginally successful organization) to 3.8, which indicates a sustainably successful entity. All of the individual scores for each level of the pyramid improved. The sign test or the Wilcoxon signed-rank test for nonparametric statistics indicates that this difference is statistically significant and is unlikely to have occurred by chance alone.[13]

Successfully Building the Pyramid: The Example of Starbucks

Starbucks (formerly "Starbucks Coffee Company") is one of the truly great entrepreneurial success stories of the past few decades. The scope and speed of its success are reminiscent of Apple, Nike, Microsoft, Amgen, and Google.

Starbucks is a classic example of an organization that has been very successful because it was effective in building the entire Pyramid of Organizational Development at a relatively early stage of development. It has achieved success as an organization through its development of the six key tasks of organizational development, not only each task individually but the effective development of the pyramid as a whole. This section will use the development of Starbucks to illustrate the process of building a sustainably successful organization by using the pyramid as a template, as described below.

Formulate the Business Foundation

The original Starbucks began as a local roaster of coffee. In 1972, the company had two retail stores that sold coffee beans: one opened in 1971 near Seattle's Pike Place Market, and the other, opened in 1972, was located in a shopping center across from the University of Washington's campus. This original Starbucks did not sell coffee beverages. It sold fresh-roasted coffee beans, teas, and spices. However, sometimes the individual behind the counter would brew some coffee and serve it in paper cups as samples.

Howard Schultz was not the original founder of Starbucks. He joined the company as Director of Retail Operations and Marketing in 1982. About one year later, Schultz visited Milan, Italy, to attend a trade show. While strolling on Milan's streets, he was struck by the ubiquity of the Italian coffee bars. He was drawn into them, and realized that the coffee bars were an extension of people's homes and a part of the Italian culture. He saw the opportunity to develop something like what he had seen in Milan back in the United States. In April, 1984 Starbucks tested Schultz's idea by opening a coffee bar inside a Starbucks retail store, and it was an instant success. Despite the experiment's success, the original founders of Starbucks decided not to adapt it to Schultz's vision: an American version of an Italian coffee bar. Schultz left to create his own company called Il Giornale, which was founded in 1985. In August 1987, Schultz went back to Starbucks with a buyout offer and a vision of taking the company national. Il Giornale acquired the assets and name of Starbucks, and changed its name to Starbucks Corporation.

In brief, Schultz's business concept for Starbucks was of a national specialty retailer/café, or, as noted above, an American version of an Italian coffee bar. During its very early years, there was not an explicit strategic mission in the way it has been defined here. Implicitly, the strategic mission was to establish the company. Similarly, there was not an explicit core strategy. However, the core strategy was to change the nature of the coffee café to an experience. Both the strategic mission and core strategy were developed later, as discussed in Chapter 6.

Identify a Market and Develop a Product

In terms of the Pyramid of Organizational Development, Schultz perceived the market not for coffee per se but for a different kind of retail/café experience. Thus the product was not just coffee but the atmosphere and experience of the Starbucks store. The store itself was part of the product experience for the customer, not just the place where the product was purchased. It was part of the coffee-related experience. Schultz also realized that customer service was part of the overall product or experience to be delivered in a Starbucks store. As a result, Starbucks emphasized its unique brand of customer service from the beginning.

Neither coffee nor cafés were new products, but Starbucks had redefined them in some magical way. Schultz had, indeed, solved the first two challenges of building a successful enterprise: he had identified a market and developed a product. This, in turn, led to the rapid growth of Starbucks, and created the next set of challenges: resources and operational systems.

Acquire Resources and Develop Operational Systems

Unlike many entrepreneurial companies, Starbucks paid a great deal of attention to the acquisition of resources and the development of operational systems. From the beginning, Schultz believed that he had a big opportunity, and he thought that Starbucks had the potential to become an enterprise with one billion dollars in sales.

He realized that if the company was going to fulfill its potential, he would need all of the resources and systems required of a large company, including financial, physical (plant and equipment), technological, and human resources. As he stated: "We could not have gotten where we are today if we had not had the commitment to build a national company with a national brand from the beginning. If you are going to build a 100-story building, you've got to build a foundation for 100 stories."[14]

The first step was to raise money, and this became a continuing challenge as Starbucks rapidly grew. Schultz spent considerable time finding investors, and without the "bucks" there would be no Starbucks! The financial resources were used to hire people capable of building Starbucks into a national brand and a national company. This was not only true of a strong senior management team, but also the acquisition of people at the operating levels, such as real estate, finance, and retail operations. Funds were also used to upgrade the company's roasting plant, its logistics and manufacturing systems, and its overall day-to-day operating systems.

Starbucks' investment in a strong operating team as well as the related aspects of infrastructure paid off for the company in many ways. The strong real estate team led the company to choose solid locations and avoid the real estate problems of other similar organizations such as Boston Market and Koo Koo Roo. The company's investment in developing strong financial systems led to a deeper understanding of store economics, and, in turn, a healthy business from a financial standpoint.

Development of Management Systems

In 1994, Howard Schultz and Orin Smith (then CFO and later COO of Starbucks) read the second edition of this book and invited Eric Flamholtz to visit Starbucks and assist the firm with its "growing pains."[15] This, in turn, led to the development of a more sophisticated set of management systems for Starbucks, including a strategic planning system similar to that described in Chapter 6, and a revised organizational structure. In 1995, Starbucks also developed its management development and performance management systems. Before that, there was a strategy and plan but not a formal, integrated planning system. There was training for customer service personnel but no management development. In addition, there was an incentive system for people but no well-developed performance management system.

Taken together, these things (planning, structure, management development, and performance management systems) all comprised the overall management systems for Starbucks, and completed the development (at least for this stage of the company's growth) of the fifth level of the Pyramid of Organizational Development.

Manage the Corporate Culture

The highest level in the Pyramid of Organizational Development, and the sixth task required to develop a successful enterprise involves culture management. From the beginning, Schultz and Starbucks had a clear idea that culture was important in building a successful enterprise. In addition, Howard Schultz had a well-defined concept of the kind of organization he wanted to build. Accordingly, Schultz articulated a set of "Five Guiding Principles" that was intended to serve as the foundation for Starbucks' culture. Subsequently, a sixth guiding principle was added: "Embrace diversity as an essential component in the way we do business." The six guiding principles which comprised the core of Starbucks' stated culture are presented below:

Starbucks Corporation Six Guiding Principles

1. Provide a great work environment and treat each other with respect and dignity.
2. Apply the highest standards of excellence to the purchasing, roasting, and fresh delivery of our coffee.
3. Develop enthusiastically satisfied customers all of the time.
4. Contribute positively to our communities and our environment.
5. Recognize that profitability is essential to our future success.
6. Embrace diversity as an essential component in the way we do business.

In addition to the stated guiding principles of Starbucks, there are also some other facets of its culture that are important. Schultz believed that the kind of organization that Starbucks was, and, in turn, the way it did business would become a source of sustainable competitive advantage. In effect, Schultz understood the role of culture as a building block of organizational success. Although he was not then familiar with the concept of "corporate culture" per se, he understood it intuitively. This led Starbucks to be concerned about the treatment of people employed by the firm. Ideally, he wanted everyone employed by Starbucks to behave like "owners." The notion was: The way we treat our people will influence the way they treat our customers, and, in turn, our overall success. This led Starbucks to a number of different personnel practices, including providing full benefits for all people working more than 20 hours each week, and providing opportunities for stock ownership.

In other words, the company developed ways to manage its culture so that it would be embraced by its employees.

The Pyramid as a Whole

Starbucks is an illustration of a very successful entrepreneurial organization. The discussion above shows that Starbucks understood the need to develop all aspects of what we have termed the Pyramid of Organizational Development and not merely focus upon products and markets. Prior to 1994, the company had done an excellent job of developing five of the levels of the Pyramid of Organizational Development; that is, everything except management systems. As we shall see later in this book, this is the classic pattern of successful entrepreneurial companies. Beginning in 1994, at about $175 million in sales, Starbucks began to develop the management systems that were required to facilitate its continued successful development. This completed the developmental work prescribed by the Pyramid of Organizational Development.

What happened to Starbucks? By the end of its fiscal year 2014, Starbucks had grown to more than to $15 billion in net revenue and more than 21,000 stores worldwide. Clearly, successful development of the Pyramid of Organizational Development pays off.

The Secret to Starbucks' Success

Starbucks did not invent or develop coffee. Starbucks was not even the first to create the American version of a café/specialty retail company. Starbucks grew out of Peet's Coffee. Starbucks did not have the advantage of a proprietary product like Microsoft or Amgen, or even the first mover's advantage. So how did Starbucks become Starbucks—the leading brand and world-class company? The answer comes directly from Howard Behar, who joined Starbucks as a Senior Executive in 1989 when the company had just 28 stores and over his tenure with the company served as President of Starbucks International, President of Starbucks North America, and also as a Board member. In 2007, Behar published a book titled: *It's Not the Coffee: Leadership Principles from a Life at Starbucks.*[16] As the books title suggests, the secret to Starbucks' success is not the coffee per se; it is the way Starbucks has been managed.

Boston Market: A Contrast with Starbucks

In the 1990s "Boston Chicken" (later renamed Boston Market) had people's mouths watering for more than just their food. The company was supposed to become "The McDonalds of the '90s." It never happened. Instead, Boston Market filed for Chapter 11 reorganization under the bankruptcy law. While Starbucks was earning quite a few bucks for its investors, Boston Market was costing its investors and franchisees lots of money.

What was different about the two companies? While Starbucks successfully focused upon all of the six key aspects of the Pyramid of Organizational Development, Boston Market did not. Boston Market did identify a market and had developed a good product, but the emphasis was upon selling area franchises rather than truly building a solid business. In other words, the focus was on the bottom two layers of the Pyramid of Organizational Development versus the pyramid as a whole. While Starbucks' skilled real estate team identified good locations and negotiated sensible deals, Boston Market was perceived as overpaying for real estate. While Starbucks' financial people were analyzing costs of store build-outs and operations, Boston Market never got the economics of their stores under control. Their stores were expensive to build and operate, and they were not profitable. Although the restaurants were losing money, Boston Market was showing a profit for a period because of the heavy franchise fees charged. But the firm's reported profitability was a mirage, which finally disappeared. In brief, Boston Market simply did not effectively execute all of the six required tasks of organizational development and ultimately paid the price.

This discussion is not intended to imply that Starbucks neither made no mistakes nor was without problems, but simply that it did a significantly better job in performing the required tasks to build a successful organization. Boston Market failed to focus on several of the key tasks of organizational development, and went bankrupt. In 1998, Boston Markets was sold to McDonald's and in 2007 was acquired by Sun Capital Partners. Some of the stores continue to operate, but it never became anything close to what Starbucks has achieved.

Summary

This chapter has presented a framework or lens for understanding what makes an organization successful, effective, and profitable. The foundation of this framework is the organization's business foundation—that defines the nature of its business, what it is working to achieve, and how it will compete. Building upon this foundation, an organization must focus on six areas if it is to succeed over the long term. These are: (1) markets, (2) products or services, (3) resources, (4) operational systems, (5) management systems, and (6) corporate culture. For organizations to be successful, they must first identify their business foundation. Then they must deal not only with each of these six areas individually and in sequence but also with the six as parts of a whole. We use the image of a Pyramid of Organizational Development to describe this holistic approach.

The chapter has also presented a tool for assessing the extent of strategic development of a company in terms of the pyramid. It has provided a data set for readers to assess their organization vis-à-vis other companies in quantitative terms.

Starbucks Coffee Company ("Starbucks") illustrates the power of developing a company in a way that is consistent with the Pyramid of Organizational Development—that is, an organization that is positioned to be sustainably successful. In the next chapter, we examine the different stages of growth and the different emphasis on each part of the pyramid that is required at each stage for an organization to be successful over the long term.

Notes

1. Michael Hiltzik, "A Chain that Lost Its Concept," *Los Angeles Times*, December 3, 2014, B1–2.
2. Eric G. Flamholtz, "Towards an Integrative Theory of Organizational Success and Failure: Previous Research and Future Issues," *International Journal of Entrepreneurship Education* 1, no. 3 (2002–2003): 297–319.

3. Google website/Company Overview/ Our History in Depth, 2015. http://www.google.com/about/company/.

4. Spencer Jakab, "Starbucks Still a Coffee Achiever," *Wall Street Journal*, January 22, 2015, C1.

5. Eric Flamholtz and Yvonne Randle, *Corporate Culture: The Ultimate Strategic Asset* (Stanford, CA: Stanford University Press, 2011).

6. Ibid.

7. Ibid.

8. For information about the Organizational Effectiveness Survey, see www.mgtsystems.com/surveys.

9. At the time of publication of this book, the database consisted of almost 2,000 organizations.

10. Eric Flamholtz and Stanford Kurland, "Strategic Organizational Development, Infrastructure and Financial Performance: An Empirical Investigation," *International Journal of Entrepreneurial Education* 3, no. 2 (2005): 117–142.

11. The exchange rate between Chinese currency RMB (renminbi) and U.S. dollars is approximately 6.1 yuan (RMB) to $1.

12. Both surveys, developed by Eric Flamholtz, have been validated and have demonstrated predictive validity to financial performance.

13. Sidney Siegel, *Nonparametric Statistics for the Behavioral Sciences* (New York: McGraw-Hill, 1956), 68–83.

14. Howard Schultz and Dori Jones Yang, *Pour Your Heart Into It: How Starbucks Built a Company One Cup at a Time* (New York: Hyperion, 1997), 140.

15. Ibid., 161, 201–202.

16. Howard Behar with Janet Goldstein, *It's Not About the Coffee: Leadership Principles from a Life at Starbucks* (New York: Portfolio, 2007).

CHAPTER 3

Identifying and Surviving the First Four Stages of Organizational Growth

All organizations pass through various stages of development. These stages are, at least in part, determined by the organization's size, as measured by its annual revenues (or for nonprofits, in terms of annual budget). This chapter presents a framework for identifying and explaining the major stages through which all organizations grow and develop as they increase in size. It should be noted that this framework applies to a division of a large company, as well as to an independent organization.

First, we identify the seven stages of organizational growth comprising the entire life cycle and then, in this chapter, examine the first four stages from the inception of a new venture to organizational maturity. We identify the emphasis on each level in the Pyramid of Organizational Development that is required at each growth stage and explain the nature of the transitions to different stages. Throughout the discussion we will present selected examples to illustrate success and failure at each stage. Then, we discuss the differences between an entrepreneurship and a "professionally managed" organization and what must be done to make the transition between these major growth stages. Next, we present a case study of a company (99 Cents Only Stores) from its inception as a new venture through its transition to become an entrepreneurially oriented, professionally managed organization. Finally, we discuss the keys to success at Stages I to IV. We will discuss the remaining three stages of growth (stages V to VII) in Chapter 4.

Stages of Organizational Growth

Like all things, organizations have a life cycle. Based upon our research, we have developed a life cycle model that identifies seven predictable stages of organizational growth. The seven stages in our model are:

I. New Venture

II. Expansion

III. Professionalization

IV. Consolidation

V. Diversification

VI. Integration

VII. Decline and Revitalization

The first four stages characterize the period from inception of a new venture or start-up to the attainment of organizational maturity. This period includes the development of an entrepreneurship through the stage when the business becomes a professionally managed organization. Stages V through VII all deal with the period of a company's life cycle after the attainment of organizational maturity through decline and revitalization.

This chapter focuses on the first four stages of organizational growth, because they comprise a complete era of growth from inception of a new venture to early organizational maturity or young adulthood. We return to the last three stages in Chapter 4, which presents the challenges posed to continue success after an organization has reached maturity.

At each of these stages, one or more of the critical tasks of organizational development identified in Chapter 2 should receive special attention. The stages of organizational growth, the critical development areas for each stage, and the approximate size (measured in millions of dollars of sales revenues for for-profit companies and in terms of annual operating budget for nonprofits) at which an organization will typically pass through each stage are shown in Table 3.1.

Table 3.1   Stages of Organizational Growth

Stage	Description	Critical Development Areas	Approximate Organizational Size (millions of dollars in sales)	
			Manufacturing Firms	Service Firms
I.	New Venture	Markets and Products	Less than $1	Less than $0.3
II.	Expansion	Resources and Operational Systems	$1 to $10	$0.3 to $3.3
III.	Professionalization	Management Systems	$10 to $100	$3.3 to $33
IV.	Consolidation	Corporate Culture	$100 to $500	$33 to $167

A key word in this statement is *typically*. What this means is that for approximately 90% of manufacturing firms that have revenues in the range of $10 million to $100 million, they will typically have to encounter the critical issues of Stage III.

There are, however, certain organizations that will have to face these problems at an earlier stage in their development, or much later. For example, there may well be a $3 million manufacturing business that is facing the need to professionalize its management systems. Or a few organizations may well reach $1 billion in annual revenue without really having to face the need to professionalize their management systems. Accordingly, we need to view the relevant range as designated for the transition to occur at each stage of development as a normal curve. In statistics, a normal curve designates the percentage of observations that fall under the area of the curve. This means that statistically 68% of the cases will fall under one standard deviation of the normal curve, while 95% of the cases will fall under two standard deviations of the normal curve. There are, of course, always certain exceptions to this. Similarly, there are exceptions to the revenue parameters used to mark the various stages of growth.

It should also be noted that in Table 3.1 we use two different ranges of annual revenue to designate the various stages of growth. Our experience and research indicate that each stage of growth is reached somewhat earlier for service companies than for manufacturing businesses. This occurs because of the greater complexity of a service company relative to a manufacturing company with the same annual revenues. This is, in turn, caused by the fact that manufacturing companies typically purchase materials that are semi-finished and use them in their manufacturing process. Accordingly, the manufacturing company's revenues include a return for the components of cost of goods sold that are derived from other organization's work. This means that the manufacturing company's value added is less than the comparable value added for a service company at a given size of annual revenues. This does not mean that the manufacturing company makes a lesser economic value-added contribution than a service company; it merely means that the service company with more employees and no raw materials to be recouped as part of sales revenue has a relatively more complex operation than a comparably sized manufacturing company.

As a result of this phenomenon, we have found it useful to convert a service company's revenues into the comparable units of those of a manufacturing company. This process is similar to the conversion from the imperial system to the metric system or from dollars into any foreign currency. Thus to convert a service company's revenues into comparable units of a manufacturing company, we multiply the service company's revenues by a factor of 3 (as reflected in the figures shown in Table 3.1). This means that the typical service company is three times more complex to manage than a comparably sized (in revenues) manufacturing company. Alternatively, it means that a $5 million service company is the rough equivalent of a $15 million manufacturing company. It should be remembered that this is an experienced-based adjustment that we have found useful rather than a strict formula.

Most nonprofit organizations can be classified as service organizations (providing services or funding for services to specific populations). Further, many nonprofits—particularly foundations, charities, and organizations that are government-funded—do not have any revenue per se. In these cases, the organization's annual operating budget can be used as a surrogate for revenues. The budget, in this case, represents the size and complexity of the business, in terms of clients served, projects funded, and so on. We focus specifically on the growth and development of nonprofits in Chapter 11.

In the following discussion, for convenience, we refer to an organization at a given stage using the parameters for manufacturing companies as a base. The reader can adjust for service companies by using the service company adjustment factor of 3, or can simply refer to Table 3.1. Financial institutions, such as banks, savings and loans, and mutual funds, can be viewed as service companies under the framework. Distribution companies can be viewed as a hybrid manufacturing-service organizations, and a multiple of 2 can be used as an adjustment factor. (In other words, a $5 million distribution company is the same as a $10 million manufacturing company and is, therefore, nearing Stage II of its development.)

Stage I: New Venture

Stage I of organizational growth involves the inception of a new venture. Stage I typically occurs from the time an organization has virtually no sales until it reaches approximately $1 million in annual sales for a manufacturing firm (or $0.3 million for a service firm). During Stage I, the organization has to perform all the critical tasks necessary for organizational success, but the greatest emphasis is on the first two tasks: defining markets and developing products. This is represented schematically in the organizational development pyramid shown in Figure 3.1. These two tasks are critical to the organization's survival because without customers and products or services to provide to them, it simply cannot exist. The ultimate purpose of this stage is to establish proof of the business concept.

Many businesses have succeeded as new ventures because the entrepreneur was able to identify a viable market and product. For example Brian and Jennifer Maxwell, both runners, created

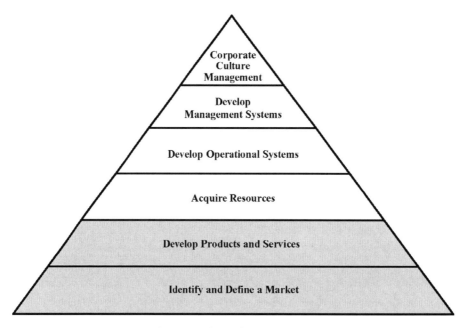

Figure 3.1   Developmental Emphasis in a Stage I Organization

PowerBar first for their own personal use as a source of competitive advantage, and then developed it into a business. This product led to the creation of an entire new category—the energy bar category.

Similarly, Jerry and Goldie Lippman, the founders of GOJO Industries (the inventor of PURELL® hand sanitizer) saw the need for something that would serve as a hand cleaner and sanitizer. The idea for the company's first product came from Goldie while she was working in one of Akron's (Ohio) rubber plants during World War II. Many of the traditional male rubber workers had gone off to war, and the women who replaced them needed a better way to remove dirt from their hands than the harsh industrial chemicals used at the time. Jerry, with only a 10th grade education, sought out chemistry professor Clarence Cook at Kent State University, and together they invented a product that would remove dirt without irritation. This was sold as GOJO® Hand Cleaner, and the couple's first customers were Goldie's co-workers in the rubber factory. With Goldie handling administrative matters, Jerry began selling to automotive service and manufacturing distributors and, within a few years, a new product category, heavy-duty hand cleaner, was established. The market remained small because of the high cost of the product, relative to the "free" cleaning solvents readily available. Jerry solved this problem by developing a portion-control dispenser and adopting a razor/razor blade approach to placing dispensers and selling proprietary refills. Today, GOJO is the world leader in institutional hand hygiene and healthy skin.

Other examples of new ventures that came about when an entrepreneur perceived a market need to be served include Noah's Bagels (fresh bagels of the highest quality in the western United States), Federal Express (overnight delivery of packages and mail), and Google (an online search tool that would enable customers to quickly find and use information).

Once in a while, a new "transformational technological platform" emerges that can be "leveraged" by entrepreneurs or existing organizations to create a plethora of new ventures. The Internet is such a platform. It has helped spawn many new ventures including Amazon.com, Facebook, Netflix, and Alibaba. For example, Netflix and Amazon.com leveraged the Internet to enable anyone with access to the Internet to see a movie or other media content at any time.

Many other new ventures are reasonably successful and profitable but not as famous or glamorous. They include businesses engaged in executive search, landscape design, printing, financial planning, restaurants, graphic design, repair services, catering, equipment leasing, specialty retailing, and many more fields. An example of one of these new ventures is EEZYCUT, founded by David Jones and Laura Mayes.[1] David was university-educated and had even completed an MBA degree course while working for Bayer PLC. Looking back, David could see that he was not yet mature enough for a commercial life and still describes himself as a cave diver (explorer) and social drop-out.

David perceived the need for a new type of cutting tool that divers could use. The old style diving knife then in use rusted immediately and blunted quickly. While on a "deco stop" (which is a pause while rising to eliminate dissolved inert gases from the diver's body and avoid the bends), David pondered how to make a better device than the one offered at the time. The first design was a failure, and David found himself starting again. It was a simple engineering design that resolved the problem with the first cutting device and made the new device (the Trilobite diver's knife) an attractive choice for emergency cutting tools. The Trilobite was the first on the diving market that provided exchangeable blades for the consumer.

David had designed an emergency cutting tool that was intended for use by divers. However, other non-divers saw the knife and found it had many other applications. This led to another design called QuattroPod, aimed towards emergency rescue services. EEZYCUT's Trilobite has been used by skydivers, hang-gliders, paragliders, kayaking, fire and rescue services, fishermen, yacht owners, gardeners, prison guards, special forces, ski patrol, public safety officers, emergency room workers and paramedics, as well as scuba divers. It has also been used in animal rescue of marine life caught in fishing line!

While David focused on the design and deal aspects of the business, Laura's role was ubiquitous. Laura was involved in the business with David from its conception. Since they are married, the business relationship developed through physical proximity. Their apartment was full of boxes and sewing machines. Laura took the phone calls, read the emails, paid the bills, and shipped the product. According to David, "Laura pretty much did everything, and kept the ship running" while he barked orders at her from behind the machines. Also, David is a self-described hermit, and Laura was his only sounding board. So she was fully informed and involved in strategy, business direction, contracts, and so on. They are a working partnership as well as a family. With no prior distribution experience, the pair has built their company into a Stage II business selling the EEZYCUT Trilobites around the globe.

Entrepreneurs do not always have to be first to identify an unserved market segment. Often they can enter a market with a better product or service. The classic example of an entrepreneur who succeeded after others failed is Herb Kelleher, founder and former CEO of Southwest Airlines. Although others had identified the market for low-cost airfare, Kelleher was the first to find the successful formula for low-cost, no-frills airfare—a market segment that Southwest has grown to dominate. Coffee is certainly not a new product, but Starbucks has grown to dominate the retail coffee bar segment. Although girls have played with dolls for many decades, if not throughout history, Isaac Larian, founder of MGA Entertainment, created Bratz Dolls to appeal to "tween" girls and grew his business to one of the largest toy companies in the world.

Keys to a Success at Stage I. At stage I, the two keys to success are the ability to identify a present or potential market need (defining a market) and the ability to develop a product or service that will satisfy that market need on a profitable basis. Taken together, these two things are necessary to establish proof of concept.

Stage II: Expansion

If an organization successfully completes the key developmental tasks of Stage I, it will reach Stage II, which involves rapid expansion in terms of sales revenues, number of employees, and so on. For most manufacturing firms, Stage II begins at about the $1 million sales level and extends to the $10 million level. (For service firms, this stage typically begins at approximately $0.3 million and continues through $3.3 million in revenues.)

Stage II presents a new set of developmental problems and challenges. Organizational resources are stretched to the limit when increasing sales require a seemingly endless increase in people, financing, equipment, and space. Similarly, the organization's day-to-day operational systems for recruiting, production or service delivery, purchasing, accounting, collections, information, and payables are nearly overwhelmed by the sheer amount of product or service being "pushed out the door."

The major purpose or challenge of Stage II is "organizational scale-up." This means that the business concept has been demonstrated to be valid (Stage I), and the organization must now acquire the resources and develop the systems required to facilitate growth. For example, EEZYCUT (described earlier) is beginning Stage II. Its founders, David Jones and Laura Mayes (husband and wife) are currently in the process of what they term "upgrading" the infrastructure of EEZYCUT to better handle the challenges they face in Stage II of their business. As David states, "It is a lot to handle!"[2]

The major problems that occur during Stage II are problems of growth rather than survival. It is during this stage that horror stories begin to accumulate:

- Salespeople sell a product they know is in inventory, only to learn that someone else has grabbed it for other customers.
- One vendor's invoices are paid two and three times, while another vendor has not been paid in six months.
- A precipitous drop in product quality occurs for unknown reasons.
- Turnover increases sharply just when the company needs more personnel.
- Missing letters, files, and reports cause confusion, loss of time, and embarrassment.
- Senior executives find themselves scheduled to be in two widely separated cities on the same day at the same time, or they arrive in a distant city only to learn that they are a day early.
- The computer system crashes frequently, leaving users without access to valuable information, basically shutting the company down for hours or sometimes days.

These are what we call growing pains.

The classic organizational growing pains that are typical of Stage II and later-stage companies are discussed in detail in Chapter 5. The relative emphasis on each key developmental task appropriate for Stage II is shown schematically in Figure 3.2.

Many companies experience a great deal of difficulty during Stage II and even disappear. Although it is established that 50% of companies survive until stage II, there are not sufficient data on the percentage that survive until Stage III. We believe (or hypothesize) that about 50% of the original 50% surviving companies at Stage II will again survive to stage III. This means that 25% of the original start-ups will survive until Stage III.

When failure at Stage II occurs, it is usually because the founding entrepreneur is unable to cope with the managerial problems that arise as the organization grows. A Stage II company needs an infrastructure of operational systems that lets it operate efficiently and effectively on a day-to-day basis. Unfortunately, many entrepreneurs are not interested in such organizational plumbing.

Some businesses that are fortunate enough to have discovered an especially rich market find themselves growing very rapidly. Although most of the development of resources and operational systems ought to occur during the period when the organization is growing from $1 million to $10 million in annual revenues, it is not unusual to find companies with $30, $40, $50, or even

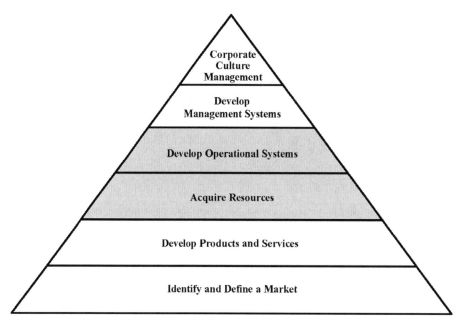

Figure 3.2   Developmental Emphasis in a Stage II Organization

more than $100 million in annual revenues with the operational systems of a Stage II organization. This kind of discrepancy between an organization's size and the degree of development of its operational systems leads to serious problems, but these may be masked in the short term by rapidly rising revenues. This often proves to be the case in some of the most spectacular examples of organizational failure, such as Osborne Computer.

Today the name "Osborne Computer" is largely unrecognized, except by "Boomers." Yet it was once as high-profile as Apple or Starbucks. Adam Osborne was an entrepreneur who perceived the need for "portable PCs," which are now known as "laptops" (even though his product weighed 28 pounds and had a screen about 6 inches wide). He developed a company, which grew to $100 million in revenues within two years, but then went bankrupt in its third year. It was a classic example of meteoric success followed by meteoric failure, brought about, at least in part, by underdeveloped operational systems. In an article on the rise and fall of Adam Osborne, Steve Coll states, "In retrospect, it seems clear that the company's accounting procedures were so slipshod that no one knew how things were."[3]

The lesson of what happened to Osborne and his fleetingly successful company needs to be learned by all entrepreneurs. Many companies continue to make the same mistakes, and the end results are similar. For example, system crashes experienced by several online brokerage firms are a warning that both the product and related infrastructure are not sufficiently developed to serve as a sound platform for future growth.

Since rapid growth can create problems as well as opportunities it is essential to be prepared for it. Preparation for growth typically requires the acquisition of resources of various kinds including money, people, and equipment. It means the development of the day-to-day operational systems to do what the business is in business to do. We term this the "operational infrastructure," which refers to the resources and day-to-day systems required to operate the business.

Keys to Success at Stage II. The keys to success at Stage II are fundamentally different from those at Stage I. Stage II is all about expansion or scale up, and successful scale up requires operational infrastructure. The level of infrastructure needs to match the size of the company as measured by its revenues. It also needs to be designed so that it will support the organization's continued growth. If the required infrastructure is in place, the organization will operate well; if not, it will experience a variety of organizational problems, which we term "growing pains." Growing pains are described further in Chapter 5.

Stages I and II Together

Taken together, Stages I and II—the new venture and expansion stages—constitute the entrepreneurial phase of organizational development. It is during these two stages of growth that the classic skills of entrepreneurship are most relevant. It is also during this phase that the need to make the transition from an entrepreneurship to an entrepreneurially oriented, professionally managed organization begins to occur.

Stage III: Professionalization

Somewhere during the period of explosive growth that characterizes Stage II, senior management realizes (or ought to realize) that a need for a qualitative change in the organization is arising. The company cannot merely add people, money, equipment, and space to cope with its growth; it must undergo a transition or metamorphosis and become a somewhat different type of organization.

Until this point, the enterprise generally will have been totally entrepreneurial. It has operated with a considerable degree of informality. It may have lacked well-defined goals, roles, plans, or controls but still prospered. However, once a critical size has been achieved, many of these practices and procedures must be increasingly formalized. The need for this transition typically occurs for manufacturing organizations by the time they have reached approximately $10 million in sales. (For service firms, the need for this transition typically arises when they have reached $3.3 million in revenues.) At this level of revenues, the sheer size of the organization requires more formal planning, regularly scheduled meetings, defined organizational roles and responsibilities, and performance management systems. The people who manage the company and its operations must also change their skills and capabilities. Until this point, it was possible to be more of a doer or hands-on manager than a professional manager. At this stage, however, the organization increasingly requires people who are adept at formal administration, planning, organization, motivation, leadership, and control. In brief, the focus at this stage of development should be on developing the management systems required to take the organization to its next stage of development. Developing and implementing these systems, in turn, requires a planned program of organizational development. It also requires using the managerial tools described in Chapters 6 to 9.

It is at this stage that the company must make a transition from an entrepreneurship to an entrepreneurially oriented, professionally managed organization. This means that the organization, while still maintaining its entrepreneurial spirit, will also need to develop the infrastructure and professional management capabilities required to continue its growth successfully.

This is a delicate balancing act. An organization must *never* lose its entrepreneurial mindset or spirit, but it must begin to develop the infrastructure and management systems required to facilitate its future growth. Although some people equate professional management with bureaucracy, we believe they are mistaken. It is true that if professional management exists without an entrepreneurial mindset or culture, it can *become* bureaucracy. But it is also true that if entrepreneurship is carried to an extreme in large companies, it can result in chaos, and chaos ultimately leads to organizational difficulties and even bankruptcy.

As we discuss throughout the remainder of this book, making the successful transition from an entrepreneurship to a professionally managed organization requires some delicate surgery. At this point, the key thing we want to point out is that, based on our research and experience, this transition is not a choice but a requirement or imperative for continued organizational success and that it involves the development of management systems. We shall provide examples throughout this book of both organizations that have made this transition successfully and thrived, as well as others that have failed to make this transition and experienced great difficulties (such as Osborne Computers and Boston Market).

The relative emphasis on each key developmental task appropriate for Stage III is shown schematically in Figure 3.3. As the figure indicates, the most important task during this stage is the development of management systems.

Figure 3.3   Developmental Emphasis in a Stage III Organization

Although the professionalization and related development of management systems of an organization ought to occur during the period when sales are growing from $10 million to approximately $100 million, the rate of growth often outstrips the rate at which the enterprise's management systems are developed. This can lead to serious problems, which can either limit the potential development of a business or cause failure. This was the case at Starbucks Coffee Company in 1994.

At that time, Starbucks was essentially a Stage II company in the process of making the transition to Stage III (in terms of its organizational infrastructure), even though its corporate revenues were more than $100 million (Stage IV). As a result, the business was beginning to experience significant growing pains, which could have hampered the company's development and ultimate success.[4]

Similar problems occurred at the same stage of growth at Jamba Juice, Noah's Bagels, and Power-Bar. Other examples include Apple Computer (revenues of more than $2 billion in 1985 but only Stage II in terms of infrastructure) and Maxicare (revenues of about $1.8 billion). Apple lost market share to IBM, and Maxicare had to downsize and ultimately file for bankruptcy. This company had grown rapidly through acquisitions but had not taken the time to develop an operational and management infrastructure that would support the much larger organization that it had become.

As noted in Chapter 1, the entrepreneurial personality can be a barrier to success at Stage III. Making the transition from an entrepreneurship to professional management involves more than just the development of operational and management systems. It requires a profound mindset change on the part of people, especially the entrepreneurs who founded the company. We have been working with companies to help them make this transition for nearly 40 years. One of the classic obstacles to this process is typically the entrepreneur; many fear becoming bureaucratic, and then confuse bureaucracy with systems. Some of this is deeply rooted in their personalities; they do not want to be controlled by anyone or anything—not plans, not role descriptions, not policies, not procedures.

Because they have been successful in launching a new venture without these things, they assume (either explicitly or implicitly) that they are not necessary and that they are, in fact, barriers to success. What they fail to realize is that the game needs to be played differently at different stages of the organizational life cycle. Without systems or plans or role definitions, the organization will definitely experience increasing confusion and quite possibly chaos. In spite of what one author has written, no one thrives on chaos indefinitely![5]

As noted in Chapter 1, when Orin Smith (then CFO of Starbucks) invited one of the authors to work with Starbucks Coffee Company to assist them in making the transition to professional management, he stated that the biggest challenge would be getting Howard Schultz to buy in to the concept that a firm could be better managed without losing its entrepreneurial spirit. He cautioned that Schultz might not have the patience for much process and systems. In fact, Howard Schultz embraced these notions very quickly. They were consistent with his belief that if you are going to build a large building, you need a strong foundation.

This issue of the psychological acceptance of the need to transition from early-stage entrepreneurship to professional management is a traumatic one for many, if not most, entrepreneurs. It requires a leap of faith because their early experiences suggest that systems are not essential to success. Without making this leap, however, the entrepreneurs may put what they have built at risk of decline or even failure.

While some entrepreneurs resist the changes required to transition to professional management, there are others who readily embrace this notion. Among those who readily embraced the idea of transitioning to professional management are:

- Brian Maxwell, founder of PowerBar
- Yerkin Tatishev, founder and CEO of Kusto Group (Kazakhstan, Russia, Ukraine, Vietnam, and Israel)
- Tim and Jud Carter, Bell-Carter Foods, Inc.
- James Stowers, Jr., Founder of American Century Investments
- Melvin and Herbert Simon, Simon Property Group

One of those cited above was James Stowers, Jr. (now deceased), founder of what is now American Century Investments. The experience of American Century Investments and its founder James Stowers, Jr., in making the transition to professional management is an excellent example of how this process can be done successfully. It is described in detail in Chapter 13.

Keys to Success at Stage III. In summary, the keys to success at Stage III are (1) the ability to recognize the need to transform from an early-stage entrepreneurial venture to an entrepreneurially oriented, professionally managed organization; and (2) the ability to develop the managerial capabilities and management systems required for future sustainable growth, including all of the tools to be described in Chapters 6 to 9. Chapters 6 to 9 also present case studies of how leaders of Stage III and beyond organizations developed and used these tools to support continued success.

Stage IV: Consolidation

Once the organization has made the transition to professional management—with workable systems for planning, organization structure, management development, and performance management—leadership must turn its attention to an intangible but nevertheless real and significant asset: corporate culture. Management of the corporate culture is the main task of Stage IV of organizational development.

The key challenge at Stage IV is to help consolidate or institutionalize the cultural aspects of the transformation from an entrepreneurship to a professionally managed organization. As the organization makes the transition required of Stage III and develops management systems, a cultural transition is also in progress. The company is going from a very loose, free-spirited organization to a more disciplined one; from an organization with a strategy and perhaps a plan to one with a well-defined planning process; from one with vague goals to more specific, measurable goals; from one with loosely defined roles to one with more formal role descriptions; and from one with limited accountability to one with more accountability. Explicitly or implicitly, this involves a cultural change, and it is a change that must be managed if the transition is to be made successfully.

Corporate culture can have a powerful effect, not only on day-to-day operations but on the bottom line of profitability as well.[6] During the growth that was necessary to reach Stage IV (which typically seems to begin at about $100 million in sales for manufacturing firms), the organization has brought in new waves of people. The first wave probably arrived when the organization was relatively small and informal, during Stage I. During this period, the organization's culture (values, beliefs, and norms) was transmitted by direct day-to-day contact between the founder and personnel. The diffusion or transmission of culture was a by-product of what the organization did. Virtually everybody knew everybody else. Everybody also knew what the company wanted to achieve and how.

During Stage II, the rapid expansion of the enterprise most likely brought in a second wave of people. The first-wave personnel transmitted the corporate culture to this new generation. However, at an increased level of organizational size, especially if the organization develops geographically separate operations, this informal socialization process becomes more attenuated and less effective. The sheer number of new people simply overwhelms the socialization system.

By the time it reaches $100 million in revenues, a third wave of people usually has joined the organization, and the informal socialization is no longer adequate to do what it once did so well. At this stage, leaders must develop a more conscious and formal method of transmitting the corporate culture throughout the organization, monitoring it and managing it. This is the key challenge faced by Stage IV organizations. The relative emphasis on each key developmental task appropriate for Stage IV is pictured in Figure 3.4.

Keys to Success at Stage IV. In summary, the keys to success at Stage IV are (1) the ability to change the corporate culture or mindset to support the professionalization of the enterprise; and (2) the ability to develop effective systems for communicating, managing, and reinforcing the culture. Chapter 10 examines the management of corporate culture in greater detail and presents examples of companies that have done it successfully and unsuccessfully.

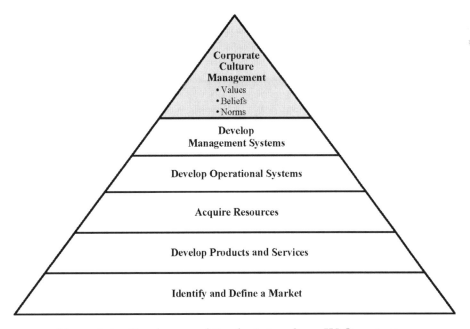

Figure 3.4   Developmental Emphasis in a Stage IV Organization

Differences between Entrepreneurial and Professional Management

Stages I and II, taken together, make up the entrepreneurial phase of organizational development, while Stages III and IV make up the professional management phase. As an organization passes from one of these phases of growth to the other, a variety of changes need to occur. There is a qualitative difference between an entrepreneurship and a professionally managed firm. The former tends to be characterized by informality, lack of systems, and a free-spirited nature. The latter tends to be more formal, to have well-developed systems, and to be proud of its disciplined, profit-oriented approach.

The most important differences between an entrepreneurship and a professionally managed organization involve nine key result areas: (1) profit, (2) planning, (3) organization, (4) control/performance management, (5) management/leadership development, (6) budgeting, (7) innovation, (8) leadership, and (9) culture. Table 3.2 summarizes the principal characteristics of professional management, as compared with entrepreneurial management in each of these key result areas. We now describe these differences in greater detail.

Profit

In a professionally managed organization, profit is an explicit goal; it is planned, rather than being a residual or whatever is left over at the end of the year. In an entrepreneurial organization, profit is sought, but it is not an explicit goal to be attained. The entrepreneur may be willing to invest and sacrifice current profits for a future big hit.

Planning

Unfortunately, in many entrepreneurial organizations, the plan, if there is one, is in the entrepreneur's head. A professionally managed organization has a formal, written business plan. Planning becomes a way of life as the organization's leaders develop and use a formal, written strategic plan as the "roadmap" for success. In addition to strategic planning, operational plans and budgets are developed. Contingency plans also are developed. The practice of informal, superficial, ad hoc planning is replaced by a regular planning cycle.

Organization

An entrepreneurial organization has an informal organizational structure with overlapping and undefined responsibilities. People are expected to do whatever is necessary, without regard to job titles or positions. This is fine when a company is small. But as it grows, chaos can set in, with people simply not knowing what they are supposed to do. A professionally managed organization has a set of written role descriptions that clearly state responsibilities. These descriptions are designed to be mutually exclusive and exhaustive. They are intended to help people understand what their roles are and to give focus to their efforts and use of time. There is also a formal organizational chart that accurately provides information about reporting relationships and helps people understand how this structure should work.

Table 3.2 Comparison of Professional Management and Entrepreneurial Management

Key Result Areas	Professional Management	Entrepreneurial Management
Profit	Profit orientation; profit as explicit goal	Profit as a by-product
Planning	Formal, systematic planning: • Strategic Planning • Operational Planning • Contingency Planning	Informal, ad hoc planning
Organization	Formal, explicit role descriptions that are mutually exclusive and exhaustive	Informal structure with overlapping and undefined responsibilities
Control/ Performance Management	Formal, planned system of organizational control, including explicit objectives, targets, measures, evaluations, and rewards	Partial, ad hoc control, seldom with formal measurement
Management and Leadership Development	Planned management development: • Identification of requirements • Design of programs	Ad hoc development, principally through on-the-job training
Budgeting	Management by standards and variances	Budget not explicit; no follow-up on variances
Innovation	Orientation to incremental innovations; willingness to take calculated risks	Orientation toward major innovations; willingness to take major risks
Leadership	Consultative or participative styles	Styles varying from very directive to laissez-faire
Culture	Well-defined culture	Loosely defined, "family"-oriented culture

Control/Performance Management

In an entrepreneurship, control of operations tends to be lacking or at least is often piecemeal. The organization usually lacks formal measurement or performance appraisal systems. A professionally managed organization, by contrast, has a formal, planned system of organizational control or performance management. This system makes full use of explicit objectives and goals, measurements of performance, feedback, evaluation, and rewards.

Management and Leadership Development

Management and leadership development is planned in a professionally managed organization. There is a conscious, planned effort to develop the managerial and leadership skills of individuals and to prepare a pool of managers that will help take the organization into the future. In an entrepreneurship, however, management and leadership development is unplanned and tends to occur, if at all, through on-the-job experience. Although the entrepreneurial organization may avoid the cost of management development programs, people may become victims of the Peter Principle (being promoted beyond their competence) and cost the company through inefficiency, mistakes, and replacement costs.

Budgeting

In an entrepreneurship, budgeting tends to lack detail. There is little follow-up on variances or deviations from the budget. A professionally managed organization's budget system focuses on standards and variances. Managers are held accountable for performance, compared against budget goals. Budgets are not cast in concrete but are there to guide performance.

Innovation

By definition, entrepreneurial companies are oriented toward innovation. Many are willing to make major innovations in products, services, or operating methods. Some entrepreneurs even "bet the company" on an innovation because of the possibility of a high payoff for success. They tend to need quick hits, or fast payoffs. Professionally managed organizations tend to be oriented more toward incremental innovations. They are less likely to bet the company, and they often spread their risk among a portfolio of different products or projects. They are willing to take calculated risks, but they may seem relatively averse to risks, at least in comparison to entrepreneurial companies. There are exceptions to this, and established professionally managed companies such as Boeing and IBM are famous for having bet the company on new technologies a number of times during their history. Many of the best-managed companies, however, are oriented to continuous, incremental improvements and long-term support of major innovations that do not require fast payoffs.

Leadership

In entrepreneurial companies, leadership typically ranges from very directive styles such as autocratic or benevolent autocratic to very nondirective styles such as laissez-faire. In a professionally managed organization, the tendency today is toward more interactive styles, such as consultative and participative management, or, in a few instances, to consensus or team-oriented styles. Entrepreneurial organizations are more likely to have charismatic leaders than are professionally managed companies because of the nature of the process of selection for promotion in large organizations.

Culture

Culture tends to be loosely defined in entrepreneurial organizations and sometimes it is not explicitly managed. Often the culture of an entrepreneurial organization is oriented toward a family feeling, which is feasible because of its relatively small size. Professionally managed organizations are more likely to treat organizational culture explicitly as a variable to be managed and transmitted throughout the enterprise. They tend to understand that culture is a source of sustainable competitive advantage.

Relevance of Differences

Our discussion of the differences between entrepreneurial and professionally managed organizations is intended to be descriptive rather than evaluative. Both types of organizations have strengths and limitations. The significant point is that different ways of operating are appropriate at different stages of organizational growth.

From an entrepreneurial organization's standpoint, it is clear that something inevitably will be lost as the organization makes the transition to professional management. However, something will also be gained. Just as a plant that has been successful in its pot must be transplanted if it is to continue to grow and develop properly, an organization that has outgrown its infrastructure and style of management must also make a transformation. Failure to do so will lead to a variety of problems.

Discrepancies between Growth and Organizational Development

As we have seen, two independent dimensions are involved in each stage of organizational growth: (1) size and (2) the extent to which the enterprise has developed the systems required to support its size in each of the six critical development areas included in the Pyramid of Organizational Development. An organization can be at Stage III in terms of size, as measured in annual revenues, but only at Stage II in its internal organizational capabilities. In other words, its infrastructure is not developed to the extent that it needs to be to support the enterprise's size. For example, after only a very few years of existence, Osborne Computer was a Stage IV company in size, but it was only a Stage II company in terms of its infrastructure. The lack of infrastructure to support the firm contributed to significant problems, which ultimately resulted in the firm filing for bankruptcy.

An organization will face significant problems if its internal development is too far out of step with its size. As shown in Figure 3.5, the greater the degree of incongruity between an organization's

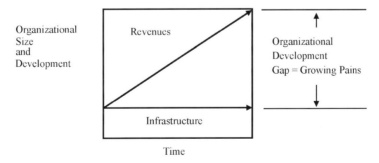

Figure 3.5   Causes of Organizational Growing Pains

size and the development of its infrastructure, the greater the probability that it will experience organizational growing pains (the topic of Chapter 5). Such an organization is like a 12-year-old boy who is well over six feet tall: He has the body of a man but, most likely, the mind of a child. As a senior manager in one organization stated, "We are essentially a $30 million company that happened to have $350 million in sales." The manager meant that the firm had the operating systems and developmental structure of a $30 million company, but its growth had given it revenue that greatly exceeded (by more than 10 times) its infrastructure's capacity. Predictably, the company was in difficulty and was ultimately purchased by a competitor.

Managing the Transition between Growth Stages

What can management do to help make the transition required between growth stages? There are four steps by which the senior managers of a growing enterprise can help their company make a smooth transition from one stage of growth to the next and, ultimately, make the transformation from an entrepreneurship to professional management. They are as follows:

1. Perform an organizational evaluation or assessment of the company's effectiveness at its current stage of development.
2. Formulate an organizational development plan.
3. Implement the plan through action plans and programs.
4. Monitor the programs for effectiveness.

We now examine each of these steps in detail.

Perform an Organizational Evaluation or Assessment

An organizational evaluation or assessment consists of systematic assessment, by means of data analysis and interviews with organization members, of the extent to which systems are adequate to meet the company's current and anticipated future requirements. While this evaluation may be performed by the organization's management team, many companies prefer to have independent consultants conduct the assessment in order to obtain greater objectivity or benefit from their experience with similar companies facing similar issues. The findings of the evaluation represent a diagnosis of the organization at its current stage of development. This assessment might include administering and using results from surveys, such as the Organizational Effectiveness Survey© described in Chapter 2 and the Growing Pains Survey (which will be described in Chapter 5).

Formulate an Organizational Development Plan

Once the organizational evaluation has been completed, management must develop a master plan or blueprint for building the capabilities needed for the organization to function successfully at its current or next stage of development. This is the strategic organizational development plan, which will be described in Chapter 6.

Implement the Organizational Development Plan and Monitor Its Progress

The third and fourth steps in helping an organization make the transition to a new growth stage are implementing the changes set forth in the organizational development plan and monitoring their effects. This includes both developing new organizational systems (planning, organization, and performance management) and developing management's capabilities through corporate education programs. Management development programs may focus on administrative skills (such as planning), leadership skills, or both. We examine the development of these management systems and capabilities in Part Two of this book. Once the development program has been implemented, management needs to monitor its progress in meeting developmental needs. Such monitoring helps senior managers identify and address any problems related to achieving organizational development goals.

These four steps—diagnosing, planning, implementing, and monitoring changes in organizational capabilities—are the keys to making a smooth transition from an entrepreneurship to a professionally managed enterprise. The steps are the same regardless of the size, industry, or current stage of development of an organization. As such, they can also be applied to organizations that have grown beyond Stage IV.

It should be noted that these steps may appear simple, but they are often quite complex in practice. The transition process typically requires one to two years for a Stage I firm; three years or more may well be required in a Stage IV firm. Some aspects of the change process (such as changes in personnel—voluntary or otherwise) can be difficult to handle. However, where the process is suitably designed and well-executed, the organization will almost always emerge from it stronger and more successful than ever.

Failure of senior management to take the necessary steps in negotiating transitions between each of the stages can have significant consequences. These range from stagnation and blocked growth to removal of the founders, as has happened at many companies. Or the company may experience bankruptcy or takeover, as happened with Osborne Computer. However, if the proper steps are taken, then organizations can experience a great deal of success. Starbucks and Microsoft are good examples of this.

Case Example of Growth from Stages I to IV: 99 Cents Only Stores

This section presents a case example of a company from its inception as a new venture through its transition to become an entrepreneurially oriented, professionally managed company. The company is 99 Cents Only Stores.

Origins of 99 Cents Only Stores

The late Dave Gold and his wife, Sherry, are a classic American entrepreneurial success story. In 1945, Dave's father, an immigrant from Russia, opened a tiny liquor store in downtown Los Angeles. In 1957, Dave's father received an offer to sell his store for $35,000, but he sold it instead to Dave and his brother-in-law for $2,000 as a down payment, with the rest being paid with no interest over a long period of time.

The Precursor to 99 Cents Only Stores

In 1961, the two entrepreneurs opened another liquor store nearby in the Grand Central Market of downtown Los Angeles. As did other, similar stores, they sold beer, wine, and hard liquor for a variety of prices.

As part of the process of doing business, they noticed that items priced at 99 cents were selling so fast that they could not keep them in stock. They decided to experiment with pricing, selling all wines priced between $0.89 and $1.29 at a fixed price of 99 cents. They advertised: "Wines of the world for 99 cents." The experiment was a great success. They found that those items formerly sold at 89 cents sold *more* when priced at 99 cents! Dave Gold had some additional insights from this experiment: (1) Customers preferred the digit 9 in pricing, and (2) customers prefer fewer digits in the price.

Dave Gold had a natural genius for business. He did a number of unorthodox things that worked quite well. For example, he advertised certain products as "the world's worst." He advertised cigarettes as "the world's worst cigarettes for 99 cents." People bought the cigarettes to see how bad they really were! He also advertised certain wines as "the world's worst wine for 99 cents," and people bought those, too, to see just how awful they were.

The Next Phase

In 1972, the two partners divided the business, with each receiving two liquor stores. Now Dave could go his own way. He could buy as much as he wanted and experiment however he wanted.

The Opportunistic Buyer. Dave Gold was an aggressive buyer. He was confident he could sell what he bought, and he was willing to buy in large quantities, including things he had never sold before. In 1973, Dave bought a supermarket that was going out of business at an auction. The purchase included many items that Dave had never sold before. He then purchased a general merchandise store in the Grand Central Market in Los Angeles near his liquor store. This was the beginning of a diversification of his business, and it ultimately led to the development of 99 Cents Only Stores.

Another example of Dave's willingness to buy occurred in 1976. Kimberly Clark, manufacturer of Kotex, had overproduced the product. Dave purchased six truckloads of Kotex. There was, however, one little problem: there was no place to store all of this merchandise. At the time, Dave's father owned an old garage located in Skid Row in Los Angeles. He let Dave use it as a warehouse to store the product, and there was also space for more storage of products.

Diversification. After a few months, small retailers began coming to the warehouse to purchase products. This led, in turn, to the creation of a business unit (which still exists today) called Bargain Wholesale, which sells merchandise at below-normal wholesale prices to retailers, distributors, and exporters.

The Genesis of the Concept of 99 Cents Only Stores

It has been said that success is the result of preparation meeting opportunity. One of Dave Gold's greatest strengths as an entrepreneur was his willingness to experiment and take risks. He learned from both successes and difficulties encountered. Since his original experimentation with selling wines and cigarettes for a fixed price of 99 cents, Dave had been flirting with the idea of creating a store that would sell everything for 99 cents. His belief that this would be a good idea was enhanced by an experiment that he conducted at trade shows.

It is a common practice at trade shows for exhibited items in a booth to be sold at deeply discounted prices rather than being carted back after the show is over. Dave tried an experiment. Instead of selling the products he brought to a trade show at a variety of prices, he separated his products into three tables with three price points: $1, $2, and $5. The experiment had two significant outcomes: (1) total sales exceeded sales of previous years where things were sold at a wide variety of prices, and (2) the "$1 table" sold the most. Dave was still not ready to launch his idea of a "99 Cents Only Stores" concept. The idea would, however, continue to intrigue him.

Stage I: Accidental Launch of 99 Cents Only Stores

Dave had been talking about this idea for a very long time with a number of people, including an old friend named Jimmy Wayner. One day in 1982, while driving near the airport, Dave and Jimmy spotted a store for lease. His friend said, "I am sick of you talking about your 99 cents idea. You either rent this building, or you never talk about this with me anymore!"

Dave rented the 3,000-square-foot facility and 99 Cents Only Stores was born. This first store would be the initial seed of the company that would ultimately become 99 Cents Only Stores. Such was the accidental launch of the 99 Cents Only Stores concept—the first of its kind in the United States.

Stage II: Expansion of 99 Cents Only Stores

Dave and Sherry acquired a warehouse to store merchandise and proceeded to expand the business by opening more stores. Dave and Sherry traveled to trade shows and auctions to find products, which they purchased for 50 cents per unit; they had a van or truck there so they could ship everything back to Los Angeles.

The company was aided in its development of the business by a great deal of free publicity. Because the concept was novel, the media were interested. The *Herald Examiner*, a Los Angeles newspaper, put the company on the front page with a story. The company also received coverage from various local channels, as well as CNN.

Dave and Sherry raised three children: Howard, Jeff, and Karen. In 1984, Dave and Sherry opened their second store. All of Dave and Sherry's children were involved in the business from an early age, and all occupied important positions in the firm.

By 1996, 99 Cents Only Stores had a total of 36 stores—all in Southern California. In May of 1996, the company did an IPO and became a public company on the NYSE, trading under the symbol NDN. One long-time observer of the company expressed the belief that a major reason Dave Gold took 99 Cents Only Stores public was to give employees a chance to participate in the value created by the growth of the company. In fact, the company launched a stock option program in which employees can participate.

Even after going public, the members of the Gold family were committed to the success of NDN. In addition, the family knew a great deal about the business from its many years of involvement.

For almost a decade after the IPO, family members continued to be the driving force in the business. By 2004, the company had grown very large and more complex. It now had more than two hundred stores and was operating in four states (California, Nevada, Texas, and Arizona).

Like all companies experiencing rapid growth, NDN was beginning to experience some of the classic growing pains that will be described in Chapter 5. Management focused on dealing with the company's growing pains and preparing to take NDN to the next level of success. The company added new members to its board, added additional depth to its management team, initiated a new process of strategic planning, developed more sophisticated supply chain operations, revised and upgraded its operational systems, and put into effect a number of other initiatives designed to strengthen the company and build on its existing strong foundation. In doing so, the company applied many of the concepts and tools presented in this book.

Stage III: Transitioning to Professional Management

By 2005, under Dave Gold's leadership, 99 Cents Only Stores had grown to 225 stores and almost $1 billion in revenues. The innovative business concept pioneered by Dave Gold had also spawned a number of imitators and, in fact, had created a new business category: the $1 store concept.

After more than 50 years of involvement in the business and its precursor, Dave Gold made the decision to retire on December 31, 2004. This led to a management succession at the executive levels of the company. Dave Gold continued as chairman of the board. His son-in-law, Eric Schiffer, who holds an MBA from Harvard Business School and joined the company in 1991, became CEO. Dave's son, Jeff Gold, who has been involved in the business for many years, became president and COO and took over responsibility for day-to-day operations. Howard Gold, also involved in the business for many years, became executive vice president (EVP) for special projects. In addition, the company hired a new CFO and created the position of EVP for supply chain operations. It also recruited experienced professionals in several other areas of the company, including human resources.

Stage IV: Consolidation

Under the new leadership of Eric Schiffer and Jeff Gold, the company developed a culture statement to formalize the values that had been underlying its operation for many years.

Conclusion

The inception, growth, and transition to professional management of 99 Cents Only Stores is truly an impressive business success story. The company created its business concept and defined a new business space. The company successfully made the transition from a family-driven business to a publicly held, professionally managed enterprise.

In 2012, the company went private, in a purchase by Ares Management and the Canada Pension Plan Investment Board as well as the Gold-Schiffer family in a deal valued at $1.6 billion. At the time of the buyout, the company had approximately $1.5 billion in revenues. The company still operates throughout several western states as well as its home state of California.

Summary

This chapter presents a framework to help senior managers understand and guide organizations at different stages of growth and development. It describes the first four major stages of organizational growth, from the inception of a new venture (Stage I) to the consolidation of a professionally managed organization (Stage IV). It examines the degree of emphasis that must be placed on each level of the Pyramid of Organizational Development at each stage of growth. It also examines the differences between an entrepreneurial and a professionally managed organization and describes the steps that must be taken to make a successful transition from one stage of growth to the next.

In the next chapter, we examine the remaining three stages of growth comprising the organizational life cycle: diversification, integration, and decline-revitalization.

Notes

1. Personal communication with David Jones, February, 15 2015.
2. Ibid.
3. Steve Coll, "The Rise and Fall of Adam Osborne," *California Magazine*, November 1983, 92.
4. Howard Schultz and Dori Jones Yang, *Pour Your Heart into It: How Starbucks Built a Company one Cup at a Time* (New York: Hyperion, 1997).
5. See Tom Peters, *Thriving on Chaos* (New York: Alfred A. Knopf, 1987).
6. See Eric Flamholtz, "Corporate Culture and the Bottom Line," *European Management Journal* 19, no. 3 (2001): 268–275.

Managing the Advanced Stages of Growth

Τ he previous chapter dealt with the issues encountered by growing entrepreneurial organizations as they move through the first four stages of growth: from a new venture (Stage I) to consolidation of an established business (Stage IV). If management has accomplished the developmental tasks described, then on completing Stage IV, the enterprise will have become a professionally managed organization. This chapter continues the discussion of the organizational life cycle and presents a framework for identifying and managing the advanced stages of growth: Stages V to VII.

Some businesses will have the opportunity to grow in size beyond Stage IV, and this growth will present a new set of organizational development problems that are quite different from those during Stages I through IV. This chapter is intended to assist the senior managers of such organizations in planning for the future development of their enterprises by examining the stages of growth that occur beyond Stage IV. It can also help senior managers of organizations that have already reached those stages of growth and are either encountering certain developmental problems or wish to avoid the classic problems at each stage.

We first describe the nature of each of the advanced stages of growth and then examine the key problems and challenges that organizations must confront as they advance to each of them.

Nature of Problems beyond Stage IV

Prior to Stage V, the organization's management problems all center around the issues of locating an initial market, developing a product, and building the operational infrastructure, management systems, and corporate culture needed to run a business that has reached approximately $100 to

$500 million in annual revenue (for manufacturing firms) or approximately one-third of this for service firms. On reaching Stage V, the firm's problems change in nature. The entity must now reestablish itself as a different type of entrepreneurial company—one that is professionalized, but at the same time is entrepreneurial and focused on finding new markets and/or developing and offering new products or services to support its continued growth. Ideally, the business will have retained its entrepreneurial orientation throughout Stages I through IV. In some cases, however, organizations may have lost their entrepreneurial spirit to some degree and must now seek to reestablish it. Once the challenge of developing new products or services has been met, the organization must then focus on developing an infrastructure capable of supporting the now-diversified company it has become.

For most organizations, growth beyond Stage IV will involve or require diversification. The core business might reach limits in terms of available market share, or the core business might simply provide opportunities for expansion into new areas. For example, Starbucks has continued its growth of retail cafés, but has also expanded into selling coffee in groceries, and creating joint ventures to sell its café concept in different venues such as airports. It has also expanded into other products like juices and bakery items (through, in some instances, purchasing existing companies). Google has diversified into many different areas from its core business in search. The company now offers software including Gmail, social networking, cloud storage, and even Google Glasses, an eyewear device for accessing the Internet. Microsoft has diversified from the Windows PC platform to web-based services.

Growth beyond Stage IV

In this section, we describe, in depth, the stages of growth beyond Stage IV: Stages V, VI, and VII. They represent the transitions that must be made by all entrepreneurially oriented, professionally managed organizations if they are to continue growing successfully. The advanced stages of organizational growth, the critical development areas for each stage, and the approximate size (measured in dollars of sales revenue or budget for nonprofits) at which an organization should pass through each stage are shown in Table 4.1.

Stage V: Diversification

After an organization has completed the consolidation stage, the next developmental challenge it faces is to diversify. This can occur either because the organization's product life cycle has reached the mature part of the S-curve, or because the core product has simply created new opportunities.

Diversification Attributable to Product Maturation and Competition. If the company's original product or product line has become relatively mature and will not facilitate sufficient future growth to sustain the organization at its current rate of growth, its historical rate of growth, or its immediate future growth expectations, the solution is diversification. This problem is simply a result of the phenomenon of market saturation.

When a business initially introduces a product as a new venture, the market is typically unsaturated, and there is relatively little competition. As the organization becomes successful, it inevitably attracts competitors. A classic example was Apple Computer and the development of the personal

Table 4.1   Advanced Stages of Organizational Growth

Stage	Description	Critical Development Area	Approximate Organizational Size (in Sales)	
			Manufacturing Firms	Service Firms
V	Diversification	New products for existing market, new markets for existing products, or both	$500 million to $1 billion	$167 to $333 million
VI	Integration	Integration of different business units through developing a new infrastructure to support them (managing resources, developing appropriate operational and management systems, and creating a culture consistent with the needs of the "new company")	$1 billion plus	$333 million plus
VII	Decline and Revitalization	Revitalization of organization at all levels of the Pyramid of Organizational Development	Varies	Varies

computer. Apple Computer found and developed the market for the personal computer (they were the first to offer a product that required little assembly) but attracted a host of competitors, including IBM. The presence of competition decreases the firm's profit margins and erodes its market share over time. Similarly, Google developed Google Glass, and then Microsoft developed the HoloLens.

Sometimes a company can have the market or playing field to itself, with limited competition, for a very long time. For example, Mattel dominated the market for dolls for young girls for many years with its iconic doll, Barbie. Since 2001, MGA Entertainment has taken away a significant portion of Mattel's market share with its edgier, multiethnic Bratz dolls. Another example of how a company can have the market to itself is in the biotechnology business. Companies such as Amgen or those specializing in orphan drugs can patent their drugs (or molecules) and create a virtual monopoly for the products, at least for a limited period of time. Amgen owns patents for its products such as Epogen and Neupogen, and has an army of lawyers to protect its intellectual property. While the patent remains valid, Amgen has a market protected from competition and can earn high profit margins. The same is true for so-called orphan drugs, which are drugs that treat relatively rare but serious diseases. Such diseases would not be profitable for investment and development by pharmaceutical companies if competition were permitted. Once a drug has been patented, it has special status and is relatively protected.

As the market for the new product becomes increasingly saturated, the new venture's rate of growth cannot be sustained for its given product vehicle. A classic historical example of this phenomenon was the highly successful dBASE II—one of the first software products for database management, marketed by Ashton-Tate, a company that no longer exists. As the potential users of dBASE II were reached, and as new competitors entered the marketplace, it was necessary for Ashton-Tate to identify new products to continue its growth. Ultimately, the company was unsuccessful in accomplishing this task and was, as a result, sold to Borland, which in turn was ultimately purchased by another company. In contrast, Oracle Corporation, which is itself built on a platform of database management software, has been able to deal successfully with the challenge of product diversification through software applications to become a dominant multibillion-dollar company.

One way of thinking about the difference between the issues faced by a company during Stages I through IV and the issues faced in Stage V is to consider the analogy of a product as an oil field. The central problem in petroleum exploration is finding new oil fields. Once an organization has found an oil field, it builds up an infrastructure to tap the oil well and convert it into marketable products. As the size of the business increases, the firm has to build its business around that oil well. The central issues here are developing the capability to tap the oil well and marketing its products. From this standpoint, the oil well is essentially a resource that the firm is drawing on. However, this resource has a finite life, which means it will not last forever—only until all of the oil has been pumped out.

Most consumer and industrial markets are very much like oil wells, in that they will not last forever. They may produce a gusher that leads to very rapid growth for an organization, but over time the oil wells inevitably play themselves out. When a company builds up its organizational and management infrastructure to tap an oil well, it usually does so with the intention of remaining a going concern. This means that if the organization is to continue to exist, it must find other oil fields that it can begin to extract resources from. Accordingly, if the company is to become more than a one-time venture, it must use some of the resources earned from tapping the oil well to invest in exploration of other oil fields. It should be hiring geologists to search for additional oil fields, spending additional resources in drilling test wells, and so forth.

Companies in totally different businesses from petroleum exploration and refining will find it useful to think of their business in terms of the oil well analogy just described. A company's entrepreneur identifies a new market, which is analogous to a petroleum corporation finding an oil field. The company develops a product that is accepted by consumers, which is, again, analogous to a firm beginning to tap the oil in the field. The organization then builds up the operational management infrastructure necessary to operate the day-to-day business, while simultaneously preparing an infrastructure that is necessary to continue the operation after its first product has been used up. Thus the challenge of Stage V is essentially long-run organizational sustainability. This is analogous to finding another oil well. If the organization is prudent, it will not wait until its markets are sufficiently dried up to begin locating markets and building new products. Accordingly, it will be engaged in a process of research and development designed to identify new oil fields and begin their production while its current oil fields are still producing.

Typically, an organization can only expect that a given product vehicle will carry it to the range of $100 to $500 million in annual revenue. As discussed previously, this is simply the normal curve for this phenomenon, and certain companies may not experience the need for a new product vehicle until significantly after $500 million in revenue is reached. A number of companies have reached

$1 billion in annual revenue before they experienced the need for a new product vehicle; however, these are the exception rather than the general rule. The upper limit for growth through a single product or line of business may be reached well before a company generates $500 million in annual revenues. For example, Bell-Carter Foods—a family-owned business that is the largest producer of table olives in the United States and the second-largest in the world—faced this problem at about $100 million, because at that size they had captured about 80% of the market for their core product (ripe black olives).

A variation on this problem was experienced by Amazon.com. The cost of developing the infrastructure to operate the business of selling books over the Internet was sufficiently great that the company needed to diversify its product line. Today, Amazon sells a variety of products over the Internet, including magazines, music, DVDs, videos, electronics, computers, software, apparel and accessories, and shoes—as well as books.

If the diversification is attributable to a decline in growth, the transition to Stage V will require a redeployment of entrepreneurial skills. The entrepreneurship that was the basis of founding the business in Stage I must reemerge and become a dominant force in Stage V. Because the original product vehicle was sufficient to carry the company along in its chosen market, the managerial problems of Stages II through IV involved building the operational and management infrastructure to support the growing organization. However, the need to diversify translates into the need to be entrepreneurial again.

Unfortunately, it may not be possible for the company to simply go back to its original entrepreneur and have that person repeat the entire process that began some time ago in Stage I. In some cases, the entrepreneur is no longer with the organization and may be deceased. For example, when The Walt Disney Company required revitalization and diversification, its founder and namesake Walt Disney was deceased and so a new team of executives needed to lead this effort.

There are many examples in business where the original entrepreneur has not been available to grow with the firm as it developed from one stage to the next. For example, Steve Jobs and Steve Wozniak both left Apple Computer. Jobs returned in the late 1990s and, in fact, served as the champion of that company's diversification through the development of its "i" line (iPod, iPad, etc.) of products. Even if the entrepreneur is still with the company, a significant amount of time has usually elapsed, as it has passed from Stage I through Stage IV, and at this point the entrepreneur is now burdened by a significant number of organizational activities. This means that the entrepreneur may not have the time or mindset available for thinking entrepreneurially about new products and markets.

It is often, then, extremely difficult for entrepreneurs to repeat their earlier success. There are many examples of companies where there was a brilliant entrepreneurial success but a failure to repeat that success at any significant level. Accordingly, what is needed is to reestablish entrepreneurship in the organization, but it must be done in a different way. Rather than looking to a single entrepreneur, organizations at Stage V must develop a cadre of so-called entrepreneurial managers.

An entrepreneurial manager is different from a pure entrepreneur. Howard Schultz, the late Steve Jobs, Jack Ma, and Michael Dell are relatively pure entrepreneurial types—very different from professional managers. As described in Chapter 1, an entrepreneur is typically someone who is above average in intelligence and has a very strong sense of the way he or she wants things to be done in the organization—that is, has a high need for control. Some people might even consider the entrepreneur to be a workaholic or to have an obsessive personality. Nevertheless, these are the very personality traits that are both necessary and useful to a company during its early stages of growth. Although a Stage V organization needs to develop a cadre of entrepreneurial managers, it is not necessary for these managers to have the same personality as an entrepreneur; rather, what is necessary is to train the entrepreneurial manager to mimic or simulate some of the behavioral patterns of the entrepreneur.

A number of organizations have experimented with the reintroduction of entrepreneurship and the training of entrepreneurial managers. The term *corporate entrepreneurship* has been used to distinguish this process of reintroducing entrepreneurship through entrepreneurial managers from the entrepreneurs required to start a new company. The entrepreneur is someone who can create a new business where none existed previously. In contrast to the entrepreneur, the corporate entrepreneurial manager is someone who can create a new business venture within an established organization. The challenge, then, is to create development programs that will help people make the transition to being entrepreneurial managers. Further, the company must develop systems and a way of thinking (a culture) that supports corporate entrepreneurship. 3M is the classic company that has demonstrated this as a core competency. This company's focus on corporate entrepreneurship has resulted in many innovative products—including Post-it, which has become a multimillion-dollar business.

Diversification Attributable to New Opportunities. Diversification can also occur simply because the core business creates opportunities for expansion in quasi-related areas. For example, Tommy Bahama, a men's clothing line, developed Tommy Bahama as a lifestyle brand. The iconic advertising figure of Tommy Bahama and its South Seas image led other companies to seek license relationships with Tommy Bahama and has led to Tommy Bahama stores that sell not just clothing but watches, cologne, and related accessories. It also led to the development of a Tommy Bahama restaurant chain and Tommy Bahama furniture.

Another example of diversification attributable to extension of an organization's core capabilities is Techmer PM (Techmer). Founded in 1981 by John Manuck, a chemical engineer who had worked for Monsanto, Techmer PM provides design and technical support for colorants and various additives that modify and enhance the physical and visual properties of plastic products that are used by automotive, home furnishing, hospital supply, food packaging, construction, and many other industries. By 2014, the company had grown to over 600 employees and had manufacturing sites in California, Tennessee, Ohio, Illinois, Kansas, Georgia, and Pennsylvania, as well as a presence in many international markets.

In 1982, Techmer PM began selling colorants to industrial trash bag producers. Manuck noticed that while the trash bag makers normally purchased the cheapest colorants they could find, they occasionally purchased red colorant at a much higher price. He learned that the red was for a new market segment to indicate biohazard—the variation of shade was unimportant, as long as it was red. The other important property was the high opacity of the bag so that you could not see the physical contents. With a flash of brilliant insight, Manuck had the idea of developing a specially formulated red colorant by adding a low-cost iron oxide pigment to the usual red formula that dramatically increased the opacity while lowering the cost. The only negative was that the bright red color became a dull red color. When the customer pointed out the change in color, he was asked if he would be interested in trying a test run using 20% less of the colorant to achieve his desired opacity while paying the same price per pound that he had been paying for his previous red. It became an instant success and quickly became known as Techmer hospital red.

There is also a more recent example of diversification at Techmer PM. In 2014, Techmer became involved with the new technology of 3D printing because this manufacturing process utilizes specific polymer properties. Also, it is an example of innovation via collaboration. Techmer's largest facility is located in Tennessee and is about 20 miles from the Oak Ridge National Laboratory (ORNL). In early 2014, Techmer and ORNL began working together to produce parts using Big Area Additive Manufacturing (BAMM), large parts that are 3D printed. In December 2014, they produced a 3D-printed electric motor version of the 50th anniversary Shelby Cobra. The thermoplastic/carbon fiber composite used for the chassis was designed and produced by Techmer. This innovation was viewed as sufficiently important that it led to a visit by President Obama to the Techmer plant in Clinton, Tennessee, one month later.

Another example of diversification concerns the authors' own firm, Management Systems Consulting Corporation (Management Systems). Founded in 1978 by Eric Flamholtz to assist organizations in applying the methods and tools presented in this book, Management Systems engages in research to develop methods and tools to help build sustainably successful organizations®. Our clients have ranged from start-ups to members of the Fortune 500 — including Amgen, American Century Investments, Baskin-Robbins, City National Bank, Guggenheim Partners, The Disney Store, IBM, Kusto Group (Kazakhstan and Singapore), Li-Ning (China), Navistar, Neutrogena, 99 Cents Only Stores, Mövenpick Gastronomy International (Switzerland), PIMCO, PowerBar, Princess Cruises, Simon Property Group, Starbucks, Techcombank (Vietnam), The Riverside Group (China), Westfield, Wolfgang Puck Food Company, and many others.

For many years, Management Systems received inquiries from consultants around the world who were interested in becoming affiliated with the firm and in licensing its methodology and tools to apply them in their own countries. Finally, in 2011, at the request of Vladimir Kuryakov, associate professor at the Russian Presidential Academy of National Economy and Public Administration, our firm initiated a program to license, train, and certify affiliates to deliver our methodology and tools in their countries.

By 2015, Management Systems had licensed and certified affiliates in Argentina, Bulgaria, Italy, Israel, Kazakhstan, Poland, Russia, and the Ukraine as well as in the United States, and Canada. In addition, the firm had associates who represented it in Australia, China, Hong Kong, and Vietnam.

Management Systems' global affiliates business was a diversification from its core business of researching and developing methodologies and tools to deliver directly to companies to enhance their effectiveness. By 2014, approximately 50% of Management Systems' revenues were derived directly from royalties paid by affiliates for its intellectual property and/or indirectly from client referrals created by its affiliates business.

Failure to Achieve Diversification. When an organization fails to diversify successfully, the result can be stagnation, sale of the company, or even bankruptcy. Even companies with well-established iconic brands can ultimately suffer or meet their demise. A classic example is Cuisinart.

Cuisinart was an upscale brand well-known for its food processors that were highly popular in the 1970s. Yet, the company filed for bankruptcy under Chapter 11 of the federal Bankruptcy Code in 1989. The food-processing business had become saturated, and though the company still controlled about 45% of the food-processing market, it experienced difficulties.

Cuisinart had not done effective strategic planning and failed to capitalize on its famous name. By the time it filed for Chapter 11, the company had only recently begun branching out to items such as cooking utensils, hand blenders, and other cooking products. Cuisinart had defined its business as the "food-processing business," rather than more broadly, and unfortunately its traditional market dried up before it found a new one. It should be noted that Cuisinart was purchased by Conair Corporation in 1989, rebuilt its brand and business, and became a company offering what it refers to as "culinary tools," including bakeware, coffee makers, microwaves, and, of course, food processors.

Two other companies that had iconic brands but suffered due to lack of diversification were Smith Corona and Schwinn. A leading maker of typewriters, Smith Corona filed for bankruptcy, in part, because the market for typewriters disappeared. Typewriters had been replaced by personal computers, and the company had not effectively responded with new products to meet changing customer needs. This company no longer exists. Schwinn, once a leading brand of bicycles, failed to recognize the changing needs and preferences of potential customers. The type of cycle that had become popular was quite different from those offered by Schwinn, and the company filed for bankruptcy in the early 1990s and was purchased by another company.

Starbucks Illustrates Successful Diversification. One spectacular example of a company that has taken both internal and external routes to achieve successful diversification is Starbucks. The company has diversified from its original core product (coffee) with the addition of other beverages and products sold within its cafés/stores. It has also leveraged the Starbucks brand with other products such as ice cream (a joint venture with Dreyer's) and has made acquisitions in the United States and Europe. Starbucks had the infrastructure to do this. Even though Starbucks seems to have saturated the U.S. market for cafés, growth in stores continues with its expansion into teas, juices, and food.

Apple Illustrates Successful Diversification. Apple illustrates that successful diversification can occur in technology as well as in more basic products like coffee and restaurants. With one of its founders, Steve Jobs, serving as CEO and champion of new products, Apple diversified from its early dependence on computers with the development of the iPod and then the iPhone. The "i" products have been spectacularly successful and have led Apple to become an iconic company with a loyal following. Its products have achieved what some manufacturers dream of—becoming "cool." Among its constituency, the use of an Apple product conveys prestige on its user and marks the user as a member of what can be termed Apple Nation©.

Apple has continued its diversification development with the Apple Watch and Apple Pay. Apple was not the first to try to enter the mobile payments industry with their Apple Pay services; however, they were the first to successfully reach mass adoption. Within the first three days of its launch, Apple Pay had already become the largest mobile payment system with more than 1 million credit cards registered.[1] The success of Apple Pay is largely due to Apple's leveraging its mobile hardware, dominant position, and clout in the mobile phone market, and (rather than trying to challenge them) partnering with the major credit card companies (American Express, MasterCard, Visa) and several of the large banks.[2]

The Apple Watch was introduced at the same time as the Apple Pay system. The Apple Watch was designed to integrate with many of Apple's other products and services. It provides functionality beyond telling time, including fitness tracking, mobile alerts, handling messages and calls, providing directions, and running third-party apps. The majority of the watch's functionality is dependent on the iPhone, and each is intended to be integrated with the other.

Keys to Success at Stage V. The central problem of Stage V is to diversify the business so that it is no longer dependent on its initial product vehicle or the initial market. The key to success in Stage V is to identify and produce one or more new products (or services) and/or to identify and effectively enter one or more new markets. This might involve diversifying outside of the organization's initial business segment. The company may be developing multiple businesses (typically, but not always through the creation of new divisions). Thus Stage V is a time when the business should be making two transitions: (1) from one product, service, and/or market to multiple products, services, and/or markets; and (2) from a single business to a set of businesses. This can be accomplished through internal development of new products, identification of new markets, or acquisition of other organizations. This is not a trivial challenge, and many companies fail to achieve it. However, once Stage V has been successfully completed, the next challenge is to effectively integrate these new businesses, which is the focus of stage VI.

Stage VI: Integration

In the process of making the transition to Stage V, an organization sets in motion the forces that require it to move to Stage VI—the stage of integration. During Stage V, the entity will have made the transition from a single product line (or service line) company to a multiproduct (or multiservice) company, and/or it will be operating in very different markets. This means that by the time the organization completes the diversification process begun in Stage V, it will consist of a number of individual business entities. As a result, it will need to develop an infrastructure that will support managing each of these individual units as part of an integrated whole.

Developing an infrastructure to support this new business becomes the key challenge of Stage VI. The organization now needs to focus on ensuring that it has the appropriate resources, operational systems, management systems, and corporate culture to support the now very different company that it has become. A new kind of operational and management infrastructure must be created and implemented. These new systems at the corporate level must be designed to manage a set of businesses, rather than just one business.

Issues to be Resolved in the Integration Stage. Several different but related issues must be addressed during this stage of organizational growth. One issue involves the process of strategic planning, both at the corporate level and within each division, and the problems involved with integrating both. There are also issues involving the proper organizational structure of each division and of the company as a whole. By the time an organization completes Stage V, for example, it will most likely be (or need to be) organized into divisions (that is, it will be "divisionalized") and this brings the need to clearly define the role of "corporate" versus the roles of each division. There are also issues related to how performance management systems should be designed and implemented within the now larger, diversified business. The organization needs to focus on ensuring that the operational systems at both the corporate and divisional levels of the company promote effective and efficient operations.

Another issue involves questions of managing the corporate culture. Specifically, each of the separate divisions within a company may have somewhat varying cultures. The systems and culture of each division may need to be, in some cases, blended so as to promote the cooperation needed to achieve goals; in other cases, the company needs to promote the belief that differences in systems and culture between divisions will be maintained in the service of meeting the organization's long-term goals. A key challenge at this stage, then, involves deciding how best to integrate the systems and corporate culture of the various units created in Stage V.

A critical issue underlying the design of the management system for a Stage VI organization involves the degree of centralization or decentralization of authority accorded to each division. Companies vary widely in the amount of decentralization that they grant to their operating divisions. This issue can be viewed as points on a continuum. At one end of the continuum are firms that attempt to control virtually everything their operating divisions do. At the other end of the continuum, a corporation essentially operates as a passive investor with a "portfolio" containing various companies. The strategy here is to defer strategic decisions and daily operations to the divisional general managers, while requiring a specified performance in terms of return on investment or amount of profit. In between are companies that strike a balance between controlling everything and being a passive investor. This type of managerial philosophy has been used for many years at Johnson & Johnson.

For example, at Johnson & Johnson, divisions may be required to achieve a 15% pretax return on investment. The methods of achieving this target return are left to divisional managers. The corporation also requires that various management systems be in place, such as a planning process. In addition, Johnson & Johnson has used its Signature of Quality Award process to motivate the development of operational and management systems at its individual companies. Companies must apply for the Signature of Quality Award, and they are evaluated on, for example, business competitiveness, organizational alignment, and information competitiveness. The specific details of these categories are less significant than the process that Johnson & Johnson is using to motivate operating divisions to develop their infrastructure.

The phenomenon of having a number of businesses within a larger entity is not only found in large, established companies such as Starbucks, Johnson & Johnson, Procter & Gamble (which now owns Gillette), GE, Citicorp, IBM, Apple, and Microsoft; it also exists in many smaller organizations. For example, Infotek—a rapidly growing Stage III company, with $40 million in revenues—had three independent divisions. Similarly, Starbucks had four divisions when it had approximately $350 million in sales.

Special Issues in Integration of Acquisitions. Another version of the need for integration of different businesses arises from the acquisition of other companies. In fact, some organizations use acquisitions as their main vehicle of growth. For example, Emergent BioSolutions—a publicly traded biopharmaceutical company focused on developing, manufacturing, and commercializing vaccines and therapeutics that assist the body's immune system in preventing or treating disease—regularly acquires smaller biotech companies as part of its overall growth strategy.

When an organization grows by acquiring other companies, it faces the need to integrate. There are many examples of failed or disappointing acquisitions attributable to the failure of effective integration. The typical cause of this integration failure is incompatible cultures.

There are, however, some companies (such as Johnson & Johnson) that have developed a core competency in the successful integration of acquisitions. Johnson & Johnson (J&J) has had a long history of successful acquisitions that includes companies such as Alza (drug delivery products), Centocor (biotechnology), LifeScan (diabetic monitoring equipment), Neutrogena (personal care and cosmetics), and Scios (biotechnology). For example, when Johnson & Johnson acquired Neutrogena, it put a J&J person in place to manage the acquisition. The person who became CEO of Neutrogena was told (in effect), "We put a lot of chips on the table. Don't screw it up."

As illustrated in this brief example, a key to Johnson & Johnson's success is that they acquire companies that generally fit their culture and gently bring them into the "J&J way" of doing things. This has contributed not only to successful growth and integration of companies but has led to the consistent recognition of Johnson & Johnson as one of the most admired companies.[3]

When acquisitions are used as all or part of the process of diversifying the business, it might also be the case that certain corporate-wide systems will need to be adjusted to meet the needs of a new division while at the same time maintaining control. In one $100 million division of a Fortune 500 company, for example, problems were created because the corporate parent mandated that certain operating systems would be used that did not adequately meet the needs of the smaller firm. Further, the parent company's culture promoted cautiousness, while the subsidiary needed to respond quickly to take advantage of market opportunities. Finally, the compensation system of the parent could not reward behavior that contributed to business development; it was structured to maintain the status quo. Without careful management and negotiation with the parent organization, such practices can adversely affect a division or subsidiary's ability to succeed.

Overall Aspects of Integration. Problems faced by organizations in Stage VI are, to a great extent, a function of organizational size, complexity, and geographical dispersion. The greater the revenues (and, in turn, personnel and transactions), the greater the degree of geographical dispersion, and the greater the degree of business variety, the greater the problems of organizational integration are likely to be.

There is a considerable payoff for successfully meeting the challenges associated with this stage. Once an organization has completed this stage of development, it will typically have achieved more than $1 billion in revenue. Our research data (discussed in Chapter 5) suggest that the probability of continuing to operate successfully after an organization has reached $1 billion or more in revenues is enhanced. Although some organizations experience difficulty and even fail, organizations are more likely to continue to grow successfully after completing Stage VI. At that point, they have become "institutions," with a variety of self-perpetuating capabilities.

Companies that have been successful as institutions of this kind are Starbucks, GE, Nestlé, Procter & Gamble, and Johnson & Johnson. All are companies with self-perpetuating capabilities.

Keys to Success at Stage VI. The central problem facing corporations in Stage VI is how to integrate a set of diverse divisions into one unified business entity. Successfully meeting the challenges of this stage involves integrating the operations of the new businesses created or acquired during Stage V, while maintaining the organization's entrepreneurial spirit.

During the integration stage, the company has a simultaneous need to have some degree of centralized control over the diverse operating units and to allow divisional managers sufficient freedom to be entrepreneurial in managing their operations. Many companies do not do a good job of striking this delicate balance and lean too heavily toward organizational control. The price is a loss of entrepreneurial instinct and culture, and the creation of institutional bureaucracy that is more concerned with form than with substance.

Stage VII: Decline and Revitalization

The final stage in the organizational life cycle is Stage VII—Decline and Revitalization. The key issue facing management at Stage VII involves revitalization of the entire organization.

In contrast to most of the other stages, which constitute a sequential hierarchy as an organization grows in size, an organization can jump to Stage VII from almost any other stage. Although it is typically the larger organizations that are most in need of revitalization, there are examples of organizations at $30 million, $50 million, and $100 million that have reached Stage VII and are in need of revitalization. By the time a company has reached the multibillion-dollar level, however, it is sure to have the seeds of future potential decline within, even though it appears to outsiders to be at the apex of its success and power.

The stage of organizational decline and revitalization seems to be inevitable. All organizations, regardless of their greatness or past success, inevitably experience a period of decline. In the late nineteenth century, the railroads were the dominant enterprises, but they failed to use their resources to move into other aspects of transportation. In the early part of the last century, United States Steel Corporation was the hallmark of the U.S. economy, but it did not retain that position. In the 1950s, General Motors was at its apex, yet it, too, experienced decline. Other once-great corporations that have experienced organizational decline include IBM, AT&T, Sears, Kodak, National Lead, International Harvester, Xerox, Levi Strauss, and Ford.

This phenomenon occurs not only in the United States but in other parts of the world as well. Examples of once-great companies in other parts of the world experiencing decline include Reuters, Allied Domecq, Toyota, and Mövenpick. For some, decline led the company to the brink of bankruptcy; for others, it merely led to stunted growth; for still others, it led to their demise.

Causes of Organizational Decline. The problems that lead to decline and the need for organizational revitalization are frequently caused by an organization's own success. With organizational success comes an increase in the organization's size. Increases in an organization's size seem to create a certain degree of resistance to change. This can result from the vested interests of people who control the organization, or it can be that the organization's size has made it very ponderous, creating lengthy delays between the time the organization identifies a trend or problem and the time it takes action. For example, Kodak, which has a distinguished history as a successful company, missed major new markets (such as instant photography, videotape recorders, and digital photography) because its size, structure, and culture all made it move too slowly. It eventually went into bankruptcy and sold off its patents to a group of companies that included Apple, Facebook, Microsoft, and Amazon.

Organizational size does not seem to protect against decline; indeed, size itself may be one of the major factors creating the need for revitalization. A wide variety of organizations, including American Express, Hewlett-Packard, General Motors, and Sears have all faced the need for organizational revitalization, despite their many billions of dollars in assets and revenues. Even such an outstanding organization as IBM has faced the need for a revitalization effort.

Organizational decline is typically a product of many complex factors. Historically, some of the most common factors include increasing competition in a business's markets, loss of competitive skills from an erosion of leadership, a sense of complacency that inhibits organizational change, and, as described throughout this book, the inability of management to build an organizational infrastructure sufficient to keep pace with the demands of organizational growth. In addition to these classic forces of decline, there is also the risk of a "disruptive" new technology, such as the Internet.

Sudden Decline from Disruptive Technology. The development of the Internet and the related businesses that utilize the platform has caused many companies to experience decline. This can be thought of as a "sudden decline syndrome."

Amazon has taken market share away from traditional retailers in many spaces. For example, Amazon's sale of books has led to disruptive change and decline for traditional book sellers such as Barnes & Noble and Borders (a company that actually went into bankruptcy and closed its last store in 2011). Similarly, Netflix and others have leveraged the Internet to do video streaming for at-home movie viewing. This, in turn, led to the loss of visits to movie houses, and the closure of many. It has also led some movie chains to reconceptualize their business as more than movies. Some chains such as Landmark Theatres have created a broader "entertainment experience" by using sofas and providing alcoholic beverages and light meals at the seat.

The phenomenon of a disruptive new technology is not new. It is an essential feature of business. In the nineteenth century, the development of electricity disrupted the dominance of artificial lighting via kerosene. It led to a business war between J. P. Morgan, who sponsored the research and development of Edison, and John D. Rockefeller, who was the entrenched dominant player with kerosene.

Decline from Market Saturation. The most common causes of decline—competition and the related phenomenon of market saturation—tend to increase throughout an organization's life cycle. During the early stages of growth after a new market has been identified, an organization typically grows and prospers, simply as a "reward" for having found the market for that product or service. For example, Apple found the market for personal computers and grew to approximately $1 billion in annual revenues. During this period, IBM—potentially a major competitor for Apple—kept telling its customers that there was no need for personal computers. Once the market was developed to the point where it was large enough to attract IBM's interest, IBM brought out its own version of a personal computer and took 30 to 35% of the total market, squeezing Apple's sales and profitability. Further, the IBM operating system became the industry standard and put additional pressure on Apple. Eventually, a number of other companies entered the market with IBM-compatible PCs. When Apple had the market virtually to itself, it earned premium profitability. Once competition increased, Apple no longer had the profit cushion that would mask its underlying organizational problems. While IBM was highly successful with its PCs, competition from Dell Computer ultimately reduced their market share and led them to sell their PC business to Lenovo in 2005.

Decline from Leadership Erosion. Unfortunately, the longer organizations exist and the larger they grow in size, the greater the likelihood that they will outgrow their founder's capabilities.

Sometimes, this occurs because there has been inadequate focus on leadership development. In other cases, it might be that the company has simply increased in size at such a rapid pace that there hasn't been time to develop the needed skills. Leadership erosion can also occur when strong and capable leaders retire and need to be replaced. Phil Knight has retired from Nike, Bill Gates has retired from Microsoft, and Sam Walton is deceased and long gone from Walmart. When strong leaders like these are present and have guided their companies for a number of years, the organization will face the challenge of replacing them.

Decline from Dysfunctional Culture. Still another contributing cause of organizational decline is a cultural problem—an increasing sense of complacency. When an organization is successful, people reasonably expect to be rewarded. Sometimes the rewards are too great for the organization to sustain. Moreover, the very fact that success has persisted over time may lead people to come to expect rewards as an entitlement. This form of managerial hubris can create a self-congratulatory atmosphere that produces a resistance to change and ultimately leads to decline. In many firms, this is reflected in a lack of concern about whether or not there are new products in the pipeline. It may also be reflected in an attitude of, "We know best what the customer wants," without actually listening to customers. Further, and perhaps more dangerous, is the feeling that the company is somehow invincible. This attitude can be disastrous when a firm competes in markets where others have systems in place to both monitor and respond to customer needs. In one $150 million firm, for example, the belief was, "We found the market and we produce the best product. No one can catch us." As the firm basked in the glory of its own success, it watched as competitors slowly took away a significant percentage of its market share.

Decline from Inadequate Infrastructure. A final, major contributing factor to organizational decline is the inability of management to develop an organizational infrastructure sufficient for the organization's stage of growth. This problem will be one of the key themes throughout this book. Indeed, the problem is the crucial issue of Stages II through IV, and when management is unsuccessful in meeting these developmental challenges, organizational decline is inevitable.

The Challenge of Revitalization

An organization in decline must rebuild itself almost from the ground up. This, in turn, requires that the enterprise become entrepreneurial in nature once again. It also can require a company to reconceptualize its business. An example of a company that was able to successfully revitalize by conceptualizing its business is Barnes & Noble. After suffering lost sales to Amazon, Barnes & Noble has diversified from the sale of only books with the creation of Nook (an e-book reader) as well as the sale of toys and games and music. In brief, it has reconceptualized its business. In contrast, Borders, which like Barnes & Noble was also in the book business, went into bankruptcy and no longer exists.

Some organizations try to achieve revitalization by acquiring other companies that are more entrepreneurial than the purchaser. For example, in a bid to revitalize, Bank of America bought Charles Schwab & Company but later sold the company back to Schwab, who has continued to build it into a brokerage powerhouse. The attempt to "buy" entrepreneurship is unlikely to succeed in most companies. A total revitalization, including a major cultural transformation, is likely to be the only effective strategy.

Companies such as American Express, The Walt Disney Company, Hewlett-Packard, Simon Property Group, and IBM are all examples of successful revitalization efforts. For example, during the 1990s, IBM, a pioneer and leader of computing, transformed from a company where hardware was the core to a company emphasizing a collection of services and software. In 2015, under the leadership of CEO Virginia Rometty, the company that once thought of itself as a "big iron" business because of its mainframe computers, has been transforming again. The company jettisoned its PC and server operations (once high-margin businesses that had become commodities) to focus on cloud services, analytics technology (so-called Big Data), and mobile devices. The company also paid Global Foundries to take over IBM's semiconductor manufacturing business.[4]

It is becoming increasingly recognized that beyond a certain point, size may not be a strategic advantage. For example, one company founder and CEO stated: "I would rather see our billion-dollar company . . . be ten $100 million companies, all strong, growing healthy, and aggressive as hell. The alternative is an aging billion-dollar company that spends more time defending its turf than growing."

The Process of Revitalization

Although there are a number of issues involved in any case of organizational decline and revitalization, the basic problem that makes revitalization so difficult is that an organization at this stage must focus on all six of the key organizational development areas at the same time and may also need to focus on changing its business foundation. The organization must now simultaneously rethink "who it is," what it should be working to achieve, how it should be competing, its markets, its products and services, its resources, its operational systems, its management systems, and its corporate culture. Although organizations at every stage must give some attention to all six levels in the Pyramid of Organizational Development, at Stage VII, it is critical that an organization *simultaneously* concentrate on all six areas plus the business foundation, and this makes revitalization complicated and challenging. Each aspect of the revitalization process (beginning with the business foundation) is examined next.

Revitalizing the Business Foundation. To exit decline and revitalize, some organizations may need to broaden, narrow, or completely change their business concepts. For example, Hewlett-Packard, which was originally in the test and measurement equipment business, is now in the business of providing personal computers, printers, enterprise server and storage technology, software, and a wide range of related products and services to individual and enterprise customers worldwide. If the business concept is changed, the strategic mission will also change because now the company will be focused on either a broader or more narrow segment of a market or will be operating in, perhaps, a completely new market. In most cases, however, the strategic mission will be focused upon "getting our house in order" and getting back to profitability. The core strategy—or overall way that the company competes—will also need to be examined and may need to be redefined to reflect the organization's current status, including the environment in which it is competing and its internal capabilities. We will explain these concepts further and describe how to develop them in Chapter 6. The bottom line is that for the organization to survive, it needs to be willing the change the very basics of how it operates and what it is in the business to do.

Two examples of successful revitalizations that involved a change in business concept were Disney and Nike. Under Michael Eisner's leadership, Disney revitalized from a distressed family-oriented motion picture and theme park company into a global entertainment powerhouse (a change in business concept). Similarly, Nike broadened its focus from athletic shoes to athletic wear and built a so-called power brand or "super" brand. Both companies did this as part of revitalization efforts.

There are also examples of companies who were unable to exit decline because they were unable to effectively create a solid business foundation. For example, the unsuccessful revitalizations of Radio Shack, Sears, and Kodak can all be traced to a problem in the business foundation, and in particular the business concept.[5] None of these companies were able to redefine their business concepts in a workable way. This in turn had an impact on what they could be expected to achieve (the strategic mission)—particularly in the competitive markets that each faced. If the foundation of a building or a business is weak, then the structure built on top of it will also be weak or crumble. That is what happened in all three cases.

Revitalizing Markets. Once the business foundation has been reconceptualized, if it is necessary to do so, the next task is to revitalize markets. This involves finding ways to more effectively meet customer needs within the traditional market or identifying new markets to serve. During Stage I, a business is able to establish itself because it has been successful in identifying a single market. In Stage V, diversification efforts lead to the development of new markets. One of the fundamental reasons a Stage VII company experiences difficulty is that the organization's size has gotten out of sync with its ability to derive revenue from its traditional (or existing) market segments. The organization is now typically operating in one or more mature markets, meaning that the rate of growth in these markets is decreasing, with profit margins being squeezed. The business is trapped in a scissors effect, facing decreasing revenues from its markets on the one hand and rising operating costs caused by its increasing size and related inefficiencies on the other. With both blades of the scissors simultaneously closing in on the organization, management is busy doing its best to hold them apart.

The primary task now facing management is to identify markets that offer the most potential—in terms of growth rates and profit margins. IBM achieved this by changing its business concept from a manufacturing company providing computer equipment to an information solutions company, with a heavy emphasis upon information technology–related services.

Revitalizing Products/Services. Organizations in decline may need to significantly refine or update existing products and services or develop new ones. A company that is in decline and needs to be revitalized may have a product or set of products that have reached the mature stage. It might also be the case that the products and services being offered have become or are becoming obsolete due to new technology or new products being introduced by competitors. The critical problem in this situation is that the moment a company becomes aware that its products are no longer competitive in the marketplace, it has already lost a sufficient amount of lead time needed to react.

Thus the organization is forced into a crisis. At a time when it needs additional revenues to invest in new directions, it finds that its revenues are declining for competitive reasons.

Revitalizing Resources. One of the relative advantages of established organizations is that they should have had the opportunity to accumulate resources over a period of time. At the same time, however, as an organization enters decline, these resources can dwindle very rapidly. The challenge for an organization in decline is to find the resources needed—including time—to invest in revitalization. At a minimum, senior leadership needs to find the time to devote to developing a revitalization plan. Resources might also need to be invested in product research and development, new technology, and, perhaps, new people.

A company facing revitalization may have a significant amount of resources at its disposal, but some of these resources will be redundant or obsolete. In brief, they may not be the type of resources that the company needs to support its exit from the decline stage. Some of its inventory, its plant and equipment, and even its people will not be appropriate for the new challenges it faces. The company may also find itself with the need to redeploy some of its assets from one market segment to another. At this stage, the company may need to make major investments to revitalize the organization, and unfortunately it may encounter internal resistance to investing in the resources needed to revitalize itself. While it is important to exercise care in making investments at a time when the company may be losing money or, at a minimum, experiencing significant challenges in continuing to successfully grow, these investments in people, technology, equipment, and so on, will be critical to the organization's very survival.

Revitalizing Operational Systems. Organizations in decline frequently have well-established operational systems—which can be both a blessing and a burden. It is a blessing because the company has systems in place. The problem is that they may not be effectively designed to meet the organization's current needs, and they may not be as efficient as they need to be. During revitalization, the leadership team may find that one or more of the company's operational systems simply "don't work" anymore, or have become obsolete. In these cases, the company may literally need to abandon some of its traditional systems and invest in implementing new ones. The time needed to replace old with new systems can also create problems as people learn how to use them and as they are debugged. In the shorter term, this might add to the company's already significant problems.

An effective strategy for identifying the steps that need to be taken to improve a company's operational systems in the context of a revitalization is to complete an assessment of the current systems' effectiveness. This assessment can be conducted by external consultants, by convening an internal task force, or a combination of both. If an internal task force is used, care must be taken to prevent members from protecting their vested interests in preserving certain systems, which may be beneficial to those members but hurt the overall organization.

A traditional area for operational system problems involves product development. Organizations needing revitalization frequently possess a functional organization structure in which the responsibility for product development is divided among production, sales, and engineering. This structure tends to create a very lengthy product development cycle. The revitalization period requires a unity of purpose within the organization. Accordingly, new products need to be developed with centralized coordination of engineering, manufacturing, and sales. The structure most appropriate for this is a divisional structure. In our judgment, it is not an accident that many of the revitalization efforts occur in organizations that have been using functional organizational structures.

Revitalizing Management Systems. Companies in decline may need to revise or completely change their planning systems, their structure, their performance management systems, and the processes that they use to develop management capabilities. These companies may have well-developed planning systems, but these systems may not be designed to focus leadership on managing all six factors that drive long-term success. In fact, the reason that the organization entered decline may be because its planning system is flawed. This might have led to the company "missing" or ignoring key environmental trends that contributed to their own products' obsolescence, to a lack of focus on developing important operational systems, and to ineffective management of the company's culture. An ineffective planning process can also contribute to poor decision making and poor execution of key goals—which in turn can lead a company into decline. During revitalization, the existing planning process may need to be refined or completely replaced. Chapter 6 describes an approach to planning that can be used to both minimize the probability of decline and assist an organization in decline in identifying and effectively managing the key factors that will lead to revitalization.

The company's structure may also be contributing to its decline and may therefore need to be revised. The leadership team needs to assess the extent to which the structure—including functional and individual roles and responsibilities—is aligned with the current strategy (which may need to change to support the company's revitalization). When there is a lack of alignment, the leadership team should develop a plan for changing the structure to better support the organization's revitalization and continued success. The process for managing structure is described in Chapter 7.

Inadequate management and leadership development (including both how the company has recruited management talent from the outside and how it has been developed within) may have been a contributing factor to decline. Simply stated, there are not enough "good managers." When this is the case, there needs to be a focus on acquiring or developing the appropriate management skills to take the business into the future. In other cases, it may be that there are not enough entrepreneurial managers who can help identify and implement new products or services and new ways of doing things—skills that are absolutely critical to an organization that is in need of revitalization. When either of these situations exists, there needs to be a focus on designing and delivering a leadership development program to "close the gaps" and position the company to exit the decline stage. Strategies for designing and implementing effective leadership development programs will be discussed in Chapter 9.

Underdeveloped or flawed performance management systems can significantly contribute to an organization's decline. Specific problems that can contribute to decline include having systems that measure the "wrong things," inadequate or inaccurate reporting of results, underutilization of measurement results, and lack of action being taken when results suggest that adequate progress is not being made. Developing or refining performance management systems should be a priority because these systems will provide the information needed to help assess whether the plans being put in place are, in fact, helping move the company out of the decline stage. The design and implementation of effective performance management systems will be discussed in Chapter 8.

One of the critical factors in any revitalization effort is, of course, leadership. If existing management is unable to mount a successful turnaround, companies are likely to seek new leadership.

For example, Louis Gerstner was recruited from outside to IBM to lead the revitalization process after an earlier effort led by an insider had failed.[6] Similarly, first Carly Fiorina and later Mark Hurd were recruited by Hewlett-Packard to lead a revitalization process after an initial effort led by company insiders was unsuccessful. Fiorina was responsible for Hewlett-Packard's merger with Compaq, but she was replaced by Hurd when the company encountered difficulties in making the merger work effectively.

Revitalizing Corporate Culture. Culture can also contribute to organizational decline and, as a result, may need to be revitalized. One of the typical problems of established companies is that, unintentionally, the culture begins to emphasize politics and avoidance of conflict and risk more than performance, quality, customer service, innovation, and profitability. Many people will have well-entrenched positions, and some are likely to resist making required changes, even though they are needed by the organization.

When the culture promotes the status quo versus innovation, ideas that might have prevented decline are not shared, and so problems go unresolved until it is too late. Sometimes, a company's success creates the belief (although is it usually a false belief) that "no matter what we do, we will be successful." This belief can result in leaders ignoring very real environmental threats (e.g., changing customer needs, competitive products that are reducing market share or making the organization's product obsolete) or not focusing enough attention on ensuring that the company's infrastructure is aligned with current needs. In brief, a culture that promotes the belief that "we will always be successful," can actually be a major factor in eventually sending it into decline.

A major focus of revitalization, then, needs to be on creating and managing a culture that fits with the new goals of the organization—that is, that promotes revitalization. This will include a strong focus on embracing change, on being willing to make tough decisions in the interest of preventing further decline, and on holding people accountable for performance against revitalization goals.

Revitalization of Simon Property Group. During the early 1990s, Simon Property Group (formerly Melvin Simon & Associates)—one of the largest shopping center developers in the United States—was experiencing a variety of growing pains. The size of the company had outstripped the managerial capabilities of its founder, Melvin Simon, and his brother, Herbert Simon, who were both primarily real estate developers.

The company began a program of revitalization that lasted about five years. This included the introduction of strategic planning, changes in organizational structure, the implementation of a formal management development program, and the redesign of the company's performance management systems. It also led to the introduction into the company of its current CEO, David Simon (Melvin Simon's son), who had an MBA from Columbia University and was more oriented to being a professional manager than either of the two elder Simons, who were primarily deal-oriented. The company culminated its successful revitalization by going public as Simon Property Group .

In 2013, David Simon was selected as one of 30 people listed in *Barron's* "World's Best CEOs."[7] During his tenure as CEO, Simon Property Group has had annualized profit of 17.4%.[8] In contrast, the return for the S&P (Standard and Poor's) 500 was 8.7% during the same period. The company's stock price increased from $24 per share in 1995 to $160 per share in 2013.

Keys to Success at Stage VII. The overall challenge for a Stage VII organization is revitalization. The key to success at Stage VII is the ability to entirely reconceptualize and redevelop an enterprise. This involves becoming entrepreneurial again and being willing to change, if needed, everything about the business and how it operates. It also involves having the ability to rebuild the entire enterprise from the business foundation to its culture. This is an enormous challenge, which many companies fail to meet.

Summary

Once an organization has completed the development challenges required to take it through Stages I through IV, it has become a professionally managed organization. However, its life cycle is not completed, and the organization must now deal with the problems and challenges posed by the advanced stages of growth—Stages V through VII.

Stage V involves efforts to diversify the company because it can no longer rely on its initial products (or services) or market for continued profitability. The organization's success has attracted competitors, and its products or services are now competing in a saturated market. The company must develop new products (or services) and/or enter new markets to "restart" another cycle of success. A prudent leadership team has not waited until this stage to begin the process of diversification and has been investing a portion of the company's profits into the development of new products (or services). Because the original entrepreneur is often no longer available, many companies are training managers to mimic the behavior of entrepreneurs, thereby creating "intrapreneurs" who will serve as catalysts for diversification.

Stage VI involves integrating the new businesses that were created around the new products, services, and/or markets developed in Stage V. These new businesses may be only partially related. The challenge is to coordinate these entities while allowing each unit sufficient independence to derive the benefits of acting in an entrepreneurial manner. Such issues as the amount of centralized control over divisions, integrating the separate planning activities, and managing the overall corporate culture must be addressed.

Finally, an organization in Stage VII—which can, in fact, be entered from any other stage of growth—must focus on revitalizing its entire business. The factors that led to decline—market saturation, an erosion of management's entrepreneurial skills, the inability to develop an organizational infrastructure to support the growth realized from previous stages, a feeling of complacency, and so on—need to be identified and effectively addressed. Revitalizing the business involves focusing on all six levels of the Pyramid of Organizational Development simultaneously.

In the next chapter, we examine the nature of organizational growing pains and present a method for measuring and interpreting them. Recognition and identification of these growing pains is a necessary part of the organizational evaluation process, which is the first step of the transition from one stage of growth to the next.

Notes

1. Nathaniel Popper, "Banks Did It Apple's Way in Payments by Mobile," *New York Times*, September 11, 2014.

2. Lisa Eadicicco, "It Took Apple Just 3 Days to Sign Up 1 Million Credit Cards on Apple Pay," *Business Insider*, October 28, 2014.

3. Vito J. Rancanelli, "The World's Most Respected Companies," *Barron's*, June 28, 2014, S30.

4. Don Clark and Ann Maria Armetal, "At IBM, a Weak Streak Persists," *The Wall Street Journal*, January 21, 2015, B1–2.

5. See Eric Flamholtz and Yvonne Randle, *Changing The Game: Organizational Transformations of the First, Second, and Third Kinds* (New York: Oxford University Press, 1998).

6. Louis V. Gerstner, *Who Says Elephants Can't Dance: Leading a Great Enterprise through Dramatic Change* (New York: Harper Business, 2002).

7. Andrew Bary, "World's Best CEOs," *Barron's*, March 24, 2013, S32.

8. Ibid.

CHAPTER 5

Recognizing Growing Pains and Assessing the Need for Change

When an organization has not been fully successful in developing the internal systems it needs at a given stage of growth, it begins to experience growing pains. These growing pains are problems in and of themselves. However, they are also symptoms of a deeper, systemic problem: the need to transition to a different infrastructure to support the current and anticipated growth and size of the organization.

This chapter examines in detail the most common organizational growing pains, showing through examples how these growing pains emerge in real-life companies. It also presents a self-scoring method of measuring organizational growing pains and a way to interpret the extent to which they signal the need for further organizational development. The chapter then discusses the degree to which different sizes and types of businesses experience growing pains. We also include information about the percentage of companies at each level of growing pains scores, based on an analysis of a database that includes more than 5,000 companies. Next, we examine the relationship between growing pains, company growth rates, and infrastructure. We will also discuss the relationship between growing pains and financial performance. Finally, the use of growing pains scores as a tool in helping to facilitate organizational transitions and measure their effectiveness is illustrated in the case example of Guangzhou Construction, previously introduced in Chapter 2.

The Nature of Growing Pains

Growing pains are problems that occur as a result of inadequate organizational development in relation to business size and complexity. They are symptoms that something has gone wrong in the process of organizational development. As such, they are a signal or alert about the need to make the transition from one stage of organizational development to the next. They are, as discussed later in this chapter, a set of leading indicators of future financial performance.

Ironically, growing pains are problems resulting from organizational success rather than failure. Nevertheless, they are simultaneously problems in and of themselves, and signs or symptoms of an underlying systemic problem in the organization. The underlying problem is the failure of the organization's infrastructure to match or keep up with the size and complexity of the business. This means that the organization's resources, operational systems, management systems, and culture (the top four variables of the Pyramid of Organizational Development) have not been developed to the extent necessary to support the size, complexity, and growth of the enterprise.[1]

A simple rule of thumb is that when an organization doubles in size (measured either in terms of revenues, production volume, annual budget, or number of employees), it requires a different infrastructure. When this adjustment in infrastructure does not happen, organizational growing pains will increase in number and severity.

If the root causes of the organizational growing pains are not dealt with appropriately, even organizations that are successful undoubtedly will experience difficulties and possible failure. To deal with growing pains, we must first be able to identify them and assess their severity.

The Ten Most Common Organizational Growing Pains

The ten most common (or classic) organizational growing pains are listed here:

1. People feel that there are not enough hours in the day.
2. People are spending too much time "putting out fires."
3. Many people are not aware of what others are doing.
4. People have a lack of understanding of where the company is headed.
5. There are too few "good" managers.
6. Everyone feels "I have to do it myself if I want to get it done correctly."
7. Most people feel our meetings are a waste of time.
8. When plans are made, there is very little follow-up, and things just don't get done.
9. Some people have begun to feel insecure about their place in the company.
10. The company has continued to grow in sales, but not in profits.

Each of these growing pains is described in the pages that follow.

People Feel That There Are Not Enough Hours in the Day
One of the most common organizational growing pains is the complaint that there is never enough time. Employees feel that they could work twenty-four hours per day, seven days a week, and still not have sufficient time to get everything done. They begin to complain about overload and excessive

stress. Both individuals and departments feel that they are always trying to catch up but never succeeding. The more work they do, the more there seems to be, resulting in a never-ending cycle. People feel as if they are on a treadmill.

The effects of these feelings can be far-reaching. First, employees' belief that they are being needlessly overworked may bring on morale problems. Complaints may increase. Second, employees may begin to experience physical illnesses brought on by excessive stress. These psychological and physical problems may lead to increased absenteeism, which can decrease the company's productivity. Finally, employees may simply decide that they can no longer operate under these conditions and may leave the organization. This will result in significant turnover and replacement costs related to recruiting, selecting, and training new people.

When many employees feel that there is not enough time in the day, usually no one is suffering more from this than the company's founding entrepreneur (if he or she is still present). The entrepreneur, feeling ultimately responsible for the company's success, may work sixteen hours a day, seven days a week in an effort to keep the company operating effectively and help it grow. As the organization grows, the entrepreneur begins to notice that he or she can no longer exercise complete control over its functioning. This realization can result in a great deal of personal stress.

The presence of this growing pain can suggest that the company lacks or has an underdeveloped planning system, that there is a lack of a formal structure (in which roles and responsibilities are clearly defined), or that individuals do not understand how to effectively manage their time. It might also suggest that the company does not have enough of the right resources to support current and anticipated future operations or that its operational systems are underdeveloped.

People Spend Too Much Time "Putting Out Fires"

A second common growing pain shows itself in excessive time spent dealing with short-term crises. This problem usually results from a lack of long-range planning and, typically, the absence of a strategic plan. Underdeveloped or weak operational systems can also contribute to this growing pain. For example, when these systems do not produce the accurate and timely information managers need to make decisions, there may be a number of "fires to fight." This growing pain can also result from the tendency to hold on to a culture that rewards fire fighters, rather than planners. Individual employees and the organization as a whole live from day to day never knowing what to expect. The result may be a loss of organizational productivity, effectiveness, and efficiency.

Examples of the putting-out-fires problem are easy to find. In one $10 million service firm, a lack of planning caused orders to be needlessly rushed, resulting in excessive pressure on employees. Drivers had to be hired on weekends and evenings to deliver orders, some of which were already overdue. At one residential real estate company, lack of planning resulted in shortages of salespeople. Because of these shortages, the company was forced to hire new people and put them to work almost immediately, sometimes without adequate training. This, in turn, contributed to short-term productivity problems because the new people did not possess the skills necessary to be good salespeople. The lack of personnel planning in a $100 million manufacturing company also created problems but for different reasons. There, personnel were hired to take up the slack when business was good. Once the crisis was over, the company found it had a number of people it simply did not know what to do with.

Fires were so prevalent at one $75 million manufacturing company that managers began to refer to themselves as fire fighters, and senior management rewarded middle management for their skill in handling crises. When it became apparent that managers who had been effective in "fire prevention" were being ignored, some of them became "arsonists" to get senior management's attention. The arsonists set fires that could be fought as a way of showing that they were contributing to the organization.

Many People Are Not Aware of What Others Are Doing

People are increasingly unaware of the exact nature of their jobs and how these jobs relate to those of others. This creates a situation in which people and departments do whatever they want to do and say that the remaining tasks are "not our responsibility." Constant bickering between people and departments over responsibility may ensue. The organization may become a group of isolated and sometimes warring factions.

These problems typically result from the lack of a formalized structure, including an organization chart and well-defined roles and responsibilities. Relationships between people and between departments, as well as individual responsibilities, may be unclear. People can become frustrated by this ambiguity and begin creating their own definitions of their roles, which may not always be in the company's best interests. The president of one of our clients vividly described this phenomenon when he said, "We were a collection of little offices working toward our goals without consideration for the good of the company."

The isolation of departments from one another may result in duplication of effort or in tasks that remain incomplete because they are "someone else's responsibility." Constant arguments between departments may also occur over territory and organizational resources. This was a problem at a large technology company where there were eighteen different divisions, each focusing on its own product line to the exclusion of the overall corporate goals. Even as product lines evolved and began to overlap, the salesforce continued to focus only on its own line to the exclusion of others. This resulted in some customers being called on by three or more salespeople, each representing a different product group and sometimes even offering similar services for different prices. In essence, the company competed against itself. Ultimately, the company lost control of its own destiny and was acquired by one of its competitors.

People Lack an Understanding About Where the Company Is Headed

Employees may complain that "the company has no identity" and either blame upper management for not providing enough information about the company's future direction or, worse, believe that not even upper management knows what that direction will be. This can result from the inability of senior management to agree about the company's future direction or can be due to a communication breakdown.

When insufficient communication is combined with rapid changes, as is often the case in growing enterprises, employees may begin to feel anxious. To relieve this anxiety, they may either create their own networks for obtaining the desired information or come to believe that they know the company's direction, even though management has not actually communicated this information. In one company, employees' speculations, as well as real information obtained from people who were close to senior management, circulated freely on the company's grapevine. Rumors were rampant, but in fact very few people really knew why certain changes were being made. Hence, employees experienced a significant amount of anxiety. If anxiety increases to the point where it becomes unbearable, employees may begin leaving the company. It should be noted that turnover of this kind can be very costly to an organization.[2]

The primary factor underlying this growing pain tends to be inadequate strategic planning. Either the organization has an inadequate or underdeveloped planning process, or plans that are made are not effectively communicated throughout the organization.

There Are Too Few "Good" Managers

Although a business may have a significant number of people who hold the title of "manager," it may not have many good managers. Managers may complain that they have responsibility but no authority. Employees may complain about the lack of direction or feedback that their managers provide. The organization may notice that some of its divisions or departments have significantly higher or lower productivity than others. It may also be plagued by managers who constantly complain that they do not have time to focus on managing their team or their department because they have too much technical work to do. When any or all of these events occur, something is wrong with the management function of the organization.

Problems like these suggest that the company has not adequately defined managers' roles or is not providing sufficient training to ensure that those in these roles have the skills needed to effectively fulfill them. If there are unclear role descriptions, those in management positions may not understand what they are expected to do. In an effort to "do something," these individuals may revert to re-creating their old roles—focusing too much attention on doing work, rather than managing it. If training exists, the company may be relying too much on on-the-job training rather than on formal management development programs. In some companies, this on-the-job training is carried to such an extreme that companies literally or figuratively walk the new manager to his or her office and say, "Here's your department. Run it."

Management problems may also result from real or perceived organizational constraints that restrict a manager's authority. In one company, the perception that only top management could make decisions greatly affected lower-level managers' effectiveness. One person at this firm described the managers as "people with no real responsibility." The feeling that only upper management has decision-making responsibility is common in organizations making the transition to professional management. It is a relic from the days when the founding entrepreneur made all decisions.

Everyone Feels "I Have to Do It Myself if I Want to Get It Done Correctly"

Increasingly, as people become frustrated by the difficulty of getting things done in an organization, they come to feel that to get something done, they have to do it themselves. The underlying cause of this growing pain is typically a lack of clearly defined roles, responsibilities, and linkages between and among roles. It may also result from a lack of resources (e.g., there are not enough people or enough of the right people to get the job done) or the inability (or unwillingness) of managers to relinquish control over results to others.

As was discussed previously, when roles and responsibilities are not clearly defined, individuals or departments tend to act on their own because they do not know whose responsibility a given task is. They may also do the task themselves to avoid confrontation, because the person or department to whom they are trying to delegate a responsibility may refuse it.

Operating under this philosophy, departments become isolated from one another, and teamwork becomes minimal. Each part of the company does its own thing without considering the good of the whole. Communication between management and lower levels of the organization and between departments may be minimal because the organization has no formal system through which information can be channeled. The lack of coordination between areas can lead to productivity problems and inefficiencies.

Most People Feel That Meetings Are a Waste of Time

Recognizing that there is a need for better coordination and communication, the growing organization may begin to hold meetings. Unfortunately, in many companies these meetings are, at best, nothing more than discussions among people. They have no planned agendas, and often they have no designated leader. Participants may be allowed to take cell phone calls, check email, "work" on their computers, hold side conversations, and focus on many things other than the content of the meeting. Meetings become a free-for-all, tend to drag on interminably, and seldom result in decisions. The same agenda items appear again and again. As a result, people feel frustrated and conclude that "our meetings are a waste of time."

The impact of ineffective meetings can be significant. For example, after five full days of work, a $150 million technology company's senior management team had yet to finalize its strategic plan. Why? Each day of meetings was constantly interrupted by "today's crisis," which took one or more members of the team (including the CEO) out of the meeting for an extended period of time. Executives continually checked email, resulting in a lack of focus on the discussions taking place. When each executive tuned back in to the discussion, the rest of the group had to spend time helping him or her catch up. Each executive had a specific agenda of items that needed to be discussed and, instead of listening to and staying focused on the topic that was on the table, decided to share whatever was on his or her mind. As a result, the discussion jumped from topic to topic, with only limited resolution of issues. After five days of meetings, over a period of three months, the team decided that the plan was good enough, simply because they didn't have the time to finish it.

Other complaints about meetings involve lack of follow-up on decisions that are made. Some companies schedule yearly or monthly planning meetings during which goals are set for individual employees, departments, and the company as a whole. These sessions are a waste of time if people ignore or fail to monitor their progress toward these goals. At one residential real estate company, the budgeting process suffered from this condition. In a frustrating yearly exercise, managers met and set goals, then met again the following year with no idea of whether they had achieved the previous year's goals.

Although the problems listed result from too many meetings or meetings that are poorly managed, at the other extreme are companies where meetings are seldom held. In these situations, there is limited communication and coordination. As a result, the company frequently suffers from productivity problems, including duplication of effort.

When Plans Are Made, There Is Very Little Follow-Up, So Things Just Don't Get Done

As an organization grows, company leaders may recognize the need for and actually embark on a formal process of strategic and operational planning. Unfortunately, there are times when people may go through the motions of preparing these plans, but the things that were planned just do not get done. In one amazing case, there was no follow-up simply because the plan, after being prepared, sat in a drawer for the entire year until the next year's planning retreat. When asked about the plan, one senior manager stated: "Oh that. It's in my desk. I never look at it."

Sometimes, there is no follow-up because the company has not yet developed adequate systems (that is, performance management systems) to monitor progress against goals. For example, many companies desire to monitor financial goals but have not developed an accounting system that can provide the information needed to do so.

In other cases, follow-up does not occur because personnel have not received proper training in setting, monitoring, and evaluating goals. They set goals that cannot be achieved or cannot be measured, or they do not know how to evaluate and provide useful feedback on goal achievement. These problems tend to appear most often in the performance appraisal process. This issue is discussed further in Chapter 8 (which deals with how to design and effectively use performance management systems).

Some People Have Begun to Feel Insecure about Their Place in the Company

As a consequence of the other organizational growing pains, employees begin to feel insecure about their places in the company. In some cases, the entrepreneur (if he or she is still present in the company) has become anxious about problems facing the organization and has therefore hired a "heavyweight" manager from outside. This action may have been accompanied by the termination of one or more current managers. Employees feel anxious, partly because they do not understand the reasons for these and other changes. When anxiety becomes too high, it may result in morale problems or excessive turnover.

Employees may also become insecure because they are unable to see the value of their position to the company. This occurs when roles and responsibilities are not clearly defined and terminations are also occurring. Employees begin to wonder whether they will be the next to get the axe. In an attempt to protect themselves, people keep their activities secret and do not make waves. This results in isolation and a decrease in teamwork.

Entire departments may come to suffer from the need to remain isolated in order to protect themselves from being eliminated. This can lead to a certain amount of schizophrenia among employees. They begin to ask, "Am I loyal to my department or to the organization at large?" In one company, a Stage IV firm, an employee expressed her sense of anxiety this way: "This company could give me a trip around the world for free, and I would think they were trying to get rid of me." In this same organization, people indicated that they were afraid they would be fired if they said anything controversial. However, when pressed about the extent to which people had been terminated for speaking up, no one could identify a specific case. In effect, the culture of the organization had become one that promoted anxiety and fear. It also created a situation in which people spent more time covering their own vested interests than working toward achieving company goals.

The Company Has Continued to Grow in Sales, But Not in Profits

If all the other growing pains are present, this one final symptom may emerge. In some instances, sales continue to increase while profits remain flat, so that the company is succeeding only in increasing its workload. In the worst cases, sales increase while overall profits actually decline. Companies may begin to lose money without having any idea why. The business loss can be quite significant, even though sales are up.

In a significant number of companies, the decline in profits may be the result of an underlying philosophy that stresses sales. People in such companies may say, "If sales are good, then profit will also be good," or "Profit will take care of itself." Profit in these companies is not an explicit goal but merely whatever remains after expenses.

In sales-oriented companies, people often become accustomed to spending whatever they need to in order to make a sale or promote the organization. For example, at one prestigious magazine publishing company, employees believed that it was important to the company's image to always "go first class." They made no effort to control costs, because they believed that no matter what they did, the organization would always be profitable. Organizations may also suffer because of systems that reward employees for achieving sales goals rather than profit goals.

For nonprofits, this growing pain can be restated as, "Our administrative costs have increased more rapidly than our funding (budget)." This growing pain can result from inadequate focus on fund acquisition (for example, in some nonprofits only a very few people are responsible for fundraising), from a belief that sources will continue to provide the same level of funding year after year, or from underdeveloped budgeting processes that do not provide the information needed to track administrative costs. The result is a lack of balance between "what we have" and "what we need" to support ongoing operations which can, at times, lead to the nonprofit's demise.

Measuring Organizational Growing Pains

Growing pains are not just binary, meaning they exist or not. There are degrees of severity of growing pains.

To assist management in measuring their organization's growing pains, we have developed and validated the Growing Pains Survey, shown in Exhibit 5.1.[3]

This survey instrument presents the ten organizational growing pains that have been identified in a wide variety of entrepreneurial companies with annual sales revenues ranging from less than $1 million to over $1 billion. Responses to the survey are entered on a Likert-type five-point scale, with descriptions ranging from "to a very great extent" to "to a very slight extent."[4] By placing check marks in the appropriate columns, the respondent indicates the extent to which he or she feels each of the ten growing pains characterizes the company.

Scoring the Survey

Once the survey has been completed, the number of check marks in each column is totaled and recorded on line 11. Each item on line 11 is then multiplied by the corresponding weight on line 12, and the total is recorded on line 13. For example, Exhibit 5.1 shows four check marks in column B. Accordingly, we multiply 4 by the weight of 4 and record the result, 16, on line 13 of column B.

Exhibit 5.1 Growing Pains Survey

Growing Pain	A To a Very Great Extent	B To a Great Extent	C To Some Extent	D To a Slight Extent	E To a Very Slight Extent
1. People feel that there are not enough hours in the day.			X		
2. People are spending too much time "putting out fires."			X		
3. Many people are not aware of what others are doing.	X				
4. People have a lack of understanding of where the company is headed.		X			
5. There are too few "good" managers.		X			
6. Everybody feels, "I have to do it myself if I want to get it done correctly."		X			
7. Most people feel our meetings are a waste of time.				X	
8. When plans are made, there is very little follow-up, and things just don't get done.		X			
9. Some people have begun to feel insecure about their place in the company.				X	
10. The company has continued to grow in sales but not in profits.	X				
Scoring					
11. Add the total number of responses in each column.	*2*	*4*	*2*	*2*	*0*
12. Multiply the number on line 11 by the number on line 12 and record the result on line 13.	*5*	*4*	*3*	*2*	*1*
13. Result of line 11 times line 12.	*10*	*16*	*6*	*4*	*0*
14. Add the numbers on line 13 in columns A–F and place the result on this line.	*36*				

The next step is to determine the sum of the numbers on line 13. This total represents the organization's growing pains score. It can range from 10, which is the lowest possible or most favorable score, to 50, which is the highest possible or most unfavorable score.

Interpreting the Severity of Growing Pains Scores

Drawing on our research concerning the degree of seriousness of problems indicated by different growing pains scores, we have developed the color-coding scheme shown in Table 5.1. This table shows five different levels of severity of growing pains from a very healthy organization to one that is at grave risk of failure.

More detailed interpretation of score ranges is as follows:

- A *green score* represents a fairly healthy organization. It suggests that everything is probably functioning in a manner satisfactory for the organization at its current stage of development.

- A *yellow score* indicates that the organization is basically healthy, but there are some areas of concern. It is like hearing from your doctor, "Your cholesterol is in the normal range but on the high side." It's something to watch and be careful about but not an immediate concern.

- An *orange score* indicates that some organizational problems require attention and action. They may not be too serious yet, but corrective action should be taken before they become so.

- A *red score* is a clear warning of present or impending problems. Immediate corrective action is required.

- A *purple score* indicates that the organization is having very serious problems and is in crisis. The organization is in distress and may be on the verge of collapse. There may not be enough time to save it.

If an organization's score exceeds 20, a more in-depth analysis to identify problems and develop recommendations for future action is warranted. Such a score may be a signal that the organization has reached a new stage in its development and must make major, qualitative changes. Failure to pay attention to a score of this magnitude can produce very painful results.

Growing Pains Scores for Different Business Sizes and Industries

Table 5.2 presents average organizational growing pains scores of companies with different annual revenues, based on our extensive research and data collection over almost 40 years. Interestingly,

Table 5.1   Interpretation of Organizational Growing Pains Survey Scores

Score Range	Color	Interpretation
10–14	Green	Everything okay
15–19	Yellow	Some things to watch
20–29	Orange	Some areas that need attention
30–39	Red	Some very significant problems
40–50	Purple	A potential crisis or turnaround situation

Table 5.2   Organizational Growing Pains by Company Size

Size (Revenues)	Stage	Average Growing Pains Score
Less than $1 million	I	27.00 (Orange)
$1–$9 million	II	29.00 (Orange)
$10–$99 million	III	29.00 (Orange)
$100–$499 million	IV	32.00 (Red)
$500 million–$1 billion	V	34.00 (Red)
More than $1 billion	VI	27.00 (Orange)

these results have been very stable over this period and virtually without change. As can be seen, organizations of every size experience some growing pains. Our data suggest that growing pains tend to increase in severity as companies increase in size from less than $1 million to $1 billion in revenues. However, organizations that reach $1 billion have (on the average) reduced growing pains. This suggests that, at revenue levels greater than $1 billion, an organization has developed the "critical mass" sufficient to bring these problems under a greater degree of control.

Table 5.3 shows scores broken down by type of industry. Figure 5.1 graphically depicts these scores, showing the trends in growing pains as revenues increase. Clearly, timing of the occurrence of significant organizational growing pains differs across industries.

Table 5.3   Organizational Growing Pains in Different Industries

Size (Revenues)	Overall	Service	High-Tech	Low-Tech	Finance
Less than $1 million	26.52 Orange	26.98 Orange	25.95 Orange	26.27 Orange	24.30 Orange
$1–$4 million	28.00 Orange	27.93 Orange	28.23 Orange	27.26 Orange	27.87 Orange
$5–$9 million	29.47 Orange	29.30 Orange	28.38 Orange	31.31 Red	28.74 Orange
$10–$24 million	29.32 Orange	27.78 Orange	28.09 Orange	29.24 Orange	31.57 Red
$25–$99 million	29.22 Orange	29.88 Orange	30.11 Red	26.79 Orange	30.21 Red
$100–$499 million	31.67 Red	31.17 Red	34.12 Red	29.17 Orange	33.67 Red
$500 million–$1 billion	33.57 Red	33.93 Red	32.00 Red	26.10 Orange	36.00 Red
More than $1 billion	27.43 Orange	28.42 Orange	27.53 Orange	17.00 Yellow	25.75 Orange

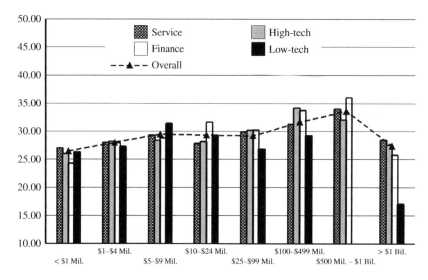

Figure 5.1 **Organizational Growing Pains by Company Size (Revenue) in Different Industries**

In the service industry, growing pains become severe when an organization reaches $5 to $9 million in revenues (Stage III for a service firm) and diminish slightly as revenues exceed $10 million. This dip in severity of growing pains may indicate that $10 to $24 million in revenue is an easier service company size to manage than those over $24 million and those between $1 and $9 million. Growing pains begin to increase in severity again as the company's revenues exceed $25 million and remain significant until revenues exceed $1 billion.

High-tech companies appear to experience significant problems when they reach the $25 to $99 million range of revenues (Stage III). Problems then continue into the $500 million to $1 billion range, after which they begin to drop. Low-tech companies, in contrast, experience the most significant problems in the $5 to $9 million revenue range. Growing pains in low-tech companies also drop significantly at revenues over $1 billion. In fact, low-tech companies with revenues greater than $1 billion experience the least severe growing pains of companies in any industry at any size.

Companies in the financial industry begin experiencing significant growing pains when revenues reach $10 to $24 million (Stage III for financial firms), which continue through the $500 million to $1 billion revenue range. Financial companies with revenues exceeding $1 billion experience a significant drop in growing pains.

The information presented here suggests that companies in different industries need to be concerned with growing pains at different periods of their organizations' lives. For organizations in the finance industry, critical periods occur when revenues begin to exceed $10 million. For high-tech companies, significant growing pains begin when revenues are at $25 to $99 million, whereas, for service companies, they appear at $5 million in revenues and again when revenues begin to exceed $25 million. For low-tech companies, this critical point occurs when revenues are between $5 and $9 million. These data also indicate that large ($500 million to $1 billion in revenues) financial companies experience the most severe organizational growing pains, whereas large low-tech companies (in excess of $1 billion in revenues) experience the least severe growing pains.

Although the data presented in Table 5.3 and Figure 5.1 indicate that there are certain stages of growth in which organizational growing pains are likely to be severe, growing pains at any stage can be alleviated. This is best done through early detection of problems and careful plans for handling them.

The data suggest that growing pains typically increase as an organization's size increases to approximately $1 billion in revenues. Although companies with more than $1 billion in revenues do encounter difficulties and even fail (for example People Express, Boston Markets, Borders, and Maxicare), this appears to be a critical size for reduced growing pains. We can hypothesize that when an organization exceeds $1 billion in revenues, it may have achieved the critical mass and resources necessary to deal with its problems and overcome its growing pains, and that the probability of continued survival is increased. In brief, most companies that achieve this size are likely to have become professionally managed and have a high probability of continued success.

Distribution of Growing Pains Scores by Degree of Severity

Since 1980, we have been collecting Growing Pains Survey results from companies of all sizes in a variety of industries. The companies in our database were either clients of our firm, Management Systems, clients of one of our affiliates, or were participants in seminars or university-based education programs. We have also analyzed our database of growing pains survey results (which consists of over 5,000 companies from around the world) to identify the distribution of growing pains scores at each degree of severity. Table 5.4 shows the percentage of companies in our database with each of the five different levels of severity of growing pains from a very healthy organization to one that is at grave risk of failure.

As can be seen in Table 5.4, fewer than 3% of companies have a growing pains score of 14 or less, and 7% have scores between 15 and 19. Most companies have scores in the range of 20 to 39 (88%). Only 2% of companies have scores 40 or greater, the highest level of growing pains risk.

Our data and experience indicate that companies with growing pains scores greater than 40 are at considerable risk. If the underlying business conditions that are causing these scores are not treated, these organizations have about 12 to 18 months lead time before they face economic disaster, or bankruptcy.

Table 5.4   Percentile Scores for Overall Growing Pains

Growing Pains Score	Percent of Companies in This Range
10–14	3%
15–19	7%
20–29	50%
30–39	38%
40+	2%

Use of Growing Pains Measurements in Making Transitions

The Growing Pains Survey and related data presented here are important tools in helping organizations manage transitions successfully at different stages of growth. They indicate the degree of distress being experienced by an organization and can function as an early warning of serious problems to be encountered by an organization, such as those ultimately experienced by Borders, Osborne Computer, People Express, and Maxicare.

We have been using the Growing Pains Survey since 1980 as part of our consulting practice to help organizations of all sizes identify the need to make the transition from one stage of growth to the next. Measures of growing pains are useful in creating the motivation for change. Without the measurements, there can be a vague awareness of organizational problems, but the growing pains measures identify the issues with clarity, and, we have found, are more likely to serve as a stimulus to action. This is consistent with the theory of "data-based change," developed by the University of Michigan's Institute for Social Research.

The survey can be used as part of the first step in the process of transition required between growth stages (described in Chapters 3 and 4). This is the evaluation of the company's effectiveness at its current stage of growth. It also serves to create a "baseline" against which progress can be assessed, as we shall see in the example of Guangzhou Construction Company later in this chapter. In fact, many of our clients have used repeated measurements of growing pains over several years to assess their progress in organizational development. Progress is assessed not only with respect to the overall score but for each individual item as well.

Organizational Growing Pains, Growth Rates, and Infrastructure

As we have noted in this and in previous chapters, when an organization's growth outstrips its infrastructure, growing pains will result. The faster an organization is growing, the more difficult it will be for management to keep the company's infrastructure at a level required to support this rate of growth.

Based on our work with a wide variety of organizations, we have identified five different rates or "categories" of growth. Growth at the rate of less than 15% a year can be thought of as normal growth. This is relatively unspectacular growth, but the organization will double in size in approximately five years if it is growing at a rate of 15% per year. A growth rate of between 15 and 25% per year can be thought of as rapid growth. A rate of growth from 25 to 50% per year can be considered very rapid growth. Growth at a rate of 50 to 100% per year can be thought of as "hypergrowth." If the organization is growing at a rate greater than 100% per year, it can perhaps be regarded as experiencing "light-speed growth."

Based on our experience, it is extremely difficult for organizations to deal with growth rates greater than 50% per year. When the rate of growth equals or exceeds what we have characterized as hypergrowth, an organization can come very dangerously close to choking on its own growth. This has happened to a number of companies, including Osborne Computer, Maxicare, and People Express.[5]

Growing Pains and Financial Performance

Our empirical research has found that there is a statistically significant relationship between growing pains and financial performance.[6] The data derived from this research indicate that there are threshold levels of growing pains that are unsafe or unhealthy for future financial performance. The results also suggest that there appears to be a maximum level of growing pains beyond which organizational financial health is at risk. Specifically, the maximum healthy level of growing pains appears to be around 30. This means that to optimize the chances of being profitable, an organization ought to keep its growing pains score to less than 30. In terms of the color-coding scheme used with the Growing Pains Survey, this means keeping the score below the red zone. These findings have significant implications for management theory and practice.

Minimizing Organizational Growing Pains

Most entrepreneurs are concerned primarily with the risk of failure if revenues are insufficient to cover expenses. However, many ignore the equally damaging risks of choking on their own rapid growth. To avoid the problems accompanying hypergrowth, a company must have an infrastructure that will absorb that growth. If a company anticipates rapid growth, then management must invest in building the required infrastructure *before* it is actually necessary. It is very difficult, and sometimes impossible, to play catch-up with organizational infrastructure if the company is growing very rapidly. Some companies, such as Starbucks, had their infrastructure in place prior to their explosive growth and reaped the benefits of this investment.

This strategy of building the infrastructure prior to growth is not merely appropriate for large companies but for relatively small entrepreneurships as well. For example, in 1992 one of the authors met with the president of a service firm specializing in insurance-based benefit programs for executives when the firm had approximately $3 million in annual revenues. At that time, the author advised the CEO that it was probably premature to build the infrastructure to the extent that was being contemplated. However, the CEO indicated that he wanted his firm to grow to $50 million in revenue by 1997. He then proceeded to invest in professionalizing his company before it was actually necessary. This was a wise move, because the company grew to more than $65 million in revenue by the late 1990s.

The Risk of Growth with Inadequate Infrastructure

When a company (large or small) does not have an adequate infrastructure, it is at risk. One of the most difficult things to tell an entrepreneur is that the company is not really prepared for growth, and that he or she needs to slow down the growth plan. As advisors, we have done this several times. As an example, we were asked by Dr. Tim Bain—an entrepreneur whose business involved holistic medicine—to help assess the extent to which his firm was ready for growth. His business was very successful and he was about to embark on a major expansion. Having read Howard Schultz's book, *Pour Your Heart into It: How Starbucks Built a Company One Cup at a Time*, Dr. Bain was aware of our work with Starbucks and in 2011 he engaged the authors to assist with the process of scale-up for his company.[7]

Our first step was to do an organizational assessment to identify the company's strengths, limitations, and the extent to which the infrastructure was in place to support Dr. Bain's growth plan—which included taking new leases on stores where his services were delivered, representing a major financial commitment. Our conclusion was that although promising, the business was not prepared for this type of growth and that it would entail considerable financial risk. We recommended that Tim begin a strategic planning and organizational development process, introduce a performance management process, develop clear role descriptions for all positions, and systematize the delivery process of his services prior to expansion (all aspects of infrastructure).

Dr. Bain accepted our conclusions and deferred his growth plan. He focused instead upon building the infrastructure required to support profitable growth. We worked with him for one year, and he continued the work on his own after that. By 2015, Dr. Bain had redefined his business concept and grown his business to $15 million in annual revenues. In 2015, as a stronger enterprise, he was planning further expansion both in terms of services offered as well as in the size of the business.

Growing Pains at Guanzhou Construction

This section examines the use of growing pains scores as a tool in helping to facilitate organizational transitions and measure their effectiveness. We will do this by continuing the example of Guangzhou Construction, previously introduced in Chapter 2.

Organizational Growing Pains at Guangzhou Construction

As noted in Chapter 2, the Growing Pains Survey was administered twice at Guangzhou Construction—first in 2009 and then again in 2010 to measure progress after an organizational development program was conducted. As seen in Table 5.5, overall, in 2009, the growing pains of Guangzhou Construction were virtually in the red zone. The score of 29.5, while technically in the orange zone with rounding placed the company in the red zone, indicating the existence of some very significant problems. The consultant team working with Guangzhou also calculated the severity of *each* growing pain and found that five of the ten growing pains were ranked red. The complete scores are shown in Table 5.5.

As seen in Table 5.5, five growing pains were in the "red zone" (that is, over 30) in 2009. The measurement of growing pains is like taking someone's temperature—that is, it is possible to determine if there is a "fever" (if growing pains are high), but identifying the exact cause of the fever (or the growing pains) requires additional research and analysis. At the same time, however, it is possible to identify some of the factors that might be leading to these results, as described below.

At Guangzhou Construction, the most severe growing pain in 2009 (35.0) was that there are *too few good managers*. This, in fact, is a common problem among companies in China, where it is typically ranked as the number 1 or number 2 growing pain. Although typical in Chinese enterprises, it is still a serious problem. The underlying problem is typically a lack of focus on management and leadership development.

Table 5.5   Guangzhou Construction Growing Pains Survey Results, 2009 versus 2010

Growing Pains	Rank		Score		Change (−, 0, +)
	2009	2010	2009	2010	
There are too few "good" managers.	1	1	35.0	33.3	−
People feel that there are not enough hours in the day.	8	1	26.7	33.3	+
People are spending too much time "putting out fires."	3	3	31.7	30.8	−
Everyone feels "I have to do it myself if I want to get it done correctly."	4	4	30.0	30.0	0
Most people feel our meetings are a waste of time.	6	5	28.3	28.3	0
The company has continued to grow in sales but not in profits.	4	6	30.0	25.8	−
Many people are not aware of what others are doing.	2	7	33.3	25.0	−
When plans are made, there is very little follow-up, and things just don't get done.	8	7	26.7	25.0	−
Some people have begun to feel insecure about their place in the company.	6	9	28.3	22.5	−
People have a lack of understanding of where the company is headed.	10	10	25.0	17.5	−
Overall	−	−	**29.5**	**27.2**	−

The high scores on two growing pains—*People are not aware of what others are doing* (33.3), and *Everyone feels that they need to do everything themselves* (30.0)—suggest that there are opportunities to enhance the effectiveness of the organization's structure (through, among other factors, clarifying roles and responsibilities) and increase the effectiveness of the company's communication and coordination processes. In addition, people feeling that they need to do everything themselves combined with the high score on "too few good managers," might indicate that there are opportunities to help managers better understand and embrace their roles (that is, make the transition from "doing" to "managing").

The high score on *People are spending too much time "putting out fires"* (31.7) suggests that there are opportunities to develop and implement a more effective strategic planning process (which would minimize the fires). It also suggests that there is a need to ensure that the culture of the company promotes and reinforces effective planning versus fighting fires.

Most significant, perhaps, is the very high score the company received on *The company has continued to grow in sales, but not in profits*. This suggests that there are significant infrastructure problems that are now affecting the company's financial performance. This is a significant "warning" that there is a need to identify and address these issues in a timely manner.

The remaining growing pains were all in the orange zone (with the lowest score being 25.0). This suggests that there are additional infrastructure improvements that need to be made. These include improving the effectiveness of meetings, creating and implementing effective performance management systems (to decrease the extent to which people feel that there is no follow-up on plans, once they are made), and helping everyone on the team understand (through effective planning and effective communication of plans) where the company is headed.

Overcoming the Growing Pains

The Growing Pains Survey results and findings from the Organizational Effectiveness Survey (discussed previously in Chapter 2) served as the catalyst for Guangzhou Construction's CEO to embark on a program of organizational development, as described in Chapter 2.

Results of the Organizational Development Initiatives

Within two years of the organizational assessment (which included the administration of the two surveys), Guangzhou Construction had dramatically improved its management systems. More important, profits had tripled. About one year after first administering the Growing Pains Survey, it was readministered to members of the organization. The results were dramatic: Guangzhou Construction's score had improved by a full color band, going from the red to the orange zone. Further, seven of the ten individual growing pains had decreased in severity as shown in Table 5.5. Two remained unchanged, and only one growing pain increased in severity—*People feel that there are not enough hours in the day*.

It typically requires two years to make significant progress in organizational development and reduce growing pains; however, Guangzhou Construction had made considerable progress in just one year.

Summary

Some people believe that the solution to the problems of growth is to avoid it. Unfortunately, very soon after an organization is founded, it must grow, or it will die. Managers can control the *rate* of growth, but it is unrealistic to try to remain at a given size or stage of development. This means we must learn how to manage growth and the inevitable transitions it requires.

This chapter presents an in-depth discussion of the most common organizational growing pains. It also presents a method for assessing the extent to which a company suffers from these growing pains. The company's score on the Growing Pains Survey can suggest both the extent of its problems and specific need for action. The chapter provides data on the degree of organizational growing pains experienced by companies of different sizes and in different types of businesses. Variations exist here, but it is clear that organizations of all sizes and types experience some growing pains. As we have suggested, the severity of these problems can be affected by the rate of growth experienced by the organization. Managers of rapidly growing companies of any size or type must learn to recognize organizational growing pains and take steps to alleviate them so that their organizations can continue to operate successfully. Finally, we have provided a case study of a company that experienced growing pains (Guangzhou Construction) and initiated action to improve its organizational effectiveness.

Notes

1. Although the primary focus of this book is for-profit organizations, nonprofits can and do experience the same types of problems.
2. For a discussion of how to quantify these costs, see Eric Flamholtz, *Human Resource Accounting: Advances in Concepts, Methods, and Applications*, 3rd ed. (Norwell, MA: Kluwer, 1999).
3. This survey has been validated. See Rangapriya Kannan-Narasimhan and Eric G. Flamholtz, "Growing Pains: A Barrier to Successful Corporate Entrepreneurship," *Silicon Valley Review for Global Entrepreneurship Research* (SVRGER) 2, no. 1 (2006), 4–24.
4. Rensis Likert developed the so-called Likert Scale. It is validated as an "interval level" measurement instrument.
5. See, for example, Adam Osborne and John Dvorak, *Hypergrowth: The Rise and Fall of the Osborne Computer Corporation* (Berkeley, CA: Idthekkethan, 1984).
6. See Eric Flamholtz and Wei Hua, "Strategic Organizational Development, Growing Pains and Corporate Financial Performance: An Empirical Test," *European Management Journal* 20, no. 5 (2002): 527–536.
7. Howard Schultz and Dori Jones Yang, *Pour Your Heart Into It: How Starbucks Built a Company One Cup at a Time* (New York: Hyperion, 1997), 161, 201–202.

Mastering the Tools for Building Sustainably Successful Organizations®

Part One of this book presented the key factors that determine organizational success and provided a framework for understanding the stages of organizational growth. Part Two focuses on a set of tools that can be used by company leaders to promote successful growth and development. Specifically, we will discuss some of the major elements of an organization's management infrastructure—its management systems and corporate culture. Management systems and corporate culture were described briefly in Chapter 2, and their places on the Pyramid of Organizational Development were shown in Figure 2.1.

An organization's management systems consist of (1) the planning system (including the strategic planning process), (2) the organization structure, (3) its system for management and leadership development, and (4) the company's control or performance management systems. Management systems have a critical influence on an organization's current and future performance and profitability.

A planning system includes the processes for strategic planning, operational planning, budgeting, and contingency planning. The strategic planning process is a critical resource or tool for managing organizational growth and development. Chapter 6 presents concepts and methods of strategic planning. It also explains the role of strategic planning in promoting long-term success and provides a case study example of how to develop and use this tool in practice. Finally, it examines an organization's requirements for strategic planning at different stages of growth.

The way people are organized in a business enterprise can have a critical impact on overall operating effectiveness, efficiency, and, in turn, bottom-line profitability. Chapter 7 discusses the nature of an organization's structure and examines the alternative forms of structure. It also identifies criteria for the design and evaluation of organizational structure as well as presents case studies of structural issues at different stages of growth.

Control or performance management systems are another critical component of the organization's management systems. Chapter 8 discusses the need for control and the nature and role of organizational control and performance management systems. It also presents a model of the key components of a performance management system and explains how they function to motivate and control behavior. Finally, it examines the design of performance management systems at different stages of growth.

Ensuring that those in leadership roles have the skills needed to manage organizational transitions is critical to long-term success. Management and leadership development can be used not only to help managers and leaders develop the skills they need, but it can also help to shape or reshape the corporate culture. Chapter 9 examines the tools and functions of management development and presents case studies that illustrate how companies can use the leadership development process to enhance organizational performance and support long-term success. It also describes the design and focus of leadership development programs at different stages of growth.

The nature and management of a company's culture also has a significant impact on organizational success. Culture influences an organization's ability to develop the systems needed to support its growth. Like other variables in the Pyramid of Organizational Development, culture must be effectively managed to promote long-term organizational success. Chapter 10 describes the nature of corporate culture and how it is manifested in organizations. It also presents techniques for managing this variable effectively and describes the nature of corporate culture at different stages of organizational growth. Finally, it presents a case study of the steps organizations should take to better understand and manage their cultures.

Part Two, then, gives a basic description of some of the most important concepts and tools that can help leaders successfully manage organizational transitions and build a successful enterprise over the long term. Figure II.1 summarizes schematically the relations among the key components of an organization's management system. As seen in the figure, the management process begins with the planning system, which articulates an organization's business concept, strategic mission, objectives, and goals. The company's plan drives (should determine) how it is organized (organizational structure). This, in turn, enhances the organization's operational systems and leads to results, which are measured by the performance measurement system.

The performance measurement system is a component of the company's performance management system, which also includes objectives and goals from the planning system as well as performance appraisals and rewards (compensation). Performance review meetings, as well as information, are the mechanisms through which these components of the overall management system operate. The management and leadership development system supports the other components of the management system by training leaders in the skills required to do planning, to use the various forms of

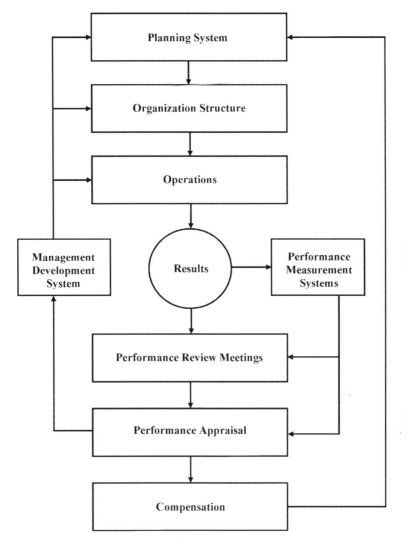

Figure II.1   The Management System

organizational structure, and to manage day-to-day operations. Input about the skills that need to be built through management development is received from the performance appraisal process.

Leadership—a key component of the management system—is not shown explicitly in Figure II.1, but it should be viewed as a part of the various components such as strategic planning (strategic leadership), operations, performance review meetings, and performance appraisal (operational leadership). (We will discuss leadership in more depth in Chapter 12.) Similarly, corporate culture is not explicitly shown in Figure II.1, but it must be recognized that corporate culture affects and is affected by all of the components of the management system.

CHAPTER 6

Strategic Planning

Effective strategic planning (or what we refer to as "strategic organizational development planning") plays a critical role in long-term organizational success. It is not only an important tool for managing organizations; it is also part of the process through which organizations make the transition from one stage of growth to the next.

Strategic planning is one of the major tools by which management can create a shared vision of what a company (whether for-profit or nonprofit) wants to become. The strategic planning process can also help to shape the corporate culture. The very act of instituting such a process, when one was not used in the past, signals to the organization's members that things are changing—that planning must now become a way of life. When done effectively, strategic planning provides a sense of direction for a company and its employees, as well as specific goals to motivate and guide behavior.

This chapter provides a proven framework and a step-by-step approach for strategic planning that helps ensure that a company's leadership is focused on all key drivers of long-term organizational success (identified in the Pyramid of Organizational Development, which was described in Chapter 2).[1] As will be explained in this chapter, our approach differs significantly from traditional strategic planning.

This approach has demonstrated its value in a wide spectrum of companies globally. It has been used by companies ranging from start-ups to members of the Fortune 500 over the past 40 plus years, including Starbucks Coffee Company, Amgen, American Century Investments, Jamba Juice, Noah's Bagels, Navistar, PowerBar, Bell-Carter Foods, Simon Property Group, Techmer PM, Tommy Bahama, Wolfgang Puck Food Company, the Kusto Group (Kazakhstan), The Riverside Group (China); and Beton 6, DESCON, and Coteccons (Vietnam).[2] It has been applied in almost every type of industry from biotechnology to financial services, software, technology, manufacturing, retail, and mining. It has been used by our affiliates in Bulgaria, Canada, Kazakhstan, Poland, Russia, Ukraine, and the United States. We have found *no limitations on its applicability in any country or type of industry or size of company.*

This chapter begins by defining the basic concepts of strategic planning in this approach. We then describe the steps involved in developing a strategic plan using our method and explain the advantages of using this approach, versus a more traditional one. Throughout the chapter, we use case examples from several organizations to illustrate this approach in practice. Finally, we describe the strategic planning process at each stage of growth.

The framework and approach to strategic planning presented in this chapter include some familiar concepts, but there are subtle and *important* differences, which we point out. As there is a great deal of semantic confusion in the language of strategic planning, we are careful to clearly define our concepts and terms, and then tie them together as a true planning system. Although some people are critical of the concept of strategic planning, the approach presented here has actually been used by thousands of organizations (both for-profit and nonprofit) all over the world. The method works if a serious commitment is made to apply it; but *it must be applied as we present it.* It has been carefully constructed, with well-defined concepts; it cannot be modified in an ad hoc manner and still be expected to work.

Strategy Defined

Although the term *strategy* is widely used, it is frequently either undefined or loosely defined. Everyone knows what it is when they see it, but they can't define it. The first challenge, then, that managers face in trying to implement a strategic plan is to define what is meant by the word *strategy*.

Strategy can be defined as "the different, yet integrated courses of actions that will be taken by a company or business unit to compete effectively in its chosen markets in order to obtain desired results." Thus strategy implies both competition and intended achievement. Taking this definition a step further, strategy consists of (1) *where* (in what markets) a company chooses to compete, and (2) *how* the company will compete in its chosen markets in order to achieve the best results. We come back to this definition a little later in this chapter.

The Nature of Strategic Planning and "Strategic Organizational Development Planning"

An organization can have a strategy and not have a strategic plan or a strategic planning process. The process of strategic planning involves deciding about the future direction and the capabilities that will be needed to achieve the organization's goals. It involves analyzing the organization's environment to assess future opportunities and threats, assessing the organization's capabilities, identifying the longer-term mission to be achieved, and developing objectives and goals that will promote the achievement of this long-term mission. The deliverable of any strategic planning process should be a written document that serves as a guide or roadmap to the future. In a sense, it is the company's "play book." An effective strategic planning process also includes a system for monitoring performance against the strategic plan, which converts it into a strategic management system.

In most traditional approaches to strategic planning, the focus is almost exclusively on "Who we are going to target/serve" (customers), "What we are going to give them" (products/services), and "What we are going to receive in return" (financial results—revenue, profit, etc.). In our approach, the focus is not just on products and markets, but also on organizational resources, operational systems, management systems, and culture—that is, on all levels in the Pyramid of Organizational Development because (as described in Part One of this book) these are the factors that drive long-term success measured by financial performance. In this sense, the term *strategic planning* is more appropriately viewed as a process of "strategic organizational development." It simultaneously deals with both the strategic aspects of markets and competition, and the organizational infrastructure—the capabilities required for long-term organizational success, as described in Chapter 2. In developing a strategic plan, if a company's leadership focuses *only* on markets, products/services, and financial performance, there is a high probability that important infrastructure problems will be missed and performance issues will arise as the company continues to grow and develop.

There are three critical aspects of strategic planning: (1) strategic issues to be addressed, (2) the "flow" of the process itself, and (3) the components of the strategic plan. We discuss each in turn.

Strategic Issues

Although many people think of strategic planning as a number-crunching exercise, its primary focus should be on identifying and resolving strategic and related organizational development issues. To articulate its future direction and strategy, it is necessary for the leadership team to address a wide variety of issues related to the company's market, competition, environmental trends, and organizational development.

Each organization will have a number of strategic issues that are specific to its market, how it will compete, and the internal systems that it needs to have to support its development. There are, however, seven generic questions that *must* be addressed by all organizations, regardless of their size and their industry:

1. What business are we in?
2. What are our competitive strengths and limitations?
3. Do we have or can we develop a true market niche?
4. What do we want to become in the long term?
5. What is our strategy for competing effectively in our chosen markets and for achieving our long-term mission?
6. What are the critical factors that will make us successful or unsuccessful in achieving our long-term mission?
7. What goals shall we set to improve our competitive effectiveness and organizational capabilities in each of these critical success areas?

The answers to these questions result in the development of key components of the company's strategic plan. For example, the answer to the first question becomes the company's *business concept*; addressing the fourth question leads to the development of the company's *strategic mission statement*.

We examine how these questions are addressed in the discussion of the steps or flow of the strategic planning process. We will also describe the process for answering these questions in a case study later in this chapter.

Management Systems' Strategic Planning Method

As shown in Figure 6.1, there are six steps in our proven approach to developing and implementing effective strategic plans. While the exact nature of the execution may differ, the same six steps should be used regardless of the organization's size, industry, or geography (country). These six key steps are (1) complete the environmental scan, (2) complete the organizational assessment, (3) resolve key strategic issues, (4) develop the strategic plan, (5) develop the budget (to support the strategic plan), and (6) conduct plan reviews on at least a quarterly basis.

The first two steps of this process involve collecting information about the environment in which the company has chosen to compete and about its internal capabilities. We term these

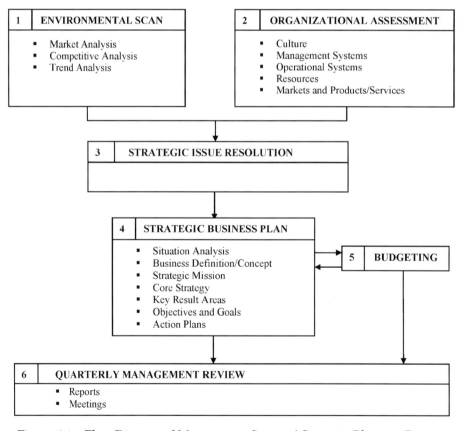

Figure 6.1   Flow Diagram of Management Systems' Strategic Planning Process

an "environmental scan" and an "organizational assessment." These two related steps replace and improve upon the conventional notion of a SWOT analysis, where "S" is strengths, "W" is weaknesses, "O" is opportunities and "T" is threats, as explained below.

Using the information collected in the first two steps as input, the third step involves identifying and working to resolve key strategic issues (including those identified earlier). In the fourth step, the management team is actually producing the organization's plan. A budget to support the plan developed in Step 4 is created in Step 5. The final step in this process is of critical importance in making the planning process really work. This step involves periodic monitoring of performance against the plan. It provides a company's management team with the opportunity to make adjustments, as needed, so that it can continue to achieve the best results.

Step 1: The Environmental Scan

As seen in Figure 6.1, the first step in the planning process is the environmental scan. This step involves collecting information on (1) the market in which the company competes, (2) the company's competition, and (3) key environmental trends that may affect the business (positively or negatively) over the next three to five years. This step replaces and improves upon the opportunities and threats component of the conventional SWOT analysis. It improves upon it because, rather than merely a general notion of opportunities and threats, the approach focuses on three key dimensions (the market, competitors, and trends) that lead to a more in-depth analysis, as explained below.

Market Analysis. The first step of the environmental scan is to collect and analyze information about the company's current and potential market. In brief, this step involves collecting information on the nature of the company's customers, their needs, how they buy, and the potential of different market segments. The output of this analysis should be a very clear picture of the company's present and potential customers, their needs, and the extent to which the company is meeting (or, in the case of potential customers, might meet) customer needs. In addition, the market analysis should identify the threats and opportunities that exist within the company's present and potential markets.

Competitive Analysis. The next step in an environmental scan is to assess the competition. The first step in this process is to identify who the company's most significant present and potential competitors are. These key competitors should be those that pose the most significant threats to the company's ability to be successful in its chosen market. The next step is to identify the strengths and limitations of each competitor—not just in terms of the products or services it provides or its ability to understand and meet customer needs (that, in turn, leads to how customers view each company); but also in terms of the extent to which it has built the infrastructure (has the resources, operational systems, management systems, culture, and culture management systems) needed to support effective and efficient current and future operations. While information about competitors' infrastructures can be difficult to obtain, it can be quite valuable from the standpoint of a core strategy (which will be discussed later in this chapter).

Identifying Market Segments: One Output of the Market and Competitive Analysis. The information collected through the market and competitive analyses can be used as the basis for understanding where a company is competing or might compete within its market—that is, its

Horizontal Segments	Vertical Segments				
	Sedans	Sports Cars	SUVs	Light Trucks	Minivans
I	Rolls-Royce Lexus BMW Jaguar	Porsche Ferrari Lamborghini	Hummer Mercedes Lexus Range Rover Escalade		
II	Honda Accord Toyota Camry Ford Taurus	Toyota Celica Volkswagen Jetta	Ford Explorer GMC Blazer Jeep Cherokee	Toyota Tacoma Ford Ranger	Toyota Sienna Ford Windstar
III	Toyota Corolla	MINI Cooper	Toyota RAV4 Suzuki Samari		

Figure 6.2   Where You Play "The Game": Analysis of the Strategic Board

market segments. A market segment is defined in terms of the product or service categories a company offers, or will offer, as well as the tier of the market in which the organization will compete. These two dimensions of the market come together in what we call the *strategic board*, which identifies the segments that are included in the market in which a company is competing. An example of a strategic board for the automobile industry is presented in Figure 6.2.

The market for any product or service typically exists in terms of three different tiers or levels of the market (shown on the vertical axis of Figure 6.2). In order to position themselves effectively, companies must understand that customer wants differ at each tier.

The primary concerns for a Tier I buyer or customer are quality, service, and prestige of the product/service or brand. Customers in this tier are less concerned with price or even price differentials than they are with the other factors. While these customers may seek to obtain the "best" price, they will not settle for less in terms of quality, service, or prestige (of the brand). For example, a Tier I automobile customer may consider a Mercedes, a Jaguar, or some other luxury automobile and might negotiate with the salesperson on price. This customer, however, wants a luxury automobile and will pay what is needed to obtain it. Viewed figuratively, the customers in this tier are those who might purchase products and services ranging from a Cadillac to a Rolls-Royce. This is true not only for automobiles per se but for all products and services that fit this particular categorization by quality. The same kind of demarcation can be true for retail (e.g., Saks Fifth Avenue, Barney's), legal services, health care, or products provided by aerospace firms.

The second tier of the market is usually significantly larger than Tier I in terms of the number of customers in this segment. In Tier II, the buyer is concerned with a combination of quality, service, prestige, and price. Typically, the buyer is making tradeoffs between two or more of these variables. The products in this category figuratively range from Volvo down to a Chevrolet. As before, this tier of the market is not just applicable to automobiles but to a full range of products and services.

In Tier III, the typical buyer is concerned primarily with price. Quality, service, and prestige are relatively unimportant. The buyer may still strive to obtain the highest quality of product or service, but he or she only has so much money to spend. In most markets, this tends to be the largest of all three tiers of the market. The buyer in this tier is looking for a serviceable product or service. It may well be a commodity or a generic brand. This tier can be symbolically represented by looking from lower-priced Ford products down through Hyundai, Kia, and used (previously owned) automobiles.

To illustrate the fact that the three tiers of the market do not merely apply to tangible products such as automobiles but to all other products and services as well, consider some examples, such as legal services, medical services, aerospace, and retailing. In Los Angeles, there is a well-known law firm by the name of O'Melveny & Meyers. This firm operates in the Tier I segment, and to paraphrase a well-known saying, "If you have to ask the price, you probably cannot afford it." In Tier III we have a firm that specializes in being a legal service supermarket: Jacoby & Meyers. And in Los Angeles, there are certainly many Tier II law firms (probably several with a "Meyers"!). With respect to medical services, community or public clinics occupy Tier III of the market, PPOs occupy Tier II, and HMOs occupy the lower portions of Tier II and upper Tier III. Many private physicians are in various levels of Tiers I and II. The upper end of Tier I tends to be occupied by some of the elite private hospitals, as well as by certain private physicians. In the aerospace sector, Hughes Aircraft had traditionally occupied Tier I of the market. It specialized in being able to do whatever was required by its customers, which were subunits of the U.S. Department of Defense. Quality, rather than cost, was the primary consideration. Today, most aerospace firms occupy Tier II, because the customer is concerned with the tradeoff between price, quality, and service; a few aerospace firms operate in Tier III. In the retailing sector, Saks Fifth Avenue and Neiman Marcus occupy Tier I. Stores such as JCPenney and Macy's occupy Tier II, while Tier III is served by Walmart, Kmart, and 99 Cents Only Stores.

It is typically very difficult for companies to compete in all three segments of the market simultaneously. Only some of the largest have traditionally been able to accomplish this feat. For example, General Motors begins with its lower-priced Chevrolets and moves its customers all the way through its product ladder to the Tier I version of its Cadillac. However, in the lower reaches of Tier III, General Motors has not traditionally competed with some of the less expensive foreign imports, and it does not compete in the highest levels of Tier I with products offered by Mercedes and Rolls-Royce.

Developing and analyzing the strategic board can help a company's leadership team understand where it currently competes and with whom it competes. This can then help a company focus on the strengths and limitations of its most significant competitors rather than assume that it competes with "everyone." If a company competes in Tier II of the retail market, it should be most concerned with understanding the strengths and limitations of others in this segment. Companies competing in Tier I or Tier III of this market should be of less concern unless there is the possibility that they might move into Tier II. For example, Starbucks does not see itself in competition with McDonald's. Starbucks envisions itself in Tiers I and II, and sees McDonald's as a Tier III business. Analyzing the strategic board can also lead to the identification of "open segments"—that is, segments in which the company might compete because no others have yet entered them.

Trend Analysis. The final step in the environmental scan is to clearly identify key environmental trends that may affect the company in the future, and the impact that these trends might have on the company's success (that is, the threats and opportunities presented by these trends). This involves addressing questions such as: What will our industry be like in five years? What emerging trends in demographics, workforce values, the economic and political environment, technology, and so on might affect our organization? What potential opportunities and threats are implicit in those trends? What actions can or must we take to deal with them?

Specific areas of focus in the twenty-first century relate to technological trends, social media trends, and the social and psychological differences of different age cohorts (e.g., what Millennials versus Gen Xers are looking for in their jobs). In addition to these types of trends, each business will have specific trends that are most important to them. For example, Navistar and other heavy and medium truck manufacturers need to be concerned with environmental regulations around emissions. Fast food restaurants like McDonald's and Burger King need to be concerned with (and have adapted to) changing consumer preferences and the trend toward "healthy eating." Retailers need to track how customers purchase their products, as well as the products that consumers want to purchase.

Many organizations initially missed the significance of the Internet for their business. For example, Borders, a brick and mortar bookstore, went bankrupt. Sears abandoned their catalog business just before direct sales via the Internet exponentially expanded and led to Amazon becoming a giant net-based "e-tailer."

Even in the technology space, an understanding of trends is critical. The challenge for technology companies is to continuously adapt or perish. Once-powerful technology companies have been weakened or have even perished because they missed trends. Examples include IBM, which initially missed the significance of the personal computer and mini-computers for its core business in mainframes; Microsoft, which initially missed the significance of the Internet; and Intel, which initially missed the significance of the trend to mobile devices. As this book is being written, cloud computing is the emerging trend in technology that will be disruptive. As stated by Tiernan Ray (who writes a weekly column on Technology for *Barron's*), "The Challenge for Internet Companies Now: Adapt or Die."[3] The challenge to adapt to cloud computing faces companies like Salesforce .com, Oracle, IBM, and many others in the technology space.

Step 2: The Organizational Assessment

The second step in the strategic planning process is to conduct an organizational assessment. This consists of identifying the company's strengths and limitations at each level in the Pyramid of Organizational Development, described in Chapter 2: markets, products and services, resources, operational systems, management systems, and corporate culture. This step replaces and improves upon the strengths and weaknesses component of the conventional SWOT analysis. It improves upon the conventional SWOT because (rather than merely a general notion of strengths and weaknesses) our approach focuses on the key dimensions comprising the Pyramid of Organizational Development, which have been validated as drivers of financial performance, as explained in Chapter 2.

The organizational assessment may be done in several ways. It may involve a self-assessment of strengths and limitations in each area, using the tools provided for this purpose in Chapter 2—that is, both the qualitative and the quantitative pyramid analysis. It can also involve the use of surveys (such as the Growing Pains Survey, presented in Chapter 5) to be completed by a sample of people in the organization or by all of its personnel. Some companies use independent consultants like the authors to perform the organizational assessment. These consultants interview personnel, analyze operational data, and may use other surveys such as the Organizational Effectiveness Survey discussed in Chapter 2. We have described this process in Chapters 2 and 5.

Output of the First Two Steps

The output of the environmental scan and organizational assessment should be a summary of the information collected, along with an analysis of what this information suggests about areas that the company needs to focus on in order to continue its success into the future. Typically, this is done in some type of report that presents:

- A clear picture of the company's current market (that is, customers) and an evaluation of the extent to which the company is currently meeting customer needs. This might also include identification of specific threats and opportunities presented by the market.

- The identification of key present or potential competitors and each competitor's strengths and limitations (from the standpoint of meeting customer needs).

- Analysis of the most significant trends that might affect the business and the opportunities or threats presented by each trend.

- An assessment of the company's most significant strengths and limitations at each level in the Pyramid of Organizational Development.

By analyzing the information collected through the environmental scan and organizational assessment, a company may also identify specific strategic issues that should be addressed in Step 3 of the strategic planning process.

Step 3: Analysis and Resolution of Key Strategic Issues

Once the environmental scan and the organizational assessment have been completed, the next—very critical—step in the strategic planning process is to identify and work to resolve key strategic issues facing the company. It is important that during this step, attention be focused on addressing the seven issues previously identified.

What Business Are We In? This is one of the most fundamental and important strategic issues that needs to be addressed. This is a deceptively simple question, but it is one of the most critical strategic decisions an organization's leadership must make, because it defines the platform or scope of the business. If the answer to this question is too broad or too narrow, it is of no real strategic value. Many organizations fail or at least do not prosper because they do not really understand the nature of their business, because they view it too narrowly, or because they are not focusing enough attention on identifying and adapting to environmental changes.

To illustrate this point, we will cite some important historical examples. During the nineteenth and early part of the twentieth century, the railroads were successful and powerful. However, they viewed the answer to the question, "What business are we in?" as obvious and fairly narrow: We are in the railroad business. Unfortunately for them, the obvious answer was not correct. They ought to have viewed themselves as being in the *transportation* business—the business of transporting people and goods. By defining their business as being railroads, they completely missed the significance of the development of other forms of ground and then air transportation, which ultimately eroded their strength.

While railroads are an example of defining a business too narrowly, there are also examples of companies that defined their businesses too broadly. For example, at one point AT&T defined their business as the "telecommunications business." While this was literally correct, it had no strategic value because it did not provide any focus.

Another important historical example is Curtis Publishing Company, which was a great success during the early part of the twentieth century but later failed because of a poorly conceived business concept. Cyrus Curtis, a great entrepreneur, built a publishing empire with major properties such as the *Saturday Evening Post* and the *Ladies' Home Journal*. Unfortunately, the company eventually failed because it had defined its business as the "publishing business." It failed to realize that in consumer media, advertising follows consumers, and one of its principal revenue streams was from advertisers. The managers of Curtis did not appreciate the implications of the new medium—television—and its impact on advertising revenues. Thus they chose to purchase a printing plant to vertically integrate the firm's operations, turning down opportunities to acquire NBC and CBS—a disastrous decision.

A more recent example of this problem concerns RadioShack. As noted in Chapter 2, RadioShack was once a very successful enterprise, serving several generations of electronics hobbyists; but its business concept became outdated leading to a long period of irrelevance in the market suggesting that it is ultimately destined for extinction like the dinosaur or dodo bird.

An organization that is trying to decide what business it is in must understand what its present and potential markets are and what the customers in those markets need. It must answer these major questions: (1) Who are our present and potential customers? (2) What are their needs? (3) How do they acquire our products or services? and (4) What do they consider to be of value in a product or service? To effectively address these questions, a company's management should use the information collected and analyzed in Steps 1 and 2 of the strategic planning process. The analysis of the strategic board, along with the information collected about the company's internal capabilities (through the organizational assessment) can assist in effectively answering this first strategic question. For example, if the railroads had thoroughly analyzed the trends in their market (for example, the advent of new technology to move people and products from one location to another), they might have recognized the need to broaden their business definition. A magazine publishing company such as Curtis must recognize that it serves two related but distinct groups of customers: subscribers, who read its publications, and advertisers, who wish to reach particular groups of people in order to market their own products or services. An organization must understand the needs of all its different segments of customers, especially when those needs differ significantly.

The resolution of this issue results in a business definition (or concept) statement, which is incorporated into the company's strategic plan. The creation of this statement is a complex and subtle exercise, requiring time and skill. Management teams may spend several days—over a period of weeks of months—discussing and debating this issue until they get it right. This is discussed further in Step 4 of the strategic planning process.

What Are Our Competitive Strengths and Limitations? The competitive analysis, along with the organizational assessment, provides the information needed to address this question. The leadership team needs to objectively identify those areas where the company is strong, as well as those areas where it is faced with a competitive disadvantage. In addition, there needs to be a focus on identifying those factors that truly distinguish the company from its competition. For example, both Apple and Microsoft differentiate themselves from others based on their technologies and brands—and both devote a great deal of time to protecting these strengths. Identifying strengths is an essential step even for successful companies, because in order to continue its success, an organization must understand what caused it. One $250 million manufacturing company, for example, has recognized that it has strengths in the areas of management systems and culture that none of its competitors have. As a result, for over 20 years, these have been significant areas of focus for the company.

The resolution of this issue is incorporated into the strategic plan in two ways. First, the key differentiators are used as input to developing the core strategy for the company—that is, the strategy around which all other strategies are based. Second, specific objectives and goals should identify what the company will do to maximize its key competitive strengths and minimize its key competitive limitations.

Do We Have or Can We Develop a True Market Niche? Although many people use the terms *niche* and *segment* interchangeably, in our opinion they are *not* synonyms. A *market segment* is any subdivision of the market defined by the tier of the market in which the company competes and the products or services it offers (as discussed previously).

A *market niche* is a place within a market segment where an organization has developed a sufficient number of sustainable competitive advantages to control a portion of that market. A competitive advantage is something (tangible or intangible) that gives an organization a superior opportunity (however marginal) to compete in the market. It can range from a proprietary product (such as a drug under patent) to a well-known brand. Potentially, anything can be a source of competitive advantage: greater resources, speed in execution, a new technology, better customer service, superior management systems, greater skill in strategic planning, or a company's culture.

We view a competitive advantage as sustainable if it will last for at least two years. This is analogous to a fixed asset under generally accepted accounting principles. Just as a current asset is something that will last or be consumed within one year, and a fixed asset is something that will last for more than one year, a sustainable advantage is essentially an organizational resource that will provide the enterprise benefits for at least two years. It can be tangible or intangible, reflected in financial statements or not, but it is still real. Accordingly, just by being the first in a market does not mean the company will establish a sustainable competitive advantage.

At times, the source of sustainable advantage can be the business model (or way the company does business) adopted by an organization. For example, Southwest Airlines has a unique business model that could be described as low-cost airfare plus a positive corporate culture. Southwest focuses a great deal of attention on both keeping its costs down and on effectively managing its company culture. Employees are all owners and, as such, are invested in helping to make the company a success.

The concept of a market niche and, in turn, the notion of a sustainable competitive advantage is important for two strategic reasons. From an offensive standpoint, the primary advantage of a niche in a market is typically that the price (and, in turn, the gross margin) of products is superior to that of competitors. This results in greater profitability and in the opportunity to reinvest those profits in a variety of ways. From a defensive standpoint, during periods of economic decline holders of a market niche tend to suffer less than their competitors. Their products tend to sell to a greater extent than those of more generic or less-established products and services.

A niche is also important defensively if a competitor wishes to invade the company's market segment. Southwest, for example, has been able to remain profitable and to grow as competitors have also begun to match the company's low fares. The reason is that Southwest's niche is not based purely on its fares (which can be easily, although not necessarily profitably copied). It is also based on its ability to effectively manage its positive culture—something that cannot be copied. Passengers experience this culture in how they are treated by employees.

Another example of the defensive value of a market niche is demonstrated by 99 Cents Only Stores, the dominant deep discount retailer of foods and household items in Southern California. It has a true market niche. California is one of the world's largest economies in terms of GDP. In 2012, it ranked 10th in the world in GDP, just behind Italy and just ahead of India.[4] Southern California contributes 60% of California's GDP. 99 Cents Only Stores achieved revenues of $1.8 billion in 2011. It so dominated the Southern California market for discount retail foods and household items that other national and regional chains have chosen not to enter and compete in that market.

A key point to keep in mind in identifying or working to create a market niche is that the most sustainable advantages are those that exist in the upper levels of the Pyramid of Organizational Development. If a company has a competitive advantage based on its culture, this will be extremely difficult to copy. For example, Walmart sells the same products that Kmart sells, but it has an advantage that has been extremely sustainable (because they have focused on it)—that is, a well-managed culture that stresses customer service.

A company whose only competitive advantage rests with the products it offers leaves itself extremely vulnerable to competition. Any product or service can be copied, thus taking away the advantage. At one time, IBM was a major player in the personal computer (PC) market. As companies like Dell Computers began producing similar products at lower cost, IBM lost its advantage. After posting an $8 billion loss in 1993, IBM began a process of revitalizing the company, which ultimately led to a reconceptualization of its business. As result, in 2005, IBM sold its PC business to Lenovo.

A market niche does not have to be small, as conventional usage of the term implies; it can be very large. For example, Microsoft has a true market niche because of its dominance in operating systems, and this niche is very large. Apple has a large market niche based in part on the "i" brand and, in part, on its ability to consistently produce innovative products.

The answer to the question of whether an organization has a market niche is incorporated into the company's strategic plan as a part of the core strategy. As will be discussed later in this chapter, the core strategy identifies how the company will use its key competitive differences (that create the market niche) to win within its market.

What Do We Want to Become in the Long Term? We define the "long term" as three to five years out, although it is possible to plan in terms of the "very long term" or more than 10 years out. The identification of what a company wants to become should be grounded in the analysis of data from the environmental scan and the organizational assessment. In brief, the answer to this question helps the company's leadership team define where it is going. The output of this discussion is what we call a strategic mission statement, which will be included in the company's plan. We discuss this later in this chapter.

In 1994, when Starbucks was still a relatively small company, it established a strategic mission to become the leading brand of specialty coffee in North America by the year 2000. This was strategic because it was intended to allow Starbucks to achieve a size and critical mass that would be defensible against potential competitors. The debate within management in 1994 centered around whether this could be accomplished if Starbucks achieved $1 billion in revenue and approximately 1,000 stores, or whether a larger number of stores and more revenue were required. The final decision was to target $2 billion in revenue and 2,000 stores by the year 2000. The strategic intent was to prevent a large company like Nestlé or McDonald's from copying the Starbucks formula and controlling the market before this could be achieved by Starbucks itself.

What Is Our Strategy for Competing Effectively in Our Chosen Markets and for Achieving Our Long-Term Mission? Once a company has identified the market in which it will compete (its business concept or definition), its competitive strengths and limitations, and what it wants to become (its strategic mission), the next question involves determining *how* it will compete in order to achieve the desired results. This involves identifying three levels of strategy that will guide the behavior of the team toward desired results within the chosen market. These three levels constitute a strategy "wheel," which is shown in Figure 6.3.

The first level of strategy is what we call core strategy, which defines the overall concept of how the company or business unit will compete. In developing a core strategy, a company's leadership

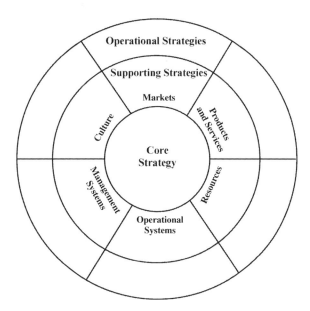

Figure 6.3   How You Play "The Game": Three Levels of Strategy

team should consider the results of its environmental scan and organizational assessment. This information will help determine how realistic the strategy is.

For example, Starbucks' initial core strategy was something like "to redefine the coffee café and blanket the United States." With the exception of small, local roasters, there was really no competition in Starbucks' initial market. In other words, there were no true national chains of coffee cafés. Southwest Airlines' initial core strategy (now somewhat changed) was something like to provide "no-frills, short-haul, high-frequency discount air travel in relatively noncompetitive markets." When Southwest began to expand its operations from its base in Texas (where it had perfected the short-haul, no-frills concept), most airlines were losing money. Southwest's strategy was not to go head-to-head with the majors but to stay in noncompetitive markets, offering potential customers low-cost air travel. The strategy has been successful; Southwest has remained profitable as it has grown to serve markets throughout the United States. Walmart's core strategy is to be the price leader, as reflected in its marketing slogan "Always Low Prices."

The second level of strategy is called *supporting strategies*, which describe what a company or business unit needs to do in each level of the Pyramid of Organizational Development to support its core strategy. The supporting strategies a company will pursue at each level in the pyramid tend to be defined in one or two sentences. They are "big picture" strategies, not a list of to-dos. Examples of supporting strategies for Southwest Airlines (based on its initial core strategy) are shown in Table 6.1.

Operational strategies identify how a company will implement its core strategy. Operational strategies might be thought of as tactics, action steps, or "to-dos." However, they should focus on the most critical to-dos versus everything that the company needs to focus on to make its core strategy a reality. Examples of operational strategies for Walmart are presented in Table 6.2.

What Are the Critical Factors That Will Make Us Successful or Unsuccessful in Achieving Our Long-Term Mission? Once its strategy has been identified, the leadership team then needs to identify where it should focus to maximize results over the long term. This typically involves clearly identifying those factors that will support or detract from the company's ability to execute its strategy. These factors (which, as explained later, are termed "key result areas") might include aspects of the company's internal operations or environmental factors that are presenting threats or opportunities. Again, the answers to this question are typically derived from the results of the environmental scan and organizational assessment.

What Goals Shall We Set to Improve Our Competitive Effectiveness and Organizational Capabilities in Each of These Critical Success Areas? The output of addressing this final strategic question is a list of goals that the company will focus on to continue its success into the future. These goals will become part of the strategic plan (which is discussed in the next section).

Step 4: The Strategic Plan

The fourth step in the strategic planning process involves preparing a strategic plan or what we term, a "strategic organizational development plan." This is a written statement of the future direction of an enterprise based on the environmental scan and the organizational assessment. While there are a variety of methods for creating and presenting strategic plans, we have a very specific and proven approach, as will be detailed below.

Table 6.1   Sample Supporting Strategies for Southwest Airlines

Markets: Products and Services

- Enter only noncompetitive markets.
- Keep fares competitive with, or lower than, other airlines' prices.
- Offer high customer service but few amenities (for example, offer only drinks and snacks on board rather than full meals).
- Stick to short routes.

Resources

- Use only Boeing 737 jets (one type of plane means easy turns, fuel efficiency, mechanics' ease to service).
- Hire people who fit culturally.

Operational Systems

- Do own ticketing.
- Do not engage in "interline baggage" (transfer of baggage directly to other airlines).
- Ensure speedy aircraft "turns."
- Focus on cost-control operations.
- Use HR selection devices and rigorous interviewing that help identify attitudes rather than skills, producing new employees that fit well into the organization.
- Focus on customer service.

Management Systems

- Focus on recognition to motivate employees and to manage and guide employee behavior.
- Utilize and manage a profit-sharing program for all employees.
- Pursue a strategy of controlled growth consistent with Southwest's core strategy.

Culture

- Create a family-like, fun culture that governs day-to-day life, as well as how employees relate to customers.

Key Differences between Our Approach and Traditional Strategic Planning. As alluded to earlier in this chapter, our approach to creating a strategic plan—which has been successfully used by organizations of all sizes and types for more than 40 years—differs in some very significant and important ways from other approaches.

First, each component of our plans is distinct, adds value, and is clearly defined. This is not always the case in other approaches. For example, some companies build their plans upon "Mission,

Table 6.2 Sample Operational Strategies for Walmart

- Purchasing through central computer, based on in-store data input
- A specific number of departments in each store
- Approximately 95% of merchandise branded
- "No questions asked" policy on returns
- Employees polled for their views on what merchandise to include and how to display it

Vision, and Values." While, as one of our clients told us, "everyone knows what Mission, Vision, and Values are," a quick Internet search reveals that this is clearly not the case. In some cases, mission statements identify a company's purpose; in others, they define what a company wants to achieve. When terms are not clearly defined or consistently used, the power of the concept is reduced. Simply put, those developing and implementing the plan aren't sure what they are supposed to be developing, why it is important, or how to use it. In fact, this same client, when asked about how Mission, Vision, and Values were used in plan implementation replied, "We really don't need to worry about them. The real focus of planning is on our objectives and initiatives." The follow-up question might have been, "Then, why bother?" In our approach, every component is important, and we help leaders understand how to use them to enhance the plan and the plan's implementation effectiveness.

Second, our approach focuses a company's leadership team on all of the key factors that drive long-term success—that is, the six levels in the Pyramid of Organizational Development, plus financial results. As stated at the beginning of this chapter, the focus of traditional strategic planning is primarily on markets (customers), product and services, and financial performance. Our approach helps ensure that something important—like effective management systems and a positive, well-managed culture—is not missed.

Third, our approach links strategy with tactics. In some companies, there is the strategic plan, which is managed by the senior leadership team; and then there are the operational or tactical plans that are managed by department or team leaders. Sometimes, there is little or no direct link between what happens on a day-to-day basis and what the company is working to achieve over the long term. As will be explained in more depth below, in our approach, there is a very clear link between a company's long-term (as reflected in the strategic mission and objectives) and short-term goals (as reflected in specific, measurable, 12-month goals that support each objective). Our plans are designed so that there is very much a focus on achieving long-term desired results.

Fourth, in our approach, there is a very specific, user-friendly template for documenting and presenting the strategic plan that is built around the Pyramid of Organizational Development. The long-term strategy, objectives, and goals are presented very clearly and concisely, and it is easy to locate information related to a specific organizational success factor (e.g., markets, resources, etc.). In other approaches, the strategic plan is what we have sometimes described as "a PowerPoint presentation for the leadership team or board." In other cases, the plan is a lengthy document that provides a great deal of background on strategy without a lot of detail about what, exactly, the company will be working to achieve over the longer term or how it is going to achieve these long-term goals (through what is being done on a shorter-term basis).

Finally, in our approach, planning is a process, not an event. In some approaches to strategic planning, plans are completed every three to five years and are not really examined or updated until the end of that planning period. At the operational level, there may be planning that takes place annually, but the plans developed may be shelved and only examined at the end of the year. In our approach, there is regular review of progress against plans—with a specific focus during the year on the achievement of annual goals. At the end of each year, there is also an update of the longer-term (three- to five-year) goals—using as input the results of an updated environmental scan and organizational assessment. In brief, in our approach, strategic plans are "living" documents and realistic playbooks that are based on the current situation in which a company finds itself.

Components of the Strategic Plan (Strategic Organizational Development Plan)

In our approach to developing strategic plans, there are eight components:

1. The Situational Analysis
2. The Business Definition/Concept
3. The Strategic Mission
4. The Core Strategy
5. Key Result Areas
6. Objectives for Each Key Result Area
7. Goals for Each Objective
8. Action Plans to Attain Each Goal

Note: Action Plans are not typically included in the strategic plan document, but are instead developed and used by the "goal owner" to promote the achievement of a specific goal—as will be explained below.

These eight components of the business plan are presented in Table 6.3 and described in the sections that follow.

Situational Analysis. The intent of the situational analysis is to provide background that will help the reader understand why the company is pursuing the courses of action defined in the remainder of the strategic plan. The situational analysis should include a brief overview of key findings from the environmental scan and organizational assessment, along with a summary of what these findings suggest about where the company needs to focus to continue its success into the future. If needed, more detailed information can be presented in an appendix to the plan.

Table 6.3   Elements of the Strategic Plan

1.	Situational Analysis	Brief overview of the key threats and opportunities presented by the company's current environment and the company's internal strengths and limitations. Should also include a brief summary of the implications this information has for the company's future development and success.
2.	Business Definition/Concept	Statement of what business the organization is in.
3.	Strategic Mission	Broad statement of what the organization wants to achieve during the planning period. Should be dated (three to five years out) and measurable.
4.	Core Strategy	The overall definition of how the organization is going to compete.
5.	Key Result Areas	Performance areas that are critical to achieving the organization's mission—that is, the six levels in the Pyramid of Organizational Development, plus Financial Results.
6.	Objectives	What the organization wants to achieve over the next 3 to 5 years (by the due date of the Strategic Mission) in each Key Result Area.
7.	Goals	Specific, measureable results to be achieved in the short term (typically within the next 12–18 months) to support the achievement of a specific Objective.
8.	Action Plans	Activities that must be performed to achieve a specific Goal.

Business Definition or Concept. The output of addressing the first strategic issue will be a statement that answers the question, "What business is the company in?" Answering this question effectively involves clearly identifying the company's target customers and what the business is seeking to do *for them.* The purpose of the business definition is to provide focus: It helps everyone on the company team understand what the company does (and doesn't) do.

The business definition or concept should be broad enough to encompass anything that the company might pursue over the next three to five years (based on an analysis of environmental scan and organizational assessment data), but not be so broad that it is meaningless. The railroads, for example, could have stated that they were in the "transportation business," versus the "railroad business." The former might have contributed to taking advantage of, versus being the victim of, new modes of transportation.

While railroads illustrate the risk of a narrow business definition, there are also problems with business definitions that are too broad. When a company tries to be everything to everybody, it will ultimately experience problems because this goal is unachievable. In one $250 million distribution company, for example, any and all businesses were viewed as potential customers—regardless of the amount of product purchased—and all were provided with the same hands-on service. It was only after three years of declining profits that the company realized that they could not service small "mom and pops" with their current business model. They narrowed their business definition to focus on higher-volume customers, and their profits improved.

The business definition/concept statement should be viewed as the basis for making decisions about which opportunities to pursue—which can be particularly challenging when a company is growing rapidly. When an opportunity is presented that does not fit with the business definition/concept, leaders need to be disciplined enough to analyze the impact that this new opportunity might have on the existing business.

The business definition/concept statement can be used as a basis for branding and marketing efforts, but it should not be written as a marketing statement per se. It should be written as a description of what the company is in the business to do, and ideally it should consist of no more than one or two sentences so that people can remember it.

A good example of a concise business definition statement is that developed by a rapidly growing health care products manufacturer: "We are in the business of solving nurses' problems." To implement this concept, the company stayed in close contact with nurses to learn about their problems and develop products that were actually solutions to these problems. Another example, from a very different industry is from an infrastructure development company in Vietnam: "DCC is a reliable contractor and subcontractor for investors and large-scale foreign general contractors in Vietnam. We support our customers to achieve optimum investment return through providing the complete construction product and service solutions with good quality at lower price, on time and safely." In both examples, it is clear who the customer is and what it is that the company is working to do for them.

The business definition/concept is not a "forever" statement. Instead, it should be written such that it identifies the business that the company will be in for at least the next three to five years (that is, over the life of the plan). Business definitions/concepts can and do change as a result of environmental changes (new opportunities and threats) and as a result of changes in the company itself. Examples of changes in business concept or definition that have worked well include (1) Nike, which transformed from a footwear company to an athletic-wear company; (2) Disney, which transformed from an animated motion picture company to a global entertainment enterprise; (3) Microsoft, which has moved from a concept of software for microcomputers to a broader notion of software for e-commerce; and (4) IBM, which transformed from a hardware company to a "total information technology" company providing hardware, software, and services. Starbucks is another company that has transformed its business concept. Founded as a café/specialty retail business, it has transformed into a coffee and related food products company. It now offers quality coffee, tea, and other beverages along with a variety of food items (bakery, sandwiches, etc.) both through company-owned and licensed stores as well as grocery outlets, restaurants, and other venues (i.e., airlines, airports).

Strategic Mission. A strategic mission is a broad, measurable, time-dated statement of what an organization or subunit wants to achieve during a planning period and is the output of addressing the fourth strategic issue. The purpose of the strategic mission is to provide an overall sense of direction for company employees. In brief, it helps them understand "where we are headed" and what the company wants to achieve.

We are very precise in our definition of strategic mission—which should not be confused with a philosophical mission. In our approach, a strategic mission specifies what the organization will be working to *achieve* three to five years from the current time, and it should clearly define this time period (e.g., "By FYE 20xx, we will . . . "). We recommend that the strategic mission be broken into "quantitative" and "qualitative" components. The quantitative aspect should identify one or more "big picture" measurable results to be achieved. For-profit enterprises will typically include revenue and profitability targets in the strategic mission. Revenue targets are important because they provide employees with a sense of how much the company is expected to grow over the planning period. As described in Chapters 3 and 4, this information can help managers at all levels work to develop the infrastructure needed to support anticipated future operations. The qualitative aspect will focus on results that are important but that may not be measurable. For example, in 1994 the qualitative strategic mission for Starbucks was to become recognized as the leading brand of specialty coffee in North American by the year 2000.[5] The quantitative aspect was to achieve $2 billion in revenue and 2,000 stores by the year 2000. This was a very ambitious strategic mission, and it was actually achieved by 2001, only six months later than planned. Today, the qualitative aspect of the *long-term* strategic mission for Starbucks might be, "To become recognized as *the* leading brand of specialty coffee in the world by 2030." The quantitative aspect of the strategic mission might be, "To grow to $30 billion in revenue and have 30,000 points of distribution by the year 2030."

Another example is a mining company in Eastern Europe that developed the following strategic mission:

By December 31, 20XX:

Qualitative: To become the low-cost leader and "most wanted" enterprise in the mining industry in the region, dominating the market in terms of efficiencies and technology.

Quantitative: To achieve production output of 600,000 tons, maintain cost of production within 5% range for every year, and increase labor efficiency by 15% over FYE 20XX.

By including the date by which the mission will be achieved, as well as measurable big-picture targets to aim for, the company is providing employees with a clear sense of direction, which is important from the standpoint of motivating people. The company will be able to measure whether or not it attained its strategic mission and, hence, its success. Mission statements that are vague, by their very nature, are not as motivational.

The type of strategic mission developed for an organization will, at least to some extent, depend on its size, scope of operations, and the extent to which the company has developed the infrastructure needed to support its current stage of growth. As described in Chapters 3 and 4, at each stage of growth, there is an implicit overarching mission that needs to be focused on and in some way embedded in the strategic mission. For example, a company in the expansion stage may include in their strategic mission something like, "Develop the operational systems needed to support continued growth," while a company in the consolidation stage might include something like, "Develop the systems needed to effectively manage our company culture." The strategic mission might also include a focus on closing infrastructure gaps and reducing growing pains. For example, a number of years ago, we worked with a rapidly growing, $750 million real estate developer, who was experiencing significant growing pains. This company's qualitative strategic mission was simply, "Get our house in order."

Mission statements can be developed not only for the organization as a whole but for specific sub-units as well. For example, the mission statement for the human resource department of a $1 billion high-tech company is as follows:

By December 31, 20XX, the HR team will:

- Fill 90% of open headcount annually by becoming a magnet attracting the best talent in our field.

- Reduce turnover to 3% to 5% or less.

- Be nationally recognized for our world-class HR practices.

- Provide our employees and managers with HR tools to improve efficiency.

- Partner with the company's leadership to sustain and enrich the company's culture.

Core Strategy. As defined earlier in this chapter, *strategy* refers to how the organization is going to compete, and there are three levels of strategy: core, supporting, and operational. In our approach to documenting a company's strategy, the core strategy—that is, the overall way that the company will compete—is incorporated as a specific statement that serves as a foundational element of the plan and as the theme for the development of supporting and operational strategies. Supporting strategies are reflected in Objectives and, if they are more short-term, in Goals. Operational strategies are typically incorporated into the way that the company does business—that is, in policies and procedures (see the example of Walmart operational strategies presented previously). If the company needs to develop a new system, process, policy, and so on to support an operational strategy, this might be included as a goal in the strategic plan.

The purpose of clearly defining a core strategy within the plan is to help employees focus on and support the overall way that the company will be working to achieve its mission. Many organizations do not have a core strategy, or at least cannot clearly identify one. When this happens, an organization can become somewhat chaotic as it reacts to the challenges of its competition, rather than proactively determining how it will defend or attack. These companies can also miss major opportunities and run the risk that a competitor will take their market from them (because they have not developed a clear understanding of how they should compete). A company that lacks a clearly defined strategy for competing in its chosen market is analogous to a major college or professional football team entering a game without a scouting report on the rival team and no concept of how to deal with their strengths or to take advantage of their weaknesses. In the absence of a great deal of luck, these teams are destined to lose the game. This is true in business, as well. Sam Walton, founder of Walmart, studied the strengths and weaknesses of Sears and Kmart before formulating his strategy of competing via operational systems (i.e., logistics and information systems). Today Walmart has not only surpassed Sears and Kmart but has also developed world-class logistics and information technology capabilities.

The starting point for developing a core strategy is to identify—based on answers to the second and third strategic issues—the company's present or potential competitive advantages and strengths and the extent to which the company has a market niche. Next, the company's leadership team should identify how they will use these competitive differentiators to win within its markets. For example, Starbucks' initial competitive difference was, in a sense, that they "created" a new market—that of a "coffee café experience." Their core strategy was to leverage this proven concept and quickly expand across the United States before any potential competitor would be able to copy their concept.

Core strategies should typically be stated in one or two sentences that clearly define the overarching way that the company is going to compete. As an example, a $250 million technology firm defined their strategy in the following way: "Leverage our proven supply chain processes and technologies to deliver customized and comprehensive solutions that provide obvious cost advantages to our customers, thus becoming an indispensable business partner."

When a core strategy is unique, it can be sufficiently powerful not only to fuel a company's growth but also to force competitors to change the way they do business. For example, Michael Dell's core strategy in founding Dell Computer was to sell personal computers that were built to order directly to customers and avoid the markup of retailers. As his company grew, it forced huge competitors such as IBM, Hewlett-Packard, and Apple to change the way they do business. Southwest Airlines perfected the low-cost airfare model and even drove larger competitors such as United, American, and Delta out of certain markets because of their inability to match its low fares.

The cost of the failure to define a suitable core strategy can be quite high. In one family-run $125 million consumer-products company, senior management spent years trying to determine not only what business the company should be in, but what its strategy should be. Even though this company saw a major competitor rising within its market and major opportunities being created within its existing market, senior management developed no concrete strategy to attack its rival or defend its position. Over a period of five years, the competitor grew to national dominance of its market, while the first company continued to lose market share and to argue about whether they could or should take advantage of new market opportunities.

An organization's core strategy should be supported by what we call *supporting strategies* at each level in the Pyramid of Organizational Development. Most strategies are built around markets and products, but powerful strategic advantages can be derived from other levels of the pyramid as well. For example, Walmart has competed with Kmart and other discount retailers, not just in products and market selection but at all levels of the pyramid, including operational systems, management systems, and culture.

Organizational culture can be an important component of core strategy. For example, Starbucks believes that it is competing not just with its coffee but its customer service as well, and its customer service depends, to a great extent, on how the company treats its people. This is also true at companies like Ritz-Carlton, Charles Schwab, American Express, Delta Airlines, and Southwest Airlines—all of which have strong customer-oriented cultures and superior customer service. We will explain how culture can be a sustainable competitive advantage in Chapter 10.

Key Result Areas. One significant and important difference in our approach to strategic planning is the incorporation of an element that we call key result areas. Key result areas are defined as "Areas or aspects of the enterprise in which performance has a critical impact on the achievement of the overall strategic mission." Based on our published research and experience in working with organizations over the past 40-plus years (as described in Chapter 2), in our approach to strategic planning, the key result areas for any organization consist of the levels in the Pyramid of Organizational Development (because these factors have been shown in empirical research to have a very significant impact on long-term success), plus financial results management (because no matter what "business" the organization is in—including nonprofits—it cannot continue to function in the absence of adequate financial resources). In brief, in our approach all plans include and are organized by these seven key result areas—markets, products/services, resources, operational systems, management systems, culture management, and financial results management.

The rationale behind this is that the six key aspects making up the Pyramid of Organizational Development are all critical phases of the "business game" and must, therefore, all be focused upon—individually and as a system. As described in the first part of this book, whether they realize it or not, all organizations are competing at *all* levels of the pyramid. Competition is not only in products and technology; it is in management systems and culture as well. By clearly identifying and focusing an organization's leadership team on these key drivers of organizational success, our approach to planning increases the probability that nothing significant is missed. In brief, if a company ignores *any* of these critical success factors or key result areas, it leaves itself vulnerable to the competition. This means that many traditional approaches to strategies planning are potentially "flawed" because they do not help leadership teams effectively focus on all factors that drive success. Instead, they focus almost exclusively on markets, products/services and financial results. It should be noted that there can be additional key result areas, but the six levels in the Pyramid of Organizational Development plus financial results management *must* be present to promote effective planning and long-term success. For example, some companies will include additional key result areas like "Mergers & Acquisitions" or "Strategic Partnerships."

The concept of key result areas can also be applied to divisions, departments, and individual position holders (as will be described in the next chapter when we discuss roles). Divisions of the company (because each has profit and loss responsibility) should use the seven key result areas discussed above as the basis for their planning. At the departmental level, key result areas will tend to be more specific in nature. They tend to define, using a few categories, what the department is responsible for. For example, the key result areas for the human resources department of the $1 billion high-tech company were the following:

1. Recruiting and Selection
2. Staff Development
3. Compensation and Benefits Administration
4. Human Resource Information Systems Management
5. Staff Retention
6. Employee Relations
7. Regulatory Compliance
8. Corporate Culture and Organizational Development Support
9. Staff Planning

A detailed discussion of the methodology for departmental planning is beyond the scope of this book, but it should be noted that the approach to planning outlined in this chapter can, with minor refinements, be applied at the department level as well. For example, in department plans, objectives and goals (described next) will be organized by the department's key result areas, and the overall department plan will be designed to support the achievement of the company's (or, if appropriate, division's) strategic mission.

Objectives and Goals. In our approach to strategic planning, objectives are broad statements of what an organization or subunit wants to achieve in the long run (that is, by the "due date" of the strategic mission) in each key result area. Goals, by contrast, are specific, measurable, time-dated results that the organization wants to attain to achieve its objectives.[6]

For example, an objective for a medium-sized manufacturer of electronic components might be "To increase our annual sales volume," while a specific goal might be "To increase sales volume from the current level of $150 million to $180 million in 20XX." Similarly, an objective in the area of facilities and equipment might be "To increase our capability for inventory storage," while a specific goal might be "To handle 150% more inventory than existing facilities by 20XX." In the area of profit, an objective might be "To earn a satisfactory return on investment." A specific goal might be "To earn a minimum of 18% ROI before taxes in each operating division by fiscal year-end."

While objectives reflect a company's (or business unit's) strategy, goals typically define results to be achieved within the next 12 to 18 months, and they might therefore be described as more tactical in nature. To help leaders understand what is required to set effective goals, we use the acronym SMART. In brief, an effective Goal should be:

- Specific—Define a specific outcome to be achieved.
- Measurable—Include a standard against which performance can be assessed.
- Accountable—Assign a specific individual on the planning team to be responsible for ensuring that the goal is achieved and for reporting on progress being made.
- Results-Oriented and Realistic—Focus on results to be achieved versus action to be taken; set at a level that the individual responsible can achieve with effort.
- Time-Dated—Clearly identify the due date for completion.

While the criteria for effective goal-setting reflected in this acronym look simple enough on the surface to meet, it can be quite difficult to do so. Effective goal setting does not come naturally to most people—that is, most people do not naturally think in terms of results. Instead, most people think in terms of activities. Learning how to set effective goals—particularly from the standpoint of making sure that they are measurable and truly results-oriented—can require practice. Our experience suggests that it can take sometimes a year or more for all members of a company's planning team to become experts in the goal-setting process, but once they do, the impact on their organizations can be quite significant. In brief, having and using effective SMART goals ensures that the planning team and the company as a whole are focused on results and nothing is more important!

Action Plans. Action plans specify the particular activities or steps that must be performed to achieve a goal. Although action plans are not necessary for all goals, they are useful for achieving relatively complex projects or tasks. In brief, action plans detail what must be done, who must do it, and by when to achieve a particular goal. Action plans can be thought of as sets of to-do lists. The steps in these plans appear in chronological order, and no step in an action plan should extend beyond the date at which the goal is due.

In most cases, we recommend that companies avoid putting detailed action plans in their corporate strategic plans. Instead, the action plan should be developed and retained by the person whose name appears on the goal—that is, the "goal owner." If a problem arises with respect to achieving a particular goal, the more detailed action plan can be reviewed by the team and adjusted, as needed.

Step 5: Budgeting

Once the strategic plan has been developed, the next step is budgeting. Budgeting involves translating what might be termed the "nonfinancial" plan (that is, the strategic organizational development plan) into financial terms. It should be noted that the development of a strategic plan and budget is an iterative process—that is, the strategic plan may need to be adjusted, based upon the level of financial resources available to support it. This can involve, among other things, moving due dates out on goals, reprioritizing goals, or adding goals (if there are more financial resources available).

Once developed, the budget (financial plan) can serve, along with the strategic plan (the nonfinancial plan) as the basis for evaluating performance. As used here, budgeting includes "capital budgeting" as well as operating budgets.

Step 6: Plan Review

The final, but very important, step in our strategic planning process is plan review—the process by which senior (in the case of the overall company plans) and departmental leadership (in the case of unit plans) regularly assesses progress against the plan and makes adjustments, as required. The focus of plan review is primarily on the progress being made against annual goals—although it can include, as appropriate, discussion of other aspects of the plan (e.g., objectives). In the absence of this step, planning is an event and not a true process. Plan review typically includes two components: (1) preparation of reports on progress being achieved and (2) a plan review meeting.

Each "goal owner" (that is, the person who is accountable for the goal) should be asked to prepare a summary of progress being made in achieving his or her goals. This should include a summary of any goals achieved during the past quarter, updates on goals that are in progress, and the identification of any current or anticipated problems with respect to making adequate progress against goals. This information should be shared with all members of the "planning team" (typically consisting of the CEO/President and his or her direct reports at the company level, or the unit manager and his or her direct reports at department level) in advance of the plan review meeting.

The purpose of the plan review meeting is to (1) review and discuss progress being made against goals; and (2) discuss and resolve specific strategic issues. Generally speaking, it is not a good use of leadership time to review the plan "page by page." Instead, plan review should consist of asking questions and discussing specific issues that have been identified—based on the review of goal owner reports (which should occur before the meeting). In addition to plan review, agendas for these meetings may include one or two specific strategic issues that the planning team needs to resolve to make progress in achieving its strategic mission, minimize long-term organizational problems, or reduce environmental threats. These issues should be identified and, to the extent possible, researched in advance of the meeting. Meeting discussion time should focus on resolving the issues. The resolution of each issue will become new objectives or goals that will be included in the company's strategic plan.

One output of the plan review meeting should be an updated plan document that contains a summary of progress that has been made to date and reflects any changes to existing goals that have been agreed to by the planning team. Changes to goals can include moving due dates up, reprioritization, deletion of goals, and/or the addition of new goals. This is not to suggest that goals should be constantly changing—because this would suggest that there was not effective planning done up front—but, over the course of the year, there may be a need to make some changes to better support the achievement of long-term goals and ultimately the realization of the company's strategic mission.

We recommend that plan review occur no less frequently than once a quarter (although some companies prefer to conduct some type of review more frequently). At least once a year—typically sometime during the last quarter of the company's fiscal year—there should be a comprehensive review and update of the plan. This involves reviewing and updating the environmental scan and organizational assessment, reviewing and refining (if appropriate) the business definition/concept and core strategy, establishing a strategic mission for the next three to five years, reviewing and refining objectives, and establishing SMART goals for the next year. The output of this annual meeting is the creation of a written document that provides the company's plan for the next three to five years.

The use of quarterly reviews helps to reinforce the idea that strategic planning is a way of life in a company and makes it part of the organization's culture. It also helps hold individual managers accountable for results that will support the achievement of the company's strategic mission.

International Truck Dealerships: Development and Implementation of Strategic Organizational Development Plans

Since 1980, hundreds of companies throughout the world have adopted and used the approach to planning described in this chapter. From 2007 to 2009, we had the unique opportunity to introduce this methodology to over 100 senior executives of International Truck dealerships from throughout the United States, Canada, and Latin America who were participants in a six-week leadership development program that we designed and delivered in consultation with Navistar, the company that manufactures International trucks and buses (the products that the dealerships offer their customers). This case study describes the steps that were taken by these senior executives to develop and implement their plans—steps that can be taken by any company to effectively implement a strategic planning process.

A Brief Overview of Navistar and International Truck Dealerships

The company that has become Navistar was founded in 1831 by Cyrus McCormick, the inventor of the mechanical reaper. By the beginning of the twentieth century, the company had branched out into other types of farm equipment (including tractors) and had joined with four other companies to become International Harvester Company.

In 1907, International Harvester began manufacturing trucks, and this business would eventually expand to the point where the sale of heavy and medium trucks was greater than that of the farm equipment. By 1910, International Harvester had reached sales of $100 million and by 1950, sales were $1 billion.

Due to a variety of factors, including loss of market share and several years of losses, in 1985 International Harvester sold off the farm equipment business (now owned by Case Corporation) and began to focus exclusively on heavy and medium truck and diesel engine production. It also changed the name of the company to Navistar International Corporation. In 2001, Navistar formed IC Bus Corporation, which was a consolidation of American Transportation Corporation school-bus body business and International Truck and Engine chassis business. Idealease is a company that was founded in 1982 to offer leasing and rental of International Trucks through the company's dealers.

Navistar is represented in the local market by "International Dealers." In brief, the International name did not leave the dealership. Dealers are independent business owners—*not* corporate employees. They are under contract to the company for whole goods (trucks) and parts. Many dealerships are very much family businesses. In some cases, the current dealer is the third (or maybe fourth) generation of the family to work in the business. Typically dealers come up through sales, with a few coming from a financial background. According to one dealer, "We tend to be affable, open, engaging—good front people for the business."

The dealer network—at one time over 800 strong in the United States and Canada—has been one of Navistar's competitive strengths. Historically, dealers might have had one to three locations. By the early 2000s, the dealer network had consolidated to approximately 300 in the United States and Canada—driven, in part, by Navistar corporate—with some dealerships having more than nine locations that were, in some cases, fairly geographically dispersed. While specific locations may differ somewhat in terms of the products and services offered, each dealership (comprised of several different locations) typically offers new trucks (heavy and medium), used trucks, service, parts, financing, and leasing. Most of the dealerships (distribution/services companies) that participated in the 2007–2009 leadership development program were in or moving into the consolidation stage—that is, they were or soon would be at $50 million+ in annual revenues (and some already had annual revenues in excess of $100 million). Many were facing both competitive as well as internal infrastructure challenges. Some of the types of infrastructure challenges being faced included finding and keeping enough technicians to provide timely service on customer vehicles, upgrading facilities, developing strategies to manage a large, geographically dispersed business, and finding ways to enhance efficiency by implementing more effective operational systems.

The Approach to Developing Dealer Plans

Two key deliverables for each participant from the International Truck dealer six-week leadership development program would be a strategic plan and the ability to effectively implement the plan within their company. Three days of the program would be devoted to plan development, with one-on-one coaching and feedback from program instructors provided as needed to each participant.

One full day in the first week of the program was focused on introducing participants to the strategic planning process described in this chapter. Another day of this first week was devoted to helping participants understand how to use the Pyramid of Organizational Development as a lens for assessing their company's effectiveness—that is, as a tool in completing the organizational assessment. These sessions were highly interactive and included a number of workshops during which participants—all of whom were either the CEO of the company or a very senior executive (e.g., CFO, VP of a specific function, general manager of a location, or a manager in training)—could apply what they had learned to their dealerships. One objective of these first two days of planning was to help participants understand the steps in the process and the language of planning used in our approach. A second objective was to help participants understand the nature of the information that they needed to collect to develop their dealership's strategic plan.

As a follow-up to this first program week, participants were asked to collect the information needed to develop their plan. During the second week of the program, participants used the information collected to develop drafts of their strategic plans. Following the second week, participants worked with other members of their company's senior leadership team to finalize the plans and were then provided with the opportunity to share, discuss, and solicit feedback from other participants during the third week of the program. During week three, participants were introduced to tools for creating effective performance management systems that would support effective plan implementation.

A more detailed explanation of the steps that participants in the International Truck dealer leadership development program took to create their plan—which provides a good roadmap for others to use—is presented below.

Developing the Strategic Plan: The Environmental Scan

For the most part, all participants in the program had a very good understanding of their markets and key competitors. They were also able to draw upon Navistar corporate for additional information. As most participants had been in the business for a number of years—as stated earlier, some represented the third or fourth generation of the family in the business—they understood their customers and their customers' needs. They also had a fairly good understanding about the extent to which they were meeting customers' needs. Most had not systematically incorporated an analysis of key environmental trends into their planning process—but there was a keen awareness of the impact that changes in the regulatory environment (in particular, emission standards) might have on the business.

As a part of the program, participants were given an assignment to work with their dealership team to complete a formal, systematic assessment of the environment in which their dealership was operating. The data collection actually began during the introductory session of the program as participants worked in small groups to identify and discuss their customers, competitors, and key environmental trends. As a follow-up to this first day of planning, participants were given worksheets that could be used to collect the data, and during the introduction to planning, the larger group of participants discussed possible sources of information about customers, competitors, and trends. During the next week of the program—which occurred four months later—participants were given the opportunity to discuss and analyze the information that they collected, and it was used as input to creating their plans. Excerpts from one dealer's environmental scan (disguised for the purpose of this illustration) are presented below.

Sample Environmental Scan Analysis Excerpts

Our Market: The customer base within our geographic market—which encompasses two states—consists primarily of class 6–7 customers who need trucks to move products. Although we have some class 8 business, it is made up of only a handful of customers. Our intent is to gradually expand in our geographic market both to the east in State X and to the south in State Y.

Our strength is in our employees, most of whom have more than 10 years of service with our dealership. Our limitations are the same—finding, training, and keeping employees has become a priority. The climate in our geographic service area calls for harsh winters and we have found competitors in southern states have been placing ads in local newspapers offering competitive salaries without the weather issues.

Competition: Our dealership has a strong Freightliner (XYZ Freightliner) and Mack (ABC Mack) presence in all locations, with Peterbilt (RST Peterbilt) present in our State X market. In every location there are small repair shops that have discounted labor rates and strong parts competitors. The Freightliner dealer is also an equipment dealer who carries several lines of road equipment. The Mack dealer currently has the State Y Department of Transportation (DOT) contract and has sold approximately 100 new Mack's to the DOT in each of the last three years.

The Freightliner dealer has several distractions and oftentimes pays more attention to road equipment than he pays attention to trucks. In addition, this dealer seems to have a significant turnover in personnel and appears to worry more about how our company is doing things rather than paying attention to his business. Although the Mack dealer is well respected in our area they seem to have serious service department issues and excluding the DOT contract they do not have a good market share in central State Y.

Our strategy continues to be to keep tabs on the local competition, but not to over-focus on their successes and failures. Our primary objective is to continue to service our customers and exceed their expectations in new, used, parts, service, and lease/rental.

Trend Analysis. There are several key environmental issues that everyone in the truck industry will continue to face going forward. The price of fuel is on everyone's mind and it appears as though $3 plus per gallon is here to stay. A second issue is the continued EPA regulations that require better, more expensive emissions on all diesel engines, which will continue to drive up costs.

The threat from these environmental issues is that there will be fewer people in the trucking business, which will tend to drive margins down. We would expect about the same number of dealers will be chasing fewer customers and many of these customers seem to be moving out of state.

Our strategy is to educate customers on how the industry is changing and why that will translate into higher cost when purchasing a truck. In addition we will attempt to convince customers that preventive maintenance programs will not only keep their trucks running better, but could possibly increase the time of their buying cycle.

Developing the Strategic Plan: The Organizational Assessment

While many participants in the program could identify their dealership's most significant strengths (what they did well) and most significant limitations, very few had done a comprehensive assessment of their internal capabilities. During the first week of the leadership development program, a full day was devoted to helping participants understand the Pyramid of Organizational Development framework and how it can be used as a tool to assess the level of infrastructure development. This included training in the framework, application of the framework to a case study of an International dealership (developed for use in this program), and then application of the framework to each participant's dealership.

Prior to the session, each participant and a small sample (10) of other managers at his or her dealership had completed both the Organizational Effectiveness Survey (described in Chapter 2) and the Growing Pains Survey (described in Chapter 5). Each participant received his or her results and was provided with instructions on how to interpret them. A summary of the overall group's results was also presented and discussed, so that each participant could see how his or her individual results compared to those of the larger group. Particular areas of strength identified through these surveys included:

- A very clear understanding of the competition
- A willingness to "do whatever is necessary" to meet customer needs
- The ability to make effective day-to-day decisions
- A strong focus on managing financial results

Not surprisingly, the most underdeveloped aspects of the dealerships—based on survey results—were at the operational systems, management systems, and corporate culture levels. The most significant opportunities to improve included:

- Finding ways to better collect and use information about customers and competitors
- Increasing the effectiveness of human resource management systems
- Implementing a more systematic approach to developing managers
- More effectively documenting and communicating the organization's structure
- Better linking the rewards people received to the performance they achieved

Following the session, participants were asked to build upon their own thoughts—documented and shared during the session—to complete an organizational assessment for their dealership. In brief, they were asked to collect and summarize the key strengths and limitations at each level in the Pyramid of Organizational Development and bring this with them to the next session. In completing this assessment, participants were encouraged to solicit input from other managers within their dealerships. Some did this by holding meetings during which the team worked together to complete the assessment. Others asked specific members of their team to complete a survey that was designed to collect this information and then prepared a summary of the information collected. As was true of the environmental scan, worksheets were provided on which each participant could capture the strengths and limitations of their company at each level in the Pyramid of Organizational Development.

Developing the Strategic Plan: Putting the Pieces Together

During the second week of the program, participants focused on analyzing their environmental scan and organizational assessment results and used this as the basis for creating the strategic plan for their company. As is true of most of the organizations in recent years who have adopted our approach to planning, the duration of these plans was three years.[7] The resolution of the seven strategic issues described earlier in this chapter occurred in the context of developing specific components of the strategic plan as described below. Please note that we have "genericized" the example of each component presented so as not to reveal any particular dealership's strategy.

Developing the Business Definition/Concept (Addressing the Strategic Issue—"What Business Are We In?"). Each participant used information collected about his or her market (customers), customer needs, and information about their organization's internal capabilities to develop the business definition/concept for their company. An advantage that this group of participants had was that they were all basically in the same business—but were located in different geographic areas. A sample business definition/concept statement for an International Truck dealership is presented below.

Sample Business Definition/Concept

ABC International is an International Truck dealership located in the Midwest that provides full service transportation solutions for our customers, who are our top priority, ranging from small business owners to large fleets.

In this example, it is clear who the customer or target customer is (small business owners to large fleets) and what the dealership is doing for them (providing not just trucks or service on trucks, but "transportation solutions"). This definition was broad enough to encompass expansions into other service offerings to better meet customer needs. In fact, some of the participants in the program were exploring the feasibility of providing mobile (roadside) service to customers.

Developing the Strategic Mission (Addressing the Strategic Issue—"What Do We Want to Become in the Long-Term?"). With a focus on the next three years, each participant identified what his or her dealership would be working to achieve. During the time of the program—2007 to 2009—the United States entered the Great Recession, which definitely had an impact on truck sales. The focus for most participants was on modestly growing overall sales—not just through truck sales, but also through parts and service—while working to maintain an acceptable profit level. Many saw opportunities to build their brand and work to become a leader in their market.

An example of a strategic mission for one dealership that includes both a qualitative and a quantitative statement of long-term results to be achieved is presented below:

Sample Strategic Mission

Qualitative Strategic Mission: To become the leading truck dealership of choice in the markets we serve by 2010 through leveraging our exceptional abilities to provide a superior customer experience.

Quantitative Mission: To achieve $250 million in sales with 4.5% return on sales.

In this example, it is clear what this dealership is working to achieve. There are clear metrics for success in the quantitative strategic mission, which will provide the company's leadership with the ability to assess performance.

Developing the Core Strategy (Addressing the Strategic Issues—"What are Our Competitive Strengths and Limitations?" and "Do We Have or Can We Develop a Market Niche?"). In developing the core strategy for their businesses, participants were asked to examine information collected about their competitors and to answer the question "What are, or could be, our true competitive differences?" Because dealerships can't directly control the design or production of the trucks that they sell, most participants focused their core strategy on delivering and building a reputation for high-quality service. An example of a core strategy developed by a participant in the program is presented below:

Sample Core Strategy

To provide a customer experience that exceeds customer expectations by such a high margin that our dealership becomes the exclusive "dealer of choice" for our customers.

Identifying Key Result Areas (Addressing the Strategic Issue—"What Are the Critical Factors That Will Make Us Successful or Unsuccessful in Achieving Our Strategic Mission?"). In organizing their strategic plans, participants in the program used the six levels in the Pyramid of Organizational Development—markets, products/services, resources, operational systems, management systems, and culture—plus financial results, as the seven key result areas. Some participants combined markets and products/services into a single key result area because it was difficult to separate the customer from the service provided. In addition, some felt that at the dealership level, they could not really control the design or production of their "product" (trucks).

Developing Objectives and SMART Goals (Addressing the Strategic Issue—"What Goals Shall We Set to Improve Our Competitive Effectiveness and Organizational Capabilities in Each of These Critical Success Areas?"). During the second week of the program, there were a series of workshops designed to help participants analyze and use the environmental scan and organizational assessment data they had collected as input to developing objectives and SMART goals. The purpose of these workshops was not to help participants complete their plans. Instead, it was to train them in these methodologies so that they, in turn, could work with their planning teams to create objectives and goals for their dealership. Excerpts from one participant's plan (disguised) are presented in Table 6.4.

Table 6.4   Sample Objectives and Goals—Excerpts from an International Truck Dealer's Strategic Plan

Key Result Area 1.0: Markets

Objective 1.1: Establish and grow the construction business.

> Goal 1.1.1: Sell at least 1 truck to each of 10 construction accounts by 12/31/09 (new truck sales manager).

Objective 1.2: Increase penetration in small customer activity.

Key Result Area 2.0: Products/Services

Objective 2.1: Increase new truck business.

> Goal 2.1.1: Sell a minimum of 30 medium trucks by 12/31/09 (new truck sales manager).

Objective 2.2: Increase overall parts business.

Key Result Area 3.0: Resources

Objective 3.1: Recruit, train, and retain the human resources required to achieve our strategic mission.

> Goal 3.1.1 Fill all open service technician positions within 30 days (service manager).

Objective 3.2: Continuously maintain and upgrade our equipment and technology resources.

> Goal 3.2.1: Implement an ISO process for ongoing updates of shop software by 6/30/09 (CFO).

Key Result Area 4.0: Operational Systems

Objective 4.1: Implement policies and procedures to standardize operations and provide consistent service.

Objective 4.2: Ensure that our CRM system is aligned with and meets the dealership's needs.

> Goal 4.2.1: Go live with company X's CRM system by 9/30/09 (CFO).

Key Result Area 5.0: Management Systems

Objective 5.1: Implement and continuously improve a program to create depth in management.

> Goal 5.1.1: Develop a succession plan (internal or external) for all key management positions by 10/31/09 (HR Director).

Objective 5.2: Implement and continuously improve a performance management system to build accountability throughout the organization.

Key Result Area 6.0: Corporate Culture

Objective 6.1: Implement and continuously improve a culture management system.

> Goal 6.1.1: Develop/refine a statement of our values by 12/31/09 (CEO).
> Goal 6.1.2: Survey employees annually as to whether the current culture management programs are effective—no later than 11/31/09. (HR manager).

Key Result Area 7.0 Financial Results

Objective 7.1: Meet our budget.

Completing the Written Strategic Plan

Following the second week of the program, participants worked with their planning teams (that is, the other members of senior leadership at their dealerships) to complete and finalize their strategic plans. This involved training their teams in the strategic planning process presented in the program (that is, the process itself and the language used in the process) and then working with their team to reach agreement on what the plan should be.

Each participant was given a PowerPoint presentation—similar to what was used in the leadership development program—that could be used as a tool in helping their teams understand and be able to use the strategic planning process. They were encouraged to model their training after what they had gone through during the program—in particular, we suggested that after they introduced a specific component of the process (e.g., business definition/concept) they present their draft of this component and work with their team to finalize it. Participants were also provided with a set of criteria that could be used as the basis for evaluating the effectiveness of each plan component that they developed. Finally, they were encouraged to draw up other program participants, if needed, for both feedback and for additional ideas about strategies for effectively implementing the process.

With a few exceptions, by the third week of the program—which was held approximately three months after the conclusion of the second week—all participants were able to complete their plan. During the third week, participants had the opportunity to share and discuss their plans with other participants and to participate in a one-on-one coaching session with one of the program's instructors.

Following Week 3 of the program, participants were encouraged to work with their planning team to develop action plans to support the achievement of the goals in their strategic plan. Tips and tools for developing action plans were presented in the second week of the program and built upon during week three. Some participants created fairly sophisticated approaches to developing and managing action plans—including having each owner capture the action plan for a specific goal on an Excel spreadsheet that was stored in a specific location on the company's intranet, and devoting some time at each leadership team meeting to discussing action plans for specific goals.

Developing the Strategic Plan: The Budgeting Process

Participants in the program had a very strong focus on their company's financial performance. In addition, Navistar had historically provided all dealers with both information and tools to develop and manage their budgets. During every week of the program, at least a half-day was devoted to providing participants with training in and tools for financial management. These sessions were facilitated by a member of Navistar's Dealer Operations team to ensure that the information being provided was relevant and user-friendly. There was a specific focus on helping participants understand how to align their financial plan with their nonfinancial plan to maximize their ability to achieve their company's strategic mission.

Implementing the Strategic Plan: Quarterly Management Review and Plan Implementation Meetings

During the third week of the program, a day was devoted to performance management systems design and implementation (a topic that will be discussed in Chapter 8). This session included a segment on how to prepare for, facilitate, and follow up on quarterly review/plan implementation meetings. Participants were given a sample planning calendar (which included key events in preparing for, holding, and following up on these meeting) and asked to create their own for the coming fiscal year. For each meeting, key items that needed to be scheduled included having each goal owner prepare and share a report summarizing progress being made against his or her goals, preparing the agenda, circulating the agenda and any supporting information (e.g., background on issues that will be discussed during the meeting) that needed to be reviewed before the meeting, holding the meeting, and meeting follow-up (including circulating the updated strategic plan and any notes from the meeting).

One key to success in making planning work is to ensure that planning team members make preparation for and attendance at these review meetings a high priority. As we suggest to all those who implement our approach, a participant should only miss these meetings if there is a real emergency. It is possible to "train" people not to miss scheduled planning sessions. For example, in one of our clients, a senior executive we shall call "Jerry" told the CEO at the last minute that he had to make an unscheduled business trip. Since he was an important player, the CEO asked us what to do, go ahead with the meeting or reschedule it? We recommended going ahead with the meeting. Decisions were made without the absent executive's input. When Jerry complained, the CEO told him the meeting was scheduled and held as planned. It was his choice to attend or not. Jerry never again missed a scheduled planning meeting.

The segment on performance management also included tips for effectively managing the meeting. There was also a discussion of strategies for holding team members accountable for goal achievement and for reporting on progress being made.

Taking the Planning Process to the Next Levels: Departmental and Individual Planning

As stated earlier, many of the participants in the International Truck dealer leadership development program had businesses that were multi-location and all actually had several profit centers—including new trucks, used trucks, parts, and service. To meet the needs of these complex businesses, Week Five of the program included a session on how to develop and implement effective departmental plans using an approach that mirrored that used at the overall company level. In this approach, each department has a business definition/concept (which answers the questions "Why does this department exist?" "What is its overall purpose?" and "How does it add value?"), a strategic mission statement (which answers the question "What is the department working to achieve over the next three years, and how does this support the overall company's strategic mission?"), a list of key result areas, and objectives and goals that are designed to achieve both the department's strategic mission as well as support the achievement of the overall company's strategic mission.

As was true of the overall company strategic planning process, participants were encouraged to serve as trainers and facilitators of department managers who, in turn, would be responsible for implementing the process with their teams. In addition, at the request of participants, we were asked to conduct a "mini" version of the larger six-week program for a select group of middle managers from these dealerships. One goal of this two-week program was to help participants develop and implement effective departmental plans.

Results of the Planning Effort at International Truck Dealerships

Over the years since this program concluded in 2009, we have frequently heard from participants about the positive impact that it has had on their business. Several have told us that a focus on strategic planning helped them "weather the storm" created by the 2008 downturn in the economy. Several of the dealerships have grown significantly—some growing from one to nine locations. One dealership—Tallman Truck Group—has been recognized as one of Canada's Best Managed Companies (several times, including in 2014). In 2015, Kevin Tallman, Tallman Truck Group's President, described the impact of strategic planning on his company: "Management Systems' approach to strategic planning forced our company to consider the infrastructure required to facilitate our company's continued growth. In the past five years, our company has grown from $100M in sales (2010) to $230M in sales (2015), and this focus on infrastructure has been a significant game-changer for our company's continued development."

Ongoing Functions of Strategic Planning

We have described strategic planning as an independent system. However, some of the outputs of planning are also key components of a company's performance management (or control) system, as we will discuss in Chapter 8. The company (or departmental) strategic plan specifies what the organization seeks to accomplish. Stating the organization's strategic mission or general direction provides a focus for its efforts. This in itself is a form of organizational control. A more specific statement of key result areas, objectives, and goals increases the degree and effectiveness of the control. A written plan facilitates the planning aspect of the control process by providing criteria against which performance can be measured and evaluated.

Strategic Planning at Different Stages of Growth

Previous sections of this chapter presented the basic concepts and methods of strategic planning, which were then illustrated in the description of what participants in the International Truck dealership leadership development program did to complete plans for their businesses. This section discusses how strategic planning should differ at each stage of organizational growth.

Stage I: New Venture

During Stage I, strategic planning is probably a very informal, even intuitive process done mostly or entirely by the entrepreneur. Our research has suggested that very few entrepreneurs do formal strategic planning in the sense described in this chapter because the overarching mission at this stage is simply to attain "proof of concept"—that is, confirmation from the targeted market that the products or services being offered are of value to them and that they are willing to purchase them from the company.

Many times, the entrepreneur is consciously or unconsciously following an informal strategic planning process at this stage. The entrepreneur often knows a particular business or industry, such as advertising, printing, publishing, ship repair, garment manufacturing, electronics, landscaping, insurance, or financial planning. Steeped in this knowledge, he or she perceives some market opportunity that is either not currently being served or not being served very well. For example, Steve Jobs and Steve Wozniak found a market for people who wanted a reasonably priced computer that they could use at home or school that actually "worked" when it was removed from the box. This laid the foundation for Apple Computer. After viewing the coffee cafés in Milan, Howard Schultz found the market for a national chain that would provide a "coffee experience" to its customers. Brian and Jennifer Maxwell identified the need for a portable source of energy for athletes and laid the foundation for what would become PowerBar.

Stage II: Expansion

During Stage II, the informal strategic planning process of an entrepreneurial company may begin to change in certain ways. The rapid growth of the organization places considerable demands on the entrepreneur's time and energy, and his or her focus is increasingly on day-to-day operations. This leaves less time and, most important, less emotional energy to do the strategic planning required for the future development of the company. Entrepreneurs in charge of Stage II companies often work 16 hours or more per day simply handling short-term problems and trying to keep up with the momentum of business. The entrepreneur may thus become a "one-minute decision maker," not by choice but by necessity. Unfortunately, the failure to do strategic planning is itself a kind of strategic plan, for the company that does not plan its future has implicitly chosen to allow the future to happen to the organization. As the legendary coach of UCLA's national champion basketball teams, John Wooden, would say: "The failure to prepare is to prepare for failure." Similarly, to paraphrase Wooden, we believe that the failure to plan is to plan for failure.

At Stage II, a company does not need a very formal planning system, but it does need some strategic planning. Because the entrepreneur is likely to be more absorbed in other activities than was the case at Stage I, it becomes necessary to substitute a system for what was initially a personal activity.

In essence, a formal strategic planning process is analogous to a "zone defense" in sports. If, for example, a college basketball team has a seven-foot center, the team is likely to have a comparative advantage in rebounding. If the team's center is only six-feet-six, the team is likely to be at a disadvantage in rebounding, but it may be able to compensate for this by using a zone defense. The zone defense is essentially a system in which people are positioned to perform certain tasks; in this example, they will be placed where they are most likely to give the defensive team a comparative advantage at rebounding. In effect, a seven-foot center is a one-person zone defense.

Similarly, if an organization has an entrepreneur who is brilliant at explicit or intuitive strategic planning, it may not need a formal strategic planning process. However, this presumes that the entrepreneur has the time and energy to perform strategic planning. When this ceases to be the case, the company must use a formal strategic planning process as a kind of zone defense to ensure that some strategic planning is accomplished.

During Stage II, a company's strategic planning process can be reasonably simple. In a company with between $1 and $10 million in annual revenues, the process may consist merely of a one- or two-day meeting of the senior leadership team that is devoted to developing the corporate strategic plan. The output of this planning meeting should be a written document that includes a business definition/concept, strategic mission, core strategy, objectives, and SMART goals (organized by the levels in the Pyramid of Organizational Development). The overarching mission of a company at this stage is to "scale," so a great deal of the plan will be focused upon defining strategies for acquiring the resources and implementing the operational systems needed to support continued growth.

The leadership team should also be meeting for at least a half-day each quarter to review progress against the plan and make any adjustments that are needed. Every company, even a relatively small one, ought to be able to devote one week a year to strategic planning at Stage II. If this modest amount of time and effort is not spent, there is an increasing chance that the company may not be prepared to effectively address external challenges, and may not focus the attention needed to build the internal infrastructure required for continued success.

Stage III: Professionalization

By the time an organization reaches Stage III, it needs to have or be actively working to implement a formal process of strategic planning that now includes a company plan, as well as department plans. The overarching mission at this stage is to "professionalize" the company, and strategic planning is a key system for doing this.

From approximately $10 million to $25 million in annual revenues, the major focus can be on the overall corporate strategic planning process, with departmental or functional plans done more informally. By the time an organization has reached $25 million in annual revenues, however, it needs a more extensive strategic planning process. The corporate plan should be accompanied by formal departmental plans, and the overall amount of planning time and effort should increase.

By the time a company reaches the size of $50 to $100 million in annual revenues, the strategic planning process ought to be well in place. It should be beginning to be a "way of life" in the company. Generally speaking, a minimum of two to three years are needed to institutionalize a strategic planning process in organizations of this size. The first year simply involves the process of learning the planning system's mechanics. During the second and third years, people should increase their planning skills.

How much time should management invest in strategic planning? A reasonable guideline is that management should invest the equivalent of at least one week per year on planning and perhaps up to 10% of its time. If less than one week per year is devoted to planning, management is planning to fail.

Stage IV: Consolidation

By the time a company has reached Stage IV, the planning process ought to be well institutionalized. Leaders and managers at all levels should by this time be "experts" in developing and implementing strategic plans for their areas of responsibility. To ensure that the process continues working effectively, strategic planning should be a topic that is included in the company's leadership development program.

A significant focus at this stage—assuming that the other aspects of the company's infrastructure have been reasonably "built" and are being effectively managed—will be culture management (the sixth key result area in the plan). As culture and plans to manage culture require specific skills, the company may want to have its leaders and managers participate in specific training on this topic.

During Stage IV, there can be a wide variety of refinements to the strategic planning process. At this point, for example, the company has the resources to do more extensive market research analysis and environmental scanning studies.

Stage V: Diversification

The focus of planning in Stage V will be on identifying new market opportunities, new product/service opportunities, or both. The identification of these new opportunities should be based on the results of the environmental scan, as well as the assessment of how the organization's current internal capabilities will support or detract from its ability to take advantage of potential opportunities for growth. The overarching mission of a company at this stage is to identify new opportunities to support continued growth.

The decision to pursue new markets and/or new products and services will lead to significant changes in the company's plan—beginning with the business definition/concept and continuing through the development of objectives and goals for each key result area. In brief, the company will have decided to become a new business and will need to plan accordingly. Frequently, the entrance into new markets or the introduction of new products or services will also have an impact on the organization's structure, with the company becoming divisionalized (versus using a functional structure). This will, in turn, affect how the company develops and implements its strategic planning process, as described next.

Stage VI: Institutionalization

The planning process in Stages VI will include divisional planning, as well as planning for the company as a whole and for departments. If a company has decided to pursue new market and/or product/service opportunities, it will probably have transitioned to a divisional structure—with each division having profit and loss responsibility. Each division, because it is a "business within a business," will need to develop a plan using the approach for a company as a whole, as described in this chapter—that is, each division will use as their key result areas the six levels in the Pyramid of Organizational Development, plus financial results. The overarching mission of a company at this stage is to design and implement the infrastructure needed to support a multi-business enterprise.

At this stage, the planning process typically begins with the leadership of the holding or parent company (the corporate CEO, corporate CFO, divisional general managers/presidents, and any other leaders of corporate functions) creating a strategic plan for the overall business. This can take many forms, depending upon how the roles of "corporate" and "divisions" are defined. At one Stage VI company, for example, the overall company plan focused on management systems, culture, and financial performance and also established what they termed "priority objectives" for all divisions for the coming year. The divisions were then instructed to be sure to incorporate these objectives into the development of their plans.

In developing their plans, divisions typically need to include a narrative that will help those outside of the division (other divisions and corporate leadership) understand the environment in which they operate (e.g., key threats and opportunities) and their internal strengths and opportunities to improve. This is important because no matter what divisional form is adopted—ranging from a situation in which the divisions receive little input from corporate (as long as they are delivering results) to a situation in which the divisions are managed more directly from corporate— the plan needs to help the reader understand the rationale behind why the division is pursuing certain strategies and what the return to the overall company will be from doing so. Typically, divisional plans are presented to the overall company planning team and approved before being implemented.

Within each division, there will be departmental plans and there may be, depending upon the overall company structure, plans for specific corporate functions like human resources, information technology, and finance. All plans need to align to support the overall company goals.

Plan-review meetings should occur at least quarterly at all levels—corporate, divisional, and departmental. Typically, although not true in all companies, departmental review occurs before the divisional review, which occurs before the review of overall company performance against goals. The output from the departmental review is used as part of assessing progress against the divisional plan, and the output from the divisional plan review is used as the input for overall corporate review. The process for preparing for, conducting, and following up on plan review meetings described in this chapter should be used at all levels.

Stage VII: Revitalization

A company facing revitalization needs to use the steps in the planning process to take a fresh look at every aspect of how it does business. Having a clear and honest assessment of the environmental threats and opportunities and the company's strengths and limitations is critical, because this information needs to be used in creating a plan for significantly improving results and decreasing the possibility of failure. The overarching mission of companies at this stage is, quite simply, to survive.

The leadership team of a company in the revitalization stage needs to be willing to change every aspect of the way it operates, which in turn might mean changing the business definition/concept, strategic mission, core strategy, or aspects of how specific levels in the Pyramid of Organizational Development are designed or function. Sometimes, companies enter this stage simply because they do not have an effective strategic planning process—that is, one that clearly focuses them on all key dimensions that drive long-term success and that has been described in this chapter.

Consultants and Strategic Planning Departments

A final issue involved in strategic planning concerns the role of external consultants and internal corporate planning departments in the planning process. We believe that the strategic plan ought to be based on line management's decisions rather than those of consultants or a planning department. Unless the plan is "owned" by line managers, it will tend to get ignored. Consultants or planning departments can, however, play a significant role as facilitators of the planning process. They can help to plan the overall process and serve as catalysts to its completion.

An internal planning department can serve as the source of market research and other competitive information. It can also aid in the logistical aspects of the planning process. External consultants can perform these facilitative roles, too. Moreover, because of their experience with other organizations, they can provide an independent, relatively objective perspective and raise questions that can be very useful for a company. For example, this simple inquiry can be a catalyst for a fresh look at some practice: "Other companies seem to be doing it this way. What is the rationale for your company doing it that way?"

Our experience as educators, researchers, and facilitators suggests that strategic planning can be effective and that it can be learned. A management team can develop a strategy and a strategic plan, but they need to have a process that can be easily understood and implemented. Our approach meets these criteria because we clearly outline the steps in the process, identify and define the components of an effective plan, ensure that the leadership team is focused on the key drivers of success, and help leaders understand how they can continue to use this process on an ongoing basis to support their company's successful development. One CEO of a rapidly growing entrepreneurial company with more than $350 million in revenues engaged us to facilitate a strategic planning process, and after a few months expressed pleasure with the results of the process. He stated: "I had the vision for what we wanted to become five years ago, but I was unable to convince people that I was correct. The process you have used, even though you did not know what my vision was, has led to the place where I wanted to go all along. The value to me is that now others have 'bought in' to the vision, because they created it, and that is invaluable!"

The Value of Strategic Planning

Some CEOs and other senior leaders do not perceive the real value of strategic planning. There are many reasons for this. First, many, if not most, organizations do not do strategic planning well. That in itself is a reason it can be devalued. Others do not see how they can really plan. They assume that the future is uncertain and unknowable, and therefore unplannable. The real value of strategic planning is not the plan per se; it is the process of planning and the systematic analysis, discussion, and resolution of issues. As the late Dwight Eisenhower (President of the United States and Supreme Commander of the Allied Forces in Europe during World War II) said, "Plans are nothing; planning is everything!"

Summary

This chapter provides a step-by-step approach to developing and implementing a strategic organizational development plan—which is designed to focus a company's leadership team on the key drivers of long-term organizational success. The chapter presents a proven framework for the strategic planning process, describes the components of a strategic plan, and presents a step-by-step approach for developing a written strategic plan. The chapter also illustrates the steps in developing a strategic plan by showing how a set of companies (International Truck dealerships) implemented them. Finally, the chapter discusses how strategic planning should differ at each stage of organizational growth. The goal of this chapter is to help leaders of companies at each stage of growth develop and implement an effective strategic plan that will promote long-term success.

The strategic planning method as we have presented it is a very powerful tool for building sustainably successful organizations®. One of the functions of strategy development is to create sustainable competitive advantage. Since many organizations are not wise enough, or disciplined enough, to do strategic planning or do it well, and since the method presented here is more comprehensive than other approaches to strategy, the strategic organizational development method can by itself become a sustainable competitive advantage.

Notes

1. While we frequently refer to "company" throughout this chapter, it should be noted that our approach to planning has been successfully used by many nonprofit organizations. This will be described in more depth in Chapter 11.
2. It was applied at Melvin Simon & Associates, which is now Simon Property Group. PowerBar was purchased by Nestlé. Selected other applications are described in Chapter 13.
3. Tiernan Ray, "The Challenge for Internet Companies Now: Adapt or Die," *Barron's Technology Week,* April 6, 2015, 32.
4. Bureau of Economic Analysis. June 5, 2012, 7, as cited on *Wikipedia.*
5. This strategic mission was developed in a planning meeting for Starbucks facilitated by Eric Flamholtz.
6. We should note that other approaches to planning reverse these terms—goals are defined as "long-term" results to be achieved, and objectives are defined as "specific, measurable, time-dated results." As long as there are both concepts, they are clearly defined, and used consistently, we believe that an organization can label these two components in any way that they like.
7. The reason behind this focus on three versus five years is that many leadership teams believe that it is difficult (and sometimes unrealistic) to plan for five years out because the environment in which they are operating is constantly changing.

Organizational Structure

This chapter deals with one of the critical management systems needed to create a sustainably successful organization: organizational structure. Structure relates to the way people are organized to perform productive work and help achieve the company's long-term goals. The way people are organized, then, can have a critical impact on the overall success or failure of the business. In addition, based on our research and consulting experience with organizations of all types and sizes, we have found that companies require different structures to be effective at different stages of growth. Although an enterprise might have been adequately organized at a former stage of development, success will facilitate its growth, which in turn will make it likely that a new structure will be required.

Even though structure is critical to organizational success, we have observed that in many businesses (regardless of size) structure design is frequently handled poorly. Structure often evolves by a series of ad hoc incremental decisions rather than in a thoughtful strategic way. As a result, we have observed some "organizational Frankensteins"—organizational structures that that seem patched together and not designed holistically. They seem patched together because typically they are "created" in an ad hoc way over time.

This chapter provides a framework to help company leaders understand how to design and use organizational structure optimally as a managerial tool. It is also intended to assist managers in understanding what must be done to change an enterprise's structure as it grows and is faced with the need to make a transition from one stage of development to the next. First, we define the nature and purpose of organizational structure. Then we provide a three-dimensional (component) framework for viewing organizational structure that differs from the conventional two-dimensional view of structure. Next, we examine the different types of organizational structures that can be used in companies. Then we discuss different philosophies of organizational structure that lead to different structural configurations. Then we present some guidelines for the evaluation and design of organizational structure. Next, we examine a few case studies of structural problems faced by companies at different stages of growth. Finally, we examine the nature of organizational structure changes that are required at different stages of growth.

Nature of Organizational Structure

An organization does not merely consist of people; it consists of the set of jobs or roles that have been patterned into certain specified relationships to achieve a purpose. An organization, then, can be viewed as a patterned arrangement of specified roles to be performed by people. It is something that management designs to help the organization achieve its mission, objectives, and goals.

A *role* is a set of expectations about how an individual will behave in a given job. The role consists of a group of *responsibilities* that the role incumbent is expected to perform. If properly designed, each individual role provides a unique contribution to the achievement of the organization's goals. Further, effective *role descriptions* help people understand who is responsible for what. This minimizes duplication of effort and the possibility that things will fall through the cracks because they are no one's responsibility.

The guiding principle underlying the organization of all the various roles that constitute an organization's structure is that form should follow function. This means that the form of the structure of the organization should be designed in such a way as to maximize the likelihood of achieving the overall functions that that structure is intended to perform. For example, if the function of an organization is to develop new products and services, then the structure (or form) of the set of roles that combine to make up the organization should be organized in such a way as to maximize the likelihood that this function will be attained. Similarly, if the function of an organization is to design and produce a product and then manufacture it as efficiently as possible, the organization should be designed in such a way as to maximize the likelihood of that happening. This principle also implies that there is no one best structure. In fact, any structure can work if it is properly designed and managed in a way that helps the company achieve its goals.

Three Related Dimensions of Organizational Structure

Although some people view structure simply as the boxes on an organization chart, we believe that there are really three distinct, yet related dimensions or components of structure that must be designed and managed.

The first dimension is what we call the *macro structure*. This consists of the boxes on an organizational chart and how they are arranged.

The second dimension is what we call the *micro structure*. This component consists of how the roles and responsibilities of each position-holder are defined and the methodology for defining these roles. For organizations beyond Stage II, all roles should be articulated in formal, written role descriptions. These role descriptions should be used as guides for the behavior of people within the company, not simply used by the human resource function or managers as hiring tools. We will examine this issue in more detail below and in Chapter 8 when we discuss performance management systems.

The final dimension of structure is what we call *supporting systems*, which include the operational systems of the organization, its management development process, its performance management systems, its planning system, and its corporate culture. A structure will not function effectively if these systems are not adequately designed to support it.

In evaluating an existing structure or designing a new structure, all three of these dimensions or components need to be considered. If any component is poorly designed or doesn't support the others, the structure will not function effectively, and in turn the likelihood of achieving desired results will be decreased.

The next section of this chapter focuses upon the macro-structure dimension. We will first describe the three core forms of macro structure and then examine the nature of the situations or conditions in which each type of structure tends to be most appropriate or "the best fit."

Alternative Forms of Macro Organizational Structure

There are basically three pure forms that are available to management when designing the macro structure of an organization. In addition to these three pure forms, there are an almost infinite number of hybrid forms or variations that are also available. Any organizational form carries with it certain strengths and limitations that must be managed in order for the structure to function properly.

The three basic forms of organization structure may be described as follows: (1) the functional structure, (2) the divisional structure, and (3) the matrix structure. Each of these is described next, along with its strengths and limitations.

Functional Organizational Structure

As the name implies, roles in the *functional organizational structure* are organized according to the various functions that must be performed to achieve the entity's overall mission. In a small manufacturing firm, for example, the following functions are typically found: (1) engineering, (2) manufacturing, (3) sales, (4) human resources, and (5) finance. In addition to these basic functions, there may be a variety of other functions found in the structure, depending on the size of the organization. The functional structure is illustrated in Figure 7.1.

As can be seen in Figure 7.1, the functional type of organization is basically a system in which managers of specific functional areas (for example, manufacturing or sales) report to a senior executive who is responsible for coordinating the overall operations of the company. The senior executive has the ultimate responsibility for the organization's results and its management.

A variation of the functional structure that is typically found in small entrepreneurial organizations we term a *prefunctional organizational structure*. This structure is most prevalent in the earliest

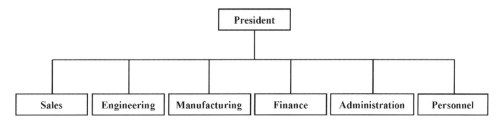

Figure 7.1   Functional Organizational Structure

entrepreneurial stages of development where there are relatively few people, and the firm has not yet differentiated and specialized into various functions; rather, the same individual may perform a number of functions or parts of functions. Accordingly, if we were to try to diagram an entrepreneurial organization at Stage I as a functional organization, we might find the same individual occupying several functions in the organization, as illustrated in Figure 7.2. For example, the president, Mark Booth, occupies three positions at Plastic Molding Corporation. He performs both the marketing and R&D functions, while simultaneously functioning as president.

The primary strength of a functional structure is that it provides for greater specialization of function, allowing people to develop very specialized skills in each area. It also allows for the recruitment of people with predeveloped specialized skills in given functional areas. Accordingly, rather than have an individual with only a general familiarity with manufacturing as its head, an organization can recruit an executive who is highly experienced and specialized in that area.

Many large organizations continue to operate under a functional structure. However, as the size of an organization increases, the many advantages of a functional structure tend to be offset by certain critical disadvantages. One primary disadvantage is that as the operation increases in size and number of products, the focus of its most senior executives (who are responsible for the entire enterprise) is spread so thin that certain products receive considerable attention while others receive significantly less. A related problem is that as the size of the organization increases, the primary concern is with the overall efficiency of each functional area (such as manufacturing or sales), rather than with a particular product segment and its related customer groups. The functions may be efficiently producing products that are out of touch with the marketplace. Large companies, ranging from Kodak to Microsoft (prior to 2000) to homebuilders like Pardee Homes (whose structure management process is described later in this chapter) have experienced these problems to such a degree that they have changed from functional structures to different forms in recent years. Because of

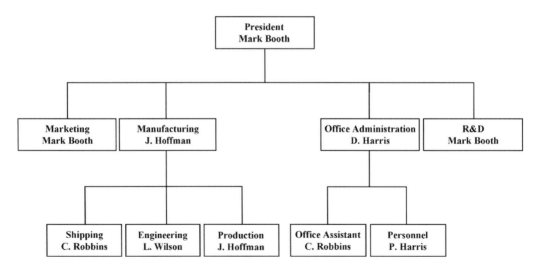

Figure 7.2   Prefunctional Organizational Structure: Plastic Molding Corporation

these problems, a different type of organizational structure has developed that strives to take advantage of key aspects of the functional system while also dealing with the problems of reduced focus and lack of in-depth concern for a particular product and customer grouping. This is known as the *divisional structure*.

Divisional Organizational Structure

As suggested earlier, the divisional organizational structure tends to group together related clusters of products and customers. A division may be set up to focus on a particular customer segment and to produce and market products that are designed for that group. Divisions can also be structured around different technologies. A classic example of divisional structure was the one built by General Motors under the leadership of Alfred P. Sloan. Sloan, who was an MIT-trained engineer, guided General Motors to supremacy in the automobile industry, replacing Ford as the number-one automobile producer in the mid-twentieth century.[1] The basic structural concept that Sloan used was to organize General Motors into several related divisions—Chevrolet, Pontiac, Buick, Cadillac, and so on—with each division focusing on a different customer market segment. The idea was to grow customers from one General Motors product to the next, up to the ultimate, which was produced by the Cadillac division. Each division had some of its own functional aspects, but there were certain overall functions performed for the divisions by the organization as a whole.

When Steve Ballmer became CEO at Microsoft, he "recognized that the company had become unwieldy and over-centralized."[2] To help the company continue moving forward, he created seven divisions, each with profit-and-loss responsibility. In late 2005, the company was again reorganized. Three divisions—Platform Products & Services, Business Division, and Entertainment & Devices Division—were created. Each had a president and, according to the Microsoft press release, the structural change was intended to "drive greater agility in the execution of (the company's) software and services strategy"[3] (a clear reflection of the need to align strategy with structure). The company was again restructured in 2013 into a dozen operating groups that would, according to Ballmer, "enable us to innovate with greater speed, efficiency, and capability in a fast-changing world."[4] The statements made by Ballmer in both cases suggest that Microsoft understands and is managing their structure so that it supports their strategic goals.

As illustrated by these examples, the basic concept of the divisionalized structure is to create divisions that focus on particular customer segments to drive results. In most cases, divisions are provided certain common services at the corporate level. Typically, these include capital allocation, finance, legal, and administrative services, among others. An example of a classic divisional structure is presented in Figure 7.3. As shown in the figure, InfoEnterprise is a producer of computer hardware and software, and provides consulting services to its customers. A general manager heads each division, and each division uses its own functional structure. The corporate services group also reports to the president.

There is wide variation in the way organizations implement the divisional concept. Some organizations have large corporate staffs that are involved to varying degrees in the affairs of the divisions, including helping to set the strategic direction for the division and reviewing its performance. It might also include ensuring that all divisions have cultures that are aligned with the overall company culture and ensuring that divisions effectively develop their management capabilities.

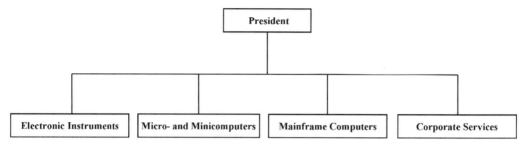

Figure 7.3   Divisional Organizational Structure: InfoEnterprise

This may be termed the *M-type divisional structure* because of the active management from the corporate staff. This model is used by many large enterprises, such as Johnson & Johnson, Bristol-Myers Squibb, Allied Lyons, GE, and Pfizer. Sometimes companies use this structure so that they can get clarity of operational results. For example, in 2014, Pfizer, the giant pharmaceutical enterprise, began disclosing the financial results of operations for three business units: generics, branded drugs, and vaccines.[5]

At the other end of the spectrum, the corporation operates as a holding company, or in a certain sense as a "vertical bank." By this we mean that the larger corporation is essentially an investor, in that it buys businesses and allows them to operate in a very independent manner. In return, the businesses must meet certain performance standards, such as return on investment or cash generation. A classic model of this style is Berkshire Hathaway—a company that prides itself on having a relatively lean corporate staff. It accomplishes this because Berkshire Hathaway is essentially an "investor-type" corporate structure (*I-type divisional structure*), in which the various divisions are essentially part of a portfolio of investments. Similarly, Teledyne Technologies is an investor in many small entrepreneurially oriented companies, and the basic criterion for their maintenance is the ability to generate cash for the overall holding company.

Both of these divisional structure models (the I-type or the M-type) may be used, and both can be effective—as long as the structure is aligned with the specific company's strategy.

The primary strength of the divisional form is that it creates a focus on specific market or product segments. The primary disadvantage is that it results in duplication of functions in different divisions and creates the need for coordination among divisions. This is what leads to additional corporate staff. The divisional structure can also lead to intense competition among the general managers of each division. Therefore, it is important that if an organization decides to adopt a divisional structure, it must invest in growing true general managers who understand not only how to run a "business within a business" but also how to be an effective member of the overall corporate management team.

Matrix Organization Structure

The final "pure" type of organizational structure has been termed the *matrix*. This structure was originally developed in the aerospace industry, although similar forms might have existed elsewhere for quite some time. In concept, the matrix approach is an attempt to achieve the best of both the functional and the divisional structures. As shown in Figure 7.4, the matrix organization structure lists the various programs, projects, or products in the far left column of the matrix organizational chart.

Each of these programs has a program manager. When the organization is large enough, there is a manager who is responsible for coordinating all of the programs. On the other side of the matrix, over the vertical columns, we have the various functional areas. Each of these functional areas, such as engineering design, manufacturing, and so on, is headed by an executive who is responsible for the functional specialization. The matrix operates by having the program managers "borrow" people from the various functional areas to work on their programs. When the program is finished, the people are returned to the functional pool. For example, a large aerospace company that is involved with the design of a new aircraft for the U.S. Department of Defense will borrow engineers and assign them to that particular project. When the responsibilities of those engineers are completed, they will return to the overall engineering pool to be reassigned. In this structure, an engineer might be simultaneously involved in more than one project.

The basic strength of the matrix structure is that it permits a focus on the customer and the product, and also allows functional specialization. The major disadvantage or limitation of the matrix structure is that it requires a high degree of coordination to be effective. The keys to successfully operating a matrix structure are conducting regularly scheduled meetings to review the status of work and having the ability to deal with the inevitable conflict that arises when employees are accountable to more than one supervisor (a program supervisor and a functional supervisor) and possibly involved in more than one program (where they now report to multiple supervisors).

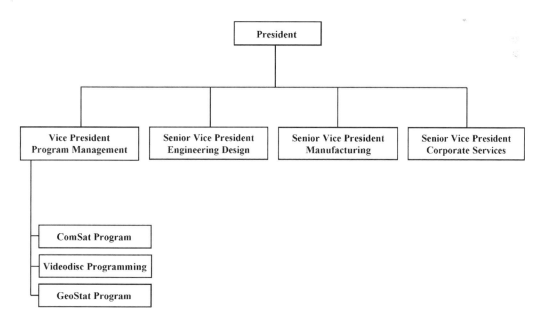

Figure 7.4   Matrix Organizational Structure: Ultraspace Corporation

Accordingly, the matrix structure requires a considerable amount of training in work-related inter-personal skills to ensure its smooth operation.

While having many advantages, a matrix structure is quite difficult to execute effectively in practice. It is a very complex structure that requires a great deal of coordination and communication to make it function properly. An organization that believes a matrix structure is best for its long-term development must be willing to invest in helping both managers and technical professionals develop the skills (for example, meeting management and team decision making) needed to help the structure function properly.

One company that has done this well as it transformed from an entrepreneurship to a professionally managed firm is Pardee Homes. Initially, Pardee was organized in a functional structure, with departments such as land development, purchasing, construction, marketing and sales, and finance reporting to a CEO and COO, who functioned as "super project managers." However, as the company grew in size, the CEO and COO found themselves spread too thin. The solution was to change the organization's structure. Over a period of about 10 years, the company evolved toward a matrix structure, as described in the section on case studies in organizational structure.

Different Philosophies of Organizational Structure Design

The use or choice among the different forms of organizational structure is not just a technical decision. It also involves issues related to the philosophy of organizational structure that spring from issues related to the nature of the business as well as leadership style and cultural practices. This section will discuss different philosophies of organizational structure that lead to different configurations of organizational design.

As noted in Chapter 4, some organizations prefer a highly centralized form of structure, while others prefer a highly decentralized structure. In addition, there are those in the middle that are more balanced between centralization and decentralization. This suggests that we can conceptually view organizational structures as a continuum ranging from highly centralized to highly decentralized with three zones of structural forms: (1) highly centralized, (2) balanced centralized-decentralized, and (3) highly decentralized. We can illustrate the various conceptual points on this continuum by using iconic companies such as McDonald's, Johnson & Johnson, and Berkshire Hathaway as examples.

McDonald's is an example of a highly centralized business. Virtually everything is decided by the corporate staff, and the individual franchisees implement the centrally designed programs, menus, and so on.

In contrast, Berkshire Hathaway manages its portfolio of businesses with what might described as a fairly hands-off approach. Berkshire Hathaway's CEO, Warren Buffett (who is in reality an investor rather than a CEO, leader, or manager) invests in companies such as Coca-Cola, American Express, and IBM or acquires companies such as See's Candy and DQ (formerly Dairy Queen). Buffett clearly does not manage the large Fortune 100 companies in which he invests, and neither does he really manage the smaller wholly owned businesses. Instead, he has a small corporate staff that he uses to select the companies that are then largely self-managed. Buffett's leadership style is, in effect, "laissez-faire" or hands-off. This means that Buffett choses to invest in companies with proven business models and experienced management. He then leaves them alone to do what they know they are supposed to do—which is to create value for the owners.

Johnson & Johnson is an example of a blend between these two extremes of style. J&J acquires companies and neither leaves them completely alone nor tries to control how they operate. For example, the companies that are part of J&J are required to create their own strategic plans, which must be reasonably consistent with overall corporate and divisional plans.

This suggests that the choice of a macro structure can be a strategic as well as a tactical decision. The tactical aspects relate to the size of the business, the extent of its geographical dispersion, and so on. The strategic aspect is the leadership style that the parent organization wishes to employ and that is appropriate for the nature of the businesses that the companies are in.

Criteria for Evaluation and Design of Organizational Structure

When structure has not been well designed, problems arise that can have a significant impact on the organization's ability to achieve its goals. As organizations grow, they add jobs and levels in a piecemeal manner to meet current needs. They also tend to design jobs around the people that they have working for them. If this process continues, the entire organization develops an ad hoc character that sometimes, simply stated, makes no sense. As a part of the organizational transition process—particularly for organizations at Stage III and beyond—there should be a focus on evaluating the extent to which the structure supports current operations and the achievement of the company's long-term goals.

Eight criteria can be used to evaluate an organization's existing structure or to design a new structure to better meet the organization's needs as it makes the transition from one stage of growth to the next. These eight criteria are described below.

To What Extent Does the Current (or Proposed) Structure Support the Organization's Strategy?

As stated previously, this is the most basic principle on which an organization's structure should be based; that is, form should follow function. Addressing this question involves developing an understanding of what the company's strategic mission and key objectives are. Then the existing structure (including the macro structure, micro structure, and supporting systems) should be evaluated for the extent to which it will help the organization achieve these goals. For example, if a company wants to move beyond offering only one product or product line and is functionally organized, it might want to consider moving toward a divisional structure. Another alternative, however, is to redesign its planning and performance management systems (supporting systems) so that they promote focusing adequate attention on developing the new product line.

To What Extent Does Each Function Add Value? What New Functions Will We Need to Better Support Our Goals?

This involves examining the roles and responsibilities of the different functions that make up the macro structure. The outcome of this analysis is to determine the contribution that each function is making to the goals of the organization. Based on this analysis, some organizations may find that certain functions have become obsolete. In one company, for example, the sole role of one functional unit was to ensure that the data input by another department was correct. As technology had evolved over time, there was no longer the need for such a control mechanism (that is, the probability that mistakes would be made in data input had become practically zero). Therefore, this unit was providing no true value to the organization. The decision was made to eliminate it and redeploy personnel to other areas.

In other cases, organizations will find that, as they grow, they need to develop new functions to better meet their needs. By the time an organization reaches Stage III, for example, it will typically find that it needs some type of formal marketing function (if it has not already developed one). Many Stage III and Stage IV businesses also find that they need to develop a formal human resource function that has responsibilities beyond payroll, recruiting, and hiring.

To evaluate whether a business has developed all of the functional units needed to support its goals or whether certain units are no longer making the contribution that they should involves determining the extent to which all key result areas are reflected within existing organizational units. For example, one key result area may be customer service. This does not necessarily mean that the organization must have a customer service unit; however, the organization must in some way have an individual or group of people who are directly responsible for the performance of customer service.

When key result areas are not effectively incorporated into the roles or functions of organizational units, they will tend to be neglected in favor of other tasks that may seem more pressing. Examples of this phenomenon have occurred in the key result area of product development, which has led to the divisionalization of many organizations. For example, Medco Enterprises, a $20 million medical manufacturing firm discussed in Chapter 1 experienced difficulty using the functional form of organizational structure because coordination problems emerged with respect to new product development. Rather than having a unit focused on a particular market segment, Medco had separate functional units for engineering, sales, and manufacturing, which created a variety of problems with respect to the timeliness and appropriateness of new products. The company ultimately shifted to an organizational structure in which one key organizational unit was responsible for the combined functions of design, manufacturing, and sales. This change shifted the focus of product development and sales to a single unit rather than require the coordination of three separate units with differing responsibilities for a much wider range of products.

To What Extent Do Individual Roles Support the Achievement of the Organization's Goals? Are There Any Changes That Need to Be Made in Existing Roles or New Roles That Need to Be Created to Assist Us in More Effectively Meeting Our Goals?

To address these questions, there must first be a clear understanding of what people's roles are. Formal, written job or role descriptions are typically used for this purpose. In some organizations, the first problem is that there are no written job descriptions. In other cases, there may be job descriptions, but they are so out of date that they no longer adequately reflect what the incumbent is expected to do. In still other cases, there are written job descriptions, but they are only used by the human resource function as tools for hiring and evaluation. They are not used as guides for individual behavior. Finally, there are cases where job descriptions are developed, based on the capabilities of the people who are currently on the team instead of being developed to reflect what the company needs to effectively achieve its goals. As is true of other aspects of organizational structure, the structure should be designed to support the company's strategy.

Effective job or role descriptions should provide those occupying a particular position with the information they need to understand what is expected of them. Therefore, each position-holder should have a copy of his or her job or role description and use it as a guide for behavior. Traditional job descriptions, however, are not necessarily designed to promote effective goal-directed behavior. Most traditional job descriptions provide the position-holder with sometimes very lengthy lists of key responsibilities. These key responsibilities appear as sentences in the job description, and sometimes there are several pages full of this type of information, with no or limited organization. In one small entrepreneurial firm (under $1 million in revenues), the office manager had an eight-page job description! The problem with developing job descriptions in this format is that important information and key responsibilities can be too easily lost as the incumbent struggles to determine what he or she should be doing.

Our approach to developing role descriptions helps clearly identify what is expected of each position-holder on the team and does so in a way that the person occupying the role can understand and use this information as a guide or a playbook. In our approach—which has been successfully used by organizations of all sizes and in all industries—individual role descriptions (and we purposely call them this to distinguish them from the more traditional "job description") are designed to mirror the format used in corporate or departmental planning (discussed in Chapter 6). In brief, they identify the mission, key result areas, and objectives for each position. (Goals are not included in the role description but are, instead, developed for each person who occupies each role in the context of the individual performance management system, which is described in more detail in Chapter 8.)

In our approach, the mission answers the questions: "Why does this position exist?" and "What is its basic purpose?" For example, the mission for the role of president might be something like, "To manage and profitably grow the overall business." Key result areas for individual positions define the categories of activities that the position-holder needs to focus on to be successful in his or her role. As was true at the corporate and departmental levels of the company, key result areas are stated in one, two, or three words. Further, each role should have between five and nine key result areas for which the position-holder is held accountable. The rationale for having between five and nine key result areas is that research suggests that most people can remember only five to nine things at any one time.[6] Therefore, to maximize the probability that people will be focused on those areas that will maximize results, we want to present this information in a manner that it can be remembered—hence, the "5 to 9" guideline. Key result areas for the role of president might include strategic planning, profitability management, new business development, supervision (people development and management), external relations, and organizational development.

Clearly defining key result areas, however, is only part of what effective role descriptions should do. They should also provide information on how people should be allocating their time among these key result areas in order to maximize results (measured in terms of the ability to achieve their own goals and help the organization achieve its goals). Finally, role descriptions should provide a description, in the form of objectives or ongoing responsibilities, of what the position-holder should be spending his or her time on in each key result area. Examples of objectives or ongoing responsibilities for the key result area of supervision might include the following:

- Recruits and selects direct reports.
- Works with direct reports to create annual goals and regularly monitors performance against these goals.
- Coaches direct reports.
- Provides annual performance appraisals to direct reports.

Evaluating structure with respect to roles begins with:

- Determining the extent to which there are existing written role descriptions.
- Evaluating the effectiveness of these written role descriptions in terms of the methodology used and in terms of the extent to which they actually reflect what each position-holder should do.
- Evaluating the extent to which the organization uses its role or job descriptions as guides for employee behavior.

The next step in evaluating roles is to look at the components of an individual's role, both separately and in relation to other roles in the organization. This is done to determine the "value-added" of each individual role to the organization. In essence, then, this analysis focuses on the contribution made by individual roles, as well as the relationship between these roles. As an organization grows, the roles that people occupy will undoubtedly change. Most of this change occurs in an ad hoc fashion. Accordingly, it is periodically necessary to do a systematic analysis of each role, both individually and in relation to the other roles that make up the organizational structure. When we have conducted such analyses, we have frequently found superfluous positions and levels within an organization, which leads to reduced efficiency and profitability.

Finally, the analysis should turn to determining whether new roles will be needed to support the organization's long-term goals. As the organization grows, for example, it will need to move from a "prefunctional" to a functional structure. This will mean the creation of new roles.

To What Extent Are Reporting Relationships Clearly Defined, and Does Each Position Holder Have The Authority Needed to Effectively Execute His or Her Role? How Should Reporting Relationships Be Defined, and What Authority Do Position-Holders Need to Support Our Long-Term Goals?

The organization chart should clearly define reporting relationships. As stated previously, however, some organizations have no organizational charts. In this case, reporting relationships need to be identified through discussions with key personnel. Even if an organization chart exists, there can be a problem with using it as the primary mechanism for understanding reporting relationships because it may not accurately reflect how the company really works. In one $100 million distribution firm, for example, while the structure on paper suggested that each middle manager reported to a specific vice president, in reality, everyone reported to the two owners of the firm. Whatever the owners asked a person to do, regardless of level within the firm, was the priority.

A further analysis of reporting relationships involves identifying the underlying rationale behind them and how they support the effective achievement of the company's goals. Reporting relationships should be clearly defined in individual role descriptions and should be designed in a way that creates a highly functional organization. When these relationships are poorly designed or defined, problems can arise. In a $500 million manufacturing firm, for example, there were a number of new product development teams that had been created by bringing in people from different functions within the company. One of the company's primary goals was to develop and launch new products, so the product teams made sense. However, each new product team reported to a different senior manager. In other words, there was no single product champion among the senior management team (which was functionally organized). Reporting relationships, in this case, were detracting from the company's ability to effectively design and release new products.

As a general rule, decision-making authority should be distributed to the lowest possible management level within a company in order to maximize its efficiency. The "lowest possible" level depends on the nature of the company and the skill levels of the management team. If, however, a company has reached Stage III and all major decisions are still being made by the president of the firm, chances are that there are opportunities to improve in this area.

In designing a new structure, both reporting relationships and the decision-making authority of each position should be carefully considered. The objective is to create an organization structure in which everyone knows what they are responsible for and understands to whom they report.

What Is the Appropriate Span of Control and Number of Levels That Should Exist within the Company to Facilitate the Effective and Efficient Achievement of Its Goals?

Span of control is defined as the number of people who report directly to a given manager. The greater the manager's span of control, the lower the cost of supervision of individual employees. The cost of supervision (per employee) decreases as the span of control increases, because supervisory costs are allocated over a greater base of employees. However, in the absence of an extremely well-developed performance management system (the subject of Chapter 8), a manager is limited in the number of employees that can be supervised before he or she begins to do an inefficient job. Conversely, it is expensive to employ more managers than is necessary. An effective span of control balances the decreasing per-employee supervisory costs against the increasing costs of managerial inefficiency.

Traditional management thought suggests that if a position has fewer than three direct reports, it is likely to be unnecessary; if it has more than nine direct reports, effective supervision is not likely to occur unless the manager is very experienced and uses sophisticated leadership methods. There are, however, exceptions to this rule of thumb. If an organization or functional unit employs highly skilled and highly motivated individuals and if there is a well-developed planning process and comprehensive performance management system, the number of people who can be supervised effectively by an individual manager might exceed nine. There are cases where managers operate effectively and achieve acceptable results while supervising 20 or more individuals. Again, however, these tend to be the exception, rather than the rule.

Span of control and the number of layers that exist within a company tend to be inversely related: The larger the span of control, the fewer the number of layers; the smaller the span of control, the greater the number of layers.

Any organization structure can also be viewed in terms of the number of levels of roles that have been aggregated to make up the structure. An organizational level consists of a group of positions that are comparable in terms of the nature of the work done. There are basically five pure (or distinct) types of levels of work in organizations, shown in Figure 7.5, and these create an organizational hierarchy. Each of these organizational levels is described briefly.

The first or *entry level* in the organizational hierarchy is the level at which technical or individual contributor work is performed. People who occupy this level of the organizational hierarchy are focused on performing technical work or "doer" work like computer programming, sales, production, data entry, or clerical tasks.

The next level may be termed the *first-line supervisory level*. People at this level may still be doing a certain amount of technical work, but a significant amount of their time needs to be devoted to supervising the technicians or individual contributors ("doers") that report to them. In performing the supervisory part of their role, they need to focus on activities like goal setting, coaching, providing feedback and planning. Individuals who are first-line supervisors have no other managerial employees reporting to them, only technical or individual contributors.

The third level in the organizational hierarchy can be termed the *middle-management level*. The function of middle management is to supervise one or more levels of other managers, which may

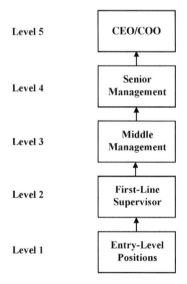

Figure 7.5   Organizational Hierarchy

include first-line supervisors or other middle managers. Organizations can ultimately have a number of levels of middle management. However, regardless of the number, the primary function for the middle managers is a supervisory and coordinating function, and a liaison between first-line supervision and senior management. Individuals in roles at this level need to spend time on activities like planning for their areas of responsibility, organizing their teams, providing coaching and feedback to the managers that report to them, and identifying ways to improve and enhance the effectiveness of their unit's operational systems.

The fourth, relatively distinct level of an organizational hierarchy is the *senior-management level*. This level tends to have two major responsibilities: (1) managing a major function within the company and (2) assisting the CEO or COO with the overall planning and management of the company as a whole. Individuals occupying roles at this level need to spend time on activities like developing and implementing the company's strategic plan, managing overall company and functional performance, providing coaching and feedback to the middle managers that report to them, and identifying opportunities to enhance overall and functional unit effectiveness.

The fifth level that can be distinguished is the *chief executive* (CEO) or *chief operating officer* (COO) *level* of the enterprise. The CEO has ultimate responsibility for the overall planning and direction of the enterprise; the COO has primary responsibility for the execution of the overall strategic plan in terms of day-to-day operations. These two positions can be treated as a single "level" of the organization to which senior managers report. Individuals occupying these two positions are spending the majority of their time on the strategic development of the business.

Organizations are not required to have all five of these levels to be effective. Small (less than $10 million in revenues) organizations may have only three levels. Larger organizations may have more than five levels.

In analyzing span of control and number of levels, the key is to determine what the optimal balance is between the two in order for the company to achieve its goals. In general, however, if a manager has less than three or more than nine people reporting to him or her, further analysis should be done to determine why. If it is the case that the organization anticipates growing a particular function, then a small span of control may be appropriate. If the organization has sophisticated planning and performance management systems in place, a span of control greater than nine may be acceptable. Generally speaking, however, organizations that operate at either extreme can have problems with respect to accomplishing their goals efficiently and effectively.

With respect to number of levels, the further removed senior management is from the customer, the higher the probability that problems will arise. If there are nine or ten levels between senior management and the organization's customers, it may be only by chance that senior management adequately understands and incorporates customer needs into their planning process. It is not impossible to stay in touch with customers when there are a large number of levels present in a company. When this is or needs to be the case—due to span of control issues—the company can develop supporting systems that provide its management team with information about customers and their needs (as well as other types of information) that can be used as input to making strategic and operational decisions.

To What Extent Do Those in Management and Technical Positions Possess the Skills Needed to Be Effective in Their Roles? What Types of Skills Need to Be Developed at Each Level of Our Company to Help Us Effectively and Efficiently Achieve Our Goals?

Answering these questions involves first determining the skill set that each position-holder should possess to effectively accomplish his or her responsibilities. Next, an assessment should be made of the extent to which existing position-holders actually possess these skills. If it is found that certain position-holders lack the skills required to be effective in their roles, then the organization may decide to provide them with training, or they may decide to move these individuals into roles that are more suited to their capabilities. The organization will then fill the open positions with people from outside the company.

It is important in examining skills that the company identify not just what it will need in the next year but what it will need over the next three to five years. Further, it is important that there be an assessment of management and leadership skills (which are different from technical skills) possessed by all levels of management. Assessment and development of management and leadership skills is the subject of Chapter 9.

To What Extent Do Interdependent Departments and Functions Effectively Coordinate with Each Other? What Types of Coordination Will Be Required to Help Us Effectively Achieve Our Goals?

Coordination (a "supporting system") can be promoted through well-designed role descriptions, the planning process, or effective performance management systems. In brief, analyzing this dimension of structure involves identifying which units within the company need to coordinate on a regular basis and then assessing the extent to which this coordination is working effectively. In some cases, functional units can work at cross-purposes with one another, either because of poor planning or a culture that promotes what can be termed "the separate islands syndrome." This can create problems for the company in terms of its ability to effectively achieve its goals.

In designing a new organizational structure, an organization's leadership team should determine what types of coordination need to take place and the timing of these events. Effective coordination mechanisms are particularly important (as explained earlier) if the organization is going to adopt a matrix structure.

What Supporting Systems Do We Need to Have in Place to Ensure That Our Chosen Structure Will Function Effectively?

If an organization is evaluating the effectiveness of its structure, it needs to examine how its planning process, performance management systems, management development process, operational systems, and corporate culture support its structure. For example, if the corporate culture promotes the idea that "we are an organization of separate functional teams that all do their own thing," a functional structure in which everyone needs to pull together toward the same common goals will be ineffective. The culture, in this case, might need to be changed (see Chapter 10) to better support the structure. If an organization adopts a divisional structure but does not have a management development process in place to grow true general managers, the structure will not function properly because the management of the divisions will be ineffective.

In designing a new structure, a key principle to keep in mind is that any structure will work as long as it has the appropriate supporting systems in place. Therefore, it is important that management take the time to consider what systems, structures, and processes will be needed to support whatever structure is adopted.

Answering the questions listed here involves performing several related analyses as part of an organizational structure assessment. These questions, as stated previously, can also be used to help design a more effective structure. The bottom line is that through addressing these questions, an organization's leadership team can identify the strengths and limitations of its current structure or any other structures it is considering adopting.

Case Studies of Organizational Structure

The next section of this chapter looks at organizational structure issues from a different perspective. Specifically, we examine cases of structure design in order to identify some of the strengths and limitations affecting organizations at different stages of growth. We focus on Stage II and Stage III companies because at these stages organizational structure becomes a critical variable. However, because organizations of all sizes must focus on designing and managing structure so as to allow the business to continue growing from one stage to the next, we examine cases at different size (revenue) levels, including larger organizations that have faced organizational structure issues.

Design Corporation

Figure 7.6 shows the organizational structure of Design Corporation—a Stage II company. This company specializes in interior design for industrial and commercial enterprises. As can be seen in the figure, the organization has three divisional units: downtown and suburban units that specialize in interior design, and a subsidiary organization that specializes in purchasing furnishings required

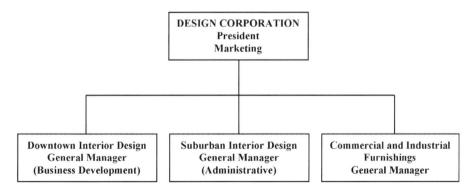

Figure 7.6   Organizational Structure of Design Corporation

for commercial and industrial organizations. At the time this organizational structure was being used, Design Corporation had approximately $3 million in annual revenues, which made it a Stage II (nearly a Stage III) company.

The basic problem facing Design Corporation was not in the design of its macro structure but in the difficulties caused by the lack of managerial and other capabilities of various people occupying key positions in the organizational structure (supporting systems). Specifically, the basic marketing strength of the organization was in the entrepreneurial founder who occupied the role of president. The manager of the downtown office had reasonable business development capabilities but was lacking in administrative capabilities, as was the president. The manager of the suburban office was lacking in business development capabilities but was an effective administrator. The operation of the third division was reasonably successful as a stand-alone entity and is not considered further here. The net result of the various skill gaps on the part of the three key managers (the two general managers and the president) meant that each individual was trying to compensate for the inadequacies of other individuals in a different part of the organization.

For example, the president was doing a great deal of marketing for the suburban division because of the lack of business development capability on the part of that division's general manager, while the manager of the suburban division was increasingly responsible for some of the administrative work of the firm as a whole. Because the president was deeply involved in the business development of one of the divisions, he did not have sufficient time to devote to the organizational development needs of a rapidly growing company.

Although none of this could be seen from looking at the organization structure on a sheet of paper, when evaluating the appropriateness of an organizational structure for any organization, we must consider the skills of the players who occupy key positions in order to determine whether the structure truly makes sense. In other words, looking at the structure on paper alone would seem to indicate that it made sense, but when we examine the skills of the various managers in the firm, this structure is one that is clearly inappropriate for this organization.

There are several solutions to the problems described in this situation. One would be to add the role of executive vice president to the firm (a macro and micro structure solution). The executive vice president would be responsible for the day-to-day administration of the organization, which would free up the president to devote time to long-range planning, organizational development, and business development, as well as to train the general managers to do business development. This solution would add to the cost of operating the organization. Another approach might be to work with each division general manager to help develop the missing skills (a supporting system issue). This might involve bringing in an outside resource to work with these individuals or sending them to training. If it was then found that they could not perform effectively in their roles, the president might decide to fill these positions with individuals possessing more appropriate skills.

Hitek Manufacturing

Hitek Manufacturing Company was a rapidly growing Stage III manufacturing company. The firm had recently achieved revenues of approximately $75 million. Up until that time, the enterprise's revenues were approximately $50 million, and it was organized in a functional fashion. The firm had developed a number of products but was experiencing certain difficulties in the coordination of new product development and with the successful introduction of these new products into the marketplace. This was due, in part, to the fact that the existing functional structure emphasized the more successful existing products. The firm's leadership team realized that it needed to have a steady stream of new products and that one way to enhance the development of new products was to have them developed in a division that was focused on a particular product market segment. Accordingly, when Hitek reached approximately $50 million in annual revenue, a decision was made to transition from a functional to a divisional structure.

Except for the president of Hitek, all the senior managers were functional specialists in areas such as sales, marketing, manufacturing, and product development. Hitek realized that to ensure the successful transition to a divisional structure, it had to develop senior managers who were capable of operating as general managers. Accordingly, part of the company's organizational development plan was focused on the development of some of its functional managers as potential general managers. By the time the firm had reached $75 million in revenue, it had two people who were thought to be very likely candidates as general managers, and a third individual who was thought to possess the capabilities of being the general manager of a smaller division. Hitek was able to successfully introduce the divisional management structure.

GoodEats, Inc.

GoodEats was a $100 million consumer-products firm, nominally organized into two divisions. One division focused on sales within the United States, while the other division sold the same product internationally. General managers headed each of the two major divisions and had profit-and-loss responsibility for their geographic territories.

As can be seen in their organizational chart presented in Figure 7.7, reporting to the general manager of the U.S. operations was manufacturing, R&D, sales, marketing, purchasing, and distribution. The general manager of the international operations had only sales, marketing, and distribution reporting to him. The general manager of international operations needed to rely on obtaining product from the manufacturing entity that reported directly to the U.S. general manager. In addition, the general manager of the international division had to rely on the R&D function that reported to the U.S. division for assistance in developing new products. In other words, while the U.S. division was a *true* division, the international division did not control all of the functional units that would contribute to its results.

Although this is not an optimal situation, it could have been managed by using a comprehensive planning process in which both general managers, the corporate CEO, and the head of finance and administration participated. The plan developed by this team would clearly articulate how functional areas that were shared by the two divisions should invest their time and resources for the good of the company as a whole. Unfortunately, the planning process at GoodEats was done in divisional silos: The U.S. general manager developed his plan, and the international general manager developed his plan, both in isolation from the other. This led to a situation in which the heads of manufacturing, purchasing, and R&D constantly felt that they were being pulled in different directions by two very strong horses. The problem was that when these managers needed to make a decision about whose directives to follow, they would, of course, follow those of their manager—the general manager of the U.S. operations. This contributed to a situation in which the company, as a whole, was

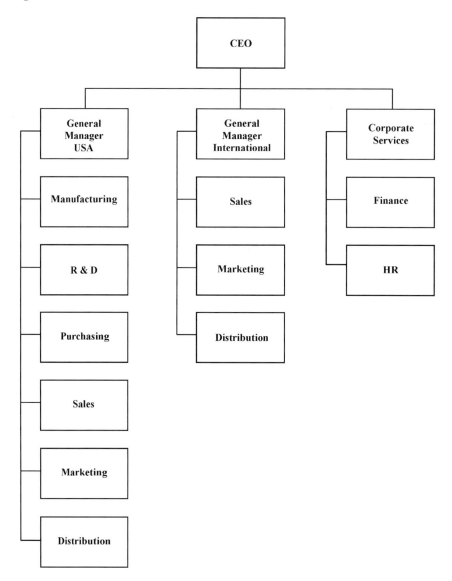

Figure 7.7   Organizational Structure of GoodEats, Inc.

not achieving the results that it might have achieved and in which the international division (even though it was viewed as a strong source of company growth) was treated like a second-class citizen.

Pardee Homes

Pardee Homes (a member of the TRI Pointe Group) is a multiregional real estate development company with a focus on developing master-planned communities and building single- and multifamily homes. The company was founded by George Pardee in 1921 as a builder of custom homes. In 1969, the company was acquired by Weyerhaeuser Company—a global leader in the forest products industry—and became the largest subsidiary of Weyerhaeuser Real Estate Company. In 2013, Pardee was acquired from Weyerhaeuser by the TRI Pointe Group.

For much of its history, Pardee Homes was organized in a functional structure, but as a result of growth its CEO and COO found themselves stretched too thin and embarked on a process of structural change that would ultimately lead to a divisionalized matrix structure.[7]

In the first phase (1996–1999) of structural change, home-building projects were structured around regional cross-functional teams. These teams were led by a project manager, who functioned more like a coordinator than a manager. Team members were specialists from architecture, construction, engineering, finance, marketing, purchasing, and sales. These team members had a direct reporting relationship to the department heads and a "dotted-line" (coordinating relationship) to the project manager (team leader). Although this structure worked reasonably well and contributed to the company's ability to achieve its growth goals, there were times when certain coordination problems arose. Specifically, sometimes a project team member was pulled in different directions by the project manager and the department head (to whom he or she had a direct reporting relationship). Managers were, for the most part, able to identify and address these problems. However, there was recognition that some supporting systems, like planning and performance management, needed to be refined to support the "new" matrix structure.

The next phase of change (2000–2004) was stimulated by the desire to grow, facilitated by a favorable housing market. One of the key differences between this phase and the prior phase was the delegation of increasing authority to regional team leaders who were informally referred to as regional managers but formally held the title vice president of community development. This was a first step toward divisionalizing the company. The company also continued formalizing the matrix component of its structure—creating systems to better support its effective and efficient operation.

The final phase of the evolution from a functional structure to a divisionalized matrix structure began in 2005–2006. In 2005, the company established a pilot project in one region to treat it as a full division (with profit and loss responsibility) and determine best practices for a full roll-out in other geographic areas. Project managers retained responsibility for managing specific projects, with team members being "matrixed in" from functions, but now project managers would report directly to the head of the division versus to the company's CEO.

As can be seen, the proper implementation of this concept takes time. It also requires a variety of supporting management systems to facilitate the structural change, including well-developed planning and performance management systems.

Starbucks Coffee

In the mid-1990s when Starbucks' revenues were in the range of $350 million, the company decided to revise its structure as a result of planning being done for its future business. Until that point, the company was essentially organized in a functional structure. However, it also had some components (mail order and specialty sales) that were divisional in nature but not treated as true divisions because they were so small. For example, mail order reported to Howard Behar, who ran retail operations. Howard Schultz was CEO, and his direct reports included several functional areas – retail operations, real estate, marketing, logistics and manufacturing, finance, human resources, and legal.

As the company began its planning for the future, it became clear that two things needed to happen: (1) the company was at the point where it needed a COO, and (2) the company was moving in the direction of leveraging its brand name and creating additional businesses. In addition, the company had just experienced a growth spurt and had hired several new executives.

In revising its structure, Starbucks switched from a functional structure to a matrix. Four business units were created: (1) retail operations, (2) specialty sales, (3) mail order, and (4) international. Retail operations included all of the functions involved in setting up and managing Starbucks' retail stores. Specialty sales involved sales of Starbucks' products and distribution arrangements outside the retail system. This included Starbucks' deals with Barnes & Noble for the distribution of coffee in their stores, with UAL (United Airlines) for distribution of Starbucks coffee on all UAL flights, with PepsiCo for joint ventures involving ready-to-drink coffee-based beverages, and with Dreyer's for a joint venture involving coffee-flavored ice cream. Mail order (also known as direct response) was responsible for coffee and other products being marketed and distributed via mail. The international unit was formed to spearhead an effort by Starbucks to expand internationally. This was to be done via joint ventures involving licensing of the Starbucks name and practices to licensees. The functional components of the matrix included the same units identified earlier.

As part of this organizational restructuring, Orin Smith, who had been CFO, became COO. Howard Behar, who had headed retail operations, became the president of the international division, and Deidre Wager, who had assisted Behar, became head of retail.

This structure was designed to facilitate and support Starbucks' growth from approximately $350 million in revenue and 350 stores to at least $2 billion in revenue and 2,000 stores. By 1998, Starbucks had grown to almost $1.4 billion in revenue and more than 1,800 stores. In 2015, Starbucks' revenue exceeded $16 billion, with more than 20,000 stores (about 50% company owned and the rest licensed) throughout the United States and internationally.

Organizational Structure at Different Stages of Growth

This section examines the organizational structure requirements at different stages of growth. It provides guidelines for the design and selection of organizational structure, rather than offering a precise formula for selecting a particular organizational structure.

Stage I

A Stage I organization usually has what we have termed a prefunctional organizational structure. This means that the typical organization at Stage I has a number of individuals who simultaneously perform a wide variety of duties. The same individual may be performing marketing and administrative tasks because the organization is not yet large enough that it can define its structure in terms of specialized functions.

Although the situation described is probably typical of most Stage I organizations, it is possible that a Stage I organization has made the transition to a functional structure. This can only be determined on a case-by-case basis, without any precise rules being given.

Stage II

A Stage II organization typically has annual revenues from $1 million to $10 million if it is a manufacturing company or from approximately $330,000 to about $3.3 million if it is a service company. Stage II organizations are usually organized according to functional specialties. They have made the transition from a prefunctional stage but are probably not yet ready for a divisionalized form of structure because their focus is usually on a single product or service line.

By the time a company reaches the mid-point of Stage II (at approximately $5 million in revenues for manufacturing companies and $1.5 million for service firms), there should be formal, written role descriptions in place that serve as guides for position-holders. There should also be a formal (written) organization chart that clearly defines reporting relationships. Finally, there should be some focus on ensuring that systems are in place to support the effective implementation of the structure.

Stage III

Organizations at Stage III, ranging from $10 million to $100 million in annual revenues for manufacturing companies and one-third of these values for service organizations, can be viewed in terms of three substage groupings: Stage III (A) from $10 million to $25 million, Stage III (B) from $25 million to $50 million, and Stage III (C) from $50 million to $100 million. During Stage III, there needs to be a continued focus on ensuring that the micro structure (formal role descriptions) and supporting systems that have been put place during Stage II continue to support the effective execution of the overall structure. This typically means revisiting and refining them.

During Stage III (A), the organization typically has a functional structure. As the company grows in size, there is an increasing need for coordination in the development of new products and services, as well as in their manufacturing and distribution. At some point, the company may begin to neglect some of its products and services. The "more important" products and services receive primary attention, while newer products, or those that are less significant in terms of current sales revenue, will be somewhat neglected. This could become a serious problem, because some of the newer products have not yet achieved significant sales revenue but may be vital to the organization's long-term development. Accordingly, sometime during this period of development, the organization may wish to consider moving toward a divisionalized structure. The primary advantage of a divisionalized structure is that it allows a group of people to focus on the development, marketing, and distribution of a common set of products and services.

For some companies, the transition from a functional structure to a divisionalized structure begins to occur during Stage III (B). (For others, this might occur much later—perhaps as late as the transition to Stage VI.) This transition involves the development of managers who will become general managers of the various divisions. Because most managers prior to this time have been technical or functional specialists in an area such as engineering, sales, or production, they now need development that will enable them to coordinate all the various functional areas. This is a task of management and leadership development, which is examined further in Chapter 9.

Another organizational problem that increasingly becomes apparent during Stage III (B) is the need for greater coordination of overall operations than is probably feasible when a single individual serves as president. Sometime during this period, the president of the organization becomes stretched very thin. This means that the individual is simultaneously involved in so many aspects of both day-to-day and long-term operations that he or she begins to feel increasingly torn apart.

What has happened is that the size of the organization and the corresponding complexity of its operations have combined to make it extremely difficult for a single individual to hold everything together. At this point the president of the organization needs to think seriously about bringing in an executive vice president or COO.

Two major transitions need to be made at this time. The first requires a role change for the president, who will give up this position to become the CEO. This involves the transition from a role focusing on both the day-to-day operational issues and the long-term development of the organization to a role in which the CEO is concerned about the organization's long-term development, strategic planning, and organizational development. The introduction of a COO who is now responsible for coordinating the day-to-day operations is the second transition.

By the time the organization reaches Stage III (C) these two transitions should be completed. This means that a COO will be in place and that the organization probably will have two or sometimes more divisions. It should be noted, however, that there are exceptions to this pattern. Many organizations reach $100 million without a COO or any divisions. There are examples of billion-dollar organizations that still have a functional organizational structure—which can be appropriate if they have a single product or service line. The continued use of a functional structure and the lack of the COO position may or may not present problems. This depends, to a great extent, on whether the structure as it is designed is aligned with the company's strategy.

Stage IV

By the time an organization reaches Stage IV, it has frequently either made the transition to a divisionalized structure or is in the process of doing so. The primary challenge at Stage IV is to consolidate the corporate culture throughout the organization. If the enterprise has become a divisionalized organization, it is necessary to consolidate the cultures in the various operating divisions, making them reasonably consistent with the overall corporate culture. These issues are further discussed in Chapter 10, which deals with the management of corporate culture.

Stage V

The focus of Stage V is diversification, either through internal development of new ventures or acquisitions. By the time a business reaches Stage V, the transition to a divisionalized structure is a "must"—that is, the transition to a divisionalized structure to accommodate the diversified enterprise it has become must be accomplished, if this has not previously been done.

Assuming that divisionalization has occurred, there needs to be a focus on clearly defining the roles and responsibilities of "corporate" and the "divisions." Supporting systems—including planning and performance management—also need to be effectively designed and implemented to promote the effective execution of the divisional structure.

Stage VI

The challenge at Stage VI is for a divisionalized organization to consolidate the various operating divisions, making them reasonably consistent with the overall corporate structure and culture. The key structural solutions to this challenge are either the decentralized type approach of Berkshire Hathaway, the balanced approach of Johnson & Johnson, or a more centralized approach (where corporate exerts more control over the division's activities). The work begun in Stage V around clarifying corporate and divisional roles, and creating supporting systems to make the structure "work" needs to continue. At this stage, there may be a need to revisit and refine existing "supporting systems" so as to increase the overall effectiveness and efficiency of the structure.

Stage VII

The challenge at Stage VII is for a company in decline to revitalize. The structural solution for such a business will depend upon what remains after the organization does "strategic surgery." For example, when the former International Harvester (now Navistar) revitalized, it sold off most of its business units such as farm equipment and construction and kept only its truck business. A functional structure seemed appropriate, and the company made this change.

It is not possible to make a general statement of structural appropriateness for all enterprises in revitalization. Some enterprises that are in revitalization will tend to be simplifying their businesses and, in turn, their structures. This might lead to a functional structure. Others will attempt to revitalize via acquisitions and thereby become more complex, leading to either divisional or matrix structures. One key to success in this stage, however, is to invest some time in identifying—based on the principles presented in this chapter—what the most appropriate structure will be to support the revitalization effort.

Summary

Organizational structure is the patterned arrangement of specified roles to be performed by people to achieve a purpose. When properly used, it is a tool that helps management increase productivity and makes it more likely that people will perform the tasks required of them to help the organization achieve its mission.

Three levels of structure must be considered when designing or redesigning an organization: macro, micro, and supporting systems. In designing structure, there are also three primary forms: functional, divisional, and matrix. Each form has its particular strengths and weaknesses, and the limitations of each can be controlled through the proper attention of management. Each of these forms of structure becomes more appropriate to use as a company progresses through the organizational life cycle. It is therefore important that management match the organization's stage in its life cycle with the appropriate organizational structure. Further, there are eight criteria outlined in this chapter that managers can use in selecting the best structure to meet their needs.

Organizational structure, as can be seen in the case examples presented in this chapter, can be a critical contributor to organizational effectiveness and success. It is, therefore, essential that managers understand how to effectively use this key management system to support their company's growth.

Notes

1. Alfred P. Sloan, *My Years with General Motors* (New York: McFadden-Bartell, 1964).
2. "Microsoft in 2004," Harvard Business School Case Study #704–508, 2004.
3. "Microsoft Realigns for Next Wave of Innovation and Growth," Press Release, September 20, 2005.
4. Andrew Goldfarb, "Microsoft Reorganizes All Divisions: Names New Xbox Head," *IGN News*, July 11, 2013.
5. Johanna Bennett, "Pfizer Could Rise 25%: A Breakup Could Unlock Value," *Barron's*, April 27, 2015, 39.
6. See G. A. Miller, "The Magical Number Seven, Plus or Minus Two," *Psychological Review* 63 (1956): 81–97.
7. For a detailed description of the process Pardee Homes used to successfully manage its structure, see Michael McGee, Eric Flamholtz, and Kathryn Schreiner, "The Transformation to Professional Management at Pardee Homes," *International Journal of Entrepreneurial Education* 3, no. 2 (2005): 185–204.

CHAPTER 8

Organizational Control and Performance Management Systems

All organizations, no matter what their stage of development, require some form of control or performance management system to motivate, assess, evaluate, and reward employees. The concepts and methods discussed in this chapter can be applied in all types of organizations from entrepreneurial start-ups to large established companies and nonprofits as well. When an organization is very small, the leader can control what is happening through day-to-day involvement and observation alone. The required coordination and information needed for personnel evaluation and decision making occurs almost by osmosis. The owner has a feel for what is happening, what the problems are, and what needs to be done, and this is enough.

As the enterprise increases in size and gains additional people, however, the entrepreneur's ability to maintain control over all aspects of its operations begins to decrease. The organization begins to experience growing pains related to ineffective control (or performance management) systems. For example, people either deny responsibility for tasks or do everything themselves because there are no clearly defined roles and responsibilities. A company can find that its profits are low, even when sales are increasing; it has no way of knowing where it stands financially because formal performance monitoring systems are underdeveloped. A business can experience a high degree of duplication of effort and decreasing productivity because of poor coordination between people and departments. The entrepreneur begins to feel that things are out of control. All these problems suggest that one of the critical challenges in rapidly growing companies is the need to be able to control what is happening. The solution is a performance management or control system.

Companies hire people, give them specific jobs and responsibilities, and expect them to perform well and achieve the enterprise's goals. However, the managers of successful organizations know that this is not enough. They realize that in order to be reasonably certain that the company's objectives will be achieved, they must have some way of influencing or channeling people's behavior. In short, an organizational control or performance management system is required. Although control and performance management systems are essential for organizational survival and growth (as described in Chapter 2), the word *control* can have negative connotations for some people. As a result, in this and previous chapters we use the term *performance management* as a proxy for control—essentially, they mean the same thing.

This chapter describes the use of organizational performance management systems as managerial tools to help build sustainably successful organizations®. First, we present a framework for understanding the nature, purposes, and components of organizational control. Then we present a framework and approach for designing and implementing effective performance management systems at the organizational, unit (department, division, team), and individual levels. We also examine some case studies that highlight performance management issues that need to be addressed at the individual and organizational levels as companies grow. Finally, we provide a description of how performance management systems should be designed to meet the needs of companies at each stage of growth.

The Nature and Purpose of Organizational Control and Performance Management Systems

The term *control* has a variety of meanings. For our purposes, it is defined as the process of influencing the behavior of people to achieve the organization's goals. An organizational "control system" is a set of mechanisms designed to increase the probability that people will behave in ways that lead to the attainment of organizational goals. An organizational control system is intended as a mechanism to help manage the performance of people in organizations, and, as a result, is also referred to as a "performance management system." This notion brings out two important aspects of organizational control: (1) it is intended to motivate people to achieve goals, and (2) it can only influence the probability that people will behave in the desired ways. Organizations use a variety of methods to gain control over people's behavior, including personal supervision, job descriptions, rules, budgets, and performance appraisal systems. These methods are all part of the enterprise's organizational control or performance management system.

A performance management system is a system designed to control some sort of organizational activity, such as sales, production, or engineering. We refer to the activities or functions that a performance management system is intended to influence as "the operational or behavioral system." This is simply the target or intended focus of the performance management system. For example, if we want to control sales, then the operational or behavioral system might be (1) a single salesperson, (2) a sales department, or (3) the entire sales of an enterprise.

Control Motivates People to Focus on Goals
The ultimate objective of organizational control is to try to motivate or influence people to achieve organizational goals—not to control people's behavior in predefined ways, but to influence them to make decisions and take actions that are likely to be consistent with the organization's goals.

Ideally, the objective of the performance management system is to increase the congruence between the goals of the organizational members (individuals and groups) and the organization as a whole. This is important, because individuals are most motivated to work toward the goals of the organization if, by so doing, they are also able to satisfy their own goals. It should be pointed out, however, that although there is usually some degree of correspondence between the goals of organization members and those of the organization as a whole, total congruence is rarely attained.

Performance Management/Control Influences the Probability of Goal Achievement

There can be no guarantee that all people will always behave in ways consistent with organizational objectives all the time. Rather, there is a specified probability or likelihood that such behavior will occur. Performance management systems are intended to increase the *likelihood* that people will behave in the ways desired by an organization. Next we examine the key tasks of performance management systems, and then discuss the components and design of these systems.

Performance Management Systems and Other Forms of Organizational Control

Performance management systems are actually only one of the ways that organizations influence or control the behavior of their members (employees). The most basic method of control is personal leadership, involving the direction of day-to-day as well as longer-term behavior. Another method is the role description and related organizational structure (discussed in Chapter 7). A role description prescribes how an individual should focus or allocate his or her time. The macro structure prescribes reporting relationships, and is another form of control. Finally, the corporate culture is another dimension of control. It identifies the values and behavioral norms desired and expected in an enterprise.

Key Tasks of Performance Management Systems

In order to motivate people to behave in ways consistent with organizational goals, performance management systems must perform three tasks. First, they must be able to influence people's decisions and actions in an appropriate direction. As we have seen, without an effective performance management system people are likely to make decisions and act in ways that fulfill their own personal needs and goals but not necessarily those of the organization. In one magazine publishing company, for example, employees and departments did their own thing without considering the needs of the company as a whole. This resulted in a number of people and departments that did nothing at all or that, consciously or unconsciously, worked at odds with the goals of the company. It also resulted in duplication of effort between departments, which contributed to increased costs.

Performance management systems must also coordinate the efforts of diverse parts of an organization. Even when people are trying to act in the best interests of a company, they may find themselves working at cross-purposes. In one $10 million service firm, there were a large number of rush orders because coordination between sales and production was poor. When orders were rushed, many had to be redone because of mistakes in production, which resulted in unanticipated delays for customers and increased costs for the company. Lack of coordination between shipping and production contributed to shipping delays and customer dissatisfaction.

The third task of performance management systems is to provide information about the result of operations and people's performance (performance measurement). This information allows the organization to evaluate results and make corrective changes as required. Even if individuals, groups, and the organization have common interests, problems may occur that require correction. In one residential real estate business, for example, managers could not be held accountable for failing to meet their budgets because the information necessary to monitor financial goals was not available. When profits began to decline, the company was unable to take corrective action because it did not have adequate information on income and expenses. In a magazine publishing company, a lack of adequate information contributed to poor performance and ineffective operations. Employees did not know how to improve their performance because managers were reluctant or unable to provide both positive and negative feedback. The result was that, even when individuals were performing poorly, they continued to operate in the same fashion as they had before the evaluation.

Key Components of a Performance Management System

The control *process* can be informal, but a performance management system is a formally designed set of parts intended to motivate and reinforce the behavior of people to achieve organizational objectives and goals. The basic components or parts of a formal performance management system are (1) key result areas for the company, department, team, or individual; (2) objectives within each specified key result area; (3) goals that define the specific, measurable, time-dated activities that should occur to support the achievement of each objective; (4) a measurement system or method for assessing performance against each goal; (5) a method for providing ongoing feedback on performance against goals; (6) a method for evaluating performance (at the end of the planning period); and (7) a method of administering rewards to motivate and reinforce performance. These seven components constitute what may be termed a company's core control (performance management) system—a formal mechanism for planning and communicating objectives and goals, measuring, reporting, evaluating performance, and rewarding performance.[1] The relationships among these seven components are depicted in Figure 8.1. We now define each component and describe how to apply (operationalize) them at the organizational, departmental, and individual levels.

Key Result Areas

As described in Chapter 6, key result areas can be thought of as critical success factors—the key factors on which achievement of the mission is based. The first step in developing an effective performance management system is to identify the key result areas for the organization, department, team, or individual.

For an organization to effectively develop and use performance management systems, key result areas need to be defined at the corporate, strategic business unit, department, and individual levels of the company. As explained in Chapter 6, at the corporate level, the key result areas consist of the

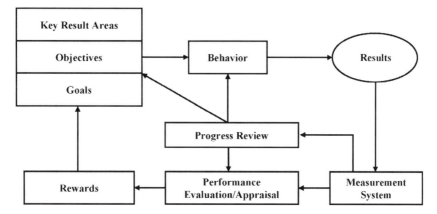

Figure 8.1   Performance Management System Design

six key strategic building blocks of the Pyramid of Organizational Development, as well as financial results. For a manufacturing plant, the key result areas might include production volume, quality, scrap, and safety. For an individual salesperson, key result areas might include sales growth, new business development, customer service, sales documentation, and professional development.

It is important to keep in mind that key result areas are *categories* of activities, not the activities themselves. They tend to be stated in one, two, or three words. Further, as suggested in Chapter 6, there should be between five and nine key result areas for the company as a whole, for individual departments or divisions, and for individual position-holders.

Objectives

As described in Chapter 6, at the organizational and department levels, objectives are broad statements of what needs to be accomplished within each key result area over the course of the planning period in order to make progress in achieving the mission. Examples of objectives at these levels include:

- To achieve a satisfactory return on assets
- To grow market share
- To continuously improve management capabilities

Objectives at the individual level, as described in Chapter 7, are ongoing responsibilities. There will be a "package" of what we typically term "objectives/activities"—as few as 2 and as many as 10 or more—that the position-holder should be performing to effectively fulfill or perform each key result area. Objectives/activities at this level, then, are intended to help the individual understand general "ongoing" performance expectations.

Objectives at all levels help to direct or channel the efforts of people in an organization to achieve certain results. They are both a means to achieve desired ends and a form of ends in themselves.

Goals

Goals are specific and measurable results to be achieved by a designated date. At the organizational and departmental levels, each goal is linked to a specific objective (as described in Chapter 6) in the context of the company or department strategic plans. At the individual level, each goal is typically linked to a specific key result area in the role description for the position that person occupies.

Goals are used to establish desired performance levels, to motivate performance, and to serve as a benchmark against which performance can be assessed. For example, "standard costs" can be used in a manufacturing plant as a goal to motivate employees to control production costs and also as a way to evaluate their performance. Goals may be based on management judgment, expectations, or historical data.

Goals at all levels—organizational, departmental, and individual—are intended to influence people's behavior both before and after actual performance. *Ex ante* (pre-performance) *control* is motivation of performance before the operation or behavioral system is executed. Goals in this area are intended to bring about desired performance levels in people. *Ex-post* (post-performance) *control* uses goals as standards in evaluating actual performance and as a basis for rewards—the seventh component of organizational performance management systems.

Measurement System

Measurement is the process of representing the properties or qualities of objects in numerical terms. In organizational performance management systems, measurement has a dual function. One purpose is to provide information that can be used for evaluating performance and making corrections in goal-directed behavior. This is the informational function of measurement. The accounting system, with its measures of financial and managerial performance, is a part of the overall measurement system that contributes to the informational function. That function also draws on nonfinancial measures of performance such as market share, production indexes, and measures of product quality.

Measurement plays another role in performance management systems. The very act of measuring something has an effect on people's behavior because people tend to pay more attention to the aspects of jobs or goals that are measured. This aspect of measurement may be termed the *process function*. It is related to Marshall McLuhan's notion that the medium is the message.[2] The medium of measurement is itself a stimulus.

There should be a system in place to measure performance against each goal in the organization's strategic plan, department plan, and individual plan; otherwise, some goals may be ignored. For example, if a store uses an incentive pay plan that compensates employees on the basis of sales volume as a performance measure, those employees will tend to compete for sales and ignore unmeasured functions such as stock work.

Progress Review and Feedback

A variety of reports, ranging from financial statements to cost reports and performance reports, provide information about the results of operations to management and others. The information contained in these reports is based on the measurements of performance. This information, in whatever form it is presented, needs to be fed back to the organization, department, or individual.

As described in Chapter 6, at the organizational and department levels, progress review should occur each quarter as the company and each unit team reviews progress against their plans. This involves having each goal owner report on the progress being achieved. It also involves working as a team to identify and address any problems being encountered in achieving organizational or department goals. Finally, it involves making adjustments to the plan, as needed, to reflect current realities and enhance the probability of achieving long-term goals (that is, the strategic mission).

At the individual level, progress review should occur on a regular basis between each manager and each of his or her direct reports. This can be provided in an ad hoc manner (immediately when the behavior is observed), in regularly scheduled one-on-ones, and, as appropriate, at group meetings to recognize good performance. The focus of this feedback should be on the individual's goals, as well as on the extent to which the individual is effectively performing his or her role on a day-to-day basis (that is, based on information in the role description).

Managers at all levels—from CEOs to those on the front line—do not always take the time to provide ongoing review of progress, which includes recognizing successes and providing constructive feedback and suggestions for improvement when needed. This can reduce the probability that desired results will be achieved. An indication that effective progress review has not occurred is when people find the results of their performance evaluation a "complete surprise."

Progress review helps the organization, department, or individual understand the level of performance that is being attained against goals. Regular feedback gives the organization, department, or individual the opportunity to take corrective action in order to increase the probability that goals will be successfully achieved. Even if performance against goals is being measured, if there is no feedback, the achievement of goals may only happen by chance.

The results or output of measurement and reporting is to provide a scorecard or scoreboard as a basis for assessing performance (which will be discussed later in this chapter).

Performance Evaluation

While measurement and feedback are occurring on a regular basis, performance evaluation occurs at the end of the planning period (that is, after the due date for all goals that have been established). Performance evaluation is a systematic process by which organizations, departments, and individuals are provided with information on how effective they have been in achieving the goals that have been established for that period of time (which, in most organizations will be a year). Typically, these evaluations include both positive feedback (to reinforce behavior consistent with the successful performance of goals) and constructive criticism (that identifies what can be done to improve performance relative to the goals—the third component of the system).

Evaluative reports generated by the measurement system (containing such items as net income, budgets compared to actual, and return on investment), as well as reports generated during the progress review process are used as input to performance evaluation at the organizational and departmental levels. At the end of each fiscal year, senior management should systematically assess overall performance against the goals in the company's strategic plan—using both the output of a "final" (year-end) measurement, as well as the progress reports that have been generated throughout the year. In larger companies, the most senior managers of each division and department should complete a similar evaluation.

At the individual level, organizations typically use performance appraisal forms as the basis for the individual performance evaluation process. While the basis for individual performance management should be specific, measurable, time-dated goals that are linked to the individual's role, some organizations adopt and use "off-the-shelf" forms that assess factors like "quality of work," "leadership," "business acumen," and so on. While these factors may be important, they have nothing to do with achieving results in a specific role. We recommend that evaluation/appraisal forms for each individual be structured around his or her position's key result areas, with the goals for each year (linked to each key result area) clearly defined and used as the basis for the performance evaluation.

While there are a variety of ways to approach the completion of performance evaluation forms and the overall performance evaluation process, at a minimum each manager should identify the extent to which each direct report has achieved his or her goals and record this information on the form. The form should then be used as the basis for a formal performance evaluation meeting between the manager and the specific direct report. If the manager has been providing regular feedback throughout the year, this process will be very easy to complete because both the manager and each of his or her direct reports has been tracking it throughout the year and therefore already knows what has been achieved.

The performance appraisal process is very tricky to execute. One specific issue relates to the use of "scores" to indicate the level of performance achieved. For example, some organizations use a 5-point scale, with 5 being "high" and 1 being "low" to evaluate performance. This can work as long as there are very clear definitions of what each score means (e.g., a "5" means 20% over the stated goal, a "4" means 10% over the stated goal) and as long as these definitions are consistently applied throughout the organization. When performance criteria are vague (e.g., there is a lack of clear, measurable goals) and/or when scoring criteria are vague, the individual performance evaluation process will become an annual exercise versus a management tool. In these situations, managers may not provide valid feedback to employees and may inflate evaluations—so that they can avoid dealing with the conflict that might arise if they provide a low evaluation.

Given these and other problems with using a scoring system, some organizations are moving away from quantitative evaluations (that is, scoring) in the context of individual performance evaluations. Later in this chapter, we will describe how one organization—SCPH—effectively accomplished this.

The Reward System

Rewards are positive reinforcers for appropriate "goal-directed" behavior. Organizations offer a wide variety of rewards, ranging from monetary items such as compensation or bonuses to recognition and promotion. Rewards can be extrinsic or intrinsic. When people perform tasks because work is interesting or challenging, their rewards are intrinsic. When people perform tasks because of the rewards they expect to receive from others, such as praise or pay, the rewards are extrinsic.

Whatever the nature of rewards, they should reinforce good performance and promote modification of poor performance. In brief, the reward received should be linked to the level of performance achieved. For something to be considered a reward, it must be valued by the individual receiving it. For example, if a person values being in charge, he or she might view the opportunity to chair an important committee or a promotion to a management role as a reward. If, however, a person values being part of a team, chairing a committee might not necessarily be viewed as a reward. Further, the rewards that are given must be *seen* as being linked to desired behavior in order to be effective as motivators.

Sometimes organizations fail to offer rewards that motivate people to behave in desired ways, or they offer rewards for one type of behavior while actually trying to motivate another. This has been called "the folly of rewarding A, while hoping for B."[3] For example, a business manager may be rewarded only for not exceeding his budget, even though the firm hopes that he will also pay attention to personnel development. Similarly, an organization that wants to motivate people to be good planners but rewards only "fire fighters" may soon find that some managers have become "arsonists."

Rewards can be useful in motivating employees before behavior occurs because of the expectation of rewards in the future. Once good performance occurs, rewards reinforce the behavior and lead to the greater probability of this behavior happening again. Behavior that is not followed by a reward is less likely to happen in the future.

The System as a Whole

All the components of the performance management system affect the operational or behavioral system for an activity. As shown in Figure 8.1, the first level of control consists of key result areas, objectives, and goals. If an organization, department, or individual does nothing but establish these expectations (and does so in an effective manner), it increases the probability of achieving desired results by about 25%. Measurement directs attention toward measured dimensions of goals. It provides information that can be used through the feedback process to help organizations, departments, and individuals take corrective action in order to increase their probability of achieving their goals. If these components (measurement and feedback) are added into the performance management system (assuming that they are designed well and function effectively), the probability of achieving desired results increases to about 50%. If the performance management system also contains the evaluation and rewards components (assuming that performance evaluations are conducted regularly and effectively and that rewards are valued and linked to desired behavior), the probability of achieving desired results increases to about 80%.

Performance Management Systems at Different Levels

As described above, there are three different organizational levels for which performance management systems should be developed: (1) individuals, (2) organizational subunits such as teams, departments, divisions, and (3) the organization as a whole. A performance management system is required to help manage the performance of people in an organization at all three levels or aggregations of people. While the design of performance management systems at each of these three levels might superficially appear to be different, *each requires the same underlying seven components identified above*. Exhibit 8.1 summarizes the source of information for each component of the performance management system at each organizational level: the enterprise as whole, business units (divisions, departments), and individuals.

Exhibit 8.1   Source of Components of Performance Management Systems by Organizational Level

Components of Control	Corporate	Business Units	Individuals
Key Result Areas ("KRAs")	Corporate strategic plan	Unit strategic plan	Key result area-based role description
Objectives	Corporate strategic plan	Unit strategic plan	Key result area-based role description
Goals	Corporate strategic plan	Unit strategic plan	Individual strategic plan
Measurement	Accounting information Other quantitative data	Accounting information Other quantitative data	Accounting information Other quantitative data
Feedback	Reports	Reports	Performance reviews
Evaluation	Periodic reviews against plan	Periodic reviews against plan	Performance evaluation
Rewards	Incentive compensation system	Incentive compensation system	Incentive compensation system

The Performance Management Scoreboard

One practical tool for implementing a performance management system is to convert it into a scoreboard or scorecard. A "scoreboard" is a device that summarizes all the key results of a game or process in terms of certain statistical measurements. At a basketball game, the scoreboard shows the points scored by each team, the number of points scored by each player, the total number of fouls by each team and each player, and the number of time-outs remaining, as well as the time remaining in the game. In brief, it shows many of the key result areas that lead to winning, or success, and the actual performance of individuals and the teams as a whole in a particular game.

Within business organizations, scoreboards can be used at all three levels of the organization to provide almost daily feedback to individual employees, departments, divisions, and the enterprise as a whole about their performance for each key result area and against each goal. A scoreboard, therefore, should contain a list of the key result areas (for the relevant unit of control), the goals within each key result area against which performance is being assessed, and the current actual measurement of performance against each goal.

Illustration of an Organizational Scoreboard

To illustrate the feasibility and utility of applying the scoreboard model of organization control just described, we examine the application of the model in a manufacturing plant. As seen in Exhibit 8.2, the plant has five key result areas: production volume, quality, safety, energy utilization, and scrap.

Exhibit 8.2   Performance Management Systems Application in Manufacturing Plant

Key Result Areas	This Year's Goals	Last Year's Goals	This Year's Performance											
			Jan.	Feb.	Mar.	Apr.	May	June	July	Aug.	Sept.	Oct.	Nov.	Dec.
1. Production Volume														
2. Quality														
3. Safety														
4. Energy Utilization														
5. Scrap														

All these key result areas are different in nature. Production volume is something that can be easily quantified. Energy use and scrap can also be measured but in a different way. Quality and safety require still a different type of measurement.

To use this scoreboard, the company would establish goals for each of these five key result areas and list them in the column titled "This Year's Goals." The scoreboard would then show last year's actual performance in the next column. In addition, this year's performance would be tracked on a monthly basis in the adjacent columns.

Virtually any company or any unit of a company can use a format similar to that shown in Exhibit 8.2 to apply the performance management system to its operations. This approach can be used for the company as a whole, a division, a department, or even an individual such as a salesperson. Indeed, one of the authors observed the application of this framework on a visit to China in 1983 in a chemical plant located in the city of Shanghai. The plant manager was using a blackboard to list the key result areas, current performance goals, prior year's actual performance, and historical best performance, as well as to track the actual performance of the plant to date. Whenever an employee walked past the blackboard, he or she got a quick glimpse at how the plant was performing to date.

Today, some companies provide similar scoreboard information to employees through their intranets. For example, in one Stage III distribution company, employees can view up-to-the-minute information related to orders (including orders shipped, orders backlogged, and so on), sales (including dollar volume, new customers, and size of purchase), and quality (for example, orders returned and defects) on their company scoreboard, which can be accessed from any desktop. This provides employees with the information they need, on a regular basis, to make adjustments in systems and in their own behavior to better support the achievement of company goals.

At an individual level, these scoreboards are most typically contained (or should be contained) in the forms that are used in the performance appraisal process. If an organization relies too heavily on more subjective measures of performance related to skills and personal attributes (like judgment, attitude, or leadership) versus more objective measures as reflected in goals that are linked to the individual position-holder's key result areas, the likelihood of achieving desired results (in terms of goals) will be diminished. Further, the evaluation process is much more difficult when individuals need to be assessed on subjective rather than objective criteria.

Beyond the "Balanced Scorecard"

The organizational scoreboard can be viewed as an improved version of the so-called Balanced Score Card ("BSC") that was popularized by Kaplan and Norton and has become widely discussed and used.[4] The core notion of the BSC is that organizational performance ought to be evaluated from more than simply a financial perspective. This premise is reasonable.

However, there is a fundamental problem with the original version of the BSC proposed by Kaplan and Norton. The original version is based on the idea that four "perspectives" ought to be used to evaluate organizational performance: (1) customer, (2) internal business processes, (3) learning and growth, and (4) financial. Although this concept has intuitive appeal, the basic problem is that Kaplan and Norton *have not provided any empirical support for these particular perspectives.* We are implicitly asked to accept them at face value, without data supporting their validity.

We do not know whether these are the correct perspectives to be used as a basis for assessing organizational performance. This can have serious consequences for organizations. Managers are implicitly being encouraged to focus on these four factors, when others might be more significant. In addition to our criticism of the Balanced Score Card, there have been other critiques of this construct. For example, Marshall Meyer, Professor at the Wharton School of the University of Pennsylvania, published a book titled, *Rethinking Performance Measurement: Beyond the Balanced Scorecard.*[5]

Instead of the four perspectives proposed by Kaplan and Norton, we believe that the six key variables that make up the Pyramid of Organizational Development ought to be used to provide a truly valid and balanced scorecard. In contrast to the four perspectives of the original version of the BCS, which have not received empirical support, there is a growing body of empirical evidence to support the six "key strategic building blocks" of successful organizations (described in Chapter 2). Specifically, the six key variables making up the pyramid should be used (in addition to financial results) to provide true balance for both performance measurement and strategic management. This should not be viewed as invalidating the original concept underlying the BSC (the notion of balanced performance measurement); but, rather, as the next logical generation or iteration of its development.[6] As we know, many products are introduced and then later replaced by improved versions. This is the case with software, where a first release is later replaced with a new and improved version. Similarly, the BSC should be replaced with our notion of a Balanced Scoreboard utilizing the variables of the pyramid as the underlying areas of focus or, in our terms, "key result areas."

Evaluation of Performance Management Systems' Effectiveness

There are two different types of criteria that can be used to evaluate the effectiveness of a performance management system: (1) technical criteria, and (2) behavioral criteria. *Technical criteria* refer to design specifications. The questions are whether the system design includes all of the relevant components and whether they are integrated into a coherent whole. *Behavioral criteria* relate to the ultimate purpose of the system per se. Specifically, does the system lead to the behaviors it is intended to lead to, and does it do so with minimal unintended dysfunctional results?

Technical Criteria for Effective Performance Management Systems Design

For a performance management system to operate effectively, each of the seven components described must be designed so as to function effectively. This means the following:

- All key result areas must be accurately identified. If one of more key result areas are ignored or not included, the organization will experience problems in achieving desired results. Certain important areas will not receive adequate focus.

- Objectives within each key result area need to reflect what the organization, department, or individual wants to or needs to achieve over the long term. In addition, care needs to be exercised to ensure that objectives within one key result area do not conflict with those in another.

- Goals need to be specific, results-oriented, measurable, and time-dated. In other words, they need to be stated in a way that performance against them can be accurately and adequately assessed. Further, all objectives need to have at least one measurable goal.

- A measurement system needs to be in place to assess performance against each goal. If, for example, an organization sets a goal that all of its products need to achieve a certain level of profitability, then the measurement system needs to provide information on product profitability. If the system is unable to do this, the goal is ineffective and either needs to be redefined or a measurement system needs to be created that will allow performance to be tracked against the stated goal.

- Feedback (based on the results of measuring performance) needs to be given on a regular basis. More important, decision makers need to use the information provided by the measurement system to take corrective action to better promote the achievement of the goals. If performance is measured but management does nothing with this information, the performance management system will break down.

- Performance evaluations need to be conducted at the end of the planning period (which is usually a year) at all levels of the organization. These evaluations need to focus on performance against goals. Further, both positive feedback (which promotes behavior consistent with goals) and constructive criticism (which should result in behavioral change) need to be provided, based on the results achieved against goals. In the absence of performance evaluations, organizations, departments, and individuals will not understand what they can do to continue their effectiveness into the future and to improve their performance.

- Rewards need to be provided, based on the level of goal achievement. It should be clear how rewards are linked to performance against organizational, departmental, or individual goals. Further, rewards should be established so that they provide something that is valued by those receiving them.

For a performance management system to function effectively, all parts of the system need to be effectively designed and connected. If any component of the system is poorly designed or is not linked with the other components, the probability that the organization, department, or individual will achieve desired results is decreased.

Behavioral Criteria for Effective Performance Management Systems Design

From a behavioral perspective, an effective performance management system meets two criteria: (1) it enhances goal congruence, and (2) it minimizes unintended dysfunctional behaviors.

Increasing Goal Congruence. The effectiveness of a performance management system is measured by the extent to which it increases the probability that people will behave in ways that lead to the attainment of organizational goals. Typically, this is the result of establishing goals in a manner that creates at least an acceptable degree of goal congruence—that is, by the individual working to achieve the organization's goals, he or she is also satisfying one or more of his or her personal goals. If a performance management system sometimes results in goal congruence and sometimes in goal conflict, it is ineffective, or at least less effective than might be desired.

To be effective, a performance management system must identify all behaviors or goals that are required to support the organization's continued development and long-term success. If the system does not identify all relevant goals and seek to control them, people may simply channel their efforts toward some desired but uncontrolled behavior. In addition, in order to be effective, the performance management system must actually lead to the behavior it is intended to (or purports to) produce. For example, a performance management system may be intended to motivate people toward achieving both a budgeted profit and personnel development. If it produces this effect, it is said to be behaviorally valid. If it leads to behavior that is in conflict with these goals, it is behaviorally invalid. In general, a performance management system cannot be expected to lead to behavior that is totally consistent with what is desired, but it must have some degree of behavioral validity if it is to be effective.

A performance management system's effectiveness also depends on the extent to which it repeatedly produces the same behavior, whether this behavior is intended or not. This quality is called the performance management system's *behavioral reliability*. A performance management system may have a high degree of behavioral reliability but lead consistently to unintended behavior, or a system may lead to intended behavior but do so irregularly.

Dysfunctional Behavior. When a performance management system is ineffective, dysfunctional behavior can result. There are two types of dysfunctional behavior: (1) goal displacement and (2) measurementship.

Goal displacement is a lack of goal congruence created by the motivation to achieve some goals sought by the organization at the expense of other intended goals. Goal displacement may be caused by several things, including suboptimization, selective attention to goals, and inversion of means and ends.

Suboptimization occurs when the performance of an organizational subunit is optimized at the expense of the organization as a whole. It is caused by factoring overall organizational goals into subgoals and holding individuals and units responsible for those subgoals. Suboptimization is a common problem and is difficult to avoid in large, complex organizations.

Selective attention to organizational goals is closely related to suboptimization. It occurs when certain goals of the organization are pursued selectively, while other goals receive less attention or are ignored. In this case, a rule or guideline that is part of the performance management system is followed absolutely, even if it contradicts or prevents achievement of the goal. The original goal is replaced by the goal of following the rules. A third type of goal displacement is caused by the inversion of means and ends. This occurs when a performance management system tries to motivate attention to certain instrumental goals, which become ends in themselves because of rewards and thereby prevent achievement of other goals.

Measurementship involves a lack of goal congruence created by motivation to "look good" in terms of the measures used in performance management systems, even though no real benefit is produced for the organization. It involves manipulating the measures used by a performance management system, that is, playing the numbers game. There are two primary types of measurementship: (1) smoothing and (2) falsifying.

Smoothing is an attempt to time activities in a way that produces the appearance of similar measures in different time periods. For example, a manager may wish to smooth the calculated net income in two adjacent periods. If profit is expected to be unusually high during the first period, this figure can be smoothed by incurring expenditures that otherwise would have been made in the second period in the prior year.

Falsification is the reporting of invalid data about what is occurring in an organization in order to make a person or activity look good in the management system. For example, Enron was charged with manipulating revenues by creating false transactions in order to show good earnings for the stock market. This and similar problems at WorldCom (now defunct) and other companies led to the Sarbanes-Oxley legislation.

Problems related to dysfunctional behavior point to the importance of designing and implementing effective performance management systems at each stage of organizational development.

Performance Management Systems in Action: Superior Security Systems Case Study

This section presents a case study of a performance management system at a Stage II company.[7] It illustrates the problems that can be created when a company's performance management system is not functioning effectively. It also identifies steps that can be taken to improve specific problems that can exist within these systems, using the framework presented in this chapter.

Superior Security Systems is a rapidly growing installer of alarm systems for homes. It also provides ongoing alarm monitoring services. The business was originally founded as an "electronics boutique," where individuals could purchase stereo systems, alarm systems, and other electronic devices for installation in automobiles and homes. With social and technological changes, the organization totally redirected its focus to the installation of these electronic systems just in homes. Later it also added a service unit for monitoring the alarms installed.

The original location of the business was a single store in a major metropolitan area in a large western state. The firm had a number of factors that differentiated it from its competition, including the use of original equipment and materials, competitive prices, rapid service, high-quality installation, and field service by means of radio-dispatched trucks. As the firm began to grow, it targeted new geographical markets. A few years later, the business had organized a franchise operation and had established 10 locations throughout the state.

Each of the franchises is organized with a branch manager, a number of installation technicians, and an administrative assistant. The administrative assistant's function is critical to the effectiveness of the operation of the branch because he or she has the primary contact with the customer and is required to relay most of the critical information concerning sales and repairs. The installation and repair technicians are also critical to the effective operation of the firm. Incorrect installation or faulty repair creates significant customer ill will and substantial cost to the company. The so-called branch manager is actually an owner-operator, who has an investment in the franchise. Depending on the size of the branch, the branch manager may also function simultaneously as an installer-technician or even as a salesperson. In some of the larger branches, there may be one or more full-time sales personnel.

Within six years, the firm had grown to approximately $25 million in annual revenue. It was growing at an average rate of 22% a year, and because of rapid growth, both in terms of the number of branch operations and in terms of the total volume of sales, there had been relatively little time to develop the infrastructure of the organization.

Incomplete Development of the Performance Management System

Certain aspects of the Superior Security Systems performance management system were more developed than others. The company had developed a relatively sophisticated strategic planning process. The company had been involved in numerous formal planning exercises over several years since its inception, including planning meetings that involved a considerable amount of discussion concerning problems facing the company, identifying alternatives, assessing their strengths and limitations, searching for information that was relevant, and formulating a broad concept of where the firm wanted to go. These sessions were the basis for the firm's decision to franchise, for example.

One problem with the planning process was, according to the organization's administrative staff as well as the branch managers, that it did not tend to result in a set of specific goals and objectives for the firm or a set of priorities to guide them in carrying out their overall efforts. The frequent complaint was that many of the plans that were made at the beginning of the year tended to be "bumped" by more immediate problems handed down by top management. The introduction of unplanned projects or crises that tended to emerge resulted in shifts in the focus of energy; the result was neglect of many of the projects that had originally been agreed to at the beginning of the year. There was a sense that the firm was making progress but that a great deal of the progress was in an ad hoc or piecemeal manner. The bottom line was that many of the participants in the planning sessions expressed uncertainty about how the content of the meetings would be translated into action.

Although the overall planning process was extensive, there had never been formal consideration of what the company's key result areas ought to be. Accordingly, although the branch managers and, in turn, the installation technicians understood in general what their role was, there was not a specific set of key result areas for which they were held accountable. Similarly, there was not a specific set of goals or objectives for which they were held accountable.

Another problem with the firm's performance management system related to the nature of its goals: *Only a few were quantifiable.* When goals were measurable, the level of performance expected was frequently unrealistic. For example, the times that were available as "standard times" for installation were thought by all but a few of the most talented and experienced installation technicians to be unrealistic. As a result, many of the employees found the standards to be demoralizing. Moreover, the enforcement of the standards was relatively uneven. Some branch managers tended to stick to standards and to evaluate installation technicians negatively whenever their performance was below standard, which was quite frequently. Other branch managers, who recognized that the standards were not wholly realistic, tended to ignore them.

One strength of the measurement system of the company was that it was organized on a "responsibility accounting basis." This meant that the business had good information concerning the profitability of each individual branch. At each branch, the company had institutionalized a monthly financial review of the data. A representative from the home office met with the branch manager and examined the monthly financial report. They also discussed issues involving branch performance on such key factors as market share.

Within each branch, however, the process of performance review was relatively uneven. With the exception of an examination of overall bottom-line profitability, there did not tend to be a review of performance in key result areas that supported that profitability. Discussions of problems would occur as they emerged. There was no systematic attempt to identify the critical success factors of the branch, to measure the branch's performance in each one of those factors, and to examine it in depth.

With respect to performance evaluation of each employee, there was an uneven emphasis by the different branch managers in evaluating their direct reports. Although it was company policy that employees were to be reviewed, based on their performance on a yearly basis, some individuals indicated that over two years had passed since their last review. They also reported that feedback on their performance ranged from some very specific, constructive criticisms to more global assessments of their performance. Many individuals indicated that they were not really sure how they were being evaluated by their managers or whether they were valued or not valued by their managers. One stated, "Well, I'm still here, so I must be doing okay."

At this stage of the company's development there was not a well-designed compensation program. The administration of compensation increases was on an ad hoc basis. Some individuals had not received a salary increase in more than two years. Further, there were no specific guidelines for salary increases that would be allocated in relation to different levels of performance, such as excellent performance, good performance, or satisfactory performance. Individuals reported that they did not have a clear idea as to how their performance would result in increases in their compensation.

Improvements in the Performance Management System

An analysis of the performance management system at Superior Security Systems indicates a number of problems in the design of that system. There are problems both in the individual components of the system and in the overall integration of the system. In this section, we examine some of those problems and make suggestions about how they can be solved.

Goals and Objectives

As described in Chapter 6, goals and objectives are the output of the organization's planning system. A company's strategic planning system should result in a statement of its mission, its key result areas, its objectives, and its goals. In the case of Superior Security Systems, the planning system did not provide a foundation for an effective performance management system in these areas. The basic problem with the planning process at Superior Security Systems was that it was not producing a well-defined statement of key result areas. The key result areas were necessary to provide an overall focus for the branch managers and, in turn, for the installation technicians and the administrative assistants. Once the key result areas for each branch were identified and defined, it was necessary to further improve the planning process at Superior Security Systems by generating a set of objectives related to each key result area. The next step would be to generate goals related to each objective, which, by definition, are specific, measurable, and time-dated. Implementing these steps would help overcome the problems faced by branch managers, installation technicians, and administrative personnel. To help avoid the problem of setting unrealistic goals, the branch manager, installation technicians, and administrative personnel should participate in the process of setting these goals. It is particularly important that great care be devoted to ensuring that the goals are measurable, specific, and time-dated. Otherwise, they will not provide an effective basis for comparison with actual performance.

Measurement Systems

A measurement system permits a company to represent the performance of a branch or individual in quantitative terms. At Superior Security Systems, the measurement system included the accounting information system, sales management system, and other sources of information. Although there seemed to be ample financial information to assist managers at Superior Security Systems, there did not appear to be an adequate source of financial information concerning performance in the branches.

To improve this, the company needed to ensure that measurements were available for each of its key result areas in order to enable it to assess performance on each of these key factors. However, this was not yet being done.

Performance Evaluation

A company should do an analysis of each of its key result areas in order to assess performance on each of these key factors. The measurements do not all have to be in dollar terms. Some can be in monetary terms, and others can be in nonmonetary terms. Some measurements can even be what may be characterized as go/no-go measurements. This means that a manager can do an informal rating of whether something has happened or not happened. For example, customer service might be assessed by the number of written complaints or letters of praise received. Ultimately, the home office might conduct a telephone sample of customers and have the interviewer generate a judgment as to whether the service provided was satisfactory or unsatisfactory. By then tabulating the number of satisfactory versus unsatisfactory responses, we can generate a measurement of branch performance in this key result area. However, little of this was being done.

Rewards

Another significant problem with the organization's performance management system was the lack of linkage between objectives, goals, measurements, and rewards. The company's compensation system did not appear to be linked to its objectives and goals. Individuals did not perceive that they were rewarded based on their ability to achieve goals. Because people did not perceive a clear linkage between goal achievement and compensation, there was unlikely to be a great deal of ownership of the goals. People may very well have been motivated, but the firm's reward system was neither enhancing nor channeling their motivation directly toward the goals and objectives that the branch sought to attain.

To improve its performance management system for this component, an enterprise should analyze its overall compensation system. To be effective, the compensation system should provide incentives for an individual to achieve the goals and objectives that the organization wants to attain. An increasing number of entrepreneurial firms are relying on compensation systems that have a significant component based on incentive compensation. In such circumstances, people are generally provided a base salary that is relatively competitive, as well as opportunities for substantial increases in compensation linked to the achievement of individual and company objectives and goals. Wherever feasible, a company should attempt to tie incentive compensation to measurable factors. However, even where this is not feasible, if management can identify the key factors it wishes people to focus on and indicate how incentive compensation will be based on those factors, it will result in enhanced motivation and performance.

Overall Assessment of Superior Security Systems Performance Management System

As can be seen in the case of Superior Security Systems, it is one thing to talk about what should be done to develop a performance management system, and quite another to review what is being done in reality. There are, as we have described above, several deficiencies or problems with the Superior Security Systems performance management system. Key problems include:

- The planning process did not result in a set of specific goals and objectives for the firm or a set of priorities to guide them in carrying out their overall efforts.
- The organization did not stick to its plan; plans that were made at the beginning of the year tended to be "bumped" by more immediate problems.
- There were problems with goals—*only a few were quantifiable*. When goals were measurable, the level of performance expected was frequently unrealistic.
- There did not tend to be a review of performance in key result areas that supported that profitability.
- Administration of compensation increases was on an ad hoc basis.

Problems in a performance management system can be identified and corrected using the model described in this chapter as a template. Similarly, the performance management systems model can also be used in any organization as a template for the design or improvement of a performance management system.

Use of Performance Management Systems at an Individual Level: The Performance Appraisal Process at Southern California Presbyterian Homes

The concepts previously presented can be used in the design of the employee performance appraisal process. A sample form that might be used in this process, developed by Southern California Presbyterian Homes (SCPH), a Stage IV nonprofit company that specializes in providing housing and other services for older adults, is presented in Exhibit 8.3. A description of how this form was

Exhibit 8.3   Southern California Presbyterian Homes Performance Appraisal Form

Immediate Supervisor: Employee:
For period ended:

Part I: Goals for Each Key Result Area

Note: Performance against the goals listed below will account for 75% of the total performance appraisal.

Key Result Area	Goals	Evaluation of Performance
1.	1.	Doesn't Meet/Conditionally Meets/Meets/Exceeds:
	2.	Doesn't Meet/Conditionally Meets/Meets/Exceeds:
	3.	Doesn't Meet/Conditionally Meets/Meets/Exceeds:
2.	1.	Doesn't Meet/Conditionally Meets/Meets/Exceeds:
	2.	Doesn't Meet/Conditionally Meets/Meets/Exceeds:
	3.	Doesn't Meet/Conditionally Meets/Meets/Exceeds:
3.	1.	Doesn't Meet/Conditionally Meets/Meets/Exceeds:
	2.	Doesn't Meet/Conditionally Meets/Meets/Exceeds:
	3.	Doesn't Meet/Conditionally Meets/Meets/Exceeds:
4.	1.	Doesn't Meet/Conditionally Meets/Meets/Exceeds:
	2.	Doesn't Meet/Conditionally Meets/Meets/Exceeds:
	3.	Doesn't Meet/Conditionally Meets/Meets/Exceeds:

Part II: Other Criteria

Note: Evaluation of performance against these criteria will account for 25% of the total performance appraisal.

Other Criteria	Evaluation of Performance
1. Job Knowledge and Task Performance: The extent to which I show that I understand the fundamentals, possess the skills, and utilize the methods and procedures required to effectively perform my responsibilities. This includes planning and organizing work to maximize my own and others' performance. Methods to Measure Performance:	
2. Judgment and Decision Making: The extent to which the judgments/decisions I make are made in a timely manner and are appropriate within the context of the situation in which they are made. Methods to Measure Performance:	

Exhibit 8.3   (Continued)

Other Criteria	Evaluation of Performance
3. <u>Leadership and Participative Management</u>: The extent to which I effectively manage/work as a member of my team in accomplishing common objectives. This includes facilitating effective communication and encouraging participation on the part of members of my team. <u>Methods to Measure Performance:</u>	
4. <u>Staff/Employee Morale</u>: The extent to which I respond to staff and employee needs in a timely and consistent manner. The extent to which I promote an environment that encourages people to work individually and as teams to accomplish goals. <u>Methods to Measure Performance:</u>	
5. <u>Willingness to Learn/Improve</u>: The extent to which I display an interest, desire and initiative to learn, attain goals, and grow in job knowledge and skills. <u>Methods to Measure Performance:</u>	

developed at this company, how it was used, and the initial response of managers to this process is presented next. This is a "classic" case that outlines the steps that can be used to design and implement an effective individual performance management system.

Like many organizations, SCPH had traditionally used an employee appraisal form that asked managers to evaluate members of their teams on factors such as judgment, leadership, quality of work, and attitude. Each year, managers were asked to provide each member of their team with a score, ranging from 1 to 5 on each of these factors. They were also asked to provide some written comments to support the score they were giving. Even though a score of 3 was considered acceptable performance, as is true in many companies where evaluation is based on more subjective criteria, most employees scored between 4 and 5. In fact, the implicit assumption was that if a person scored below 4, there was something wrong.

Whenever subjective criteria are used to evaluate performance, managers find it difficult to give employees low ratings because, as the criteria are somewhat vague, this can lead to conflict over who is really right. Frequently, then, most employees continue to receive favorable performance appraisals, even though they may not be performing at the highest level possible. Further, it is sometimes only by chance that people in these organizations are focused on achieving the organization's goals because their performance appraisal (and typically their compensation) are based on performance against subjective criteria that may or may not relate to goal achievement.

Recognizing that there was a need to develop more objective measures of performance and to focus his team more on the goals of the organization, Gerald (Jerry) Dingivan, then president and CEO of SCPH, began a program in 1997 to redesign the organization's performance appraisal process. The first step in this process was to assemble a team of senior managers representing both the home office and the company's facilities, which came to be known as the Performance Management Task Force. The purpose of this task force was to review the current performance appraisal process, including the forms used in this process, and to make recommendations about changes that would make the process more goal-oriented.

Working with one of the authors, the task force developed an understanding of what the key components (as described earlier in the chapter) of an effective goal-oriented performance appraisal process should be. Putting this process in place involved several steps, which are outlined next.

Revision of Job Descriptions

Although SCPH had traditionally had fairly detailed job descriptions, the task force determined that an effective performance appraisal process would be best facilitated by using a key result area–based role description format (described in Chapter 7). Senior and middle managers from throughout the company were provided with training in this methodology and were asked to transform their existing job descriptions into the key result area format. Once each manager had completed a draft of his or her job description, a workshop was held in which each manager was able to obtain feedback from others in order to ensure that the role description accurately reflected the key factors on which that position should be focused. The final step in this process was for each role description to be approved by the manager's immediate superior. Once managers were trained, they worked with the members of their team (supervisors, front-line workers) to help develop key result area-based role descriptions for these positions. In other words, the methodology was cascaded throughout the various levels of the company. The stage was now set to introduce the new performance appraisal forms and process.

Design of the New Performance Appraisal Forms

The Performance Management Task Force met several times to debate what should and should not be included in the new performance appraisal forms the company would use. One thing all task force members could agree on was that the forms should be as simple as possible and that they should include specific goals for which people would be held accountable. The team also felt strongly about the need to move away from numerical scoring of individual performance, at least for a short time. The task force believed that employees throughout the company had come to rely too heavily on using numbers both to just get the performance appraisals done but also as a standard for understanding their performance. The new process should focus both managers and their direct reports on performance against goals, rather than on numbers that represented this performance.

There was also discussion about the need to retain some of the subjective criteria that had been used in the previous evaluation process. The task force felt that some of these criteria were important from a cultural perspective. Five of these factors were, therefore, retained on the performance evaluation form. Although these criteria were retained, the task force also believed that managers should take the time during the goal-setting process to explain or discuss how performance would be measured in these areas. In other words, the goal was to make the evaluation of these subjective criteria somewhat more objective. A decision was made, however, that 75% of the individual's evaluation would be based on performance against goals. The remaining 25% would be based on performance against the more subjective criteria.

As can be seen in Exhibit 8.3, the form was designed to include the key components of an effective performance management system, plus space for the manager to provide an evaluation. The form provides space to list each position-holder's key result areas (taken from the role description) and space to list up to three goals for which the individual would be held responsible over the course of the coming year. The task force agreed that, at least in the first year of this new process, no individual should be held accountable for more than three goals in any key result area. It was also suggested (when the process was eventually introduced to the organization's entire management team), that managers try to keep the number of goals for any individual to no more than 10. In an effort to keep the form as simple as possible, the task force decided that there was no need to list the individual's objectives on this form (they were included on the role description). Instead, the role description would become an attachment to the form.

Evaluating performance on each goal would consist of circling one of the four statements— exceeds, meets, conditionally meets, or doesn't meet—and then providing comments about why this particular evaluation was given. (Dingivan had added the term *conditionally meets* to the form in an effort to take into account those situations where individuals had given a great effort to achieve a goal but had simply been unable to meet it.) The task force agreed that it was particularly important that comments be included on the form and that they were, in some ways, more important than whatever level of performance had been circled.

Use of the Form

To use the form, managers would meet with each of their direct reports before the beginning of the year to set specific goals. Prior to these goal-setting meetings, key elements of the organization's strategic plan (written in the format described in Chapter 6) would be shared with each manager. All those in management positions would be asked to establish what they believed their goals should be for the coming year to help the company achieve its goals. Their immediate supervisor would also prepare a list of goals (organized by key result area) for which they felt that individual should be accountable (in order to support the achievement of the company's plans). The goal-setting meeting would then take place, and an agreement would be reached between the manager and the direct report (who, in this case, was also a member of the management team) as to what the individual's goals would be for the coming year. For those who occupied technical roles (for example, housekeepers and technicians), it was decided that the "goal" column of this worksheet would contain standards of performance that needed to be met. In other words, goals for these positions would, in a sense, be pre-set. When supervisors reviewed these standards with those holding the positions, the individual in question would also have the opportunity to provide input on these expectations and include additional goals (if appropriate). The idea was to make the performance appraisals of these positions somewhat more programmable.

One concern that the task force had was how to handle a situation in which an individual might not have any goals under a specific key result area for a particular year. It was decided that, in these cases, the manager would simply write in the blank, "see role description." What this meant was that the individual would be held accountable for performance against those objectives that were a part of the key result area–based role description. These objectives would be reviewed as a part of the goal-setting meeting. While the process was being introduced to the management team, it was later decided that managers could choose to include the phase "see role description" within all key result areas if they so desired, even if specific goals were also set. In these cases, the individual in question would be evaluated both on the specific goals and on general performance within each key result area.

As a part of the goal-setting process, managers would also discuss specifically how they would be evaluating the individual's performance with respect to each of the more subjective criteria. The factors they would be looking at or the behavior they would be looking for were to be recorded in the appropriate space on the performance evaluation form.

At the end of the year, the manager would then complete the last column of the form, thus evaluating the individual's performance against specific goals, relative to the objectives listed in the person's role description and against the five subjective performance criteria. Managers would then meet with each direct report and provide their feedback. There was space at the end of the form for both the employee and the manager to provide additional comments prior to signing the form. The form would then be submitted to the next level of management for final approval before being sent on to the company's human resource department.

Training in Conducting Effective Performance Appraisals

It was important that all managers throughout the company adequately understood the new performance appraisal forms and how to use them. To facilitate the effective implementation of this process, Yvonne Randle (who had been assisting the Performance Management Task Force in the design of the process) provided several training sessions on the new performance evaluation process. These sessions took place over the course of 18 months. Sessions focused on helping managers understand the key components of effective performance appraisal systems, the design of the new form and its advantages over what had been used in the past (from the standpoint of promoting behavior consistent with helping the company achieve its goals), and how to effectively prepare for and conduct effective goal-setting and performance appraisal meetings.

Another important part of these sessions was that they provided managers from throughout the company with the opportunity to provide feedback on how effectively the new process and forms were working. They were encouraged to make suggestions for changes that might be made so that the forms and the process would better meet their needs. This feedback was collected and reviewed by the Performance Management Task Force. They responded to every idea submitted. Some were used to make minor adjustments in the form or the process that was to be used. Other suggestions for changes were not adopted, but the task force made sure to provide their rationale for not using these ideas.

Results

SCPH fully adopted the performance appraisal process throughout the company. Although some managers were, at times, still skeptical about the process, most managers described it as less cumbersome than the one previously used. More important, the new process helped the company focus individual efforts on those goals that would be most important to helping achieve its long-term mission.

Control and Performance Management Systems at Different Stages of Organizational Growth

No single performance management system is ideal for every organization. Each organization is different and requires a different type of system. The major factor that determines the nature of the performance management systems required is the company's stage of growth.

Stage I

Even the smallest organizations need some type of control, but at Stage I, control typically is relatively informal. Usually, the entrepreneur can exercise control during Stage I simply through day-to-day interaction with people in the organization. By the very fact of constantly being there, the entrepreneur is able to observe what is happening and be on top of almost everything. At this stage, the entrepreneur still knows all the company's employees and is able to observe what most of them are doing and suggest modifications when necessary.

Even in this informal stage, however, the basic functions of control need to be exercised. The organization should have a basic budgetary system and an accounting system. At Stage I, a company can get by with a relatively informal performance appraisal system, but there ought to be some regular appraisal process.

Stage II

As soon as an organization reaches Stage II, its control needs to increase dramatically. The entrepreneur no longer has the time to handle control single-handedly, nor can he or she personally interact with all of the growing number of employees. There is increased need for the kind of coordination that only a formal performance management system can bring. If the entrepreneur fails to recognize the need for a more formal system, the company is likely to experience difficulties.

During Stage II, a company ought to be beginning to develop a formal planning system that includes the basic elements described in Chapter 6. It also needs a basic performance management system to help carry out its plan that includes basic measurement systems designed to provide information that can be used in assessing progress against goals and holding regular progress review meetings. It will most likely need to change its basic accounting system to some kind of "responsibility accounting system," which provides information not only on overall financial performance but on product-line profitability and business segment profitability as well.

In Stage II, the evaluation and reward component of the performance management system must also be developed further. Job or role descriptions specifying responsibilities are required. Some sort of individual goal setting should be introduced, accompanied by a formal performance appraisal system. The organization's compensation program also ought to become more systematic and include an incentive component that is linked to performance. Failure to make these changes during Stage II may lead to the feeling that the organization is out of control.

Stage III

By the time a company has grown to Stage III, it requires more sophisticated and powerful methods of control. This is the stage at which the company must develop a formal performance management system, along with other components of its management systems.

As we have noted, planning at Stage III needs to be brought down to the level of individual products or profit centers. Similarly, the company's budgeting system needs to be brought down to the level of individual products or profit centers.

The company's accounting information system will typically need to be reconceptualized to provide a greater amount of information for management control. By the time a business reaches Stage III, it ought to have a well-developed set of management reports dealing with the nonaccounting information that is required to monitor the business. In brief, the company should have well-developed measurement systems and reporting processes that provide the accurate and timely information needed to assess performance against all goals at the organizational and unit (department, division, team) levels.

By this stage, managers at all levels should be effectively setting and using specific, measurable, time-dated goals as the basis for performance appraisals. A formal performance appraisal system should be in place, and all managers should have the skills needed to effectively fulfill their roles in this process (including having the ability to set effective goals and provide effective feedback).

If management did not lay the foundation for these systems during Stage II, they will be more difficult and costly to develop during Stage III. If the company still has not put the systems into place by the time it reaches the later phase of Stage III, it is likely to experience serious growing pains. These may be masked temporarily by continually rising sales if the company is in a favorable market. Unfortunately, when the market ultimately turns, the company may find itself facing a "scissors effect" of simultaneously reduced revenue and increased costs. This can prove fatal.

Stage IV

By the time an organization reaches Stage IV, its core performance management system should be in place. Most of the changes to be made at this stage are (or at least ought to be) merely refinements.

The planning system becomes more sophisticated. Moreover, the budget process may be refined to include features such as flexible budgeting (budgeting based on different assumptions about the economy and related level of business). The accounting information system ought to be able to generate accurate, timely, comparative data.

Performance appraisals, oriented toward performance against plan or goals, should be regularly scheduled, and employees should expect that deviations from standards will require factual explanations. The performance appraisal process described in the case study of SCPH is an example of what is appropriate for a Stage IV organization.

By the time an organization reaches Stage IV, its core performance management system ought to be well developed, functioning smoothly, and in place as an integral part of its overall corporate culture.

Stage V

The challenge for performance management at Stage V is to design performance management systems to support a multi-product/service or multi-market business. The design of each component of these systems will, at least in part, depend upon the divisional structure form adopted. For example, in a company that is highly centralized (such as McDonald's), all franchisees are held to the same performance standards, and performance is monitored on a regular basis against these standards. In a less centralized divisional structure, there may different standards of performance for different divisions (because they operate in very different markets and/or offer very different products or services). At this stage, attention also needs to be devoted to identifying how the divisions and corporate will complete and coordinate with each other with respect to performance review and what the expectations are with respect to performance evaluation. Finally, some attention needs to be devoted to designing the reward system at the corporate and divisional levels.

When diversification has occurred as a result of a merger or an acquisition, time should be spent during the due diligence process identifying the nature of the performance management system in each company and determining what the system will be once the "deal" has been completed. The new entity may adopt the performance management system of one of the companies involved or may create a new system that reflects best practices from each company involved in the acquisition or merger. This can include how the individual performance management system is designed and implemented.

Stage VI

The challenge for performance management at Stage VI is to fully integrate the systems for all the diversified units, while simultaneously having an appropriate system for each of the individual business units. For an enterprise like Johnson & Johnson, which typically has relatively mature business units, this is not that difficult. However, for a rapidly growing enterprise that has been created by acquisitions, it is far more challenging. For such diversified businesses, the core notion is that at Stage VI there probably cannot be a single performance management system where "one size fits all." Instead, the principles of each of the performance management systems must be the same, but the features might be different.

What is required in such complex situations is a custom solution to the design of a performance management system. There cannot be a "cookbook" approach.

Stage VII

The central challenge at Stage VII is to deal with organizational decline by revitalizing the entire enterprise. It is possible that one of the contributors to decline has been poorly designed performance management systems or even the lack of performance management systems per se. For example, if performance management systems are not functioning effectively, managers may not receive the information needed in a timely manner to make critical decisions. As a result, opportunities and critical threats to the business may be missed. If the individual performance management system is not functioning effectively, people may not be held accountable for results that need to be achieved. As a result, important goals are "missed," the organization begins to experience significant problems and, as a result, goes into decline.

The development of performance management systems during Stage VII will depend upon the overall plan for organizational revitalization. As in Stage VI, what is required in such complex situations is a custom solution to the design of a performance management system.

Summary

When an organization passes the size at which the leader can personally function as its control system, the owner will increasingly be stretched thin; with the addition of other employees and managers, the need for coordination will grow. There will also be a need for information about problems being encountered in various aspects of operations, including receivables, inventories (if any), and sales. Thus there will be a growing need for formal controls to supplement the personal involvement of the entrepreneur.

Unfortunately, an organization does not have to be very large before it becomes extremely difficult, if not impossible, for the entrepreneur to perform all functions of the control system. In fact, by the time a company reaches $1 million in annual revenue, it becomes highly unlikely that the entrepreneur alone will be able to exercise effective control. This chapter describes the basic concepts that leaders can use to develop and implement effective performance management systems to support the continued success of organizations at any size and stage of growth.

The framework for developing effective performance management systems presented in this chapter has been used by companies of varying sizes in different countries around the world—including Bulgaria, China, Kazakhstan, Poland, Venezuela, and Vietnam as well as the United States and Canada—to evaluate, design, and enhance the effectiveness of their performance management systems. Applied properly, the framework presented in this chapter can be a valuable managerial tool for helping to build sustainably successful organizations®.

Notes

1. For a more in-depth discussion of control/performance management systems, see Eric G. Flamholtz, *Effective Management Control: Theory and Practice* (Norwell, MA: Kluwer, 1996).
2. Marshall McLuhan, *Understanding Media: The Extensions of Man* (New York: McGraw-Hill, 1964).
3. Steven Kerr, "On the Folly of Rewarding A, While Hoping for B," *Academy of Management Journal* 18 (December 1975): 769–783.

4. See Robert S. Kaplan and David P. Norton, "The Balanced Scorecard: Measures that Drive Performance," *Harvard Business Review* (January–February 1992): 71–79.

5. Marshall Meyer, *Rethinking Performance Measurement: Beyond the Balanced Scorecard* (New York: Cambridge University Press, 2002).

6. For a more detailed discussion of the problems of the version of the balanced scorecard proposed by Kaplan and Norton, see Eric G. Flamholtz, "Putting Validity and Balance into the Balanced Scorecard," *Journal of Human Resource Costing and Accounting* (Autumn, 2003): 15–26.

7. This is a disguised version of an actual company. Significant changes have been made in the nature of the business; however, the issues described were actual problems facing this company.

Management and Leadership Development

Having managers at all levels that understand, embrace, and effectively execute their roles is a key to long-term sustainable success. This is, in fact, the overall purpose of management/leadership development. Highly successful companies (including well-known organizations such as GE, Johnson & Johnson, IBM, Starbucks, Amgen, Guggenheim Partners, Princess Cruises, PIMCO, and Navistar; and lesser known organizations such as Kusto Holdings with operations in Kazakhstan, Russia, the Ukraine, and Vietnam, Techmer PM and Bell Carter Foods in the United States, and Xu Zhou Construction Machinery Group in China) *all* recognize the critical importance of investing in enhancing the skills of current and potential leaders. In brief, leaders at all levels have the responsibility for designing and managing the key drivers of long-term organizational success and they need to have the capabilities to do so.

This chapter begins by defining the management/leadership role and "leadership effectiveness." We then identify what we term "the three-dimensional framework" for understanding management and leadership effectiveness. The chapter then provides strategies for creating and implementing effective leadership development programs and processes to help current and future managers build the capabilities needed to support their organization's long-term success. Throughout, we provide examples of what actual companies have done to utilize the tools and techniques presented.

The Management and Leadership Role

The overall purpose of a manager is to influence the behavior of people in a way that makes them more likely to achieve organizational goals (this, it should be noted, is our definition of "leadership"). Executing the management role involves, among other things, supervising and developing direct reports, developing and implementing unit or company plans, and overseeing day-to-day operations. As explained in Chapter 7, there are four levels of management included in the organizational hierarchy: first-line supervisor, middle manager, senior manager, and CEO/COO.

Those who occupy first-line supervisory or middle management roles are frequently referred to as being in "management roles."[1] The primary focus of individuals in these roles should be on executing the organization's strategy through management of day-to-day operations. Those who occupy senior management roles or the roles of CEO or COO are in "leadership roles," where the focus should be on the organization's long-term (strategic) development. It should be noted that those in management roles also play a role in strategy development and those in leadership roles also need to focus on managing day-to-day operations. As a result, we will frequently use the term "manager/leader" when we work with organizations in the design and delivery of management and leadership development programs. We will also use this term throughout the remainder of this chapter.

A Three-Dimensional Framework for Understanding Management and Leadership Effectiveness

Based on our experience in working with managers/leaders in a wide variety of organizations, as well as research on the nature and determinants of management/leadership success and failure, we have developed what we term a "three-dimensional framework" that explains management and leadership effectiveness. The three dimensions that make up this framework are:

1. Role Concept
2. Management/Leadership Skills
3. The Inner Game of Management

Each of these dimensions accounts for about one-third of management/leadership success. Therefore, to maximize success, each dimension needs to be managed in a manner consistent with the level of management/leadership occupied: CEO/COO, senior management, middle management, or first- or front-line supervisor. Each dimension is described in turn below, along with what is required to effectively manage it.

Role Concept

This dimension is defined as the way an individual thinks about and approaches his or her role. How an individual views his or her role has a direct impact on his or her behavior and, specifically, on how the individual allocates and invests his or her time.

As individuals move into a management/leadership role for the first time or as they move from one level of management to the next, they face two related challenges in adopting an appropriate role concept. First, there is the need to understand and accept that the management/leadership role is, in some ways, more ambiguous than and fundamentally different from that of a technical professional or "doer." Second, there needs to be a significant shift in how the individual allocates and manages time.

A fundamental and profound change should occur when an individual makes the transition from performing some technical job to doing the job of a manager. It is analogous to going from a player's role to a coach's role in some sport. The player's role is analogous to the doer's role, while the coach's role is analogous to the first-line supervisor's role. Unfortunately, unlike the coach's role in a sport, the manager's role is much more ambiguous in nature. Many new managers are not entirely sure what they should be doing; that is, they don't understand that this new role is truly different from the technical role previously occupied. They therefore continue doing what they have done in the past and hope for the best.

While the ambiguity of the management/leadership role is a particular challenge for new managers, it can be a problem for managers at all levels. If this challenge is not addressed when the individual is in a first-line supervisory role, problems will only increase as the individual continues "doing" work versus managing it.

This first challenge can be addressed by clearly defining roles and then taking the time to ensure that the occupant of each role understands what is expected of them. Key result area-based role descriptions (described in Chapter 7) can be used to help managers at all levels understand what they should focus on and how much time should be devoted to each of their key result areas. In doing so, these role descriptions help take the ambiguity out of the role. When an individual moves into a new management/leadership role (whether the individual is becoming a manager for the first time or is being promoted to the next level), there should be an orientation process that includes reviewing and discussing the expectations of the new role—using the role description as a guide.

The second, related challenge relates to time use. A manager/leader needs to spend a significant amount of time supervising the work of others and managing his or her area of responsibility. Time needs to be allocated to activities like planning (deciding what to do, when to do it, who should do it, and so on), reading materials and reports, meeting with people, training and coaching direct reports, working with direct reports to set goals, and monitoring performance against goals. These are very different types of activities from the performance activities of jobs such as engineer, accountant, and salesperson. And, as the individual moves beyond the first/front-line supervisory role to other levels of management/leadership, the amount of time that is allocated to these activities should increase.

To effectively invest and manage time as a manager/leader, an individual needs to overcome a "bias toward action" and replace it with what might be termed a "bias toward strategic thinking and planning." When confronted with a task, the natural tendency for most people is to "jump in" and start working on the task. This is a "ready-fire-aim" mentality. It is consistent with what we term a "doer" role. It feels good to move into action mode toward solving the problem or completing the task; it is psychologically rewarding because it seems to accomplish something. Unfortunately, this is not an effective approach for managers/leaders because their role is to effectively deploy their team to accomplish the work and achieve the goals. If the manager/leader individually or with his or her team starts "doing the work" before the situation has been assessed and a plan has been developed for addressing it, valuable resources may be wasted. Managers/leaders need to accept that their role is more strategic and involves focusing their time on planning, goal-setting, developing their team, and so on, where the pay-off of this effort might not occur immediately.

Well-developed key result area-based role descriptions can help an individual understand what the expectations are with respect to how he or she should allocate time to achieve the best results.

In addition, it is sometimes useful for the individual in the role to periodically track their actual time use. We typically recommend that this be done for a minimum of two weeks. The output of this time tracking will be the actual percentage of time that is being allocated to each key result area. A comparison of this information with the time allocations included in the role description can be used to identify areas where the individual is spending too much or too little time. An action plan can then be developed to help the individual move from current (reflected in the time-tracking results) to desired (presented in the role description) time utilization. Chapter 13 presents a case study of Bob Bennett, founder and CEO of GroundSwell Resources, Inc. who discusses the process of leadership development and the related "reprogramming" required to effectively manage role concept and the other two dimensions effectively.

Role concept is, in many ways, the foundation of becoming an effective manager/leader. As described above, effectively managing this dimension involves understanding the role and allocating time effectively. Once this is understood, the individual needs to accept, embrace, and learn to like this role.

Management/Leadership Skills

The vast majority of management and leadership education focuses on this dimension, which we define as "the people management, organizational management, and organizational development skills that an individual at a specific level of management/leadership needs to effectively execute his or her role." People management skills include motivation, communication, time management, delegation, and training. Organizational management skills include meeting management, decision making, project management, and team-building. Organizational development skills include strategic planning, structure management, performance management, leadership development, and organizational culture management. These are very different skills from those required to be effective in a technical or doer role.

Based on extensive work with managers and organizations over more than 40 years, we have developed a framework called the Pyramid of Management and Leadership Development (shown in Figure 9.1) that identifies the key skills required at each level of management and leadership—from first-line supervisor to CEO. The foundation of this Pyramid is role concept (which means that a first step in successful skill development is to have a clear understanding of and a willingness to embrace one's role as a manager/leader). Building on this foundation are five different levels of skills that managers must develop over their careers to be effective in their roles. These five levels are (1) core management skills, (2) operational management skills, (3) organizational management skills, (4) organizational development skills, and (5) transition management skills. As an individual moves from one level of management/leadership to the next, he or she needs to develop successively higher levels of skills (as defined in the pyramid). This means that someone in the CEO or a COO role should be able to effectively use *all* of the skills in the pyramid.

The *core management skills* are the skills required of all managers at all levels and within all organizations—whether it is Apple, Nike, Starbucks, or a 10-person start-up. These include communication, problem-solving and decision making, time management effectiveness, delegation effectiveness, interpersonal effectiveness, and operational leadership effectiveness (which we will

Figure 9.1 Pyramid of Management and Leadership Development™

describe in more depth in Chapter 12). These should be thought of as the foundational skills upon which all other skills are built.

At the next level of skills in the Pyramid of Management and Leadership Development are the *operational management skills*. These are skills required to manage day-to-day operations and supervise people. They include recruitment, selection, training and coaching, day-to-day supervision of people, motivation, performance appraisal, and management of meetings. Together with the core management skills, these are the skills needed by first-line supervisors to effectively fulfill their roles.

At the next level are *organizational management skills*. These skills include operational planning (including how to set SMART goals and develop action plans—discussed in Chapter 6), organizing people (including understanding how to develop and use role descriptions—discussed in Chapter 7), designing and effectively using performance management systems, developing management capabilities (because this is the first level that involves "managing other managers"), financial management, and team building. Middle managers need to possess these skills along with the core and operational management skills.

In addition to having the skills at the core, operational management, and organizational management levels, senior managers need to develop and be able to effectively employ *organizational development skills*. These skills include strategic planning (see Chapter 6), organizational planning (which involves understanding and managing the organization's infrastructure—that is, the Pyramid of Organizational Development), strategic leadership (that is, creating and managing a leadership molecule, as described in Chapter 12), and corporate culture management (see Chapter 10). These are "leadership" versus "management" skills because they focus on the long-term development of people and the organization.

To effectively execute the CEO and COO roles, an individual needs to have developed and be able to effectively use all of the skills in the Pyramid of Management and Leadership Development, including *transition management skills*. Developing transition management skills involves understanding how to identify the need for and how to manage individual and organizational transitions. Basically, these skills involve understanding how to manage change. This, too, is a leadership rather than a management skill.

While role concept relates to an individual's behavior, this second dimension relates to helping individuals develop the ability and knowledge needed to effectively execute their roles. Developing or enhancing management and leadership skills involves identifying educational opportunities that will provide the individual with what he or she needs to perform his or her role effectively. Methods to develop or enhance skills—which we will discuss later in this chapter—can range from in-house leadership development programs, to reading a book, taking a course, or working with a coach. The outcome of these efforts should be that the individual develops a clear understanding of what the skill in question is and knowledge of how to use it effectively.

The Pyramid of Management and Leadership Development framework has been the basis for programs used by many of our clients over the years, including Bell-Carter Foods (where it has been used for over 20 years), Navistar and its International Truck dealership network (as will be described later in this chapter), American Century Investments, GroundSwell Resources, Inc., Pardee Homes (then a subsidiary of Weyerhaeuser), Surgitek (a subsidiary of J & J), Techmer PM, and several Head Start agencies in the nonprofit space.

The Inner Game of Management[2]

This third dimension of the management/leadership effectiveness framework focuses on the individual's mindset and psychological needs. It is defined as "the way that the individual manages his or her need for control, source of self-esteem, and need to be liked." This is not about personality. Instead, it is about learning to *think* like an effective manager/leader. Actors understand that to effectively play a role (and management is, by definition, a role), they need to learn how to think like the character they will be portraying. Although we are not suggesting that individuals in management roles adopt the role of another person, we are suggesting that by understanding how effective managers/leaders think, they can greatly increase their effectiveness, while at the same time infusing the role with their own personality.

With respect to the need for control, those in management/leadership roles need to feel comfortable having indirect versus direct control over results—because they need to work through and with other people to achieve specific goals. In a technical or "doer" role, control over results is at a maximum. For an accountant, computer programmer, engineer, or salesperson, personal performance frequently determines the results. However, as soon as the position of first-line supervisor is reached, the relationship between personal effort and control over results becomes more indirect and tenuous. This fact is difficult for many (if not most) people to accept, and yet it must be accepted if they are to be successful in their roles as managers/leaders.

When this "decreasing degree of control" phenomenon is not accepted, a manager/leader typically tries to reestablish the feeling, if not the reality, of control. For example, the manager may want to be involved in everything or have all significant decisions checked before they are finally made. The results are typically negative in two respects. First, the manager is bogged down in detail and, in reality, is doing not just his or her own job but the work of other people as well. Second, the procedure can lead to lower productivity on the part of direct reports who are continually checking with their supervisor, as well as to their reduced motivation and professional development. The manager copes with these problems by working harder and harder.

The desire-for-control syndrome is a fundamental problem for many managers. It gets worse as a person moves higher and higher up in the organizational hierarchy, and there are CEOs of some major corporations who never fully make the psychological transition. There are, for example, CEOs of $100 million–plus companies who feel that they *must* know "every detail" and who expect their senior executives to do the same because this is the way they satisfy their need for control.

The second aspect of the Inner Game of Management concerns the individual's source of self-esteem. A manager needs to learn to derive a sense of self-worth from being the best manager/leader instead of being the best doer or technical professional. Because a manager's job is to make use of others to achieve organizational goals, the individual must increasingly derive personal satisfaction from the performance of direct reports. This is analogous to a basketball coach who derives self-esteem from the team's ability to win a championship rather than from his or her personal ability to play offense or defense.

Managers/leaders also need to learn how to feel comfortable having direct reports who possess greater technical knowledge or skills than they do—that is, they need to learn that they do not need to be the technical "star" of the team. It is a personal challenge to accept and feel comfortable in such a situation. However, the best managers/leaders understand that their success does not depend on their own technical ability. Instead, it depends on the abilities of those who work for and with them. Therefore, they seek to surround themselves with star performers who can do the work, while the manager focuses on being the best manager. People who are unable to effectively manage their source of self-esteem—that is, who believe that they need to be the "technical" star—tend to hire only weaker people, and this, in turn, can lead to team productivity problems, declining morale, and possibly failure.

While effective management of the need for control involves giving something up (control) and effective management of the source of self-esteem involves making a transition (from being rewarded by being a doer to being rewarded by being a manager), effective management of the need to be liked involves striking the right balance between striving to have everyone like you and doing what needs to be done to effectively fulfill the management/leadership role. Put another way, to be an effective manager/leader, an individual needs to learn how to manage the need to be liked so that it does not interfere with the ability to do the things that effective managers do—like provide constructive criticism, ask direct reports to do things that they may not want to do (but that are in the best interests of the team or organization), and surface and deal with conflict. If a manager's need to be liked is too high, direct reports may "walk all over" the manager and, in the final analysis, may neither like nor respect him or her.

As people are promoted to higher levels, managing the need to be liked becomes increasingly important. Senior managers must sometimes make decisions that are unpopular, but that are necessary for survival of the business. In addition, senior managers set the "tone" for the rest of the organization: If they are uncomfortable dealing with conflict or making difficult decisions, the rest of the organization will be uncomfortable as well.

The first step in effectively managing the Inner Game of Management dimension is to develop a very clear understanding of what is expected in the current role. Effective key result area (KRA)–based role descriptions—which include specific time utilization targets and clear definitions of each KRA—can be used as a tool in this process. In addition, the individual's supervisor should meet with him or her to review and discuss what the role description means in practice.

Next, there may be a need for the individual to develop or enhance his or her skills. For example, learning how to delegate effectively can help those with a high need to control a situation to "let go." Learning how to provide effective feedback (both positive feedback and constructive criticism) and manage conflict can help those with a high need to be liked to better manage this aspect of the Inner Game of Management. Learning how to effectively develop others (that is, train and coach) can help individuals feel rewarded by the role they play in growing their team and in their roles as managers/leaders (that is, this can be helpful in managing the source of self-esteem).

Finally, the individual can use a variety of tools to promote effective management of the Inner Game of Management. For example, an "individual management system"—consisting of reports from and meetings with direct reports—that provides information about progress against projects and goals can help promote indirect versus direct control. Using clear standards of performance or SMART goals as the basis for feedback makes the feedback less "personal" and can be an important tool for individuals that have high needs to be liked. Having time-utilization targets and working to achieve them can be rewarding and can, in turn, help individuals derive a sense of self-worth from managing versus doing.

Finally, it is important in managing the Inner Game of Management that each individual honestly assess how his or her needs might be interfering with the ability to effectively perform the management/leadership role. Then, the individual should develop an action plan for overcoming the problems identified.

The Nature of Management and Leadership Development

Broadly defined, management and leadership development is the process of building the capabilities of the organization's present and potential managers through hiring experienced managers/leaders from outside the organization, developing them from within, or doing both. Most successful organizations use both external recruitment and internal development. *Management development* focuses on helping individuals develop the capabilities to manage the day-to-day operations of the business (the company or their business unit). *Leadership development* focuses on helping individuals develop the capabilities needed to strategically manage the business, their unit, or their team. In this section, the term *leadership development* is used to refer to activities and programs that focus on helping participants develop both management and leadership capabilities.

To maximize its effectiveness, a leadership development program should focus not just on skill development but also on helping participants understand how to behave and think in their roles as managers and leaders—in brief, the program should focus on all three dimensions of management/leadership effectiveness (that were described in the last section). The overall results of a leadership development program should be measured in terms of the behavioral changes made by managers/leaders and, ultimately, in terms of increased productivity of these individuals' teams.

A variety of methods can be used to develop and enhance the capabilities of current and future managers and leaders including group-based training programs, self-study, and one-on-one coaching. Organizations can utilize external expertise (e.g., college professors, consultants) and/or can draw upon the expertise of internal professionals in the design and delivery of these programs. It is important that the programs provide participants with opportunities to apply what they are learning in practice and that this learning be reinforced "on the job." To maximize the impact of leadership development on individuals and on the organization, it needs to be viewed as an important ongoing process, versus as an event.

Leadership development is just as real an investment as the investment in plant and equipment. It is an investment in the human capital of an organization—the skills, knowledge, and experience of people.[3] It is an investment in the infrastructure of an organization, the managerial capabilities required to run the enterprise effectively and take it successfully to the next level.

Companies in a wide variety of industries and of varying sizes, such as Navistar and their International Truck dealership network, Kusto Group (a large holding company now based in Singapore), Simon Property Group, Bell-Carter Foods, Techmer PM, and Princess Cruises, have all created and successfully implemented leadership development programs. In addition, a number of nonprofits, such as Head Start, are working to develop the skills and capabilities needed to manage their entities as true businesses in order to continue their success into the future. The entrepreneurs and leaders of these organizations recognize that one of the critical factors in their ability to continue to successfully grow their companies will be the presence of sufficient managerial talent. As the owner of one firm that had grown in about seven years to more than $100 million in revenues stated, "We have plenty of product and expansion ideas, and I can borrow money for expansion from a bank, but my critical need is for people who will be capable of managing what we plan to become." Our global database of growing pains scores (see Chapter 5) consistently ranks "not enough good managers" as the number 5 growing pain. However, in China this is the number 2 growing pain, probably as a result of the lost generation of managers attributable to the so-called Cultural Revolution in that nation.

In response to this kind of need, Melvin Simon & Associates (now Simon Property Group)—one of the largest shopping center developers in the United States—established The Simon Institute as an in-house management development program for senior executives designed to provide advanced leadership and organizational development skills. Similarly, Princess Cruises engaged the Anderson School of Management at UCLA to design and deliver a leadership development program for its entire senior management team and then worked with the faculty of this program to design an in-house program for middle managers and officers on the ships. The Doctors Company—a medical malpractice insurance company—conducts a two-day leadership development program for its approximately 100 officers each year. The learnings from the program are supported throughout the year by the company's internally designed and delivered TDC University—which consists of content delivered online, through webinars, and through face-to-face training provided by internal and external resources. TDC University is offered to anyone in a management or leadership role.

On the nonprofit side, since 1991 Johnson & Johnson has sponsored (through the Price Institute for Entrepreneurial Studies) a two-week program each summer at UCLA, during which Head Start directors (the CEOs of their organizations) are provided training to enhance their organizational management skills.

Leadership development has also made its way around the globe. For example, 40 CEOs of highly successful, rapidly growing companies in China enrolled and participated in a "CEO Leadership Development Program" custom-designed and led by Eric Flamholtz at Cheung Kong Graduate School of Business in Hong Kong and Beijing during 2009. The program included a combination of group-based seminars and one-one-one coaching using our proprietary individual and organizational assessment tools.

Although leadership development can play a positive role in building management/leadership capabilities, it is not a panacea. It cannot be expected to turn people into managerial wonders overnight. The development of managers/leaders takes time. Consequently, it is useful to regard leadership development as a process of *building* managers. It requires a commitment on the part of the individual who participates in the programs, as well as on the part of the organization. In the absence of such a commitment, the investment in leadership development will not realize a return with respect to creating better leaders and, in turn, improving the company's overall effectiveness.

Functions of Management and Leadership Development

Management/leadership development has several important functions that support and promote successful organizational development. The most obvious is to enhance the skills of the organization's managers and leaders. Leadership development can also be used to (1) help define or redefine the corporate culture, (2) help promote the style of leadership that the organization desires, and (3) serve as a reward to or recognition of good managers.

Enhancing Management and Leadership Skills

The focus of most leadership development programs is on skill development. However, as discussed earlier in this chapter, the ability of individuals to *apply* these skills in practice is influenced by the concept of their role and their mindset. Leadership development programs that focus only on skills may not produce desired results, as skills are only part of the equation for creating effective managers and leaders.

The true test of whether a leadership development program has been successful is evidenced in an individual's ability to apply these skills in practice to achieve desired results. In other words, the desired outcome from any leadership development program is behavioral change.

Shaping the Corporate Culture

One of the most powerful uses of leadership development programs is to help articulate and communicate the corporate culture. Programs may communicate culture by various means, such as by using example cases to describe "the GE way" or "the HP way" and identifying "heroes" who personify corporate values and serve as models to be emulated.

The very act of implementing a leadership development program communicates that the company values personal development and that it expects the management team to work to continuously improve its skills. These are both values that can greatly assist an organization as it continues to grow and develop. A classic example is Starbucks. During the early years of its development, Eric Flamholtz was invited to coach the top three senior leaders at Starbucks. This signaled the personal commitment of the most senior leaders to their own growth. Later, others participated in similar coaching programs. Another more recent example is at Guggenheim Partners, where Scott Minerd, Global Chief Investment Officer, volunteered to participate in a pilot coaching process in his business unit, Guggenheim Partners Asset Management. Later, all of his direct reports and some of their direct reports participated in similar processes involving "360 reviews" and one-on-one coaching.

Promoting Leadership Style

Another major function of leadership development is to communicate the leadership style that is acceptable in the organization. Many companies promote a version of "contingency theory," which postulates that the appropriate style of leadership depends on the nature of the situation. (This approach is described in Chapter 12.) Other organizations promote a single style of leadership. One $500 million medical product manufacturer, for example, devotes time in their leadership development programs to helping leaders and managers at all levels understand how to lead the team decision-making process because collaboration is an important value.

Rewarding and Recognizing Present and Potential Managers and Leaders

Some organizations use participation in leadership development programs as a reward. Individuals are selected for participation in the program based on their performance or their potential. In some cases, organizations may even ask individuals to apply for admission to the program (much like college). A senior management team reviews applications, with participants being selected based on their merit. This approach has been used successfully at Techmer PM—a privately held company that provides design and technical support for colorants and various additives that modify and enhance the end use performance of plastic products that are used by automotive, home furnishing, hospital suppliers, food packaging, and many other industries.

In 2011, we partnered with John Manuck, Techmer's founder and CEO, to design a five-session leadership development program for current and future leaders. It was decided that the program would be limited to 25 participants—including the nine members (at that time) of the senior leadership team. Those interested in participating in the program needed to complete an application that asked the individual why he or she wanted to participate, what the benefits of the program would be to them, and how they saw their participation benefiting Techmer. Competition for the program was intense. People viewed it as a privilege and a reward to be selected. Over the next three years, the program was offered three more times so that all those in management/leadership positions and all those who had potential to be managers could develop the skills needed to be effective in their roles.

Management and Leadership Development at Different Organizational Levels

Effectiveness at each level in the organizational hierarchy (described in Chapter 7) requires that an individual adopt the appropriate role concept, deploy the management and leadership skills needed to be effective in that role, and manage his or her inner game in a manner consistent with that level of management. In fact, each of the levels in the organizational hierarchy can be viewed as a different stage of management/leadership career growth. This means, in turn, that the focus for management development programs and processes should differ, depending on the level of managers involved.

For all levels of management, the first step in any management/leadership development program or process is to help individuals understand, specifically, what is expected of them in their roles—which, in turn, will help them manage their role concepts. One of the most effective ways to communicate expectations of a role is by using a key result area-based role description (as described above and in Chapter 7). Sometimes, these role descriptions need to be created or revised as a part of the management/leadership development process because they simply do not exist, or if they exist, they are not effective in communicating expectations (particularly with respect to how time should be invested to maximize results). In fact, many of the organizations that we have worked with to design and deliver leadership development programs include a session on how to develop and use key result area-based role descriptions. This benefits not only the individuals in the program, but also the organization as a whole because these participants can then use what they have learned in managing their teams.

If effective role descriptions already exist, they need to be shared and discussed with the individual who occupies or who will occupy that role. This should include a specific focus on time utilization targets and a discussion of any potential barriers to fully implementing the role. The outcome of this effort is to ensure that each manager has a clear picture of performance expectations and, more importantly, understands how to invest his or her time to maximize results.

A very significant transition needs to be made as individuals move from the technical (or "doer") role into the first-line supervisor role. A significant amount of time now needs to be focused on managing (versus devoting 100% of time on doing), the individual needs to develop new and very different skills (those needed to manage other people versus do the work oneself), and the individual needs to adopt a very different mindset (learn to feel comfortable with indirect control, derive satisfaction from being a manager, and effectively manage the need to be liked). The focus of management development for these individuals will be on helping them understand the management/leadership role, on developing the first two levels of skills in the Pyramid of Management and Leadership Development, and on developing strategies to effectively manage their inner game of management.

The next level in the hierarchy—middle management—requires a further change in an individual's concept of his or her role, skills, and mindset. The key challenge at this level is to learn how to "manage managers." With respect to role concept, this means spending time working with direct reports (who are in either first-line supervisory or other middle management roles) developing and monitoring performance against overall unit and subunit plans, working with direct reports to develop their management skills, and participating with other middle managers (peers) in the development and implementation of plans for the larger unit within which the individual reports. Middle managers need to develop the skills in the first three levels of the Pyramid of Management and Leadership Development. With respect to the Inner Game of Management, they need to learn to feel comfortable working through other managers to "get the job done," and be able to constructively deal with conflict among direct reports. They also need to be willing to provide feedback and input to both their direct reports, as well as to their peers (who are also managing other managers) and to their supervisor. Finally, they need to learn to derive their sense of self-worth from being a manager of managers, versus a doer or a first-line supervisor.

Positions at the fourth level of the hierarchy (senior management) include vice president, senior vice president, and executive vice president. These are leadership positions because those at this level focus not only on day-to-day management of their teams and the business, but also on the organization's strategic development. Senior managers have a unique challenge with respect to role concept: they are a functional (or divisional) leader, as well as a leader of the organization as a whole. In a very real sense, they need to learn when to put their functional/divisional hat on and when to put their corporate hat on. Senior managers who do not fully understand or embrace this "dual" role can create problems for their senior management teams because they push for what is best for their functional area or division, sometimes at the expense of what is good for the company as a whole. In addition to the skills needed to manage day-to-day operations and their team of direct reports (that is, the skills at the first three levels in the Pyramid of Management and Leadership Development), senior managers need to develop the skills needed to promote long-term organizational development—which include strategic planning, strategic leadership, organizational development/planning, and corporate culture management). The dual role that senior managers should play needs to be supported by an Inner Game of Management that, in a sense, is also dual. In terms of need for control, senior managers need to be comfortable having very indirect control over day-to-day operations and execution of plans, while at the same time exerting a great deal of control over the development of these plans as a member of the senior leadership team. They need to derive their sense of self-esteem from not only what they do in their functional areas or divisions but also from the organization's overall performance. They also need to feel comfortable surfacing and dealing with difficult organizational issues—even if these are not in their specific area of responsibility. Finally, senior managers must learn how to deal with conflict at all levels, especially the conflict that arises as they attempt to help the organization transition from one stage of development to the next.

There are at least three dimensions to a CEO's or COO's role concept. First, these individuals need to devote time to managing the company as a whole, including helping senior management identify the need for organizational transitions, and then managing those transitions. Next, these individuals need to serve as managers of the senior management team. Finally, the CEO (in particular) and to a lesser extent the COO need to spend time as the representative of the organization to the outside world. In this context, the CEO might be serving on outside boards or participating in community events. He or she might also be dealing with the company's advisory board, board of directors, or a parent company (if the company is part of a larger organization). If the company is publicly held, there will be relations with investors. Failure to recognize this last aspect of this most senior management role can be deadly. In one $75 million organization, for example, the president had for too long ignored his responsibilities with respect to the parent that owned his company. The larger company flew him to their corporate offices with no explanation for the trip and promptly fired him for lack of performance.

The CEO and COO need to have developed and be able to effectively use all the skills in the Pyramid of Management and Leadership Development, including developing the skills needed to guide the organization through the inevitable transitions required during its life cycle. This means, in a sense, that these individuals should be the most skilled *managers and leaders* in the company.

With respect to the Inner Game of Management, those occupying this most senior level of the organization need to learn to live with very indirect control over day-to-day operations, while at the same time recognizing that they and their direct reports (senior management) need to exercise significant control over the development and implementation of the company's strategic plan. The CEO and COO need to derive their source of self-esteem from the entire company's results (even if the individuals in question came out of specific functional areas). They also need to understand that not everyone will like the changes that will inevitably need to be made as the organization grows and develops. They will need to feel comfortable making these changes and dealing with any conflict that might result from doing so.

Table 9.1 schematically summarizes the previous discussion linking the five different levels in the organizational hierarchy with the three critical dimensions of management success. This table shows that as the individual moves from one level of the organizational hierarchy to the next, the role concept must change from a player's role at the entry-level position of a technician to the role of a kind of head coach, as he or she reaches the level of CEO or COO. It also shows that the skills must move from technical skills directly related to the hands-on performance of the task at the entry level to increasingly higher levels of skills shown in the Pyramid of Management and Leadership Development as the individual moves up the organizational hierarchy. Finally, it shows that the individual must also make a psychological transition from playing the role of a technical professional or doer to that of a leader as he or she moves to the highest levels of the organizational hierarchy—that is, the individual must learn how to effectively play the Inner Game of Management. The primary function of management and leadership development is to help people make the transitions required at each level of the organizational hierarchy.

Case Studies of Management and Leadership Development

While effective implementation of leadership development programs can take a variety of forms—ranging from one-on-one coaching or self-development to comprehensive group-based training—all have specific factors in common. In this section, we use the International Truck

Table 9.1 Critical Aspects of Management Development Transitions

Five Levels of the Organizational Hierarchy	Role Concept	Skills	Inner Game of Management
5. CEO or COO	Company Leader—focused on managing the organization as a whole, being an ambassador to the external environment, and supervising senior managers.	All of the skills in the Pyramid of Management and Leadership Development, including transition management skills—the ability to identify the need for and manage individual and organizational transitions.	• Comfortable with working through the senior management team to achieve desired results. • Derives self-esteem from the success of the company as a whole and from the results of the senior management team. • Has ability to make tough decisions, to provide needed feedback to the senior management team, and to deal with conflict within and outside of the company (effectively manages the need to be liked).
4. Senior Manager	Manager of a major functional area or division and a "general manager" of the organization as a whole (that is, serves as a member of the corporate management team). Understands when to perform as a functional unit or divisional manager and when to act in the role of corporate leader.	All of the skills at the first four levels of the Pyramid of Management and Leadership Development, including organizational development skills—strategic planning, organizational planning, strategic leadership, and corporate culture management.	• Comfortable working through middle managers to achieve the goals of the functional unit or division. • Derives self-esteem from being both the head of a functional unit and a corporate leader. Understands when to play each role. • Understands the need to make decisions that are in the best interest of the company and knows that this may produce conflict within his or her functional unit or division. Knows how to manage this conflict.

(continued)

Table 9.1   (*Continued*)

Five Levels of the Organizational Hierarchy	Role Concept	Skills	Inner Game of Management
3. Middle Manager	A manager of other managers. Understands the necessity of working through other managers, not directly with technical professionals, to achieve results.	All of the skills at the core and operational management levels of the Pyramid of Management and Leadership Development, as well as organizational management skills: management development, departmental planning, organizing the team (including developing role descriptions), performance management system design and implementation, financial management, and team building.	• Comfortable letting the managers who report to him or her manage the technical professionals within their area of responsibility. Does not feel the need to directly control technical professionals' efforts. • Derives self-esteem from being a manager of other managers. • Is comfortable dealing with conflict and providing feedback to direct reports (that is, the managers that report to him or her).
2. First-Level Supervisor	Manager of technical professionals.	Core and operational management skills: delegation, time management, recruiting, training, performance appraisal, and supervision.	• Comfortable giving up direct control of results to technical professionals. Instead, works through them to achieve results. • Derives self-esteem from the results achieved by his or her team of technical professionals and from being the "best" manager.

Table 9.1   (*Continued*)

Five Levels of the Organizational Hierarchy	Role Concept	Skills	Inner Game of Management
2. First-Level Supervisor (*continued*)			• Is focused on and comfortable dealing with conflict and providing effective feedback to those who report to him or her.
1. Technician	Technical professional ("doer")—100% of the individual's time is devoted to doing work, rather than supervising it.	Technical skills directly related to hands-on performance of tasks.	• Has direct control over results. • Self-esteem is based on the person's individual efforts. • Believes that being liked will get him or her ahead (avoids conflict).

dealership leadership development program (introduced in Chapter 6) as a case study in how to design and deliver a comprehensive leadership development program. In describing this case study, we identify four key principles of effective design and delivery that can be applied in any organization and, where appropriate, provide additional examples of how to operationalize them.

Principle #1: Clearly Define the Goal or Focus of Leadership Development

While the overall goal of any leadership development effort is to "improve or enhance the organization's management/leadership capabilities," the specific focus can be very narrow or quite broad. Building upon the framework described earlier in this chapter, it is actually possible to create a specific progression of goals that leadership development efforts should meet. The first or foundational goal of any effort needs to be that managers/leaders at all levels understand their roles (role concept). This can, in fact, be the overall goal of the program. At Princess Cruises, for example, a program was designed and delivered to help all managers/leaders (both at corporate—beginning with the CEO and his direct report—as well as on the ships) clearly define and execute their roles. A primary focus of this effort was on developing and using key result area-based role descriptions as guides for behavior and as performance management tools.

Once this goal is met, the program can then focus on people, team, organizational management, and/or organizational development skills and the mindset required to execute them effectively. This will depend on the organization's current level of management/leadership capabilities, as well as the anticipated future growth and development of the enterprise (that is, what the organization will need in the future).

As explained in Chapter 6, Navistar and its dealer network recognized that as competition increased and as dealerships continued to consolidate (making them much larger and geographically dispersed businesses), there was a need to ensure that executives had the skills required to successfully take their businesses into the future. They also believed that even those who were reasonably effective could benefit from "refreshing" their skills and from interaction with their peers in other areas of the country. Another goal was that the executives who participated in the program would take what they had learned back to their dealerships and train others—thus fostering the development of the entire organization's leadership capabilities. The program, therefore, had the goal of helping participants develop the ability to use all of the skills in the Pyramid of Management and Leadership Development.

Principle #2: Design the Program to Meet Targeted Participant and Organizational Needs

Companies of all sizes invest valuable time and money conducting or sending managers and leaders to programs that have no real payoff in terms of providing tools that participants will actually use. The bottom line: To maximize the value of the investment in leadership development being made by the organization, the program needs to be designed to meet that organization's specific needs. This involves identifying the topics or skills to be focused on, selecting or developing content (including frameworks and tools) that will be used to help participants develop or enhance the identified skills, and then creating materials that will be used to support learning in the program.

The overall goal or focus of the program can help determine the nature of the skills or the topics that should be included in or focused on in the program. Sometimes, the goal of the program can result in a focus on a very specific skill set—as was true at Princess Cruises (described above). In other cases—as was true of the International Truck dealer leadership development program—the goal led to the focus on including a broad range of topics and skills.

Once topics are identified, the actual content to be included can be "off the shelf" (it is the same regardless of who it is delivered to) or can be customized or tailored to the specific audience. Our experience suggests that some customization is usually appropriate and that it helps to enhance the overall program's effectiveness. This typically occurs through using language that is familiar to the audience, developing case studies that are built upon actual incidents that might occur within their businesses, or creating workshops designed to address specific issues that are relevant for them.

Principle #3: Design the Program to Provide Participants with Frameworks, Tools, and the Opportunity for Application

There needs to be an underlying framework or model for each skill included in the program because this provides participants with something they can actually use. For example, the framework underlying our approach to management/leadership effectiveness has three factors—role concept, skills, and the Inner Game of Management—that need to be managed. We define each of the three factors, explain what they look like in practice, and also provide strategies for effectively using them.

Participants also need to be given the opportunity to apply what they are learning or have learned in practice. This can occur during the session in which the skill is being addressed or as a follow-up. As they put into action what they are learning, they also need to spend some time thinking about and/or discussing the results that they are achieving by doing so. When problems are encountered in using a specific skill, time needs to be devoted to identifying what might be done or done differently to address them. The bottom line: New skill development requires practice and this must be built into any program—whether it's one-on-one coaching, self-study only, or a comprehensive program like that delivered to the International Truck dealers.

Principle #4: Identify the Best Ways to Deliver Program Content

Program delivery methods can include reading articles or books, online (e-learning), one-on-one coaching, small informal learning sessions, and larger group-based training sessions. All of these methods, in fact, can promote and support leadership development. Selecting the best way to deliver the program depends on the amount of resources (including people's time and dollars) that the organization has and is willing to invest in the development effort and on understanding what will work for the targeted audience. For very small organizations (under $1 million in revenue), this might mean that leadership development is promoted through readings and "brown bags" during which participants can discuss how they will apply what they have learned. In $500 million plus companies, this might mean that there are semiannual educational programs for managers and leaders at all levels that are supported by e-learning and individual coaching.

Regardless of the methods used and the size of the organization, a key to any successful program is ensuring that it supports the notion that leadership development is a process versus an event. The message should be: Leadership development is not a one-time session; instead, it is a continuous process of learning and development.

Our experience suggests that there is a need to include in any leadership development program some face-to-face (in the "classroom") training experiences. This provides the opportunity for participants to fully engage with each other and with the instructor in discussing key concepts and in actively working together to complete specific activities that will contribute to their learning and development. Leadership involves managing people, and it is impossible to learn about managing people in complete isolation from others. Given the importance of this face-to-face learning in promoting leadership development, it is important to carefully select program faculty. Faculty need to be able to present and discuss concepts and tools, provide practical examples of their use in the context of the specific organization, engage participants in discussing strategies for using concepts in practice, and provide recommendations for addressing any problems being encountered.

The Leadership Development Principles in Action

The International Truck dealership leadership development program (called the Executive Dealership Leadership Program or "EDLP") was built on these four core design principles. Members of the program design team visited dealerships to learn about how they operated and to hear from executives about some of the challenges that they faced. This information was used as input to creating case studies and tools that could be used by participants to apply what they were learning in their dealerships. These visits also helped program faculty tailor their presentations and their facilitation process to this audience.

The EDLP was a six-week program that was designed to be delivered over a period of two years. There were four separate groups of approximately 25 participants, with the first group beginning the program in 2007. The size of the group was purposefully limited so as to promote sharing, discussion, and small group coaching that was provided by program faculty. Sessions were conducted approximately every four months, with each session being held in a different part of the United States—typically at a hotel or resort. This was done both to "keep things fresh," but also to vary the travel time and expense for participants. While Navistar subsidized the cost of program development and delivery, each participant was required to pay a fee to be a part of the program.

During each week of the program, there was a focus on developing or enhancing the skills needed to manage direct reports, as well as the skills needed to effectively manage and develop the business. There was also a focus on enhancing team effectiveness. Following each week of the program, participants were given specific assignments to complete that would help them apply what they had learned to enhancing their own or their organization's effectiveness. During the next week of the program, there were opportunities to share the results of applying what had been learned in practice. This included discussing any problems that were being encountered and then working with both program faculty and other participants in addressing them. An outline of the first two weeks of the program—which occurred in February and June 2007 (for the first group of participants)—is presented in Exhibit 9.1.

Included in the program were a number of tools that participants could use to assess their own and their dealership's effectiveness. These included four surveys to assess management and leadership effectiveness that were completed by the participant and a sample of his or her direct reports—one focused on assessing the extent to which the individual is effectively managing the three dimensions of management effectiveness discussed in this chapter (called the "Management Effectiveness Survey" or "MES"), another on assessing their operational leadership effectiveness (which will be discussed in Chapter 12), a third on assessing their time management effectiveness, and a fourth on assessing their effectiveness as a delegator. Each participant also completed and had a sample of his or her company's leadership team complete the Growing Pains Survey (presented in Chapter 5) and Organizational Effectiveness Survey (described in Chapter 2). Participants were provided with surveys and other tools for assessing the effectiveness of their organizational structures, meetings, performance management systems, and organizational cultures. They were also provided with tools that could be used to collect the qualitative information needed to develop their strategic plans (that is, as described in Chapter 6, to complete the environmental scan and organizational assessment). The information from each of the surveys was presented and discussed. And, most importantly, each participant was asked to develop specific action plans for addressing any issues identified.

There were several specific assignments that participants were required to complete and submit to program faculty for review. The purpose of this step was, in part, to promote the actual implementation of specific tools within the businesses represented in the program and, in a very real sense, to hold participants accountable for actually using what they were supposedly learning. More important, however, this allowed each participant to receive feedback from an expert who could help ensure that they understood and were using the tool effectively to support their own and their

Exhibit 9.1   Outline of the First Two Weeks of International's EDLP

Week 1	Week 2
Pre-Work	Pre-Work
• Complete the Growing Pains, Organizational Effectiveness, and Management Effectiveness Surveys • Bring a sample job description from your dealership.	• Complete a key result area-based role description for your own and one other position on your team. • Track your time for a minimum of two weeks. • Complete the environmental scan and organizational assessment for your dealership.
Day 1: Building Successful Organizations: The Pyramid of Organizational Development, stages of growth, and growing pains	**Day 1** (First 2 Hours): Workshop: Progress in implementing what was learned in Week 1 and feedback on role descriptions developed
Day 2: The three dimensions of management and leadership effectiveness (role concept, management and leadership skills, and the Inner Game of Management) and developing key result area-based role descriptions	**Day 1** (5 Hours): Effective time management (including analysis of time-tracking results)
Day 3 (Half-day): Small group (teams of 5) coaching on survey results and case study analysis	**Day 2**: Strategic Planning (Part II): Analyzing environmental scan and organizational assessment data, developing the business definition, strategic mission, core strategy, and objectives for your dealership
Day 4 (Morning): Financial analysis (half-day)	**Day 3** (Half-Day): Effective decision-making tools and techniques
Day 4 (Afternoon): Strategic Planning (Part I): The steps in the strategic planning process, the environmental scan, and the organizational assessment	**Day 4** (Half-Day): Capital investment decision and financial analysis
Day 5 (Half-Day): Setting SMART goals, implementation issues and solutions, and review of preparation needed for Week 2.	**Day 4** (Half-Day): Setting SMART goals for your dealership
	Day 5 (Half-Day): Effective meeting management and using meetings as a tool in developing your strategic plan; preparation for Week 3

business's success. Typically, this feedback was provided in either a one-on-one or a small group setting, where participants could ask and have their questions answered. Members of the program faculty were also available in between sessions to address participants' questions.

A specific deliverable from the first year of the program was a completed strategic plan for the business, which was submitted and then reviewed by program faculty. During the second year of the program, participants were asked to identify a specific business challenge or issue that they wanted to address and then use what they had learned in the program to address it. As a requirement for graduation, they needed to submit a report that summarized the issue that they focused on, how they used the tools presented in the program to address it, and the results that were obtained. These final projects were evaluated by members of the program faculty and by members of Navistar's Dealer Operations team (which is the unit that works most closely with the dealer network). Awards were given for the best projects. These were presented during a graduation ceremony that was at the conclusion of the sixth week of the program.

As discussed above, the EDLP was designed to help participants apply what they were learning in their business. Each session of the program was highly interactive. After a specific concept or tool was presented, participants were given the opportunity to apply it to themselves or their business (e.g., by analyzing a case study, completing an exercise, discussing it with fellow participants). Instructors encouraged participants to share their ideas and to ask questions if something was not understood. And, this was followed by specific assignments for applying what had been learned in their dealerships. Participants were also asked at the end of each day to provide feedback to instructors about what worked and what didn't work during that day. Based on what was learned from delivering the program to the first group, a few program modifications were made.

Instructors for the program were carefully chosen for both their expertise in specific topic areas, as well as for their ability to adapt their delivery to the specific audience. The primary instructors for the program came from our firm, Management Systems (including the authors of this book). During each week of the program, at the request of the dealer network and Navistar, a half- to a full day was devoted to managing the financial aspects of the business. A member of Navistar's Dealer Operations team was selected to conduct these sessions because he could not only describe important concepts and tools, but could also effectively show participants how they could be used within their dealerships—frequently using tools and information that Navistar could provide to them. Other program faculty included two principals from a marketing firm whose focus was on dealership marketing and branding; and three faculty members from UCLA's Anderson School who each presented a half-day session during the sixth week of the program (which was held on UCLA's campus).

Program Deliverables and Results

While there were individual differences in terms of the extent to which participants successfully implemented what they had learned in the program, there were several changes that nearly all participants made in their business. One of the most powerful changes—very much discussed during the sixth week of the program—was that they had developed significantly new ways of thinking about their role and their business. This was based on using the frameworks and models presented in the program—including the Pyramid of Organizational Development, the concept of SMART goals, the three dimensions of management effectiveness, and many others.

Second, all participants had developed and begun implementing a strategic plan for their business (as described in Chapter 6), and some were already seeing positive results by the time the program concluded. Third, most were approaching their leadership roles very differently—that is, they were focusing more time on managing versus doing. Fourth, many suggested that organizational and team effectiveness had been increased by developing and implementing key result area-based role descriptions—in brief, there was greater clarity about "who was responsible for what."

Finally, some participants had begun (some of them early on in the program) training others in some of the concepts that they had learned in the program. There was such a demand, in fact, for assistance in "taking these concepts to the next level of leadership" that a two-week program focused on departmental leadership was designed and delivered to direct reports of EDLP participants by the authors, who were the lead faculty for the EDLP.

Some participants, like Don DeVivo, President of DATTCO (an IC Bus dealer that also provides school bus, motor coach, and other transportation solutions), implemented formal management development programs within their dealerships for their own team of managers and leaders. Don described this process by saying, "It was important to get key staff to buy into the process, and we drove it down to the (front line) managers." This was accomplished by having all managers and leaders on his team participate in a formal leadership development program that was conducted by one of the faculty members from the EDLP. Leadership development has become a process within DATTCO that is focused on in the meetings that Don has with his management team "two to three times a year." He says that this helps keep "leadership development alive." He goes on to say, "The whole process that EDLP put in place is embedded in our company—particularly the SMART Goal setting process." Don also implemented and has continued to use the strategic planning process (described in Chapter 6) that he was introduced to as a part of the EDLP. He says, "There was a huge impact [on our business]—our whole management process was task-driven, not strategic. As we were growing, we were able to manage the growth." And, the results speak for themselves: Over the six years following his participation in the EDLP, Don's business grew significantly in terms of both revenue (up 50%) and profit (up 40%).

Management and Leadership Development at Different Stages of Growth

This section examines the different needs for management and leadership development that companies have at each stage of organizational growth.

Stage I

At the earliest stage of growth, most organizations do not have formal management development programs for their people. Management development takes place, if at all, through on-the-job training or through self-learning (e.g., reading a book, taking a course). While establishing an in-house training program is usually prohibitive and not really needed at this point, the company's founder (who might be, at this stage, the only "manager") might be devoting some of his or her time to self-directed learning.

Stage I is a good time for the entrepreneur (and other members of the leadership team, if they exist) to begin establishing the organization's cultural attitude toward leadership development. For example, the leadership team might devote one to two hours each quarter to a specific leadership skill. This might involve reading an article or book and then discussing its application in practice within their business. The founder and other members of the leadership team might also be using the benefits of membership in membership-based organizations (like the National Association of Women Business Owners) to help enhance their leadership skills. Most significantly, the founding entrepreneur can serve as a role model and can stress, through words and action, that leadership development is important to the organization's long-term success.

Stage II

During the early part of Stage II, an organization can continue the same approach to leadership development that was recommended for Stage I. However, there are exceptions. Dr. Tim Bain, who was discussed in Chapter 5, engaged the authors to coach him in managing and scaling up his firm. Specifically, Dr. Bain was coached in the understanding of growing pains and their risks, the process of strategic planning, the process of performance management, and the process of culture management. This coaching provided the managerial competencies for him to scale his company successfully, as described in Chapter 5.

By the time it reaches approximately $5 million in annual revenues, a company is probably ready for and can afford some form of more formal management and leadership development as well. Investment in acquiring these capabilities provides both an "insurance policy" against organizational failure as well as the tools for successful development of a business.

The principal goal for a Stage II company is to ensure that all those in management and leadership roles (including the CEO) understand their roles, have developed and can effectively deploy the core management skills, and have adopted a mindset consistent with that of an effective leader. In addition, members of senior leadership should be working to build the skills needed to effectively fulfill their roles as senior leaders—including the skills needed to implement basic strategic plans and performance management systems.

The program for helping managers/leaders develop these skills can take many forms. At a minimum, it needs to include a specific focus on clearly defining roles (e.g., using a key result area-based approach) and on providing managers with frameworks and tools to effectively delegate, manage their time, make decisions, maximize their interpersonal effectiveness as managers/leaders, and effectively influence people to achieve goals (that is, develop their operational leadership skills). Content can be delivered using any of the methods described above, but the organization should be moving toward creating its own program that can be used on a continuing basis to develop its current and future managers. The program should include ample opportunities for managers and leaders at all levels to discuss their progress and work together to solve problems. Another advantage of using a team-based approach to leadership development is that participants will, as a result of their efforts to apply what they are learning, uncover organizational issues that need to be addressed, which, in turn, can help promote long-term organizational success.

Stage III

By the time an organization has reached Stage III, it should be well on the way to establishing an in-house program of leadership development. At this stage, the key organizational development issue is professionalization, which, in turn, means implementing effective management systems (and, this will involve helping those in senior management roles develop the skills at the fourth level in the Pyramid of Management and Leadership Development—including strategic planning, organizational development, and strategic leadership).

At this stage, there will typically be multiple levels of management and leadership, and those at each level need to understand, embrace, and be able to execute their unique roles.

The founder/entrepreneur (if still present within the organization) or the CEO needs to feel comfortable having very indirect control over results—working through a team of senior managers. The entrepreneur or CEO must learn to trust his or her direct reports to perform their roles, and to manage through their direct reports (other managers) to accomplish organizational goals. This, in turn, means that these people will have to think like entrepreneurs or businesspeople rather than simply as functional specialists.

Assuming that the organization has already laid the foundation for management development in Stage II by focusing upon core management and possibly operational management skills, a major goal for a Stage III company will be to reinforce and continue to build these basic skills. Such skills are not simply learned once and then fully retained. People get into and out of habits, and skills must be reinforced. For example, one function of the five-year driver's license renewal test is simply to motivate people to read the test booklet again and remind themselves of what they ought to be doing. Although most people probably consider it a nuisance to go through the test, it is likely to make them remember long-forgotten parts of the rules of the road. Doing so reinforces the way they ought to be driving.

Reinforcing basic skills can involve designing and implementing new programs —perhaps consisting of workshops, self-directed learning, or coaching. Continuing to build management and leadership skills will involve delivering existing programs to new members of the leadership team and to those who might occupy management and leadership roles in the future; and developing new programs that focus on helping participants develop "new" skills.

During Stage III, the frameworks, tools, and language of leadership development being used by the company in its leadership development programs should become "a part of the way that we do things." All managers and leaders should have the same understanding of what it means to be effective in the performance of each skill in their business. For example, when someone says, "management effectiveness," all members of the leadership team think, "role concept, skills, and the Inner Game of Management." And, more importantly, all members of management and leadership understand how to assess effectiveness against these three factors and can identify possible steps to enhance effectiveness.

During Stage III, the organization needs to implement programs for building all of the skills in the Pyramid of Management and Leadership Development. There can be different programs for each level of management and leadership (which focus on the specific skills needed to effectively execute their roles), or all managers and leaders can participate in the same or a similar program. The four principles for creating effective leadership development programs should be used when developing these programs. At this stage, the CEO and other members of senior leadership might also be involved in individual one-on-one coaching programs that can help them both continue to develop the skills needed to perform their roles and address specific organizational development issues.

Stage IV

By the time an organization reaches Stage IV, leadership development should be a way of life—for both the organization and for its managers and leaders at all levels. There should be very specific programs or processes in place to prepare future managers for their roles and to help individuals develop the capabilities needed to assume the next level of management or leadership. These processes might include participating in specific outside training, in-house group training, self-study, and/or one-on-one coaching. There should also be processes in place to recruit and select, as appropriate, individuals with the skills needed to fulfill specific roles when there are no internal candidates available. Personal or leadership development might also be included as a specific area of focus in the individual performance management process.

Wise senior executives planning for the successful long-term development of their enterprises will focus on identifying what is needed to build the capabilities of their human assets and then will be willing to make the needed investment to do so. They will realize that their companies are competing not merely in products and technology but in people as well.

A Stage IV company might have its own human resources (or human resources and organizational development) department and staff who will take a leadership role in identifying the company's leadership development needs and in securing resources to meet these needs. In some cases, leadership development programs will be designed and delivered by internal resources. In other cases, the organization will draw upon the expertise of either outside university educators or consultants to help design and deliver management development services.

A specific focus of leadership development in Stage IV should be culture management, as this is the stage at which this key building block of success becomes most critical. As will be described in Chapter 10, leaders at all levels need to understand the important role that they play in the culture management process, and they need to develop the ability to use specific culture management tools to help culture become a strategic asset.

A Stage IV organization is large and complex. To continue its success into the future, managers and leaders at all levels need to have the skills to manage both day-to-day operations and the company's longer-term development. In brief, managers and leaders of a Stage IV company need to adopt a holistic perspective. They need to think in terms of the Pyramid of Organizational Development both for the care and feeding of the existing enterprise and for the development of new entrepreneurial ventures that will help the company move into Stage V.

Stage V

A company in Stage V needs to continue providing and refining, as needed, leadership development programs and processes that help individuals at all levels of management/leadership develop the skills needed to effectively execute their roles. In addition, a company at this stage needs to have specific programs and processes in place to build true general management capabilities.

A Stage V company is in the process of creating or has already created divisions—with each division operating in a very real sense as a business within a business. The leaders of each division—general managers, divisional presidents, and so on—need to have the skills and capabilities to manage their own businesses, but to do so in the context of a larger enterprise. Senior and middle managers within the division also need to understand how to effectively lead within a divisional structure.

As a company divisionalizes, it needs to clearly define the role of corporate and the role of each division (as described in Chapter 7). This, in turn, will influence the type of leadership development that is required to support effective implementation of the structure and the organization's overall long-term success. For example, in some divisionalized structures, there are corporate functions (e.g., legal, human resources, sales/marketing) that are responsible for establishing policy and for identifying best practices. In these structures, the senior leaders who represent these functions within the divisions need to develop the capabilities to work effectively with their divisional CEO, while at the same time working with and representing the function within their division. In all divisional structures, senior leaders of the division and of the holding company need to develop the skills needed to work effectively with each other.

Stage VI

The leadership and management development programs created in Stage V need to continue into Stage VI—that is, there needs to be a continued focus on developing general management capabilities and the capabilities needed to work within a divisionalized structure. There also needs to be a focus on sharing and using best practices across the divisions. Even when it is a holding company—where each division provides very different products or services, or operates in very different markets, or both—the organization can benefit greatly from identifying the best management and leadership development programs and processes and then utilizing them in all divisions.

In addition, if the organization has diversified or plans to diversify through mergers or acquisitions, there needs to be a focus on helping managers and leaders at all levels maximize the advantages and minimize the limitations that can result from combining two (or more) different enterprises. For senior executives, these skills include how to conduct or oversee the due diligence process, how to effectively integrate operational and management systems, and how to maintain a strong, positive culture as two (or more) companies are combined into a single entity (in a merger) or as they are acquired under a holding company structure.

Stage VII

An organization facing revitalization does not have the time or the resources to devote to management and leadership development programs because its overarching mission is to survive. Unfortunately, if company leaders and managers do not have the skills needed to effectively perform their roles at this stage, their company is probably doomed to fail. However, if there is a turnaround or revitalization team in place, it is possible for selected managers to get on-the-job experience in this process as it actually unfolds. A revitalization effort is of the level of risk and complexity of open heart surgery. Neither open heart surgery nor a revitalization process should be done by inexperienced amateurs. Unless the process is led by highly skilled and experienced professionals, the "patient" is likely not to survive.

Investment in Leadership Development

Leadership development is an *investment* that needs to be made to build a sustainably successful organization. The owner of an expensive automobile, such as a Mercedes, for example, would or should be prepared to spend 5% of the car's value on maintenance to protect the asset. Managers are frequently far more expensive than cars and other machines, yet companies fail to invest in management development, either as preventive maintenance to avoid managerial obsolescence or to enhance managers' skills and, in turn, increase the human assets' value.

Although no precise guidelines can be given, we recommend that a company invest between 5 and 10% of its annual payroll in leadership development. If an organization is investing less than 5%, it may experience productivity problems or high personnel replacement costs as either qualified technical professionals leave because their manager is ineffective, or as managers are asked to leave because they are deemed ineffective.

Some company leaders may feel that these are costly investments, and they are, but the alternative is to incur the opportunity cost of lost profit—a loss frequently caused by ineffective management. For example, one medium-sized consumer products manufacturing company that failed to invest $60,000 in a management development program for all its top managers found it cost the firm $1,500,000 in losses from ineffective management by one member of the group.

Summary

This chapter examines the role of management and leadership development in promoting long-term organizational success. We have provided a three-dimensional framework for understanding and assessing management and leadership effectiveness and have shown how it can be applied and used in practice. We have also identified four principles for designing and implementing effective management and leadership development programs and have illustrated these principles in practice, using a case study of a comprehensive leadership development program.

As we have seen, an organization does not have to be the size of GE or IBM to invest in and benefit from management and leadership development. It must, however, make a serious commitment to management and leadership development at a level appropriate for its stage of growth.

Notes

1. See, for example, John P. Kotter, "What Leaders Really Do," *Harvard Business Review*, May–June 1990.
2. See Eric Flamholtz and Yvonne Randle, *The Inner Game of Management* (New York: AMA-COM, 1987).
3. See Eric Flamholtz, *Human Resource Accounting*, 3rd ed. (New York: Kluwer Academic Publishers, 1999).

10

Corporate Culture Management

This chapter focuses on the nature and tools for managing corporate culture to build sustainably successful organizations®. We will discuss the nature of corporate culture, and then describe the key elements of corporate culture and how culture is manifested in organizations. Next, we provide a description of how culture changes and how this change process can be managed to maintain an organization's effectiveness as it grows over time. We also provide case examples of the steps that several corporations took to begin effectively managing their corporate cultures. In the final section of this chapter, we describe the nature of corporate culture at different stages of growth.

Although the concept of corporate culture is abstract and may seem somewhat elusive, it is nonetheless real and can have a decisive impact on organizational success and profitability. In fact we believe, as we shall explain in this chapter, that corporate culture is the ultimate source of strategic advantage for an organization.

Every organization, from a small entrepreneurship to a multibillion-dollar firm, has a corporate culture, whether it knows it or not. The corporate culture is much like a personality, in that it changes over time as a result of an organization's own development or changes in the environment. As we stated in Chapter 6, for example, strategic planning can shape the culture through providing a vision. However, if the organization's performance management process (control system) does not reward individuals for pursuing that vision, individuals will receive conflicting messages about their organization's culture and will be left to select their own meaning.

The basic issue is that unless the cultural change process is adequately managed, an organization can find itself with a culture that does not support the goals it wants to or needs to achieve.

The Nature of Corporate Culture

As previously defined, *corporate culture* consists of a company's values, beliefs, and norms. *Values* are what an organization considers most important with respect to its operations, its employees, and its customers—the things an organization holds most dear, strives for, and wants to protect at all costs. *Beliefs* are assumptions that individuals hold about themselves, their customers, and their organization. *Norms* prescribe how people ought to behave; they translate values into day-to-day behavior. The corporate culture is, in essence, a guide to behavior, as well as a mechanism for creating expectations for the future with respect to rewards and action.

Culture Is the Ultimate Strategic Asset

We believe that corporate culture is the ultimate strategic asset of an organization. This means that it is the ultimate source of sustainable competitive advantage, because (as discussed further below) it cannot be copied. This view of culture as not just important but as the ultimate strategic asset is shared by several leaders of highly successful companies, including Ren Zhengfei of Huawei, and Howard Schultz and Howard Behar of Starbucks.

Ren Zhengfei, founder and deputy chairman of the board of Huawei Technologies Co. Ltd ("Huawei") has stated that "Culture is the 'Nuclear bomb, of Huawei."[1] Huawei is a world-class technology company headquartered in Shenzhen, China. What does it mean that "Culture is the 'nuclear bomb' of Huawei"? The nuclear bomb is the ultimate weapon in any war. Huawei views itself as being in a battle or war with all of its competitors. It is a continuous battle for survival. What Ren Zhenfei is saying is that in the battle for corporate survival, the ultimate weapon is corporate culture.

Similarly, Howard Schultz has stated that when people ask him what the secret is to Starbucks' extraordinary success, he tells them that it is the organization's people that make the real difference. Howard Behar, who was the head of retail at Starbucks as well as president of Starbucks International, has written a book whose title states, *It's Not About the Coffee*! As the title suggests, Starbucks' success is not attributable to its fine coffee, per se, because coffee is, of course, a commodity; rather, its success is attributable to the leadership style and culture of the company, which impact the performance of its people.

Key Dimensions of Corporate Culture

Many organizations now recognize that corporate culture is important to their success. As a result, they typically articulate what they think their culture is, or ought to be, in some type of culture or values statement. For example, a corporate values statement might say: "We value speed, flexibility, creativity, employee engagement, honesty and integrity. We abhor bureaucracy and politics." On the surface, these values appear to be reasonable; but these statements do not always focus upon all of the corporate culture variables that promote success.

Specifically, our published empirical research has identified five key dimensions (or culture variables), which directly impact an organization's success, as measured in "bottom line" financial performance.[2] These areas are (1) customer-client orientation, (2) orientation toward employees, (3) standards of performance and accountability, (4) commitment to innovation and change, and (5) what we term "process orientation."

Customer-Client Orientation

The importance attached to how the company views its customers or clients, as well as the assumptions employees hold about the nature of their customers and clients, can have a profound impact on how the company operates and thus on its success.

Some companies have been very effective at developing and communicating to their employees their values with respect to customers. Employees at Disneyland, for example, refer to their customers as guests. The word was chosen carefully to send a message to Disneyland employees about the company's customer orientation. It is intended to have an impact on the way employees interact with customers; in fact, employees are trained to make customers feel at home. The goal is customer satisfaction, which Disney hopes will encourage them to return to the park in the future.

Southwest Airlines is another company that has, throughout its history, effectively managed its culture with respect to treatment of customers. The culture promotes having fun and was built on "Luv" (a play on the name of the airfield where the company was born). Customers who travel this airline, which offers no-frills, low-cost travel, experience the caring firsthand, from check-in to baggage claim. Flight attendants have been known to play games in flight (like seeing who has the most pennies) and to sing songs. Since 1988, the company has won the airline industry's *monthly* highest customer satisfaction award (the Triple Crown) over 30 times and has been on the list of *Fortune*'s World's Most Admired Companies more than 20 times.

People (Employee) Orientation

The second critical cultural area is the view people hold about themselves and others within the organization itself. Again, as was true with customer orientation, there are two components to this dimension: (1) how people are viewed with respect to their roles within the business and (2) how important people feel. Some companies devote a great deal of effort to satisfying employee needs and making them feel valued. At the extreme, these organizations develop a strong competitive team spirit that is directed at other companies and even at departments within the same company. At the other end of the spectrum are those companies in which employees are viewed as replaceable. Somewhere in between are companies where some employees are considered valuable assets (by themselves and everyone else) but where other employees are considered second-class citizens.

Southwest Airlines' culture also has a tremendous impact on its employees. While other airlines may offer higher salaries, employees remain with Southwest because of the emphasis that the firm places on valuing its employees who are, in fact, referred to as internal customers. This value is attributable to the company's former CEO, Herb Kelleher, who was famous for his antics and desire to promote fun. The company has numerous programs, including its Star of the Month (recipients have their profiles posted on the company's website) and its annual awards banquet, held to recognize the contributions that employees make to the company's success.

Similarly, the culture at Starbucks places an extremely high value on the treatment of people, who are referred to as "partners." Starbucks uses a variety of tools to manage its culture, including a formal statement of core values, as can be seen on their corporate web site: www.Starbucks.com.

Medium-sized firms like Bell-Carter Foods have also successfully managed this important aspect of culture. Bell-Carter Foods is a family business that has been in operation for over 100 years.

A significant focus of its business is on canning and distributing ripe table olives through retailers throughout the United States. In fact, the company is the largest table-olive producer in the United States and the second largest in the world. Tim and Jud Carter (the third-generation leaders of the family business) were extremely committed to creating and maintaining an environment in which employees felt valued and in which people could have fun. Jud, Tim, and their entire senior management team traditionally operated with open-door policies, which allowed any employee to bring an issue to them. At their corporate offices, Tim held monthly all-employee meetings during which any employee could discuss any issue they would like with him or other members of the senior management team. Finally, the company has traditionally made a practice of celebrating senior executives' birthdays in unusual ways. At their plant in Corning, California, Jud's birthdays were annual events in which employees tried to outdo the previous year's event. Over the years, these parties included everything from songs written especially for the occasion to having everyone "dress like Jud" (in khaki pants and a blue work shirt, complete with a red wig to represent his red hair). All these events and ways of operating helped to communicate the value that the company placed on its people. The company's people-oriented culture continues under the fourth generation of family leadership of CEO Tim T. Carter, Tim's son.

While it is easy to identify firms like Starbucks, Southwest, and Bell-Carter where people are valued, it is equally as easy to identify organizations that have problems with their orientation toward employees, because these organizations usually experience very high turnover. Conversely, organizations that are successful at making employees feel valued (by whatever means) tend to experience relatively low turnover. (We do not wish to imply that employee orientation is the *only* cause of turnover, but it is often a significant one.) In one $100 million company, for example, employees expressed much fear about the future and felt that anyone below the senior management level was a second-class citizen. Turnover was rampant, not only among the lower levels of the company but also among members of the executive team.

Performance Standards/Accountability

The next key dimension is a compound of two elements: performance standards and accountability. Performance standards include things like what and how much employees are held accountable for, the level of quality expected in products, and the expected level of customer satisfaction. Accountability refers to the process of holding people responsible or accountable for what they do or fail to do in an enterprise.

Performance standards and accountability are (or at least ought to be) two sides of a single coin. However, in practice many organizations can have explicit performance standards but still not hold people accountable.

In some companies, employees believe that they are held accountable only for coming to work on time. In others, employees are held accountable for achieving goals that will help the organization meet its mission. Sometimes the definition of *accountability* can become distorted, as was the case in one $35 million high-tech manufacturing company that had traditionally placed a high value on "commitment." Over time, employees came to believe that commitment meant spending nine to ten hours a day at work, regardless of what they were doing during that time period. The norm was to come to work early and to never leave the office prior to 5:00 (if possible, staying until 5:30) as a way of showing commitment. Although the company had many employees "working," they were having difficulty meeting their goals because employees were focused on an inappropriate standard of performance.

At other companies, like Smartmatic (a Venezuelan company), Johnson & Johnson, and GE, people are held accountable, not only for achieving goals but also for behaving in ways consistent with the company's values.[3] Similarly, we have assisted several of our clients in developing measures of culture in order to hold people accountable for adherence to key corporate values as part of their performance management systems.

Commitment to Innovation and Change

The fourth major cultural element is how a company views and reacts to innovation and change. Growing organizations that embrace change as a way of life tend to experience less difficulty in making the required transitions that have been discussed throughout this book. Those in which change is viewed as threatening tend to experience significant problems. In one $100 million organization, for example, the owner-entrepreneur nominally supported the changes needed to take his company into the future. However, when confronted with the need to make changes in his company's planning process, product line, structure (including delegating more decision-making responsibility to members of his management team), and corporate culture, he resisted. Instead of changing, he held on to the old ways of doing things until his business began to lose market share. When this occurred, he blamed his senior management team and replaced them for the second time in as many years.

Process Orientation

The final dimension of culture is what we have termed "process orientation." Some organizations believe in business processes and others are process averse. Growing organizations need a variety of processes as part of their infrastructure in order to scale and continue to grow in a healthy manner. These processes include communication processes, decision-making processes, planning processes, and many others.

Some organizations are anti-process because they equate process with bureaucracy. However, processes are required to help a company avoid choking on its own growth.

There are many examples of how processes contributed to organizational success. For example, the key to the success of Ford Motor Company in the early years of the twentieth century was not the car, per se; it was the assembly line created by Henry Ford. Similarly, the success of Dell Computer was not a proprietary computer technology; it was attributable to the process of making computers to order online and bypassing the traditional "middleman" in distribution. Finally, the growth of Walmart into the dominant retailer is attributable to its logistics and information systems, not to its products, which are identical to those sold by Kmart!

The Impact of Corporate Culture on Organizational Success and Financial Performance

Culture has a critical impact on overall organizational success. As Howard Schultz, founder and chairman of Starbucks Coffee Company has stated: "When people ask me the reason for Starbucks' success, I tell them not what they expect to hear but what I really believe. People are the key to Starbucks' success."[4] The company's culture is based on the notion that the way Starbucks treats its people affects the way its employees (called "partners") treat its customers, and, in turn, its financial performance.

Culture influences every aspect of the Pyramid of Organizational Development, and every level of the pyramid has an impact on culture. This is illustrated by the value one $500 million manufacturing firm placed on relationships. One reason this business had grown large and become so successful was that the company had developed and maintained good relationships with its customers. As the organization grew, this became not only an important part of its culture with respect to customers but also with respect to its employees. Rewards and, in fact, the organizational structure, reflected the value placed on forming effective relationships. On the company's organization charts, there seemed to be no consistent use of the titles given to positions at each level of the organization. Reporting to the president were vice presidents, executive vice presidents, and senior vice presidents. While the responsibilities of these positions did not vary a great deal, the titles were different. So what explained the variation in titles? In talking with people at the company, it appeared that the individuals at any level who had developed the best relationships with those at the next level were rewarded with the most desirable titles. The cultural belief was, "Success depends on developing good relationships," and the structure reflected this.

In this example, the structure developed out of the culture, but in other cases the culture is influenced by the structure. In another case, the organization's culture nominally promoted "being flexible." At the same time, the culture supported a belief that senior management could use any resource needed to accomplish its goals. As a result, the business did not have a formal organizational chart or job descriptions, even though its revenues exceeded $100 million. (It should also be noted that these are both examples of ineffective structure design, as discussed in Chapter 7.) As suggested by this example, because culture supports and is supported by all levels of the Pyramid of Organizational Development, an organization cannot just simply decide to change its corporate culture without making changes in its operations and structure.

Organizations that focus on culture and ignore these other areas are wasting their resources. If, for example, a business decides it is going to make the transition to a culture that rewards planning but fails to design and implement a strategic planning system in which individuals are rewarded for their performance, the culture will remain unchanged.

Corporate culture not only affects all levels of the Pyramid of Organizational Development, it also has a direct impact on financial performance. Our empirical research has found that there is a statistically significant relationship between the extent to which corporate culture is embraced (that is, the extent to which employees "live and breathe" it) in a company's business units and the overall financial performance of those units, as measured in terms of "EBIT" (earnings before interest and taxes).

This research supports the notion that corporate culture is a critical factor in an organization's success. It shows that there is a direct relationship between corporate culture and the bottom line of organizational performance.

Strong and Weak Cultures

The notion of strong and weak cultures is very important for organizational success. Some companies have strong and others have weak cultures.

A *strong culture* is one where people have a very clear sense of what the culture is. They understand it and can explain what it is. A strong culture can be positive or negative. Examples of companies with strong cultures include Amgen, Disney, Huawei (China), Starbucks, and all companies owned by Johnson & Johnson (such as Neutrogena and LifeScan), and General Motors.

A *weak culture* is one where people do not have a very clear sense of what the culture is. They do not understand it and cannot explain it. At one company, the two brothers who served as its most senior executives did not and could not agree about what the culture should be. For example, one brother's behavior suggested that being reactive and constantly changing course was important; the other brother's behavior (communicated, in part, by working with the team to develop a formal strategic plan) suggested that being proactive and planning for changes was important. Needless to say, managers who reported to them (and, in fact, employees throughout the company) were not sure what the company really valued and how the company wanted them to operate in their roles.

Functional and Dysfunctional Cultures

There are not only strong and weak cultures but also functional and dysfunctional cultures. A *functional culture* is one that has a positive impact on organizational performance and success. A *dysfunctional culture* is one that has a negative impact on organizational performance. Many companies have both functional and dysfunctional aspects in their culture.

Some examples of companies with positive or functional cultures include Amgen, Bell-Carter Foods, Huawei, Southwest Airlines, and Starbucks. At Southwest, for example, the company's focus on customer service—both external and internal—greatly contributes to its continued success.

Just as there are many examples of how a functional culture can be an asset, there are also many examples of how a dysfunctional culture can be a barrier to sustainable success. Sometimes a culture that has been functional for a long time can become dysfunctional. Examples of how formerly functional cultures became dysfunctional and impacted performance negatively include AIG, American Express, IBM, and Toyota.[5]

Perhaps the ultimate example of how a formerly functional culture became dysfunctional is General Motors (GM). GM once ruled the world of automobiles and was an icon of U.S. industrial strength. Over a period of decades, GM fell from grace. Even in the "new" GM, the CEO, Mary Barra, has publicly cited the dysfunctional aspect of the GM culture.[6] Specifically, Barra cited the so-called "GM nod" and "the GM salute" as symbolic of its dysfunctional culture. The GM nod, as described by Barra, refers to a practice of GM managers sitting in a room, nodding in agreement at steps that need to be taken, then leaving the room and doing nothing. The GM salute refers to the practice of employees keeping their arms folded and pointing outward, as if to say that responsibility lay with others, not with themselves.

Real versus Nominal Corporate Culture

Many organizations develop culture or philosophy statements that articulate their values, beliefs, and norms. These may be displayed on walls or in employee handbooks, and if an employee is asked about his or her company's culture, these sheets of paper appear. Examples of culture statements include Starbucks' "Six Guiding Principles," Johnson & Johnson's "Credo," and Southwest Airlines' "Mission Statement." Unfortunately for many companies, the information printed on these pieces of paper is, at best, a slight exaggeration of the company's real culture and, at worst, a wish list of what the company would like to be but is not. In the case of U.S. automobile companies for decades, the nominal culture was, "We produce the best automobiles in the world," while the real culture was, "If you can get it to drive out the door, we can sell it." The real culture ultimately led to the irreversible entry of Japanese automobile manufacturers into the U.S. market.

Similarly, after months of working to prepare a formal statement of its values, a medical products firm proudly unveiled it. When employees walked by the posters that displayed these values, it was all they could do to keep from laughing. While the posters stated that work-life balance for employees was one of the company's most important values, managers (and other employees) felt compelled to work on holidays and weekends as a way of showing their commitment to the company. Many managers had not taken a vacation in more than two years. The real value was, "If you want to be valued here, you need to do whatever it takes, even if it means giving up your personal life."

We refer to the statements presented on paper as the *nominal culture* and the culture that people actually operate under as the *real culture*. The difference between the nominal and the real cultures of a rapidly growing Stage III high-technology business is illustrated in Table 10.1.

Table 10.1   Nominal versus Real Culture: An Example

Nominal Organizational Culture

1. Quality products
2. Ethical dealings with vendors
3. High quality of working life for the employee

Real Organizational Culture

1. The firm is sales-oriented rather than profit-oriented.
2. Current standards of performance seem to be unrealistic.
3. The company appears overly optimistic about its capabilities.
4. There is a lack of accountability.
5. Personnel tend to avoid conflict.

The nominal culture suggests that this publicly held technology enterprise has some very positive values and beliefs that support its future growth and success. The problem is, however, that people's behavior is influenced by the real culture. The real culture led people to hide product-related problems rather than solve them (that is, to avoid conflict and responsibility), to blame other people when things went wrong, and to focus their attention on the bottom line because of the mistaken assumption that "as long as the product is selling, we must be making money."

At this company, the systems and structure were not in place to support what the leadership wanted its culture to be—in other words, the culture was not being effectively managed—and the result was that this company could not effectively influence people's behavior to achieve its goals. Among other things, it did not have a well-defined system to reward people for doing what it needed them to do, and no quality-control system was in place. Further, quality-control personnel were viewed as unneeded interruptions rather than as important members of the production team.

As this example illustrates, the real culture does not have to be the antithesis of the nominal culture; rather, it can merely bear no relationship to it. The real culture of any organization can be identified by examining a variety of factors. These manifestations of culture are discussed in the next section.

Manifestations of Corporate Culture

An organization's culture is manifested in a variety of ways. Aside from people's behavior, an organization's culture is reflected in (1) the language people use, (2) the things that act as symbols and the meaning attached to them, (3) the rituals performed within the company, (4) the rewards provided by the company, as well as the recipients of these rewards (known as "heroes"). Each of these is discussed next.

Language
The words and phrases people use to talk about themselves, events, or the organization are manifestations of the organization's culture. As noted earlier, Starbucks refers to employees as partners. This is intended to suggest an ownership relationship among employees. Other companies refer to employees as associates (Walmart), team members (Infogix), and cast members (Disney). This language is intended to have a different connotation than viewing people as employees or staff. For example, the use of the term *cast members* at Disneyland and Disney World is intended to communicate to all employees, even the maintenance people, that they are like actors playing their defined roles in a live stage production.

In many organizations, acronyms are used to share and discuss ideas. We have frequently experienced this phenomenon. Although the message behind using acronyms might seem to be that the organization is striving for efficiency and using the minimal amount of time to communicate with one another, a more subtle message is that the firm is creating a language all its own that only insiders will understand.

Culture is also manifested in the language used to talk about the organization itself. With respect to organizational development, perhaps the most feared word is *bureaucracy*. The meaning attached to this word for many employees of entrepreneurships is that of a slow-moving dinosaur that seldom gets anything accomplished. The problem is that "bureaucracy" often becomes equated with "professionalized," even though the latter is a state to be desired and an organizational form that is necessary for continued success. Managing language during the transition process, then, can be critical.

Language can also be a powerful means of communicating a change in culture. For example, employees of one Stage IV consumer products company were expected to behave professionally in every aspect of the firm's operations. People dressed very formally and spoke of and to each other very formally (for example, executives were referred to as Mr. or Ms.). Employees were very businesslike in everything that was done (even though the product produced and sold by this company had the image in its marketplace of being very friendly and fun). Executives dressed in suits and even in off-site meetings had a difficult time removing their jackets.

The old executive team was eventually replaced by a new, younger team. This team set about changing the firm's culture to one that better reflected the type of product it produced. Casual dress and casual language became a part of everyday life at the firm. Everyone from the president to front-line employees was now referred to by their first names. The president of this company was known to use such phrases as "That's a Big Wow"—something that would never had been used by the former regime. The language, then, reflected a change to a more casual working environment and a focus on the fun that had become somewhat de-emphasized by the former group of executives.

Symbols

Things within an organization to which special meaning are attached are known as *symbols*. Depending on the organization, symbols may include furniture, awards, and dress (uniform). In many companies, the type of furniture or office an individual has symbolizes his or her value to an organization. In one $100 million manufacturing business, the type of telephone people had was a significant symbol of status. One individual, who occupied an open cubicle, lobbied very strongly for a speakerphone because this symbolized a higher status than the traditional phone that had been provided. Although a speakerphone was somewhat impractical in an open environment, the meaning attached to the phone was so strong that its practicality was secondary in this individual's mind.

If managed properly, symbols can be used to motivate people to achieve the organization's goals. For example, in one $100 million manufacturing company, the field sales operations had created a traveling coffee cup that was given to a sales rep who had done something beyond the call of duty. The individual receiving the coffee cup also received a letter from the divisional manager specifying why the cup was being awarded. The recipient was permitted to keep the cup for a month, and then it was returned to the manager to await being awarded again. A coffee cup seems like something fairly trivial, but at this company it had acquired a great deal of importance. It symbolized that the individual receiving it had provided a valuable contribution to the company.

Rituals

Special events and traditional ways of doing things are what we refer to as rituals in companies. Examples of corporate rituals include retirement parties, company picnics, afternoon beer busts, and annual meetings. Generally, rituals are intended to communicate the values and beliefs related to a company's people orientation.

Many years ago, we witnessed the retirement ritual at a manufacturing business. We were in a meeting with the president, and he informed us that we would have to break in about 10 minutes because he needed to be at an employee meeting in the company's cafeteria. He explained that one of the company's employees was retiring. When we arrived in the cafeteria, it was already filled with employees sitting and standing along the walls. The retiree was seated at one of the tables nearest the front; the table was otherwise empty. The president asked us to be seated at the table, and he approached a microphone that had been set up in the front of the room. He explained why they were there (basically to honor a loyal and long-term employee), mentioned the employee's years of service, and called her up to the microphone. He thanked her for her contribution and presented her with a pen-and-pencil set embellished with the company logo and an envelope containing a monetary gift. He then told the employees that there were donuts and coffee for everyone and that they should say good-bye to the retiring employee. It is difficult to capture the spirit of the event, but the goodwill of all was evident.

Although the entire presentation lasted no more than 15 minutes, the values and beliefs it communicated and reinforced were very powerful. First, it showed that the company values all of its employees and their service. Second, it reinforced the belief that loyalty and service will be rewarded. Third, it indicated that the company believes its employees are part of a family. The sharing of food (in this case simply coffee and donuts) added to the family atmosphere. Finally, it suggested that the leadership of the company is interested in and concerned about its employees.

Celebrations held at companies as diverse as Bell-Carter Foods (birthday parties) and Southwest Airlines (annual awards banquet) are rituals that help communicate to all employees that employees are viewed as a part of the family and that fun is a very real part of the culture.

Like other aspects of culture, however, rituals must be managed, or the values and beliefs they are intended to reinforce can become distorted. For example, annual meetings can become an excuse to get away at the company's expense instead of as an opportunity to learn from each other and build the team.

Rituals can also be mismanaged when employees no longer understand their intent. Two examples of this mismanagement include (1) the afternoon get together—which becomes a time for employees to share their complaints rather than share ideas and build their team, and (2) the meeting that is held each week because "we've always had it," even though attendees agree it's a waste of time.

When, however, a ritual has been effective at communicating its message and employees embrace it, they may choose to maintain it, even at significant cost to themselves. At Hewlett-Packard, for example, during a period when the company's performance was less than expected and significant cuts were being made across various operations, employees voluntarily raised money to sponsor the company picnics. The implication of this is that employees clearly understood that the company valued them and that the picnic was only in jeopardy because of the company's performance. Further, the company had effectively communicated the belief that employee loyalty was valued, and employees chose to express their loyalty by sponsoring the picnic themselves.

Rewards and Heroes

There are monetary and nonmonetary rewards that a company can give employees for behavior consistent with the company's culture and its goals. Examples include bonuses, company-sponsored vacations, employee-of-the-month awards, certificates of appreciation, and items embellished with the company logo and presented in recognition of service of a particular kind. Many use certificates to recognize employees who complete a management development program or provide valued service to the company. These certificates help other employees understand what the company values.

Domino's Pizza is a company that uses rewards effectively to foster its values of teamwork, customer service, and high performance standards. National awards go to winners of annual competitive events and to individuals and stores with the best sales record. Recognition of a different kind is given to poor performers. The slowest delivery times are recognized by inscription of the store's name on a plaque placed near the slowest elevators at corporate headquarters. Finally, founder Thomas Monaghan's impulsive gift of his tie to an especially successful manager has become a tradition, and hundreds of these awards are presented annually.

As is true of the other manifestations of culture, rewards must be managed, or they can communicate values and beliefs and promote norms that are at odds with the company's goals. One small Stage II service firm had instituted a "manager-of-the-month" program intended to reward the "best manager." Unfortunately, the program had become a popularity contest rather than a way to recognize behavior consistent with the company's goals. The criteria for determining who should receive this reward were vague, and employees were asked to vote on who they believed to be the best manager. This process was adversely affecting morale because, although the most popular managers won, those who were working hard to meet their goals were sometimes overlooked. Eventually, it might be expected that the good performers who were not rewarded for their behavior would simply give up.

In other cases, organizations can overdo it with respect to rewards. In one large company, each time a meeting or event was held, all attendees received some type of memento: a T-shirt, coffee mug, pen, or plaque. Over time, these rewards came to have no meaning to those who received them. Employees complained that they had closets full of T-shirts and cupboards full of mugs. The president of the company, upon hearing this, decided to use rewards more strategically. He did not immediately take away all of these rewards, but he dramatically decreased their use. No one seemed to notice! The hope was that, over time, these types of rewards would again be appreciated.

Those who receive rewards and recognition can, over time, become recognized as company role models (heroes). Therefore, it is important that those who receive rewards truly exemplify the organization's values, beliefs, and norms. When they do not exemplify the organization's core values, the business can be promoting behavior that is inconsistent with its long-term goals.

It is important to also recognize that corporate heroes can be still working in the company or long since departed. These are the people that employees hold up as role models. Herb Kelleher is a living hero in the company he founded—Southwest Airlines. His behavior (which promoted fun) let all employees know what is acceptable. Similarly, Bill Gates, founder of Microsoft, but no longer active in the business, is still a living hero at that company where he represents the values of innovative product development, competition, and other aspects of the company's culture that have helped to support the company's success. Finally, at Apple, though Steve Jobs is now deceased, the legend of Steve Jobs lives on. He is still an icon and somewhat mythic figure at Apple, and his story still exerts a powerful presence.

Sadly, there are other truly heroic business figures that are not well utilized by their companies. For example, Ueli Prager, the founder of Mövenpick, a global restaurant, food, and hotel company, is underutilized as a cultural icon. If his story were told, he would be well recognized as a great entrepreneurial figure. Similarly, Nikola Tesla, a truly great technological genius, is only now getting some of the recognition he deserved because Elon Musk, the entrepreneurial founder of Tesla Motors, has named his flagship car the Tesla.

How Corporate Culture Changes

Corporate culture should change over time. In fact, culture *does* change over time as the organization grows and as new people are added; we refer to this type of change as uncontrolled change, or cultural mutations. Culture *should* change over time to support organizational growth; we refer to this type of change as controlled or managed. We discuss these two change processes in the next sections.

Uncontrolled Culture Change

The corporate culture of a start-up or early-stage entrepreneurship is dictated principally by the founder and the few people he or she initially hires. Everyone understands the culture and buys into it. It is very easy for the founder(s) to influence and maintain the culture through direct contact with all employees on a daily basis. However, by the time there are four or five generations of employees, it is almost impossible for people at the lower levels of the organization to have any direct contact with those at the top who articulate the culture. Therefore, the culture that those at the bottom of the organization adopt may be very different from the culture the founder and the original group of employees want to promote.

Such different perceptions result from the tendency of individuals to interpret the corporate culture in ways that meet their own needs. These differences in interpretation can be viewed as mutations in core values. In the absence of a well-managed culture, this process of mutation can lead to the original culture becoming very distorted. This can be a subtle—almost imperceptible—process. In addition, if the culture is not managed or is not managed effectively, there can be a clash between the old and new cultures that can affect the company's success.

In one $500 million service company, the two companies of equal size that merged to create the larger entity had extremely different cultures. One of these companies was very entrepreneurial, while another bordered on being a bureaucracy. In the entrepreneurship, managers were encouraged to do their own thing; in the other, people waited to be told what to do by their managers. In the more "professionalized" company, there were well-developed systems and processes that were consistently used; in the entrepreneurship, if systems and processes existed, they were frequently ignored. After the merger, the senior management team, consisting of the executives from both companies, worked together to develop a strategic plan for taking the new business to the next level. The team tried, unsuccessfully, to blend the two cultures but could seldom see eye-to-eye on what was needed. Over a period of about two years, the new company's performance significantly declined, and the members of executive management were replaced.

Given our previous discussion of the relationship between culture and the organization's infrastructure, any time a change is made in a particular area of the company, there will be an impact on culture, whether or not the organization has planned this change.

Planned Culture Change

If an organization is to be successful as it grows, culture must be managed at each stage of growth so that the values, beliefs, and norms support the other changes taking place. As we discussed in Chapter 3, culture does not become a critical factor until a company reaches $100 million in revenues, but that does not mean that it should or can be ignored. For example, in a $50 million manufacturing company, strategic planning was done, but because the culture and other systems did not support it, it was nothing more than a yearly paper exercise. The company had not found ways to explicitly manage its culture so that it supported planning.

Microsoft, recognized as being one of the most phenomenally successful entrepreneurial ventures of the late twentieth century, went through several periods of cultural change. Microsoft was founded in 1975 by Bill Gates and Paul Allen. At that time, Gates and Allen focused on developing the software for the first personal computer—the Altair (produced by MITS computing in New Mexico). Over the next several years, the company developed software for other computer makers, and by 1980, revenues had reached $8 million. It was in 1980 that Microsoft was selected to produce the IBM-PC operating system (MS-DOS). This system eventually became the industry standard. In these early days of the company (and for obvious reasons), the focus was on the developer, and the culture of the organization reflected this.

As Microsoft continued to grow, with sales reaching $24 million in 1982, Gates began to realize that the informal manner in which the company had operated in the past would no longer be appropriate for the future. He began to hire professional managers to help take his company to its next stage of development. Jon Shirley, a 25-year veteran of Tandy, was brought in as COO and began to help develop the infrastructure needed to run the much larger firm that Microsoft was becoming. At the same time, however, the company tried to maintain the feel of a much smaller firm. This was facilitated, in part, by a number of rituals (like the annual holiday party and company picnics), as well as the norm that any employee at any time could email Gates or Shirley directly if they had a question or concern. Gates and Shirley typically responded quickly and personally to each email received.

The organization continued to promote a family feeling, but its culture also promoted being aggressive and assertive. Conflict was not unusual and in many cases was promoted. Although at times it may have gotten somewhat heated, whenever conflict is dealt with openly, it typically leads to greater innovation and creativity—significant values at Microsoft.

Throughout the 1980s, Gates continued to be in charge of product development and demanded the most from the developers. His "Bill meetings" (a type of ritual) were opportunities for him to question and critique ideas, as well as to promote his vision for what his firm would become.

As the company entered the 1990s, it faced new challenges. Revenues were now over $1 billion and were derived not just from the organization's sales of its operating system but also from application software. However, the company had not changed certain aspects of its culture to support a firm of this size. There was still a great deal of centralized control. For example, the president of the company still signed all employment requisitions, even for temporary employees. At the same time, however, product developers in different units worked independently on their products. Gates recognized that this needed to change as the environment pushed for software products that worked together. He assumed the role of coordinating the product development efforts. The company began to focus on creating integrated products, and this meant that its product development teams also needed to be integrated.

In 1991, the company began to realize that its primary customer base had shifted from the OEM (original equipment manufacturer, who purchased Microsoft operating software for use in its computers) to the end user (who purchased its application software and who demanded support for its use). Promoting a focus on end-user service and support required not only a shift in the company's infrastructure but also in its culture. Now the company had to promote not only "reverence for the developer" (a value on which the company was founded) but also "reverence for the customer."

In 1991, the company also became more formal with respect to its security. Although it had been viewed as less than positive to wear badges in the mid-1980s, software developers began to realize that they had a great deal of valuable software and ideas in the firm that needed to be protected.

By 1999, the company had grown to over $14 billion in revenues and was continuing to experience great success. However, Bill Gates and the new president, Steve Ballmer, decided that they needed to "reinvent Microsoft," calling their initiative "Vision Version 2." This initiative was developed to address issues identified through interviews conducted with employees throughout the company. Interviews suggested that people did not necessarily understand the firm's direction and that the company had become too slow to react to market opportunities. The idea, according to Ballmer, was to "reinvigorate the vision," that computing power will be usable on any device, anywhere.

One key to the new vision was to have programmers continue developing software to support the Windows technology, while at the same time giving programmers the freedom to explore non-Windows-based software that would support the growing Internet business. To minimize the possibility that these different types of software might end up competing for customers, the company redesigned its structure into eight new groups, focused both on technology and customers. The first two groups were devoted to basic research and continued product development. Each of the remaining six product development groups targeted a different buyer.

One of the reasons behind the changes made in 1999 at Microsoft was that people had come to feel that the company was becoming too bureaucratic. Decisions were taking too long, and many felt the firm was mired in red tape. Part of the problem was that the company had continued to operate with a culture of centralization. Many decisions were "bumped" to Gates or Ballmer, who were becoming (partly because of the sheer number of decisions to be made) bottlenecks. Before the new Vision Version 2, Gates and Ballmer were involved in every decision. In the new culture, rolled out in 1999, senior managers (those below Gates and Ballmer) were now responsible for running their businesses and managing their budgets as they saw fit (as long as they met their goals). In addition, the company continued to focus its developers on better understanding and meeting the needs of customers.

In September 2005, the company again restructured, this time into three divisions. The reason, according to Steve Ballmer, then CEO, was to "align our business groups in a way that will enhance decision making and speed of execution, as well as help us continue to deliver the types of products and services our customers want most."[7] In other words, this change was intended to continue the process of refining the structure to better fit the company's culture.

On February 4, 2014, Satya Nadella succeeded Steve Ballmer as CEO of Microsoft. Nadella's leadership has led to a transformation of the company's business and technology culture from client services to cloud infrastructure and services. He has been credited with helping bring Microsoft's database, Windows Server, and developer tools to its Azure cloud. Microsoft's revenue from its Cloud Services is growing and is estimated to be $6.3 billion in 2015.[8]

How to Manage Corporate Culture

As a result of organizational growth leading to mutations in its core values and a lack of time to focus on culture management (because other systems have taken precedence), an organization can find itself with a culture that is no longer appropriate for its size and strategic intent. When this occurs, usually by the time a business reaches $100 million, culture management must become a priority.

There are six basic steps in the process of culture management: (1) analyzing what the organization's culture is now (the current culture); (2) determining what the culture should be, given the organization's current stage of growth (the desired culture); (3) identifying gaps between the organization's current and desired cultures; (4) developing a culture management plan; (5) implementing the culture management plan; and (6) monitoring changes in the culture after the plan is implemented over time. Each step is described in turn.

Assessment and Analysis of Current Culture

The first step in the culture management process is to perform a "cultural assessment" to determine what the culture currently is. Because the emphasis is on the real culture, not the nominal culture, we recommend ignoring written culture statements (at least initially) and focusing instead on what people have to say about the culture they live and breathe. As explained earlier, culture is a very fuzzy concept; asking an employee to describe his or her organization's culture usually results in the employee either pulling out the company's philosophy or culture statement and beginning to read it or looking blankly at the interviewer as if he or she is speaking a foreign language. In other words, the direct approach is not effective in gathering information on this subject.

A more indirect approach that has been very effective for researchers and managers alike is to ask employees to write or tell short stories about their experiences in the firm. Employees should be asked to tell a story or two related to critical incidents they have personally experienced or heard about that occurred at the company. Another effective method is to have them construct a story that describes their first day on the job. The construction of these stories can take place on paper, and they can then be read aloud in a group setting or told to interviewers.

The next step is to extract from the stories critical elements of the company's culture. The identification of these elements may be done by the employees themselves or by an independent observer.

Once the elements have been identified and summarized, they should be circulated to employees for further elaboration or feedback.

An example of two stories that were told by employees at a Stage IV service business, and the elements of the culture that they identify are provided in Table 10.2. As shown in the table, the stories suggest a number of elements of this organization's culture, including concern for quality, the importance of extra effort, concern for people, the importance of first impressions, the concern that people feel valued, and the importance of treating people with respect.

In analyzing stories, it is useful to identify how culture is manifested in the organization. What symbols are important to people? How do they talk about themselves, their customers, and company events (language)? What rituals are important? Who receives rewards (the heroes) and for what? What types of rewards are important to people in this firm? This is important information, not only in terms of identifying the current culture but also in terms of identifying how to manage these manifestations of culture in order to promote a strong, functional culture.

As a result of such analyses, a number of competing subcultures may be identified. For example, each department may adhere to slightly different values. This is important information in the culture management process because the goal of this process will be to blend all of the competing cultures so that they support the overall corporate goals.

In addition to story analysis, an organization may use interviews to collect information on its culture. Through a series of questions that focus on key aspects of corporate culture (for example, treatment of employees and treatment of customers), interviews can collect information on both the organization's current culture and what interviewees believe the culture should be. In most cases, it would be very difficult for someone inside the organization to effectively use this method because interviewees may not feel that they can be completely candid.

An alternative is to design and administer a corporate culture survey, which is *not* the same as an attitude survey. Culture surveys should focus only on helping to identify the organization's values, beliefs, and norms, not on things like whether employees are satisfied with their pay and benefits. Typically, these surveys should consist of no more than 40 questions, with each question representing a key element of the organization's desired culture. Those completing the survey are then asked to identify the extent to which each element of the organization's desired culture is currently being practiced.

Whatever method is used to collect information on the organization's current culture, the outcome of the cultural assessment will be a list of the elements of the current culture and their meanings. Some managers also find it useful to develop a list of the systems or structures (elements of the company's infrastructure) that promote each of the various cultural elements as a way of identifying possible targets for change.

Identification of the Organization's Desired Culture

In beginning to explicitly manage an organization's culture, the key question is, "What should our culture be, given our current stage of development?" In the final section of this chapter, we provide some general guidelines for the elements of corporate culture at different stages of development.

Whatever the stage, however, it is senior management's responsibility to answer this question. In doing so, the focus needs to be on both what the culture should be today and on what the culture

Table 10.2   Stories and Their Elements

Story 1

Not long after I began working here, I was reviewing some artwork that had been submitted. As usual, I was hoping to be able to approve the work and get the project rolling. The artwork was all right. In fact, it was probably more than just all right. But still it wasn't perfect. It fell into that gray area of being almost what you had in mind.

I showed it to my boss. Like me, she agreed that it was okay, would do the job, and be just fine. We stood a minute looking at the work, each of us wishing it were a bit something more, but recognizing that maybe sometimes okay is good enough. Then my boss turned to me and said, "I want to love this!" And in that moment we both agreed that it was worth it to get that extra something we wanted from the artwork.

Story 2

When I arrived at the company, Allan was working the reception desk, and while I was filling out my application he offered me coffee, decaf, tea, hot chocolate, milk, and water. Every time he offered, I said, "No thank you. I'm fine." When I met with the president, the first thing she asked me was if Mark had offered me coffee or tea, and I said that he had but that I didn't want anything. I was fine. After I interviewed with the president, she took me into the sales department to meet Jerry, the manager. When I met him, he asked me to tell him about myself in two minutes. I started telling him what my experience was and what I had done. He stopped me and said, "No, tell me about yourself." I was very impressed. So far, everyone at this company had been interested in who I was as well as in what I had done.

After I met with Carol, I met another member of the sales team, and the first thing he asked me was if anyone had offered me coffee or tea or something to drink. I said that they had and I was fine, really! Well, I came back for a second interview the next week, and then started work two days later.

Element of Culture Extracted from These Stories

1. We value quality in our products.
2. We take the extra effort to "do it right."
3. We care about our employees.
4. First impressions are important.
5. We want to make everyone who comes in contact with us feel that they are valued.
6. We treat people with respect.

should be in five years. From brainstorming sessions, workshops, or surveys, senior management should construct a set of values and beliefs that it deems will meet the organization's needs. These can be a set of three to five key phrases, each with a paragraph to explain their meaning, or simply a list of the key elements of the culture. If a company chooses to use a list, then senior management should develop its own written definition of each element so that there can be no misinterpretation of its meaning.

We recommend that the culture statement contain no more than five to nine key items so as to help employees remember them. However, these statements might also include brief definitions (no more than a paragraph).

Identifying Gaps between Current and Desired Cultures

Once an organization's management has identified what it wants or needs its culture to be, it then needs to determine the extent to which the desired culture is currently a reality for employees throughout the enterprise. The basic question is, "To what extent do our employees currently live and breathe the desired values, beliefs, and norms we have articulated?"

Addressing this question involves comparing the current culture (as identified through stories, interviews, and surveys) with the organization's desired culture (as articulated by senior management). In some cases, the desired culture will already be a reality. In others, the current culture will be quite different from one that will best support the organization's long-term goals (the organization's desired culture). Closing culture gaps involves developing strategies to better manage the organization's culture.

Developing a Culture Management Plan

A culture management plan focuses on ensuring that those aspects of the organization's desired culture that are already a reality are preserved. More important, however, is that this plan should focus on developing strategies for closing any gaps that exist between the company's current and desired cultures.

Developing strategies for effectively managing an organization's culture usually involves focusing on other systems, as culture affects and is affected by everything else in the Pyramid of Organizational Development. This is why it is important to identify those aspects of the infrastructure that are detracting from an organization's ability to realize its desired culture. Similarly, each time a change is made in the infrastructure, senior management needs to consider the cultural implications. To illustrate the impact that other systems can have on culture, Table 10.3 presents excerpts from a culture assessment completed for a Stage IV manufacturing firm we call Alpha Manufacturing. As can be seen in this table, a variety of other systems, structures, and processes were supporting the current culture, which wasn't necessarily the culture that the company needed to support the achievement of its long-term goals.

Sometimes the need for a culture change arises because of an acquisition or merger. In this case, senior management must perform an assessment of each of the cultures, identify areas of overlap and conflict, and determine the best way to blend the cultures. This may mean that some values of one or both companies will need to be significantly changed or, perhaps, eliminated in order to

Table 10.3   Elements of Alpha Manufacturing's Current Culture and Factors That Support Them

Treatment of Customers	
Current Culture	**Organizational Dimensions That Affect or Are Affected by Culture**
Customer and quality orientation are present but not consistent throughout the organization.	There is the perception that Quality Assurance is the "policeman," versus a valued partner in promoting quality.
	Discrepancies exist between departments as to the extent to which quality goals are effectively set and monitored.
We have a commitment to "doing it right the first time," as long as it doesn't affect the schedule.	This creates stress throughout the company.
	The product development process is adversely affected.

Treatment of Employees	
Current Culture	**Organizational Dimensions That Affect or Are Affected by Culture**
We pay lip service to balancing work and personal lives, but our actions do not support this.	The company takes on too much in developing plans. Job design may promote some people working excessive hours. Reward-recognition system may promote working long hours.
We are not "confrontational" or "aggressive." We are "polite" and "professional." There is a "kill the messenger" syndrome operating within the company: No one wants to hear bad news; we tell people what they want to hear.	This may contribute to suboptimal decisions being made. This may contribute to communication and meeting-effectiveness problems. The reward system may reinforce beliefs. Managers may not want to or know how to effectively confront poor performers.
We value training and developing our people, if we only had the time!	There is a lack of time to develop human resources. Training varies from department to department. As positions have changed, no formal system has been created to provide training in new skills.

Table 10.3 **(Continued)**

Performance Standards and Accountability	
Current Culture	**Organizational Dimensions That Affect or Are Affected by Culture**
We set high goals and will do everything to meet them.	Goal setting is reinforced by and reinforces "people working hard" and feeling that one can't say no. Human resources are stretched thin. Too many priorities are in the planning process.
People get rewarded for who they know and not necessarily for good performance (against goals). People may not always be held accountable for performing their jobs.	Managers may not be held accountable for financial resources management. People are promoted who are not qualified. People are not held accountable for following procedures. There may be problems in the goal-setting process. A lack of up-to-date job descriptions contributes to problems.
We don't take risks.	This attitude affects product and market development processes. Our cautious attitude affects development of other processes in the organization.
We don't want to become bureaucratic; we are flexible.	Product development and other systems are not adequately defined. There are insufficient formal mechanisms to communicate between and within departments. There are too many teams and individuals working on the same task. There is no formal system to develop effective managers, which contributes to managers not being prepared to assume their roles. Planning is not yet integrated throughout the company.

support the organization's growth. The culture's management is, however, essential in helping the company make a smooth transition because it has such a tremendous impact on employee morale.

For example, when American Century Investments acquired The Benham Group, they made a special effort to integrate the two companies' cultures. In the beginning, there were concerns because Benham's business focused primarily on fixed income rather than equities, whereas American Century was exclusively focused on equities. This could have created a significant cultural conflict. To facilitate the integration of the two companies and their cultures, American Century initiated a number of steps. They assigned a senior executive to devote virtually full time to the integration of the company for a planned period of approximately 18 months. They engaged the services of our consulting firm (which had worked with them for many years) to serve as a liaison between the two firms. Our firm interviewed a sample of employees from Benham during the first 18 months to obtain feedback on how the integration was going and whether there were any special concerns. Issues were identified, which were brought to the attention of the executive responsible for the integration, and they were successfully addressed. We also facilitated joint sessions for strategic planning and team building between the senior executives of both companies. Meetings were intentionally held in Mountain View, California, at Benham's corporate office, rather than in Kansas City, where American Century was headquartered. The integration was successful—made easier, in part, by the compatible sensibilities of the two CEOs, who had a number of things in common.

Although corporate culture change is a necessary part of the transition process, culture must be managed on a continual basis in order to ensure that it supports the company's goals and operations. The values, beliefs, and norms must be communicated and constantly reinforced because as a company continues to grow, new employees will need to understand what the culture is and what it means.

Senior management is ultimately responsible for the culture management process. Moreover, senior managers actually serve as role models for the rest of the company. It is important, then, that they not only communicate the culture through their words but also through their actions. At one technology company, for example, the founder and CEO decided to decentralize management decision making. Unfortunately, employees continued to complain that the founder still made most of the major decisions. The nominal culture said, "We believe in providing all of our managers with the authority they need to make decisions." But the behavior, for whatever reason, stated, "The founder will decide."

A positive example of the role senior management can play in the culture management process is that of a $35 million manufacturing firm. In this firm, employees came to equate commitment with hours worked, regardless of actual productivity. Changing this aspect of the company's culture began with a memo from senior management—sent to all employees—stating clearly that the company wanted people to work smarter, not longer hours. Senior management decided that they would no longer arrive at the office before 7:30 A.M. and would leave the office by 5:30 P.M. Through their behavior, they attempted to show their employees what the new value would be: we value productivity, not just hours worked.

A second way to manage corporate culture is through training programs. Orientation programs can serve as a way to provide new employees with an understanding of the corporate culture, as well as of how the infrastructure works to support this culture. Again, however, although the words are important, the other elements of this program—for example, whether the president welcomes them in person or in a video, the first impression left by their immediate supervisor, and the tone of the meeting—can leave a lasting perception of the company's values. In the absence of such formalized programs, employees are sometimes left to their own devices to read the handbook and identify what's important in the company.

Management and leadership development programs can also serve as a means of conveying the corporate culture, as discussed in Chapter 9. They help to build a sense of teamwork and, at a minimum, usually communicate to employees that the company values training and professionalized management. Further, management and leadership development programs provide managers with the skills they need to support and use the organization's systems in ways that reinforce the corporate culture.

Another way that corporate culture can be managed is through personnel selection. This can be proactive or retroactive. Proactively, the goal is to select personnel who will promote the values, beliefs, and norms of the firm and who are not at odds with the culture. Although this is a very time-consuming process and takes a great deal of planning and execution, it can be very effective.

Ritz-Carlton is a company that uses personnel selection to manage their culture. Southwest Airlines also uses this mechanism as one way of managing its culture. Their hiring processes focus on identifying attitudes rather than skills.

Retroactive personnel selection usually occurs during culture change. The goal is to eliminate individuals who will not support the new culture or, at a minimum, move them into positions where they can do little to harm the cultural change process. Some companies bring in outsiders, called hired guns, to perform the terminations. Usually, in these cases the entrepreneur realizes that he or she cannot do what needs to be done and either moves up or out of the company.

In other cases, the culture eventually becomes so strong that other employees force the cultural violator out. The person who refuses to adopt the new culture becomes an outsider and leaves of his or her own volition. Individuals who leave under these circumstances sometimes say that the company just wasn't any fun anymore.

Finally, corporate culture can be managed through the administration of rewards. As discussed in Chapter 8, it is important to ensure that rewards are linked to the behavior needed to achieve organizational goals and objectives, as outlined in the strategic plan. The company should be trying to create corporate heroes out of those individuals who best exemplify this behavior. These individuals can, in turn, act as role models for others. This is why it is not only important for employees to understand what they are being rewarded for but to publicize achievement as a way of motivating others to exhibit the same behavior. In some companies, the best performers are rewarded with bonuses. The reward structure and system must constantly be reevaluated to determine that it is motivating employees to be concerned with the appropriate goals and that these goals have not become distorted.

To illustrate how some of these corporate culture management mechanisms can be used to better manage an organization's culture, Table 10.4 shows the current and desired culture of Alpha Manufacturing. It also provides examples of how this company changed certain systems, structures, and processes in order to help increase the extent to which its desired culture was realized throughout the company.

In brief, Alpha Manufacturing developed a culture management plan that focused on changing other aspects of its infrastructure in order to support its new culture. In addition to developing this

Table 10.4   Alpha Manufacturing's Current and Desired Cultures and the Tools Used to Make Its Desired Culture a Reality

Treatment of Customers	
Current Culture	**Desired Culture**
Customer and quality orientation is present but not consistent throughout the organization.	A strong customer and quality orientation is present and consistent throughout all areas of the company.

Strategies for Managing This Dimension

Continue efforts to improve the company's strategic planning process, including goal-setting regarding quality.

Set individual quality-based performance goals.

Continue efforts to provide technical training on customers to employees.

Current Culture	**Desired Culture**
We have a commitment to "doing it right the first time," as long as it doesn't affect the schedule.	With respect to product and service quality, we are committed to doing it right the first time.

Strategies for Managing This Dimension

Take steps to make planning a way of life and take it down to departmental and individual levels.

Establish a process of prioritizing product ideas and managing workloads.

Formalize a process of better managing interdepartmental policies and procedures.

Continue efforts to provide effective managerial and technical training.

Treatment of Employees	
Current Culture	**Desired Culture**
We pay lip service to balancing work and personal lives, but our actions do not support this.	Our words and actions support a balance between work and our employees' personal lives.

Strategies for Managing This Dimension

Continue to improve the company's strategic planning process.

Develop more effective role descriptions, evaluate current *actual* time allocation by each position's key result areas, and develop recommended percentage time use by key result area.

Implement a formal structure and staffing plan.

Develop and implement leadership education, *including a focus on effective time management.*

Table 10.4 (*Continued*)

Treatment of Employees (*continued*)	
Current Culture	**Desired Culture**
We are not "confrontational" or "aggressive." We are "polite" and "professional." There is a "kill the messenger" syndrome at the company: No one wants to hear bad news; we tell people what they want to hear.	We address conflict and performance problems in a clear, direct, and professional manner. We encourage people to make suggestions, offer constructive criticism, and constructively challenge the majority as a way of promoting organizational and individual development.

Strategies for Managing This Dimension

Develop leadership education programs that include training in feedback and conflict management skills.

Encourage sharing of ideas on teams.

Practice effective in-process meeting management techniques that promote sharing of ideas.

Current Culture	**Desired Culture**
We value training and developing our people, if we only had the time!	We make training and developing all of our people a priority.

Strategies for Managing This Dimension

Make leadership education a requirement for all managers.

Continue efforts to provide technical training to all employees.

Performance Standards and Accountability	
Current Culture	**Desired Culture**
We set high goals and will do everything to meet them.	We set high but realistic goals and realistically prioritize our work.

Strategies for Managing This Dimension

Continue to improve Alpha Manufacturing's strategic planning process, *including setting realistic priorities and goals.*

Establish a process for prioritizing product ideas and managing workloads.

Current Culture	**Desired Culture**
People get rewarded for who they know and not necessarily for good performance (against goals). People may not always be held accountable for performing their jobs.	People are rewarded based on their performance, as measured against specific performance goals that are appropriate for their position.

(*continued*)

Table 10.4   (*Continued*)

Performance Standards and Accountability (*continued*)

Strategies for Managing This Dimension

Develop key result area–based role descriptions and clarify roles.

Use goal-based performance appraisals and provide ongoing feedback to direct reports.

Train managers in how to provide effective feedback and administer rewards.

Improve the extent to which policies and procedures are understood and followed.

Current Culture	Desired Culture
We don't take risks.	We promote and reward appropriate innovation and risk taking.

Strategies for Managing This Dimension

As a part of the strategic planning process, devote time to discussing key strategic issues and finding ways to promote entrepreneurship.

Train managers and team leaders in how to promote appropriate risk taking.

Continue efforts to formalize the product development process to enable Alpha Manufacturing to take calculated risks.

---

plan, the company created a culture management task force, made up of middle managers. Their responsibility was to further analyze the information provided by the culture assessment, monitor performance against specific goals that had been set in an effort to better realize the firm's desired culture, and provide feedback to the organization's senior management team.

Implementing the Culture Plan and Monitoring Changes

Step 5 (Implementing the culture management plan) and Step 6 (monitoring changes in the culture after the plan is implemented over time) are fairly self-explanatory. Implementation is a matter of execution of the plan. We also strongly recommend re-assessing the culture for the purpose of monitoring changes and measuring progress in achieving cultural objectives. For example, Emergent BioSolutions has used a culture survey to monitor changes in their company's culture. The survey has been administered approximately every 18 months since 2009, and the results have been used to identify specific areas that need to be focused upon and better managed.

The Importance of Cultural Norms

We have been engaged by several companies to assess why their culture was not functioning in the desired way. In each case, a key problem was that, while there was a culture statement articulating the core values of the company, there was not an accompanying set of norms that translated those values into specific behaviors. Cultural norms are the key to making culture real by having an impact on the actual day-to-day behavior of employees.

Smartmatic is an example of how cultural norms are a key to making the desired culture a reality. The company is a privately owned, multinational company headquartered in Caracas, Venezuela, that designs and deploys end-to-end, custom technology solutions to enable government agencies and large enterprises to fulfill their missions with the utmost efficiency. In 2011, it had about $200 (U.S.) million in revenue and about 250 employees. It views itself as a "Silicon Valley type" of company that happens to be located in Venezuela.

Smartmatic has developed a statement of eight core values and related behaviors (that is, norms).[9] A great strength of this approach to the management of culture is in the "definition" of the overall cultural values in terms of specific "related behaviors" that will demonstrate the value. For example, someone exemplifying the "teamwork" value is sharing information openly, listening attentively, dealing with conflict effectively, and encouraging people to work as a team.

The Smartmatic value of "excellence" is the company's value that deals with performance standards and accountability. As defined at Smartmatic, "excellence" in performance is demonstrated in terms of specific "related behaviors" when a person:

- Delivers in accordance to commitments
- Executes assigned tasks with diligence and quality
- Simplifies systems and processes to eliminate unnecessary work
- Consistently delivers with high standards of excellence with no mistakes

The strength of the cultural statement of the company's value with respect to performance standards and accountability is in the four "bullets" describing the related behaviors. Most culture statements of values refer to general concepts of integrity, innovation, and so on, without providing sufficient specificity to translate the value into actual day-to-day behavior. As stated by Victor Ramirez, Smartmatic's senior vice president of human resources, "We added behaviors to the values statements to convert the values into reality."[10]

The notion that norms are critical to implementing values was confirmed in 2014 in a culture management project that the authors' firm, Management Systems, conducted for Techcombank, the eighth-largest bank in Vietnam. Techcombank ("TCB") already had a statement of values. However, the values were not impacting day-to-day behavior of people to the desired extent.

A culture management project was conducted with Techcombank in order to assess the current culture and help implement it more effectively. As a result of the culture assessment, we concluded that while TCB had a statement of values, it lacked a culture management system to motivate people to behave in accordance with those values. We created a culture management system to help TCB manage its culture more effectively. This included the development of a set of norms to help translate the existing set of core values into actual day-to-day behavior. We also proposed linking compensation of managers to measured performance of people against TCB values.

Corporate Culture at Different Stages of Organizational Development

Although the particular elements of a corporate culture will differ, culture should change to meet the demands at each stage of development. This section discusses some of the key dimensions of culture at the various stages of organizational development.

Stage I

The culture of most small organizations emphasizes flexibility, ability to respond quickly to the environment, and the notion that the company is a family, with the entrepreneur serving as the parental figure. The organization seems to be constantly moving, and although there is a certain amount of anxiety about the company's future, there is also a great deal of excitement. In some Stage I companies, technical wizardry and innovativeness are valued, and often the technicians are the corporate heroes. In others, the focus is on sales and marketing, and those individuals who work in these areas become the heroes.

Culture is communicated through direct interactions with the entrepreneur. Employees, in fact, look to the entrepreneur for direction, so he or she is able to almost daily define and reinforce the corporate culture, as well as to monitor and correct it. Very few entrepreneurs choose to commit their values to paper at this stage of development. Although this is not an absolute necessity, it can serve as a basis for communicating values as the business grows. Whatever is placed on paper, however, should be supported by the daily operations of the enterprise.

Stage II

The corporate culture of the Stage II business is very similar to that in Stage I. The organization still values responsiveness, but now there is a tendency for this to mean "crisis management." The business still values flexibility, but now this means something like being flexible and creative enough to operate with less than adequate resources until personnel interviews are completed or until the new facilities are ready. The organization also still values the family, but now there is an extended family living within the same "house," and one's loyalty seems to depend more on which leader (regardless of level) one is most exposed to. Corporate heroes tend to become those people who are the best fire fighters and problem solvers.

It is at this stage of development that the corporate culture of most organizations begins to become distorted. Because all employees can no longer have direct contact with the entrepreneur, they are left to develop their own interpretations of the corporate culture, based on what they have heard. Because the entrepreneur cannot be there to monitor behavior, he or she must depend on other managers to do so, but those managers have their own interpretations of the culture. If the company has not yet developed the strategic planning, performance management, management development, and organizational structure consistent with this stage of development, it may be placed at a further disadvantage because, even if it can develop the appropriate culture, there will be no support for it.

At this stage of development, a company should devote at least part of its planning time to articulating the culture that will support its efforts and to devising ways to communicate it to employees. Again, if there is an existing culture statement, it may need to be revised to reflect the needs of the current stage of development. In this regard, it should mention a shift toward planning and control in at least an implicit way, as well as an emphasis on meeting responsibilities and goals. Further, as suggested in Chapter 8, the reward systems should be reviewed and changed, if necessary, in order to support the behavior required to achieve the organization's goals.

Stage III

It is at this stage of development that the culture of an organization should make a fundamental shift toward promoting professional management. The culture of a Stage III organization should promote planning as a way of life, accountability for meeting departmental and individual goals, a commitment to training employees to become professional managers, and other behavior consistent with the professionalized firm. However, if the planning, control, management development, and organizational structure systems are inconsistent with the requirements of this stage of development, then the culture will be as well.

At this stage, the culture is, of necessity, still being implicitly managed in most cases. However, senior management can increase the probability that its culture will support its professionalization efforts by at least considering the impact that proposed organizational changes will have on what it believes to be the corporate culture and how that might be managed. In other words, it can build into its change efforts a cultural component that redefines existing elements and clearly articulates new elements. However, the effort required to explicitly manage these elements may need to be postponed until the systems and structure are at least nominally in place.

Stage IV

By the time an organization reaches Stage IV, it needs to develop a formal method for managing its corporate culture. Corporate culture management should become an important part of the planning process, and resources should be devoted to (1) performing a cultural assessment to identify potential problem areas, (2) clearly articulating the existing culture and the desired culture, if different, (3) identifying gaps between the current and desired cultures, (4) developing a plan for transforming or maintaining the corporate culture, (5) implementing the culture management plan, and (6) monitoring changes in the culture after the plan is implemented over time. The latter step should include a process for monitoring the culture on a regular basis to ensure that it is supporting the organization's goals.

Stage V

At Stage V, an organization will be diversifying. It will either create new business units or make acquisitions, or possibly both. The key challenge in this will be to either acquire or create business units whose cultures are consistent with the existing enterprise. The acquisition of companies with a compatible culture is a key strategy of Warren Buffett's iconic firm, Berkshire Hathaway. When Buffett acquires a company, he is seeking established companies with a certain culture that fits his style of laissez-faire (or hands-off) management. Buffett is looking for companies that can operate autonomously and do not require management from the parent company. This style of acquisition is also used by On Assignment, a rapidly growing leading company involved in the temporary staffing space. It is a core strategy of On Assignment, led by CEO Peter Dameris, to acquire established companies that can continue to operate autonomously. This same cultural strategy was used by privately owned Citation Corporation in the foundry business, under the leadership of T. Morris Hackney.

Stage VI

The key challenge at Stage VI is to integrate the acquired or created business units into the existing enterprise. Where the culture is well defined and it is desired that the acquired companies embrace the core culture of the parent company, this will require cultural integration as well. We have worked with and assisted several companies in the cultural integration process including American Century Investments (headquartered in Kansas City, Missouri), whose acquisition of Benham was described earlier in this chapter. On the surface, the merger of a Midwestern company with a California company located near Silicon Valley seems not to be made in heaven; but it was actually both a good fit and a well-executed cultural integration, because of the extensive culture merger planning and activities described above.

Stage VII

Stage VII involves the revitalization of a business that is in decline. This might involve the re-creation of the enterprise's entire culture as well as other aspects of the business. Implementation of cultural change in revitalization requires a cultural assessment like that done for Techcombank. Ideally, it also requires culture management training of the senior leaders, and development of the new culture using the five key dimensions we have described in this chapter. Finally, it requires the development of behavioral norms to help execute these values. It also can require the development of a comprehensive culture management system, as described above.

Summary

A clear understanding of the meaning and importance of corporate culture remains elusive for many managers. Some managers choose to deny the existence of a culture in their organizations; others are intimidated by the thought of trying to identify anything so fuzzy, let alone of finding ways to manage it.

This chapter addresses these issues. We examine the nature of corporate culture and how culture is manifested in organizations. We also describe methods that can be used to identify an organization's culture and to manage it so as to increase organizational effectiveness and promote long-term success. In brief, managers must first determine what their current culture is through performing a culture assessment. Next, they must determine what their culture *should* be, given their stage of growth, and, finally, they must design and implement a plan for managing the corporate culture.

Every organization has a culture, and culture can have a profound impact on organizational success because it supports the other changes needed to make the successful transition from one stage of growth to the next. It is, then, important for managers to understand and learn how to manage the culture as their organization grows.

The culture management framework and method we have presented is a very powerful tool for building sustainably successful organizations®. Many companies do not have the capability for effectively managing their culture as they grow, and the culture mutates over time. Just as a strong functional culture can be an asset, the development of an effective *culture management capability* can also become another source of sustainable competitive advantage.

Notes

1. Eric Flamholtz, "Corporate Culture Is the 'Nuclear Bomb' of Huawei," *Management Systems Perspectives* (July 2014).
2. See Eric Flamholtz, "Corporate Culture and the Bottom Line," *European Management Journal* 19, no. 3 (2001): 268–275; and Eric Flamholtz and Rangapriya Narasimhan-Kannan, "Differential Impact of Culture upon Financial Performance: An Empirical Investigation," *European Management Journal* 23, no. 1 (2005): 50–64.
3. For a discussion of how Smartmatic holds people accountable for its values, see Eric Flamholtz and Yvonne Randle, *Corporate Culture: The Ultimate Strategic Asset* (Stanford, CA: Stanford University Press, 2011), 117–122.
4. Interview by Eric Flamholtz with Howard Schultz, at a Starbucks Café in Santa Monica, California, April 26, 1995.
5. For a discussion of how these companies, cultures were dysfunctional and impacted performance, see Chapter 9, "The Dark Side of Corporate Culture," in Eric Flamholtz and Yvonne Randle, *Corporate Culture: The Ultimate Strategic Asset* (Stanford, CA: Stanford University Press, 2011).
6. Jeff Bennett and Mike Ramsey, "GM Takes Blame, Vows Cultural Shift," *Wall Street Journal*, June 6, 2014, 1.
7. "Microsoft Realigns for Next Wave of Innovation and Growth," Press Release, September, 20, 2005.
8. Tiernan Ray, "Amazon Reveals Just How Profitable the Cloud Can Be," *Barron's*, April 27, 2015, 28.
9. For further discussion of Smartmatic's values, see Flamholtz and Randle, *Corporate Culture*, 114–122 and 137–140.
10. Ibid., 117.

Special Aspects of Organizational Transitions in Growing and Changing Enterprises

The previous sections of this book have examined the organizational issues and related managerial tools required by organizations to become sustainably successful at different stages of growth. This section of the book deals with some special issues related to these transitions.

Throughout the book, we have provided brief examples of how our concepts can be applied to nonprofits. The purpose of Chapter 11 is to provide a more comprehensive description of how the concepts, frameworks, and tools presented in this book can be used by a nonprofit to manage growing pains and build a sustainably successful enterprise. The chapter will also explore and provide suggestions for effectively managing some of the unique aspects of nonprofits—including the relationship between staff and volunteer boards. We will use case studies from actual organizations—some will be disguised—to illustrate how the concepts in this book can be effectively used by a nonprofit's leadership team to promote success.

As leadership is an important ingredient in long-term success, Chapter 12 focuses on this topic. This chapter defines leadership and describes the two types of leadership that need to be present within a successful organization—operational (day-to-day) and strategic. It then identifies the key tasks of operational and strategic leadership (what effective leaders do) and also describes how to choose a leadership style that will help influence people to achieve organizational goals. Finally, it introduces the concept of a "leadership molecule"—a true leadership team that performs the tasks of strategic leadership needed to support the organization's development and long-term success.

Chapter 13 describes the experiences of actual companies that have applied the concepts, frameworks, methods, and tools described throughout this book. Its purpose is to share insights with you that will facilitate the application of the intellectual content presented in this book to your own organization. We will describe what was done and, to the extent possible, the results. The chapter focuses primarily upon companies from Stages III to VI because that is primarily where the concepts, frameworks, methods, and tools presented in this book have the greatest impact, and those companies have been our focus in our consulting applications. In these examples, we will (to the extent feasible) discuss the issues faced at various stages of growth in each company's life cycle.

CHAPTER

11

Building Sustainably Successful Nonprofits

In the late 1990s, one of the authors (Yvonne Randle) made a presentation to the California Association for the Education of Young Children (CAEYC) titled, "Business is NOT a bad word." This title was chosen because our experience suggested that some nonprofit leadership teams believed (and some actually said), "We are not a business. We are a nonprofit, and that is different." While it is true that nonprofits are somewhat different from their for-profit "cousins," they are, in fact, "businesses" that compete for people and resources (dollars) and face similar challenges as they grow. They come in many forms—including membership-based organizations (such as the National Association of Women Business Owners, Young Presidents Organization, and Junior Chamber of Commerce), organizations that provide a specific service to a specific population at no or little cost (such as Head Start, Goodwill, and community-based food banks), foundations, organizations focused on education and community outreach, and school districts.

Throughout the book, we have provided brief examples of how our concepts can be applied to nonprofits. The purpose of this chapter is to provide a more comprehensive description of how the frameworks and tools presented in this book can be used by a nonprofit to manage growing pains and build a sustainably successful enterprise. The chapter will also explore and provide suggestions for effectively managing some of the unique aspects of nonprofits—including the relationship between staff and volunteer boards. Finally, we will use case studies from actual organizations—many will be disguised—to illustrate how the concepts in this book can be effectively used by a nonprofit's leadership team to promote success.

Applying the Pyramid of Organizational Development to Nonprofits

As is true for for-profit enterprises, the Pyramid of Organizational Development can be used by nonprofits to assess the extent to which they have built the infrastructure needed to support effective and efficient operations. In this section, we describe each level in the Pyramid—beginning with markets—and provide examples of its application in nonprofits. A discussion of the three aspects of the business foundation (discussed in Chapters 2 and 6) will be presented later, in the context of strategic planning.

Identify and Define a Market

As is true in the for-profit world, the first challenge for a nonprofit is to identify a market need. Similar to entrepreneurs in the for-profit world, founders of nonprofits typically identify this need because it is something of interest to them. One might even describe this as a "passion." The National Association of Women Business Owners (NAWBO) was created by a group of women in 1975 that saw a need to foster the development and growth of women-owned businesses. Head Start was created in 1965 as a part of President Lyndon Johnson's War on Poverty to help preschool children of low-income families prepare for lifelong learning and "break the cycle of poverty." Shelter 37 was founded in 1993 by James Washington, a former UCLA and Dallas Cowboys football player, who saw a need to help young people in Los Angeles whose lives have been affected by crime, drugs, violence, or abandonment to improve their ability to get and keep a job. InterfaithFamily was founded by Edmund Case in 2001 to help people in interfaith relationships engage in Jewish life and help Jewish communities welcome those in these relationships. Freedom Writers Foundation was founded by Erin Gruwell, a former teacher with a passion for reducing high school dropout rates, engaging at-risk youth, and increasing overall academic performance—for *all* students.

Nonprofit entrepreneurs are typically very passionate about the market that they are working to serve. James, Ed, and Erin had experiences that were significant drivers for the creation of their enterprises. James grew up in the Watts neighborhood of Los Angeles and witnessed firsthand the impact of unemployment on young people. Ed experienced the displeasure of his family and his religious community when he decided to marry a non-Jewish woman. Erin was a high school teacher who found that traditional educational methods would not engage students and create the motivation required for at-risk youngsters.

In addition to the clients, members, and families that these organizations are working to serve, most nonprofits also need to view funding sources as "customers" because they provide the financial resources to support continued operations. Successful nonprofits have a good understanding of who their funding sources are or will be and what these funding sources needs are. For example, Head Start agencies are federally funded and know that they need to meet certain performance standards to continue receiving their funding. NAWBO, at the national and local levels, obtains some of its revenue from its members and some from corporate sponsors who are interested in funding the development of women-owned businesses. Other nonprofits like Shelter 37 and InterfaithFamily receive private donations from individuals and companies interested in their work and may also apply for grants. In all cases, however, nonprofits need to find ways to attract and maintain these "customers" through the impact that they have on the people that they serve.

Develop Products and Services

Most nonprofits provide services (versus products per se) to the market that they are focused on serving. NAWBO, for example, provides training and networking opportunities to its members and advocates for women business owners at the federal, state, and local levels. Head Start provides a comprehensive set of services—educational, emotional, social, psychological—to help promote school readiness and lifelong learning. Shelter 37 provides 16- to 24-year-olds with life skill and job training and assists the participants in these programs in securing employment. InterfaithFamily provides web-based resources, training, networking opportunities and other support to interfaith couples and Jewish community-based leaders. Freedom Writers Foundation creates stories of overcoming adversity through education.

For funding sources, the "product" provided by nonprofits is "outcomes." Funding sources—whether they are individuals, corporations, or foundations—want to see that the organization they are investing in is delivering results. In some cases, these results need to be systematically measured and reported to funders (e.g., in Head Start agencies). In other cases, the "business" that the organization is in—for example, transforming the lives of young people, providing meals and shelter to homeless, or serving meals to seniors— is enough to keep funders engaged because, typically, the work being done is something that they are interested in. In these latter cases, the nonprofits' focus will need to be on continuing to keep these funding sources engaged.

Manage Resources and Develop Operational Systems

There are few differences between how non- and for-profit organizations build these two levels of the pyramid. Both types of enterprises face challenges with respect to acquiring needed human, technological, physical, and financial resources; and developing the day-to-day systems needed to support current and anticipated future operations.

There are, however, a few differences that need to be considered and managed. First, some nonprofits cannot afford to pay salaries that are competitive with for-profits that operate within their markets. This can lead to a situation where the nonprofit actually becomes a training ground to supply for-profits with skilled personnel. Sometimes, this problem can be solved by increasing salaries. In other cases, the nonprofit either needs to look to other ways of retaining personnel (e.g., a strong, inspiring, well-managed organizational culture) or accept that this is going to happen and prepare for it. This latter alternative would mean having a well-developed pipeline of potential employees to fill the vacancies when they occur.

A second difference is that many nonprofits are limited in terms of what they can invest in infrastructure development activities—including the development and implementation of new operational systems, bringing in outside resources to provide training, and (as stated above) increasing compensation—because they have very specific standards that need to be met with respect to how they allocate and manage their budgets. In some cases, these problems can be addressed through seeking and obtaining approval to allocate a specific amount of the organization's current budget to infrastructure development. It is also possible to secure new funding (e.g., small grants, donations from board members, etc.) that is specifically targeted for use in infrastructure development. For example, we facilitated a strategic planning process for one nonprofit that had obtained a grant for this purpose. In another case, a board member agreed to fund a two-day meeting to develop a strategic plan for the organization.

Develop Management Systems

All organizations need to develop effective planning and performance management systems, a structure that is aligned with their strategy, and a process for ensuring that those in leadership positions have the skills needed to effectively execute their roles. A major difference for most nonprofits in developing and implementing these systems is the presence of a volunteer board that, in effect, is part of the organization's management system.

While the board's composition and role can differ, somewhat, from organization to organization, its basic purpose is to provide input and advice to the people (typically referred to as "staff") who work in and manage the nonprofit's day-to-day operations. The most effective nonprofit boards are those where members clearly understand that their role is strategic (focused on the long-term development and success of the organization) versus tactical (involving themselves in day-to-day operations). This role is sometimes difficult for some people to embrace because, chances are, they are on the board as a result of what might be termed their keen interest or passion for the nonprofit's work. Frequently (although not always) nonprofit boards will have fiduciary responsibility—that is, they are charged with ensuring that the organization is financially sound and that resources are being wisely invested to achieve desired outcomes. At the most basic level, this role involves reviewing, approving, and holding the CEO or executive director and his or her team accountable for effectively managing the organization's budget, and, if necessary, replacing them.

For nonprofits, effectively implementing the management systems level of the pyramid involves clearly defining both staff and board roles (a part of the organization's structure). This should be done in writing (e.g., in the organization's bylaws). The role description for the board can be used to identify and engage new members as well as to remind existing board members about the boundaries of their roles.

As will be described later in this chapter, the development and implementation of the four management systems is basically the same in nonprofits as it is in for-profit enterprises—except that if a board is present, it will participate in this process. For example, the board will provide input on and in some cases will have the authority to approve the organization's strategic plan; and will sometimes have responsibility for selecting and evaluating the organization's CEO or executive director. The board may also be asked to approve structural changes—particularly if they involve the creation of new leadership positions or title changes that result in higher compensation for the occupant of the role.

Manage the Organizational Culture

Many nonprofits have a unique advantage with respect to culture management—people tend to join and remain a part of a nonprofit because they believe in and are supportive of the organization's purpose and values. People sometimes remain on the staff of a nonprofit even though they might receive higher compensation elsewhere because they are rewarded by the work that they do.

However, as is true in other organizations, this advantage can erode over time if the culture as a whole is not systematically managed. For example, in one $5 million (budget) nonprofit that had grown dramatically over a decade, the founder (who was the CEO and who was approaching retirement) simply would not let his senior leadership team do their jobs. He was critical of their performance and periodically berated individuals in front of the team. Everyone felt that they needed to be on guard against a possible outburst, and some employees came to literally hate going to work. Even though employees were passionate about the work that they were doing, many were considering leaving the organization. When the CEO "exploded" during a board meeting, the decision was made that he needed to retire or be terminated. Upon the founder's departure, a member of the senior leadership team, who had been with the organization for many years, was appointed by the board as the new CEO. The culture of the organization changed almost overnight—people felt a sense of relief, began to share and work together to address key issues, and many told the board that they were now "happy to come to work because the fear is gone."

As is true of for-profits, nonprofits need to build into their organizational planning a focus on culture and culture management. They also need to ensure that the culture, as appropriate, evolves as customer and employee needs change.

Applying the Stages of Organizational Growth and Growing Pains to Nonprofits

The seven stages of growth discussed in Chapters 3 and 4 can be directly applied to nonprofits. The only difference is that annual budget (instead of revenues) is used as the basis for identifying size. As most nonprofits are service-based organizations, this means that an organization with an annual budget less than $300,000 is Stage I, while a nonprofit over $1 billion in budget (such as Goodwill Industries—one of the largest nonprofits in the world) is at Stage VI.

As is true of for-profits, understanding the stage of growth that the organization is in and the challenges that need to be addressed in moving to the next stage should be considered when developing the organization's strategic plan. When an organization has not successfully built the infrastructure needed to support its operations, nonprofits (like their for-profit cousins) will experience growing pains. As described in Chapter 5, all growing pains apply to nonprofits as they are stated except the last—"The company has continued to grow in sales, but not in profits." This growing pain needs to be restated as, "Our administrative costs have increased more rapidly than our funding (budget)."

Since 1995, we have been collecting Growing Pains Survey results from nonprofit organizations. Table 11.1 presents the average scores for nonprofits and compares them with those of for-profits that are included in our database (described in Chapter 5).

Strategic Planning in Nonprofits

The approach to strategic planning described in Chapter 6 can and should be used by nonprofits in basically the same way as it is in for-profits. However, there are some unique aspects of nonprofits that need to be "managed" to promote effective plan implementation. First, nonprofits seem to be more prone to developing strategic plans "every five years" versus making planning an ongoing process that involves *annually* looking out three to five years. As described in Chapter 6, this is not effective because both the environment in which the organization is operating and the very nature of the organization will change significantly in this time period, thus making the plan irrelevant. Second, most nonprofits have boards typically comprised of people who volunteer their time to help promote the organization's success. Board members should be involved in helping to develop and support the implementation of the nonprofit's strategic plan. The nature of this involvement will differ, depending upon the role that the board plays, but generally speaking, the board's focus will and should be on strategy versus tactics.

Table 11.1 Nonprofit Growing Pains and How They Compare to For-Profit Companies

#	Growing Pain	Score Non-Profit	Score For-Profit
1	People feel that there are not enough hours in the day.	38.4	34.6
2	People are spending too much time "putting out fires."	34.4	32.5
3	Many people are not aware of what others are doing.	35.7	30.6
4	People have a lack of understanding of where the organization is headed.	30.7	28.1
5	There are too few "good" managers.	28.0	27.8
6	Everyone feels "I have to do it myself if I want to get it done correctly."	30.9	27.5
7	Most people feel our meetings are a waste of time.	28.3	25.4
8	When plans are made, there is very little follow-up, and things just don't get done.	27.2	26.6
9	Some people have begun to feel insecure about their place in the organization.	26.0	26.3
10	Our administrative costs have increased more rapidly than our funding/budget (for nonprofits) OR the company has continued to grow in sales but not in profits (for for-profit businesses).	27.6	25.1
	Overall	**30.7**	**28.5**

In this section, we will review the six steps in our planning process and describe how they can be applied in a nonprofit. To illustrate the process in action, we will share a number of examples of how this approach has been applied in nonprofits, but will provide a little more in-depth look at one nonprofit whose business is focused on providing comprehensive services to promote school readiness for children in their local market. This organization, which we will call "Healthy Beginnings Child Services," is a Head Start[1] grantee (meaning that it receives federal funding to deliver the Head Start program at the local level), but it also provides preschool programs that are supported by their state and other funding sources.[2] The annual budget for this organization, at the time that the plan described below was developed, was $9 million.

Step 1: Complete the Environmental Scan

The trend analysis for nonprofits will be the same as that in for-profit businesses—that is, it should focus on identifying the environmental trends (e.g., economic, demographic, regulatory) that will have the most significant impact on the organization over the next three to five years; and then identifying the opportunities and threats presented by these trends. A trend that is being closely monitored by some Head Start agencies, for example, is an aging population in the geographic areas that they serve accompanied by a decline in the number of children 0 to 5—which represents this organization's "target (service) market." With respect to the market and competitive analysis, there are some special issues that need to be addressed by nonprofits.

For nonprofits, the market analysis needs to focus on both the customers (e.g., members, clients, audiences, etc.) that the organization is working to serve (the target service market), as well as present and potential funding sources (the target funding market). In completing this part of the environmental scan, the organization's leadership team needs to work to identify the extent to which it is currently meeting both customers' needs and what might be done or done differently to enhance their effectiveness. Information about customers/clients can be collected in a variety of ways. Some nonprofits (like NAWBO) conduct regular customer (in their case, member) surveys and use this information as input to plan development and performance assessment. Some draw upon the best thinking of their leadership teams and board to identify what's working and what's not with respect to meeting customer needs. With respect to funding sources, the nonprofit's leadership team should clearly identify funding sources (present and potential) and assess the extent to which they are or can meet their needs.

It is sometimes difficult to convince nonprofit leadership that there is a need for a competitive analysis. Some believe that what they offer is unique enough that they don't really compete with anyone. Some even believe that the word "competition" has negative connotations. The fact is that nonprofits *do* compete—they compete for financial resources (funding), and they compete for people's time. While it may be true that there are no other entities providing exactly the same services to exactly the same customers, there are probably other entities that are targeting the same potential donors. There may also be entities that are serving or could serve the organization's targeted customers and/or who are providing or might provide similar services. The overall questions that need to be addressed in completing this aspect of the environmental scan are:

- Who are our present and potential competitors with respect to securing funding? That is, who might a present or potential funder give their resources to if they didn't give them to us?

- Who are our present or potential competitors with respect to serving our target market? That is, where might our targeted customers go to meet the needs that we are trying to satisfy, if they don't come to us?

- What are the strengths and limitations of each competitor?

- What can we do to minimize any potential negative impact of these competitors on our continued success?

It should also be noted that another deliverable from the competitive analysis can be the identification of potential strategic partners—that is, other organizations with whom the nonprofit might join in the provision of services to a particular customer or client base.

To illustrate these concepts, Table 11.2 presents excerpts from Healthy Beginnings Child Services' environmental scan. To preserve their anonymity, we have disguised their location and size.

Step 2: Complete the Organizational Assessment

As described earlier in this chapter, the Pyramid of Organizational Development can be used as the lens for completing the organizational assessment—in very much the same manner as it is used in a for-profit business. In brief, this involves assessing the organization's strengths and limitations or opportunities to improve with respect to each key driver of long-term success.

Table 11.2   Excerpts from a Healthy Beginnings Child Services Strategic Plan Environmental Scan

Market Analysis		
Target Customers	**Customer Needs**	**How the Organization's Products/ Services Meet Customer Needs**
Low-Income Children	Such children are at-risk for developmental issues, health issues (including obesity), and academic failure.	Comprehensive approach to serving the "whole child" and working to address all needs.
At-Risk Children	Positive school readiness experiences. Training and support for parents.	High-quality classroom experiences. Support services for parents.
Lower-Income Families	Transportation. Quality childcare. Quality preschool. Parental support.	The Head Start model not only focuses on the children but on the entire family through home visits. Working with the family as a unit to help them develop and work toward goals that will address their needs. Childcare. Quality preschool. Parental support and training.
Other Agencies	Collaboration to provide services. Prioritizing community needs. Seeking funds.	Staff sit on agency committees and boards. Assist with the assessment of needs. Can offer grant-writing assistance.
Competitive Analysis		
Competitors	**Strengths from the Customers' Perspective**	**Limitations from the Customers' Perspective**
Home Providers	Proximity to home. Hours of operation. All ages of children are served. May have rules that are flexible.	Level of quality. Range of services provided does not compare to Head Start support. Cost. Maybe training.

Table 11.2   (Continued)

Competitive Analysis		
Competitors	Strengths from the Customers' Perspective	Limitations from the Customers' Perspective
Schools and School Districts	Reputation of school district. All children could possibly be in one site. Public school student population and parents are a "captive audience." "Built-in" connection and co-location with K-12 education. Children would receive services in the building where they would eventually go to kindergarten. Have the facilities. Quality staff. Internal structure.	Limited knowledge of birth to five. May have policies that are difficult for families with young children/ transportation. Inexperience with preschool. Source/cause of increasing taxes. Costs are too high. Healthy Beginnings Child Services has over 20 years of experience in the preschool field.
Private Preschools	Can pick your home or center in relation to where you live. Time frames. Societal status. Less structure. Less regulations.	Cost. Costs to parents are higher due to state and federal programs being free to them. Potential training of staff. Transportation. Geographic limitations.

Trend Analysis		
Trend	Opportunity	Threat
Demographic: Majority of the school districts are reporting declining enrollment. Decrease in number of children in school districts. Decrease in school enrollment.	Provide space opportunities in the public school buildings which may reduce cost for space. More opportunity for space in schools.	Difficulty filling enrollment slots. Less children for enrollment.—Less money in schools means that they may begin to charge for usage of space or service. Not able to meet enrollment.
Economic: Funding cuts at the federal, state, and local levels (many of which are occurring at the 12th hour or even retroactively).	Decreased slots would mean that a waiting list would probably be a result.	Additional time must be spent planning for, anticipating, and developing contingency plans for various funding scenarios.

(continued)

Table 11.2   (*Continued*)

Trend Analysis		
Trend	Opportunity	Threat
State funding decreasing.		Decrease in overall funding means that less services can be provided. Must provide mandated services, but auxiliary services may be eliminated.
Regulatory: Increasingly restrictive. regulations—both state and federal.	Provides an opportunity to tighten our operations to meet the more stringent requirements.	Requires additional staff time spent on ensuring compliance, tracking information, documenting progress, and submitting reports.
Technology: Technology is used heavily by families (iPhone, iPads, air cards for laptops, texting, etc.)	It could provide us better coordination to get home visits completed.	Home visiting staff includes older "mother" types who are not comfortable with technology. It is difficult for them to engage families.

This information can be collected from the organization's employees—using surveys, interviews, or focus groups—and/or the organization can ask an independent consultant to assist in the completion of the assessment. The deliverable from this process should be a written report that summarizes key strengths and opportunities to improve at each level in the Pyramid of Organizational Development. An example of the output of this assessment—based on the work completed at Healthy Beginnings Child Services—is presented in Table 11.3.

Step 3 and Step 4: Analysis and Resolution of Key Strategic Issues and Development of the Strategic Plan

In developing their plans, both nonprofits and for-profit businesses need to address the same seven issues—which were identified and discussed in Chapter 6—with the resolution of each issue being incorporated into a specific element of the strategic plan. There are, however, some specific challenges that nonprofits face in addressing these issues and developing specific aspects of the strategic plan, as will be discussed below.

Developing the Business Definition/Concept Statement (Addressing the Strategic Issue, "What Business Are We In?") As is true for for-profits, answering this question involves clearly identifying the target customers and what the nonprofit will be doing to meet those customers' needs. Effective nonprofit business definitions sometimes focus exclusively on the customers that the organization is working to serve, while at other times they focus on both these

Table 11.3   Excerpts from Healthy Beginnings Child Services Organizational Assessment

Products and Services	Strengths	Limitations/Areas for Improvement
High-Quality Classroom Experiences	• Program review instruments utilized to assess classroom quality have shown that we do provide classroom experiences that are high quality. • Meet all federal and state guidelines and in some areas exceed requirements.	• Not all share the same understanding or desire to understand what it means to provide high-quality classroom experiences.
Preschool Services (Head Start, Pre-K, and Early Head Start)	• We provide a spectrum of services for all eligible children.	• Limited slots in programs and in specific centers. • Families must meet eligibility requirements.
Outcomes and Measurements	• Data available for analysis.	• Misuse of information.

Resource or Operational System	Strengths	Limitations/Areas for Improvement
Financial	• Strong, diverse financial base including funding from federal, state, and local sources; debt-free operations. • Cost allocation has permitted more opportunities for support services. • We have a highly competent, experienced fiscal department that handles cash flow, access to funds, operational budgeting, financial reporting, and accounting. • Good/excellent financial accounting system for tracking/reporting/projecting.	• We are at the mercy of the government and spending/budgeting trends. • Approved funding has decreased to prohibit nonessential purchases. Training opportunities have decreased, and raises have been limited. • Costs are allocated across all programs. If one program makes changes, it will impact all programs; not all programs will be affected in a positive manner.

(continued)

Table 11.3   (*Continued*)

Resource or Operational System	Strengths	Limitations/Areas for Improvement
Facilities	• Facilities that meet/exceed the regulations. • Healthy Beginnings owns many of its own buildings and can control the upkeep and access.	• Growth has created problems with overcrowding in office areas. • Facilities that were designed by in-house staff may be poorly designed. We should have professionals design spaces in order to best meet the needs of our clients. • Facilities could be used to better market services through targeted signage.
Equipment	• Healthy Beginnings provides each location with hardware/software, Internet connectivity to complete the technical parts of employee's jobs. • Healthy Beginnings has a fleet of vehicles, ample copiers, and a host of computers. • We are able to purchase what we need to do a good job. • Own our buses.	• The need for more computers, laptops at centers since the demand is growing for teachers/home visitors/staff to become more "online" with assessment tools, email, Outlook schedules, and so on. • Older obsolete equipment. • Budget limitation sometimes doesn't allow for replacement.
Information Systems	• Computer equipment and communications systems are state of the art in most cases. • We recognize the importance of keeping current with trends in technology. • Very limited paper files—less costly. • Knowledgeable IT staff.	• Laptops for staff would be useful. • Hands-on training for certain technology. There is no written training plan for all staff to be trained to use technology appropriately.

Table 11.3 *(Continued)*

Resource or Operational System	Strengths	Limitations/Areas for Improvement
Human Resources	• Have highly qualified and experienced staff. • We have systems in place to assure we hire qualified individuals. • There are many opportunities for formal training throughout the year, as well as an ability to focus individually as needed. • Ongoing policy and procedures updating due to changing environment/Head Start requirements.	• Lack of available and qualified staff. • Interviewing is highly structured, which can limit effectiveness with more high-level positions. • Each program designs their own training plan, but they are not synchronized so that programs could access or utilize trainings that may be occurring in other programs. • Keeping procedure manual up to date.
Public Relations, Sales, Community Outreach, New Opportunity Identification	• We market ourselves through parades, fairs, school fairs, job fairs, and local colleges. • Community organizations turn to us as we are established. • Participation on community boards and committees.	• We focus on "tried and true" events but don't regularly expand our involvement in new or planned areas of expansion (consequently, we are largely unknown in those areas). • We don't have a formal, agency-wide marketing strategy that is connected to program expansion, new markets, etc.
Quality Assurance, Control	• Good internal controls for monitoring and review. • There is a well-trained middle management group who completes frequent checks/tracking in order to make sure we are in compliance and providing quality services.	• Timeliness of information. • We have reduced some positions and increased the workload for some team members as a result of flat funding in years past.

(continued)

Table 11.3   (*Continued*)

Management System	Strengths	Limitations/Areas for Improvement
Planning and Plan Implementation	• We develop strategic plans. • Service area plans are updated annually.	• Formal planning at times falls short in the sense that plans are not always committed to writing and shared with all involved. • We have not had a formal strategic planning meeting for several years. • Everything is a priority; changing daily plans; can't plan if others change your schedule.
Organizational Structure	• The structure is very clear on who you go to for what. This includes who is responsible for what area. • Job descriptions are detailed for each position.	• Need clearer understanding of leadership roles. • Individuals seem unsure about what decisions they can make and what decisions need to be made at a level above them; often, decisions can take a long time to be made if they are not of an emergency nature.
Performance Management Systems	• We have system(s) in place to monitor child outcomes. • We have a formal appraisal process.	• We currently do not have consistent uniform systems in place to monitor progress and share findings. • Performance appraisals are limited to "meeting the standard" as the highest rating. • Challenges with how to effectively reward performance.
Management Development/Specific Management Skills	• We have managers with many years of experience, knowledge and expertise in their assigned areas of responsibility. • Training is provided to managerial staff to ensure successful completion of tasks.	• Training is not regularly or consistently provided in management skills (e.g., supervision, time management, effective delegation, etc.)

Table 11.3   (*Continued*)

Culture	Strengths	Limitations/Areas for Improvement
	• There is a strong commitment among employees to improving children's lives. • People believe in what we do. • The atmosphere is professional. • Staff are friendly and supportive on a coworker and personal level (Healthy Beginnings family)	• We "fly by the seat of our pants" by putting out fires after they've started . . . not always preplanning and communicating with the intensity that we should. • Many staff have territorial issues and become easily offended when others bring up concerns or try to help. • Some people are of the opinion that decisions are never to be questioned.

customers and meeting the needs of funders. As an example, the business definition for Healthy Beginnings Child Services is presented below:

Sample Business Definition for a Nonprofit—Healthy Beginnings Child Services

We provide eligible families with comprehensive and individualized services that support school readiness and help parents understand and embrace the role they play in their children's education and development. Our services include high-quality preschool classrooms, parent engagement opportunities, home visits, family support and training, and health, safety, and nutrition guidance.

Nonprofits face several challenges in addressing the question, "What business are we in?" and, in turn, creating an effective business definition/concept statement. First, as stated at the beginning of this chapter, staff and/or board members may not view what they do as a business, and, therefore, even using the term "business definition/concept" becomes a problem. In these cases, leadership teams agree that there is a need to clearly define what the organization is and should be doing, but the term "business definition" doesn't work for them. When this view is present and strongly held, changing the "label" of this component to something like "purpose" (while retaining the definition of the component) can be enough to address these concerns.

A second and somewhat more difficult problem to manage relates to reaching agreement on what the business definition/concept *should be*. The very strong focus on "service," "serving others," and "serving as many people as we can," can sometimes undermine the ability to clearly define what the organization does. In addition, sometimes successful nonprofits are presented with so many requests to provide their services that it is difficult to choose because it means giving something up.

In one nonprofit, for example, board and staff spent nearly four hours debating whether it was better to focus on providing their services (which included education, counseling, and peer support) to the target customers that they had been focused upon since the organization's founding 10 years before or expand their services to very different types of clients who had similar needs. Some were passionate that there should be no limitations on whom the organization should serve. Others (including the organization's CEO/executive director) believed that the potential for growth within the existing market was very high, that the organization had expertise and a reputation in this market, and that there weren't adequate resources (including knowledge of the other potential markets, as well as financial resources) to expand. As is true in many nonprofits, board and staff were very passionate about what the nonprofit was set up to do and wanted to serve as many people as possible. While this is admirable, trying to provide service to everyone can lead to significant problems. The decision was finally made to focus on the current market for the next three years and revisit possible expansion into others after that. The rationale was that by focusing on this market, the nonprofit could continue to build its capabilities and that when adequate resources were available, it would be able to expand into other areas.

How can this second challenge be effectively managed? As was true in the example above, one way to manage this issue when it arises is to revisit and discuss environmental scan and organizational assessment findings. In brief, what do they suggest about what business the organization should be in? What offers the most potential for impact? A specific area that needs to be focused on is the level of funding and why current funders are providing resources to the organization. In the example above, the fact that the organization had no experience with the other potential markets and weren't even sure that their current services would meet these market's needs was a factor that led to a more narrow business definition. Another factor that contributed to this decision was the assessment that current funders were most interested in helping to support work in the current market.

Developing the Strategic Mission (Addressing the Question, "What Do We Want to Become in the Long-Term?"). As is true of for-profits, a nonprofit's strategic mission needs to identity the big-picture results that the organization will be working to achieve in its markets (that is, with its customers), which (unlike for-profits) will not be measured in revenue growth and profitability. Instead, measurements of success can include the number of clients served, the level of funding achieved, expansion of services provided, and other factors.

Nonprofits are becoming increasingly focused on measuring and documenting outcomes—that is, tracking the impact that their services have had on their target markets. Funders, in fact, are increasingly asking to see evidence of outcomes before making an investment. Sometimes, as is the case with Head Start agencies, the full impact of their programs and services cannot be measured for many years (e.g., one measurement is a Head Start child's success in school, as well as in life over the longer term). In these cases, it may be difficult to include an outcome measurement in the strategic mission. In other cases, as is the case with Shelter 37, mentioned earlier in this chapter, outcomes are shorter-term (e.g., the number of Shelter 37 youth who have earned a high school diploma, the number of youth who have secured jobs and are still employed over X period of time, etc.).

When outcomes can be assessed within the timeframe of the strategic plan, this metric should be included in the strategic mission.

It should be noted that some nonprofits find it very difficult to identify realistic measurable and meaningful quantitative measurements to include in their strategic missions. In our work with non-profits, we encourage staff and board members to think about possible quantitative measurements of success (e.g., target funding level, numerical measurements of outcomes, etc.), but there are times when measurements simply don't exist or where the ability to achieve a target is so dependent on an uncontrollable source (such as securing funding from a governmental agency) that it just doesn't make sense to include it. Therefore, some nonprofit strategic missions will be more qualitative in nature, as illustrated in the example below from Healthy Beginnings Child Services:

Sample Strategic Mission for a Nonprofit—Healthy Beginnings Child Services

By July 31, 20XX, we will be the provider of choice for early childhood education and early intervention services in the geographic areas we serve by improving quality while operating more effectively. We will maintain quality programs and compete effectively for additional programs and services, based on need. We will be recognized by our funding sources, early childhood entities, and local communities for the dedication and specialized skill sets of our staff, high quality services, and continued program development.

Core Strategy (Addressing the Questions, "What are Our Competitive Strengths and Limitations?" and "Do We Have or Can We Develop a Market Niche?"). Having a core strategy that identifies the overall way that the organization will compete is as important for nonprofits as it is for for-profit businesses. In developing a core strategy in nonprofits, one issue that needs to be addressed, if it exists, is the belief that "we don't have any competition" (described earlier in this chapter). Once competitors are identified, there needs to be an assessment of their strengths and limitations. This assessment can then be used as the basis for identifying true competitive advantages (or whether the nonprofit has or can develop a market niche). One specific question that can be used by nonprofits to help identify their competitive advantages and whether they have or can develop a market niche is, "Why would a potential funder provide our organization with funding versus another?"

Based upon an analysis of their competitors' strengths and limitations (excerpts were presented earlier in this chapter), Healthy Beginnings Child Services' leadership team identified the following as their key competitive strengths:

- Our very good reputation in the community for providing quality service.
- The diverse and comprehensive nature of our programs and services.
- The experience and qualifications of our staff and our leadership team.
- Our culture of caring about employees and of being willing to invest in their development.
- A very strong financial base that is supported by effective management of our administrative costs.

After some discussion, they crafted the following core strategy:

Build upon our reputation for providing quality services, our ability to provide comprehensive services, and the positive aspects of our culture to grow the number of families served and attract and retain the qualified (and caring) employees needed to meet our families' needs.

Identify Key Result Areas (Address the Strategic Question, "What Are the Critical Factors that Will Make Us Successful over the Long-Term). The same seven key result areas that are used in for-profit businesses should also be used in developing nonprofit business plans (because research has shown that these are key drivers of long-term success). However, the labels used to identify these key result areas are difficult for some nonprofit leadership teams to apply and use in practice. In brief, the terminology used (not the underlying concept) doesn't seem to fit. When this is the case, the nonprofit may adopt (although we do not recommend this) a different set of designated key result areas; but if they do, they need to be very careful to ensure that the seven drivers of success are actually included in the revision. This can be accomplished by clearly defining the areas of the pyramid addressed by each key result area. As an example, one nonprofit that adopted this approach presented their key result areas as follows:

1.0 Outreach and Communications (markets, operational systems)

2.0 Advocacy (markets, products/services)

3.0 Partnerships (markets, products/services, resources, operational systems, financial results)

4.0 Program Design and Delivery (products/services)

5.0 Fund Development and Management (financial results)

6.0 Capacity and Infrastructure (resources, operational systems, management systems, culture)

7.0 Board Development (Management Systems)

Nonprofits may include one or two specific additional key result areas beyond the core seven. One of these relates to the board, per se. The strategic plan for a nonprofit should include objectives and goals related to what the organization is looking for from their board and what they will do to develop their board's capabilities (e.g., identifying what the board's composition should be, selecting new board members, providing training to their board, etc.). In some cases, as illustrated in the example above, there is a separate key result area in which objectives and goals for the board can be recorded and managed (e.g., "board development"). In other cases, the goals for the board are presented under an objective under the "management systems" key result area.

A second key result area that might be added is something like "strategic partnerships" (which can also be a distinct key result area in a for-profit plan). This is most appropriate when these strategic partnerships are serving multiple purposes—for example, they are being used to help secure additional funding, and they are also providing specific services to the nonprofit's clients.

Objectives, SMART Goals, and Action Plans. These three concepts should be developed and used in nonprofits in the same manner as they are in for-profits. It should be noted, however, that there seems to be a greater tendency in nonprofits to define goals as "broad, long-term results to be achieved" and objectives as specific, measurable, time-dated results (SMART). As described in Chapter 6, when this is the case, there is no problem relabeling the two components. It is, however, important that these two components be present and used consistently within the plan. Table 11.4 presents excerpts from Healthy Beginnings Child Services strategic plan as an illustration of objectives and SMART goals in a nonprofit.

Table 11.4   Sample Objectives and SMART Goals—Excerpts from Healthy Beginnings Child Services Strategic Plan

Key Result Area 1.0	**Markets and Products/Services**
Objective 1.1	Be the leader in providing services in early childhood education.
Goal 1.1.1	80% of all classrooms will achieve or exceed the minimum required ECERS rating (per program requirements) by 7/31/XX (Jenny).
Key Result Area 2.0	**Resources**
Objective 2.1	Utilize technology to support efficient service delivery and maintain relationships with the families we serve.
Goal 2.1.1	Implement an electronic notification system for staff and families by 11/30/XX (Ben).
Key Result Area 3.0	**Operational Systems**
Objective 3.1	Provide training to all staff to help enhance their job performance and their ability to utilize technology.
Goal 3.1.1	Have all staff achieve 75% proficiency on our "technology usage test" by 6/30/XX (Bobby).
Key Result Area 4.0	**Management Systems**
Objective 4.1	Clearly define and communicate the preschool division's structure and staff roles and responsibilities.
Goal 4.1.1	Finalize key result area–based role descriptions for all management positions by 6/30/XX (Bobby).
Key Result Area 5.0	**Culture**
Objective 5.1	Effectively communicate and manage our culture as a strategic asset.
Goal 5.1.1	Clearly define and document (in writing) our core values by 7/31/XX (Karen).
Key Result Area 6.0	**Financial Results Management**
Objective 6.1	Effectively manage expenses and costs.

Developing the Budget. For nonprofits, this step in the strategic planning process serves the same purpose as it does in for-profits—to identify how financial resources will be invested to promote the achievement of the nonfinancial (strategic) plan. While it is beyond the scope of this book to address this issue in detail, it should be noted that the budgeting process for nonprofits can sometimes be made more difficult by restrictions that are placed upon them in terms of the percentage of funding that can be allocated to G&A (general and administrative) costs.

Plan Review. To maximize the effectiveness of the planning process, the leadership of nonprofits (staff and board) needs to implement a plan review process like that described in Chapter 6. Typically, however, this process will involve two phases: (1) plan review conducted by staff, and (2) presentation and discussion with the board of results being achieved against the plan.

Plan review by staff will involve, as it does in a for-profit, preparing for and holding quarterly (or sometimes more frequent) plan review meetings. Prior to each meeting, each goal owner should prepare a written report summarizing progress being made in achieving goals, with these reports being circulated among the team. Meeting time should be devoted to discussing and resolving any problems with respect to achieving goals and to discussing any new issues. Following the meeting, the strategic plan should be updated (as described in Chapter 6), and a written report should be prepared for the board on progress being made against the plan.

The progress report or plan update report to the board should typically not include detailed progress against each and every goal in the plan. Instead, it should provide more of a big-picture look at what has been accomplished. One CEO of a nonprofit structured her report to the board based on key objectives (that had been identified as a part of the plan development process). For each of these objectives, her quarterly progress report answered the following questions: (1) What efforts have we made to achieve this objective? (2) How were we successful? (3) What are possible next steps? She and her team also identified specific challenges related to achieving plan goals that they wanted board input on.

The report to the board should be circulated in advance of the board meeting during which progress against the plan will be discussed. Some nonprofits hold plan review meetings with their boards on a quarterly basis, while others prefer to provide updates every four or six months. As the board is not (and should not be involved) in day-to-day operations, any of these options can be effective. The frequency of board involvement in plan review depends on the needs of the organization and its staff.

During the board's plan review meeting (which will typically occur in the context of a regularly scheduled board meeting), the focus should be on providing input to staff on plan achievement. This can be in the form of asking questions about information presented in the plan review report, providing input on strategies for increasing the probability of achieving key goals, and sharing ideas about what might be done to address specific problems or strategic issues. The goals of the organization should also be kept in mind during discussion of financial performance (budget review), which is a typical agenda item for most board meetings. Finally, time should be devoted to discussing how the board is performing against its goals—which should be included (as described above) in the strategic plan.

Organizational Structure and Structure Management in Nonprofits

The framework and tools for designing and managing structure described in Chapter 7 can and should be applied to support the long-term successful development of a nonprofit. This involves designing the macro structure so that it is aligned with the organization's strategy, clearly defining roles and responsibilities, and implementing systems to support the effective implementation of the structure. Some of the specific structural issues that nonprofits frequently need to focus on as they grow and develop are discussed below.

Wearing Multiple Hats

Small nonprofits (in Stages I and II, and sometimes in Stage III) frequently have people who occupy two or sometimes more roles. For example, the executive director of the organization might also be responsible for managing a specific function (e.g., IT, the delivery of a specific service, marketing). Sometimes, this is because the organization is so small that separating out the two (or sometimes more) roles doesn't make economic sense—that is, one person can still realistically fulfill both roles. Sometimes, this is the result of budget constraints—that is, there aren't the financial resources needed to support a person in each role.

Having people who wear multiple hats can be effective as long as the expectations are clear and as long as these expectations can reasonably be met. However, as the organization grows, there is a high probability that one person will no longer be able to effectively fulfill two (or more) roles due to an increase in workload. Nonprofits that have this as a part of their structures need to be aware of and manage it as a part of their strategic planning process because it can have a significant impact on overall performance. In one $10 million (budget) nonprofit that had two service delivery divisions and that had grown significantly over a decade, for example, the director (CEO) wore *at least* three hats. He was responsible for funding acquisition (including grant writing), partnership development and maintenance, managing one of the divisions, and overseeing the entire organization. While the organization, overall, was successful, the director and his board felt that significant opportunities were being missed in the market (from a funding perspective), and some team members felt that they were not receiving the direction and training they needed to be successful. The director was simply spread too thin. At one board meeting, the director and the board laid out the structure on a whiteboard. When they did, it was clear that the director's span of control was far too large (nine people) for anyone to be successful. The board voted and approved a new management position to oversee the day-to-day operations of the division, thus providing the director the time needed to focus on the strategic development of the enterprise.

The Role of Volunteers

Many nonprofits have volunteers (not employed by the organization) who help support the achievement of organizational goals. They might be involved in staffing a fund-raising event, in directly serving clients, in providing training to staff, and in many other ways. When volunteers are used, they should be included in and managed as a part of the organization's structure. This does not necessarily mean that they will be included on an organization chart. It does mean, however, that the roles that they will play and how they will be managed should be discussed and clearly defined.

The management of volunteers can be, at times, a difficult balancing act. On the one hand, the nonprofit will want to ensure that volunteers understand and stay within the boundaries of their roles. On the other hand, volunteers are not getting paid, and upsetting them can "cost" the organization in terms of the willingness of people to serve in this role in the future. Having a written description of the role each volunteer will play can be a useful tool in this process. These role descriptions do not need to be as detailed as those of full-time staff, but they do need to clearly define what the volunteer in that position should and should not be doing. The staff person to whom volunteers report (that is, the person who will be in a very real sense serving as their supervisor) should take the time to review these expectations, ask for any feedback, and answer any questions. It should also be clear to each volunteer who the staff person is that he or she should primarily be working with or for (that is, who he or she basically reports to).

Clearly Defining Board and Staff Roles

As described earlier in this chapter, the lack of clarity about board and staff roles can create specific problems or challenges for a nonprofit. These include board members' expertise being underutilized because they aren't sure what they should and should not be involved in; board members becoming or wanting to become too involved in the organization's day-to-day operations; and staff and board members being frustrated with each other because each is not delivering what the other believes they should be.

It is important that staff and board roles be clearly defined (in writing) and that these role definitions be revisited frequently. Some nonprofits include information about board responsibilities in their bylaws. Others do this less formally. Review of staff and board roles should be included as a part of the annual strategic planning process. In addition, the orientation of new board members should include a specific review of roles and responsibilities.

One tool that can be used to clarify board and staff roles is key result area–based role descriptions (described in Chapter 7). To illustrate the use of this tool, Table 11.5 presents the mission and key result areas for the board and leadership team of one nonprofit.

Management and Leadership Development in Nonprofits

There is little difference between nonprofits and for-profit enterprises with respect to the management and leadership capabilities required to support the organization's long-term success. However, there are two important (and one might argue somewhat unique) skills that the CEO/executive director of a nonprofit needs to possess, regardless of the organization's size: fund development and management of the board.

The CEO/executive director needs to have the ability to directly or indirectly (through managing the work of others) identify funding sources and complete the work (including, in some cases, preparing grants) needed to secure these funds. In addition, he or she needs to possess the capabilities to develop and manage relationships with potential and present funders. Typically,

Table 11.5   Roles of Board and Staff

Board of Directors Role

To establish the vision for the organization's continued development and provide support to management in making this vision a reality.

Key Result Areas

1. Strategy Development and Evaluation
2. Executive Director Selection/Performance Review
3. Resource Acquisition and Management
4. Fiscal Management
5. Program Monitoring
6. Community Relations
7. Board Development

Leadership Team (Staff) Role

To realize the organization's mission through effective management of day-to-day operations.

Key Result Areas

1. Strategic and Operational Planning
2. Program Management
3. Resource Acquisition and Management
4. Fiscal Management
5. Board Relations
6. Community Relations
7. Management and Organizational Development

---

the management of these relationships is something that needs to be done by the most senior executive—the CEO/executive director.

Board management leadership skills have several dimensions. First, there is the skill needed to "design" the board (that is, to identify the composition needed to support the achievement of organizational goals). Next, there is a need to understand how to attract, select, and retain board members. Finally, there is the skill set required to manage the board on an ongoing basis—including structuring and facilitating board meetings.

The development of leadership and management capabilities in nonprofits can occur through a variety of methods, including attendance at leadership development programs offered by associations to which the organization belongs, university-sponsored programs, in-house programs, and individual coaching. The leadership team needs to identify the best method to be used, given the resources available. In one Head Start agency, for example, the executive director had attended the UCLA "Fellows" program that was designed to promote the development of effective leadership and organizational development skills. Following the program, she identified the need for all of her direct reports to better embrace their roles as managers and leaders. She basically said to them, "We cannot continue to grow and be successful if you continue being 'doers.' I care a lot about results, but I also care how you achieve them. I need you to manage and grow your team, rather than do the work yourself, and I am going to help you develop the skills to make this happen."[3] She worked with one of the authors to design and implement an in-house program. This program began with an introduction to the three dimensions of management and leadership effectiveness (described in Chapter 9). Participants were also provided training in time management, delegation, operational leadership effectiveness (discussed in Chapter 12), decision making, and performance management (including how to create effective key result area–based role descriptions). Over a period of about two years, her team had made the successful transition to their roles.

Performance Management in Nonprofits

Performance management systems in nonprofits should be designed and managed in a manner similar to that used in for-profit enterprises—as described in Chapter 8. In some nonprofits (like Head Start), funding sources conduct regular reviews of the organization against well-defined performance standards. In others, the performance management system is designed and managed by the board and staff, and is built upon the foundation of the strategic plan.

One key to promoting effective implementation of performance management systems is to ensure that goals are measurable. For example, the goal of one nonprofit stated, "To achieve 95% client satisfaction by (date)." On the surface, this is a SMART goal, but when the leadership team began to discuss it, they realized that there was no system in place to actually measure client satisfaction. This realization led to the team's devoting several meetings to clearly defining and documenting the measurement system that would be used to monitor performance against each goal in their organization's strategic plan. On their "measurement specification forms," the team identified how performance would be assessed, the person responsible for assessing performance, how results of the measurement process would be reported, and how frequently performance would be assessed. This illustrates one effective way to create and implement the measurement component of the performance management system.

At the individual level, all of the strategies identified in Chapter 8 can be applied in nonprofits. A specific area of focus at the individual level needs to be on how the CEO/executive director's performance will be evaluated. Working with the board, the CEO/executive director needs to clearly define his or her goals, identify the methods that will be used to assess performance (e.g., board evaluation, self-assessment, input from the CEO/executive director's direct reports, community or client input, etc.), establish and meet dates for measuring performance and providing feedback (including who will provide the feedback and how), identify the method that will be used at year-end to evaluate overall performance, and determine how rewards will be used to recognize performance.

Most of the goals against which the CEO/executive director's performance will be assessed will be related to organizational performance, but there should also be some related to the performance and growth of the individual in his or her role. For example, this type of goal might focus on how effectively the individual is managing his or her team, on the effectiveness of board communication, or on the extent to which the individual has enhanced a specific capability. Some CEO/executive directors use a scorecard approach for presenting their individual goals (like that described in Chapter 8). This makes it very easy for the board to understand what is being focused upon, how performance will be measured, and the progress being made.

As is true in all organizations, staff and board need to focus an appropriate amount of time on the management and implementation of the performance management system. Including a review of progress against the organization's goals as a standing board meeting agenda item is one strategy for ensuring that this happens. Another thing that nonprofits need to guard against is allowing their performance management system to become focused on factors other than results. Having checklists of things that need to be done (e.g., how to open the office, how to answer the phone, how to set up a facility, etc.) are important, but they are very much day-to-day routines. They are not directly about results to be achieved.

Culture Management in Nonprofits

As described earlier in this chapter, many nonprofits have an advantage when it comes to culture management because those who join the organization—as staff or board—frequently do so because they believe in and are supportive of the work being done. They embrace what the organization does and are willing to work hard to deliver the best to their customers/clients. Even when this is the case, without effective culture management, each individual might have a different picture about what effective customer service means, and this can lead to conflict within the organization.

Culture management within nonprofits begins (as it does in all organizations) with the development of a clear statement of the organization's values. At Healthy Beginnings Child Services (the disguised nonprofit described earlier in this chapter), there had never been a written statement of values. One agenda item on an annual strategic plan development meeting was to begin the process of formally managing the organization's culture. This involved identifying the organization's values and determining the best way to make them real for the rest of the employees. Some of the elements of Healthy Beginnings Child Services' values identified during this meeting are presented below, along with how each reflects one of the five dimensions of culture discussed in Chapter 10:

1. Respect individuals as professionals (people orientation)

2. Meet them where they are and accept where they are going (customer–client orientation)

3. Follow the rules and celebrate successes (performance standards and accountability)

4. Embrace change, but do it at a pace that we can handle (openness to change)

5. Be proactive and communicate! (process orientation)

While the identification of the organization's values should begin with the senior leadership team, once documented, the values should be shared and discussed with employees throughout the organization to ensure that they are understood and make sense. This is not to suggest that the values should be changed, but the way that they are stated may need to be tailored to promote better understanding. Some nonprofit leadership teams also share and discuss the statement of values with their board before they are finalized. However, it should be kept in mind that while the board needs to be supportive of the values, they are not expected to live them on a daily basis, and this should be kept in mind in capturing and using their input to refine the values.

The process and tools described in Chapter 10 can be used to identify the extent to which the desired culture, once defined, is being lived by employees throughout the organization. This information might be collected using group discussions (best used when the organization is small and there is a culture of open sharing of information), one-on-one interviews, or surveys. Based on the information collected, the leadership team can identify gaps between the current and desired cultures. The team should then develop specific goals for closing any gaps identified. These goals should be included in the organization's strategic plan, with progress against goals being monitored on a regular basis.

The advantage that some nonprofits have with respect to staff and board embracing and living the culture can become a disadvantage as the organization grows or needs to change (to meet the needs of a different environment). Changing strong cultures that are not supportive of what the organization needs to do to be successful will typically involve implementing new or significantly refining existing systems at other levels in the Pyramid of Organizational Development, as illustrated in the case of Community Child Development Services (the disguised name of a real organization) described next.

Community Child Development Services (CCDS) was a $7 million (budget) child development agency when the executive director and associate director (who had both been with the organization for nearly a decade) recognized the need to "professionalize" their operations in the face of declining federal funding and new opportunities at the local level (including increased budget for state-funded preschool). Specific problems included lack of up-to-date technology, too much paperwork, an underdeveloped training system, lack of formalized strategic planning, poor communication, and a culture in which people were not held accountable for their performance. There was, in fact, a belief that "we never terminate anyone."

To address these issues, CCDS's leadership team worked together for six months to develop a strategic plan using the approach described in this book. The board was involved in reviewing and providing input on the organization's strategy, as well as in listening carefully to and supporting the investments in new technology and systems that would be required to promote more effective and efficient operations. With the board's support, old operational systems were replaced with new ones, and training was provided to promote the effective utilization of these new systems.

In addition to strategic planning, CCDS's leadership team and board also worked to enhance the effectiveness of the other three management systems. The executive director worked with one of the authors to design and deliver an in-house leadership development program for all managers and supervisors (including "teacher-directors" who supervised the educational centers where services were provided to children) that occurred over a period of two years. This program focused on both individual skill development, as well as on helping those in leadership positions support the implementation of new management systems. Topics included the three-factor approach to management/leadership effectiveness (discussed in Chapter 9), as well as leadership effectiveness, motivation, time management, delegation, effective goal-setting, developing effective key result area–based role descriptions, and organizational culture management.

The organization's structure was clarified by developing key result area based role descriptions for all positions. This process was led by the organization's director of human resources, with the associate director also providing input. Those in unique positions (e.g., associate director, executive director) developed role descriptions for their positions. When two or more people occupied the same position (e.g., there were 12 people with the title "teacher/center director," with each overseeing a center), they worked together to develop the role description for that position. These were submitted first to the manager of that position (e.g., the associate director submitted her role description to the executive director), and, once approved, they were submitted to the director of human resources.

Performance management systems were implemented at the organizational and individual levels. At the organizational level, the leadership team met on a quarterly basis to review progress against the plan and provided CCDS's board with quarterly updates on the progress they were making against goals—in a format similar to that discussed in this chapter. At the individual level, the performance evaluation process was redesigned to focus on the position's key results areas and on SMART goals. During the introduction of this new performance evaluation system, the executive director stressed that as the organization looked to the future, people would be held accountable for delivering on their commitments and goals.

While the implementation of all of these new systems was positive, some of the longer-term employees were resisting the changes. Some complained that "change was happening too fast." Others suggested that the new systems were going to adversely affect the "caring" nature of the organization and detract from the ability to provide the high level of service to children and their families. Still others simply said, "I don't see why we need to change, because we have been and continue to be successful." Resistance to change also came in actions. Some employees continued to use manual approaches, rather than the new, more automated systems. Some managers did not complete and submit goals on time, using as an excuse that there was "just too much to do."

The executive director responded by providing the change resisters with more information about why the changes were needed to support continued growth. She and other members of the leadership team also provided one-on-one coaching to help employees understand the changes and, if appropriate, develop the skills needed to support them—using as the basis for this work performance against goals that was documented in the revised evaluation process. Support was provided, but the executive director also sent a very clear message that "The ship is sailing, and you can choose to get on or be left behind." A few long-term employees did, in fact, leave the organization—either on their own or because they were asked to leave (due to continued underperformance).

As a result of the changes that were made, the organization's culture shifted to a focus on performance, organizational and individual development, and openness to change. This shift, in turn, was supported by and supported the required transitions in other organizational infrastructure components that were needed to promote CCDS's continued success as the organization grew over a decade to have an annual budget of nearly $10 million.

Summary

This chapter describes how the frameworks and tools for building sustainably successful organizations® presented in this book can be applied to nonprofits. While nonprofits face many of the same issues as their for-profit counterparts as they grow, there are also some unique aspects that need to be managed as a part of the organizational development process—including developing and utilizing a volunteer board and securing resources from funding sources.

We have examined the similarities and key differences for all of the managerial tools presented throughout this book. Specifically, we have provided a detailed description of how to use the approach to strategic planning in a nonprofit because this is, in a very real sense, the foundation for developing the management systems needed to support long-term success. We have examined some of the unique structural issues that nonprofits need to address, including the role of the board vis-à-vis management and the role of volunteers. We have also discussed the similarity of performance management, management development, and culture management in both for- and non-profit enterprises.

Our underlying theme in this chapter has been (based upon years of actual experience with both types of organizations) that the concepts, frameworks, methods, and tools described throughout this book can *and should* be applied in nonprofits (just as they are in for-profits businesses) to build sustainably successful organizations®.

Notes

1. For more information about Head Start, its history, and the services that it provides, visit the Office of Head Start website (www.acf.hhs.gov/programs/ohs).
2. Dr. Yvonne Randle was introduced to Head Start in 1991 when she began teaching in a program at UCLA's Anderson School that was designed to provide Head Start executive directors (CEOs of their organizations) with tools to effectively manage and grow their businesses. Over the ensuing decades, Dr. Randle has had the opportunity to work with a number of agencies in helping them develop and implement strategic plans, as well as on enhancing the effectiveness of their leadership teams, and managing their cultures.
3. The transition for "doers" to managers is discussed in Chapter 9.

CHAPTER 12

The Challenge of Leadership Throughout the Organizational Life Cycle

One of the most critical managerial functions in promoting successful organizational development is leadership. Effective leadership is, in fact, a prerequisite for building sustainably successful organizations®. This is true, not only for leadership at the very top of the organization, but throughout it as well.

There are two different types of leadership that are required to build sustainably successful organizations®— strategic and operational. Strategic leadership is focused on building the organization over the longer term, while operational leadership is focused on execution or more day-to-day operations. During the early stages of a company's life cycle, these two types of leadership are typically, but not always, provided by the same person—the founder or CEO. As an organization grows and changes over its life cycle, the nature of the leadership it requires changes and becomes more complex. To meet the challenges, a company's leadership needs to evolve from a single leader to a "true leadership team," or what we term a "leadership molecule"—described later in this chapter.

This purpose of this chapter is to identify and address the key leadership issues that companies face as they grow from early-stage entrepreneurship to larger, more complex organizations. We begin by clearly defining the concept of leadership, as well as the two types of leadership—strategic and operational—that need to be present in any organization at any size. Next, we identify six leadership styles and provide criteria that can be used to identify the "best" style for a specific situation. We then describe what we have termed the "key tasks" of operational and strategic leadership—that is, what effective leaders do. Building on the key tasks of strategic leadership, we introduce a concept we have termed the leadership molecule—a framework that can be used to assess the extent to which an organization's leadership team is focused on the most important factors that drive success and the extent to which they operate as a true team. In brief, this chapter focuses on the functions that need to be performed by leaders as their organizations grow and the form that leadership takes (i.e., whether these functions are performed by a single leader or by a leadership team). These issues are relatively neglected in the literature of leadership and organizational growth.

The Nature of Leadership

Although many people believe that leadership is an attribute of personality, this has not been confirmed by research, as we discuss later in this chapter. A more fruitful way to think about leadership is that it is a set of behaviors to be performed. In this sense, *leadership* is defined as "the process of influencing the behavior of people to achieve organizational goals." Under this definition, leadership is an ongoing process, not a set of traits that a person possesses. The process involves understanding, predicting, and controlling others' goal-directed behavior. The leader's ultimate objective is to create a goal-congruent situation—a situation in which people can satisfy their own needs by seeking to achieve the goals of the organization. Leadership, then, like organizational control, is behaviorally-oriented and goal-directed.

There are two types of leadership: (1) operational leadership and (2) strategic leadership. *Operational leadership* is the process of influencing the behavior of people to achieve operational goals. This dimension of leadership is concerned with the day-to-day functioning of the enterprise. *Strategic leadership*, in contrast, is the process of influencing the organization's members to determine the future direction of the enterprise and its long-term objectives for organizational development. Both types of leadership are essential to building sustainably successful organizations®. Managers at all levels—CEO/COO, senior management, middle management, and front-line supervisors—need to be effective operational leaders. The most senior levels of the organization—the CEO/COO and his or her direct reports (as the organization grows)—need to also be effective strategic leaders. Effectively influencing people to achieve day-to-day and long-term goals involves choosing a style that fits the situation and performing key operational or strategic leadership tasks, as will be described below.

Styles of Leadership

There is a vast body of research and theory on leadership that can be summarized into various schools or classifications of leadership theory: (1) leadership trait theory, (2) leadership styles theory, and (3) contingency theories of leadership, which has also been termed situational leadership. More than half a century of research has failed to confirm that there is one "correct" style of leadership that is best for all situations—whether these are situations being encountered by the CEO, a middle manager, or a first-line supervisor. Rather, there are a variety of styles, each of which can be effective

Directive

1. Autocratic	I'll tell you what we are going to do because I'm the boss.
2. Benevolent Autocratic	I'll tell you what we are going to do because it will be best for all concerned.
3. Consultative	I'll decide, but I'll discuss it with you to get your opinions before I make the decision.
4. Participative	We'll discuss the issues together, but I reserve the right to make the final decision.
5. Team (consensus)	We'll all meet and discuss it until everyone agrees on a decision.
6. Laissez-faire	Do whatever you want to do.

Nondirective

Figure 12.1 Continuum of Leadership Styles

or ineffective, depending on the circumstances. This notion has been called *contingency theory* or *situational leadership*.

Based on our own and others' research, we have identified six basic styles of leadership. These styles constitute a continuum that proceeds from a very directive to a very nondirective leadership style, as summarized in Figure 12.1.

It should be pointed out that this is only one of a variety of leadership classification schemes. The major point to draw from it is that in their purest form, these styles are indeed different and may therefore be appropriate for different situations with different personnel.

The Autocratic Style

The autocratic style is a very directive style of leadership. Someone using this style will make the decision or provide the direction typically without explaining the rationale behind it. This is the "just do it" style of leadership, which can best be characterized by the statement, "I will tell you what we're going to do because I'm the boss," or "Look, I'm head of the department; I'm being held responsible. I will tell you what we're going to do, and that's that." The spirit of autocratic leadership can also be captured in the exchange between a COO of a company and another high-ranking corporate leader in the presence of one of the authors: "When I say jump, you say, 'How high?'"

This was the style of leadership used by Sam Walton in the early years of his company and by Steve Jobs, during his early years at Apple and initially upon his 1997 return to the company. It is a style commonly observed in Fortune 500, as well as entrepreneurial organizations. For example, the legendary Jack Welch, the former CEO at GE, at one time was referred to as Neutron Jack because he was quick to make decisions about the firm and its subsidiaries in a very directive manner. However, Welch made the transition to using a much more participative style in his later years at GE.

The first reaction many people have to this style is negative. Why? Because beginning in the late twentieth century, managers were inundated with information suggesting that the way to achieve the "best" results was through maximizing the involvement of team members in decisions that will affect them. Although we agree with this, there are also times when managers *must* use a directive style in order to achieve the best results. For example, if a team is faced with a crisis, there may not be time to involve everyone in the decision. Someone must make it. Another example of a situation that may require a more directive style is when a manager is supervising an inexperienced or unmotivated employee. These types of employees require a more directive approach. In a sense, they *want* to be told what to do.

The Benevolent Autocratic Style

The benevolent-autocratic style is a "parental" style of leadership: The leader acts on the assumption that he or she knows what is best for the organization and the individuals involved. The degree of direction used in this style is essentially the same as with the autocratic style but is more benign. A manager who uses this style will usually explain the rationale behind decisions, whereas an autocratic leader will not. Instead of simply issuing directives, a person adopting this style might say, "I'll tell you what we're going to do, because it will be the best for all concerned." Where an autocratic leader might say, "As a condition of coming to work here, you are obliged to accept what I say," a benevolent autocrat might say, "This is what I want you to do, and here's why." This is the classic style found in many entrepreneurships during the initial stages of organizational development.

The Consultative Style

The third style of leadership is qualitatively different, at least to some degree, from the first two. This is the first of two "interactive styles" in which the manager solicits input from direct reports but reserves the right to make the final decision. Managers using the consultative style (as opposed to the other interactive style, discussed next) tend to present their teams with information and ask for their response. To illustrate this, suppose a manager is presenting the organization's goals for the coming year. An individual operating with the autocratic style might say, "This is what we're going to do. These are our goals for next year." A benevolent autocrat might approach the situation with, "This is what the organization needs, and here is how it will affect you." In contrast, a manager using the consultative style might say, "Here is what I think our goals ought to be for the next year. What's your reaction?" Having asked this question, the manager then needs to make it very clear that while input is welcome, the decision is still his or hers to make. If this is not clear, problems can arise as direct reports come to believe that the manager was using a more nondirective style in which all votes were equal.

The Participative Style

A manager using the participative style also reserves the right to make the final decision. However, managers using this interactive style will tend to ask their teams for even greater input. The basic difference between the participative and consultative styles is the manner in which others' opinions are solicited and used. In the participative style, the group actually helps to develop ideas rather than just give input on the manager's ideas. In the consultative style, the manager might come into a group and say, "Here is what I think we should do. Give me your reaction." The manager using a participative style, on the other hand, may have an idea about what the group should do but basically will say, "Here are the problems. Let's discuss them together and come up with recommendations. Then I'll make the final decision."

There are certain challenges inherent in using either one of the interactive styles of leadership. First, a manager must be open to the ideas and opinions of his or her team and be willing to change perspective, based on these ideas. If the manager's mind is already made up, everyone on the team will know this and will be extremely frustrated by the fact that the manager is making them go through the motions of providing input, even though this input will not be used.

A second challenge is helping team members understand that, although the manager wants their input, the decision is still the manager's to make. This can be difficult to communicate, especially if none of the team's input is used. Whenever this occurs, the manager should make a practice of explaining a decision to pursue a certain course of action, how the information provided by the team was evaluated, and why (in this case) it wasn't used. This will help the team understand that their input was of value and that the manager wasn't simply creating the impression of soliciting input.

The Team (Consensus) Style

The team or consensus style represents another qualitative shift along the continuum of styles. It is the first of two nondirective styles in which the manager provides team members with a great deal of authority in the decision-making process. A leader adopting this style operates as a member of a team in making the decision. The leader's vote counts no more than any other team member's vote. A person using this leadership style might say, "Let's meet, discuss the problem, and reach an agreement on its resolution." A group with a leader who uses this style is thus given more responsibility than in the other styles. This means that the leadership that is frequently exercised by a single individual under the more directive styles of leadership has been delegated as responsibility to a team of individuals.

There are two basic versions of the consensus style: (1) true consensus (or the jury) style and (2) majority rules. In the true consensus style, everyone on the team must agree on the direction to be pursued or the decision to be made. If there is even one dissenter, the "jury" must continue its deliberations until a true consensus is reached. This form of the consensus style obviously requires a great deal of time. More important, it requires that all team members be trained in how to use effective decision-making techniques. If team members do not understand the steps that should be followed in making effective decisions, they could meet forever and still not decide anything.

Finally, it requires that team members leave their egos at the door. People need to be willing to agree to disagree and not feel that they've lost if a decision runs counter to their original opinion.

The second version of the consensus style is majority rules. A team using this style will literally vote on the course of action to pursue with respect to a particular issue. Whatever course of action the majority of participants selects (again, the team leader's vote counts no more than that of other team members) is the one that will be taken. When teams choose to use this version of the consensus style, they need to agree ahead of time how ties will be broken if they occur.

Although this version of the consensus leadership style tends to be less time consuming than the consensus version, it is not without problems. First, the majority-rules version of the consensus style creates winners and losers. This can significantly disrupt the ability of a team to work effectively together. Second, the losers can, if not properly managed, undermine the team's ability to effectively implement its decision. We have witnessed more than one case of senior managers who left the room after a majority-rules decision was made and told their direct reports, "That's the worst decision we ever made."

The impact of such statements on the organization can be profound. First, the chances of the decision being implemented are reduced. Second, such statements can significantly undermine the image of the senior management team. The organization may come to believe that there is no true team directing the efforts of the company.

This is not to suggest that the consensus style should never be used. Instead, it is to point out that there are challenges in using this style (as there are in using any of the six key styles). These challenges need to be recognized and managed, if the style is to be used effectively. Although this is a complex style, an increasing number of organizations have been experimenting with it for a number of years.

The team style of leadership was used by Jim Stowers, Jr., at American Century Investments—a mutual fund, investment-management company—as he built the company from a new venture to one with more than $65 billion in assets. Stowers had long believed in the value of a team approach to portfolio management, and he extended this philosophy to the management of the company, where an increasing number of decisions were made by the firm's executive committee operating as a team. Stowers believed that teams make better decisions than individuals, and he wanted American Century's executive committee to function as a team CEO. Nevertheless, he reserved the right to use his extra vote to make certain decisions.

The Laissez-Faire Style

The most nondirective style of leadership—laissez-faire—places the responsibility for task accomplishment completely on the direct report. A leader using this style essentially says, "Do whatever you want to do," or "Do the right thing."

As was true of the autocratic style, some people's first reaction to this style is negative. Some even question whether such a style represents leadership at all. They ask, "How can a manager simply tell someone to 'do what you want to do'?" The laissez-faire style, in fact, is quite a powerful style when used in the right situations. If a manager has someone who is highly skilled and highly motivated (that is, understands the requirements of the job and has the skills to effectively perform them), then the manager can just let this person "do it." The manager does not need to devote a great deal of time to overseeing this individual's efforts. Instead, the manager's role becomes one of communicating the goals of the company to team members and letting them determine how the manager can best support them. The manager is still managing the team by ensuring that everyone is moving in a direction that will lead to the overall attainment of the company's goals. However, the amount of time that the manager needs to spend overseeing individual efforts is greatly reduced. The bottom line: If a manager can use a laissez-faire style in a given situation (if the circumstances are right), this will give him or her a great deal of time while also providing the desired results.

There are two versions of this style, one positive and one negative. A leader operating under the positive version promotes the notion that highly trained individuals do not need a great deal of direction. This type of leader thus gives his or her direct reports considerable independence. Such a leader might say, "You are a professional. You know what your job is. Do whatever you have to do to get it done." This is the version of the style that we include in the continuum of styles presented in Figure 12.1.

The negative version of the laissez-faire style might be characterized by the statement, "Do whatever you want to do. Just leave me alone." This is an "abdocratic" style—an abdication of authority and responsibility. This version of the laissez-faire style should *never* be used. It will do little to help a manager achieve desired results.

Factors Influencing the Choice of Leadership Style

It is important to understand that a manager at any level does not have to always use (and, in fact, shouldn't always use) the same leadership style. The most effective managers have the ability to use a variety of styles, each suited for a particular situation. Understanding the key factors that need to be considered in choosing an effective style to fit the situation helps managers increase their leadership effectiveness. We have found that consideration of six key factors can help an individual decide which style is best at a given time. The first two factors we discuss are the most important; they probably account for 80 to 90% of the influence on leadership effectiveness in a given situation.

Nature of the Task

One of the most important factors to consider in choosing a leadership style is the degree of programmability of the task on which the direct report will be working. A programmable task is one in which the manager can describe, in advance, all of the steps needed to complete it. A nonprogrammable task is a creative task in which it is almost impossible for a manager to define the steps necessary for its successful completion. If a task is highly programmable (that is, the optimal steps for its completion can be specified in advance), then a directive style of leadership is appropriate. If the task is nonprogrammable (that is, the nature of the work necessitates a great deal of variation in individual procedures), a directive style may be difficult or impossible to use, and a more participative or nondirective style will be required. In other words, the greater the degree of programmability of the task, the more appropriate it is for a manager to say, "This is the right way to do this task; we know it's right because we've studied it and worked out the best way to do it." Where the task is less programmable, the manager must use a more interactive or nondirective approach.

Nature of the People Supervised

In identifying the "nature of the person," a manager needs to consider three factors: (1) the level of skills the individual possesses; (2) how motivated the individual is; and (3) the extent to which the individual wants to work alone (that is, the extent to which he or she prefers to work on his or her own). When examining the nature of the situation, each of these factors should be assessed relative to the task that the individual direct report will be performing. For example, a person can be extremely skilled in one area and very motivated, but the task assigned requires a different set of skills. If a manager in this situation uses a nondirective approach, it can lead to a disaster because the person in question simply did not possess the required skills.

Taken together, these three factors comprise a single variable that we call *the potential for job autonomy*. The more highly skilled, highly motivated, and in need of independence a person is, the greater is that person's potential for job autonomy. Conversely, a person with low motivation, low task-relevant skills, and low need for independence has a low potential for job autonomy.

People with different potentials for job autonomy require managers with different leadership styles. A nondirective style (consensus or laissez-faire) will be most appropriate with direct reports who have a high potential for job autonomy, while a very directive style is appropriate with people who have low potential for job autonomy. A more intermediate style of leadership is needed when direct reports do not fit one or the other extreme.

As stated previously, these first two factors—nature of the task and nature of the person supervised—account for about 80 to 90% of what managers need to consider in choosing a leadership style. Figure 12.2 shows the relationship between the two factors we have just described and the six leadership styles described in the previous section.

Potential for Job Autonomy

	High	Low
High	Most effective style Interactive (consultative, participative)	Most effective style Directive (autocratic, benevolent autocratic)
Low	Most effective style Nondirective (consensus, laissez-faire)	Most effective style Interactive (consultative, participative)

Programmability of Task (vertical axis label, High at top, Low at bottom)

Figure 12.2   Factors Affecting Choice of Leadership Style

As can be seen in the figure, a high degree of programmability combined with a low potential for job autonomy would ideally require a directive style. At the other extreme—low programmability and high job autonomy—a nondirective approach would be most effective. The other two cells show intermediate conditions where an interactive approach would best fit the situation. For example, a person who is highly motivated and working at a job that requires a high degree of nonprogrammability but is not very skilled may require a leader who adopts a style somewhere in the middle of the continuum, either consultative or participative, at least until the person becomes more experienced.

Supervisor's Style

If a difference exists between a supervisor's preferred leadership style and the style of one or more direct reports, it will be difficult for direct reports to justify their own style unless the supervisor allows the use of it. Direct reports may even feel a need to change their own style to make it closer to that of the supervisor. In other words, supervisors have a tendency to consciously or unconsciously evaluate their direct reports on the basis of their own leadership styles. The manager in the superior position in such a situation may need to recognize that people can use different styles and still be effective. Further, when an individual finds that the preferred style (given the evaluation of the first two factors described above) is different from the supervisor's dominant style, this person may need to find a way to help the supervisor understand *why* it is important that this style be used. The bottom line: If a manager uses the wrong style in a given situation, the probability that desired results will be achieved is reduced.

Peers' and Associates' Styles

The dominant style of a peer group can also influence a manager's choice of leadership style. For example, if most managers in a particular group use a consultative style and a few use a benevolent-autocratic style, the latter individuals will feel some pressure to change their style to make it more like that of the majority. Again, however, these individuals can work to educate their peers about the reasons behind their use of a different style and its influence on results. Further, if the individuals using the "non-dominant" leadership style begin to achieve superior results, concern about their style will be diminished.

Amount of Available Decision Time

People are much more willing to accept a directive leadership style in crisis situations than in situations where nothing needs to be decided in a hurry. If someone in a room full of people says, "I see smoke," people will not expect to be asked to form groups and discuss alternatives for action. Most individuals will probably be quite comfortable with someone saying, "Stand up and calmly walk out the door, down the hall, and out into the street."

Nature (Culture) of the Organization

Each organization has norms concerning the type or types of leadership style felt to be appropriate for its members. These norms affect all members of the organization and are likely to be influenced by the styles of the organization's founder, CEO, or most successful managers.

Leadership Style Is a Choice

The bottom line is that leadership style is a choice to be made. It is a style to be selected, based on the key factors in the situation. There are six key factors (described above) that affect the choice of leadership style. They can be analyzed to determine what kind of style would be most appropriate in a particular situation with particular types of personnel. Again, however, the most important of these factors are the first two.

Two Sets of Leadership Tasks

Two different types of leadership tasks must be performed in organizations. One of these can be termed the "micro" tasks—the tasks of *operational leadership*, which include all of the day-to-day things that must be performed to influence people to produce and deliver the products and services that the organization offers to the marketplace. The other set is the "macro" tasks of leadership. These tasks comprise what we call *strategic leadership* and include establishing the organization's vision, managing the corporate culture, managing the strategic aspects of the company's operations, developing the systems needed to support the long-term development of the business, and managing change.

Key Tasks of Operational Leadership

Operational leadership tasks are the things that a manager (at any level of the organizational hierarchy) needs to do on a day-to-day basis to influence the behavior of people to achieve goals. Previous research has identified five tasks that comprise the functions of operational leadership.[1] To be effective as operational leaders, managers must perform all five key tasks on a regular basis with each of their direct reports. If any task is not focused on to the extent that it needs to be, the likelihood that desired results will be achieved decreases.

Goal Emphasis. An effective leader emphasizes the attainment of goals through setting goals, focusing on goals, ensuring the effective communication of goals, and monitoring performance against goals. The late Rensis Likert, an internationally noted behavioral scientist, pointed out that to be effective, a leader has to demonstrate a "contagious enthusiasm for the achievement of organizational goals." To be an effective leader, then, an individual needs to understand how to set effective goals and ensure that those responsible for helping achieve them understand them. The concept of effective goal setting was discussed in both Chapter 6 and Chapter 8.

In performing this task, the effective leader's style can vary widely. A very directive or autocratic leader might simply say, "Here are our goals." At the other extreme, a very nondirective or laissez-faire leader might say, "Let's agree on what our goals are, then you figure out how to achieve them." At the intermediate level, a person with a participative or consultative style might say, "Here's what I think our goals should be. What do you think?"

One of our favorite examples of the succinct application of goal emphasis was observed in an executive committee meeting at a rapidly growing medical engineering subsidiary of Bristol-Myers Squibb. The company's CEO was asked how he might implement the concept of goal emphasis. He turned to the vice president of sales and stated simply, "Sell something!"

One of the best leaders we have encountered with respect to goal emphasis is Howard Schultz of Starbucks. In the best sense, Schultz is a demanding leader. He not only wants "guns and butter" but "entertainment" as well. Specifically, Schultz wants growth and profitability. At the same time, he wants people to have fun (a cultural goal). Although these things are sometimes at odds, Starbucks has done a very good job overall at all three. This has been accomplished, in part, because goals have been established to drive results in all three areas.

Interaction Facilitation. To achieve desired results, an effective leader needs to focus on helping people work together effectively and cooperatively. This is the definition of *interaction facilitation*. Effectively performing this task involves effective meeting management and team-building.

Individuals who effectively perform this task ensure that every meeting has a purpose and clear objectives that define what is supposed to be accomplished. They understand that there should be agendas for all meetings (distributed in advance) and that all participants should be prepared for whatever discussion will be taking place during the meeting. These individuals also understand how to manage meetings in a way that desired results are achieved (for example, decisions are made, action steps are developed, etc.). Someone using a directive leadership style might accomplish this task by saying, "We're having a meeting. This is our agenda, and this is what we're going to accomplish." A more nondirective way to do the same thing might be to act as a facilitator at a meeting, helping to summarize what people are doing and asking nondirective questions.

Unfortunately, many CEOs and other executives sometimes dominate meetings, rather than facilitate the process. Either because of their personalities or because they assume it is their role, they tend to lead (direct) meetings. Where this has become dysfunctional, an outside facilitator can be of great help. The key is getting all issues and opinions on the table and then working to resolve them.

Work Facilitation. Performing this task involves providing or helping personnel obtain what they need to achieve their goals. This can be accomplished in a variety of ways, including helping to schedule a task, making suggestions about how work should be done, providing reference materials, and suggesting knowledgeable sources of information regarding task procedure. A very directive way of facilitating work might be to say, "This is the way you should be doing your job." At the other extreme, a person using a laissez-faire style might simply ask nondirective questions or suggest that people look in certain areas for help.

Supportive Behavior. This fourth task of effective leadership involves providing both positive and negative feedback to direct reports on a regular basis. Positive feedback is important because it serves to reinforce appropriate goal-oriented behavior and thereby increase the chances that the behavior will continue to be performed. Negative feedback, in the form of constructive criticism, tends to eliminate dysfunctional behavior. Providing feedback effectively involves being as specific as possible, focusing on the individual's behavior (versus interpreting what the behavior means or focusing on the person's attitude), and adjusting one's style of communication to that of the person receiving the feedback. It also involves striking the right balance between providing feedback in a timely manner and doing so in the right place (e.g., constructive criticism should be provided one-on-one versus in a team setting).

A directive leader might express supportive behavior with "No, John. Don't do it that way. Do it this way." A person using a more nondirective style might handle a similar situation with, "I'm going to have to evaluate what you do on this project. You do a self-assessment at the same time. Then, let's meet and compare notes, and we'll see where we need to go from there." An extremely nondirective approach might be to say, "You've just completed the project. I want you to review your documentation and critique it. What have you done well? What have you done poorly, and how will you better this in the future?"

Personnel Development. The effective leader helps to develop people. He or she motivates people to be concerned about their future development—working with each direct report to analyze their specific needs for development and identifying ways to meet these needs. One way of performing this task that some managers have found effective is to work with each direct report to set at least one goal on an annual basis that relates to improving the person's skills and performance.

As was the case with the other factors, the leadership style used to perform this task can range from directive to nondirective, depending on the personnel and the nature of the work being done. A directive approach might be to say, "I think you should go to this management training program." A nondirective approach might be to say, "What do you see as your developmental needs? I want you to think about them and to decide what you want to do to meet them."

Key Tasks of Strategic Leadership

Strategic leadership tasks are the things that leaders do to plan for and manage the organization's long-term development. These tasks need to be focused upon and performed by the organization's most senior leaders on an ongoing basis. In the early stages of development, these five tasks will be performed by the entrepreneur or founder. As the organization grows, the leadership team will need to share responsibility for performing these tasks and do so as a "molecule" (which will be discussed later in this chapter). Each of the five strategic leadership tasks is described, in turn, below.

Strategic Vision. Formulating and effectively communicating a strategic vision is the first task of strategic leadership. This involves clearly defining what the organization will or should be working to achieve and then effectively communicating this "vision" throughout the business. In brief, it involves creating a picture of what the future state will be like. For example, Howard Schultz's original vision was to create an American version of the classic Italian coffee bar and roll it out on a national basis, even though Starbucks then had only two retail stores in Seattle.

Although the development of a vision is a requirement for effective strategic leadership, the content of the vision does not have to be created by the entrepreneur or CEO, per se. Many strategic leaders are effective because they create an environment or process through which the leadership team develops the vision for the firm. For example, in 1995 (as discussed in Chapter 6) the senior leadership team at Starbucks created the strategic mission for Starbucks which was, "To become the leading brand of specialty coffee in North America by the year 2000." This strategic vision was intended to help Starbucks develop a niche or stronghold with sufficient strength to defend itself against competitors such as McDonald's or other large fast-food retailers with the financial resources to preempt Starbucks in the market. Once this was accomplished, Starbucks then proceeded to attempt to establish itself as a global brand with a global footprint.

Corporate Culture Management. The second task of strategic leadership concerns the management of the organization's culture. This task ultimately falls to the CEO of an entity, whether it is a corporation as a whole or a subdivision. Initially, the culture of a company is formulated and spread by the company's founder. However, when an organization reaches or exceeds a certain size (Stage IV), it must be formally managed, as explained in Chapter 3. At that point, a company needs to establish a formal system for culture management. For example, under Fuad El-Hibri's leadership at Emergent BioSolutions (a publicly traded biopharmaceutical company), the company began a formal system of culture management in 2009.[2] This included creating a statement of the company's culture and establishing culture management as a priority objective in the company's strategic plan.

In addition to ensuring that there is an appropriate system for managing corporate culture, effectively performing this strategic leadership task involves serving as a role model of the company's desired culture. Promoting values needs to be a focus of leaders on an ongoing basis, versus something that is focused upon only when there is a need to change.

Operations. Ensuring that operations are aligned with and functioning effectively to help the organization achieve its long-term goals is the third task of strategic leadership. Operations refers to the day-to-day activities that take place in the business—that is, how systems and processes are actually implemented and how people behave within their roles. However, there is a strategic aspect of operations in addition to their day-to-day execution. The strategic aspect involves the development of processes and systems required for effective and efficient day-to-day functioning. This task of strategic leadership also involves the monitoring of operations to make sure that they are functioning as planned. This task is sometimes (but not always) the responsibility of a chief operating officer.

The strategic leadership task of operations is the same regardless of the specifics of retail, financial services, manufacturing, or other industries. It involves ensuring the effective execution of the strategic plan and ensuring the smooth functioning of day-to-day business activities, or what is sometimes referred to as "making the trains run on time."

Organizational Development and Systems. The fourth key task of strategic leadership involves organizational development and related systems. In this context, the term *organizational development* refers to the whole process of influencing the members of the organization to build the various key aspects of the Pyramid of Organizational Development that have been described throughout this book.

As an organization grows and changes, it requires changes in its infrastructure. The strategic leadership organizational development/systems task involves focusing on designing and implementing the infrastructure (both operational and management systems) required by an organization as it grows. These are the systems required to support the organization's ongoing successful development versus day-to-day operations per se. For example, logistics and information systems are needed to support day-to-day operations of Walmart (and they need to be designed so that they are aligned with the company's long-term goals and are supported by other aspects of the company's infrastructure). They are implemented through day-to-day activities such as inventory counts, entering data, and truck deliveries.

This is not to suggest that effectively performing this task involves understanding all of the technical details of all organizational systems. Instead, effectively performing this task involves overseeing the development and implementation of key operational and management systems and doing so in a holistic manner. In performing this task, leaders will bring in technical experts, as needed, to assist with the details.

Innovation and Change Management. This strategic leadership task involves identifying the need for and managing organizational innovation and change. The overall goal of someone performing this task is to help ensure that change is an ongoing process (versus something that happens only periodically) and, in a sense, to champion change and innovation throughout the organization. The focus for innovation and change can be on any aspect of the company's operations—products, processes, people, systems, and so on. In a sense, this task can be viewed as the essence of entrepreneurship per se. For example, the development of the "i-technology" platform by Apple has facilitated its becoming one of the most valuable companies in the world.[3]

This task ultimately falls to the CEO of an entity, whether it is a corporation as a whole or a division. Change is inevitable in an organization as it grows or adapts to its environment.

Although the ultimate responsibility for managing change is the responsibility of the CEO, it is often managed as a group process by the senior leadership of an enterprise. This is a sound approach to the management of change that will be discussed below in the context of what we term a "leadership molecule."

The Leadership Molecule

This section examines and develops the notion of a leadership molecule, cited above. It explains the role the molecule plays as companies pass through the various stages of organizational growth. It begins, in other words, to develop an alternative theory of leadership in organizations, which is termed "the leadership molecule hypothesis." This hypothesis is the outgrowth, as we shall explain, of inductive observation of actual business practice. We also cite some empirical research that tested and supported the leadership molecule hypothesis. Finally, we shall examine the implications of this construct for the management of organizations as they grow through the organizational life cycle.

The Conventional Paradigm of Leadership

The conventional paradigm of business leadership is based upon the notion of a single leader such as Howard Schultz at Starbucks, Richard Branson at the Virgin Group, or the late Steve Jobs at Apple. Although such leaders do undoubtedly exist (especially during the early stages of entrepreneurial growth), they are often, like the tip of an iceberg, the most visible component of an unnoticed or unrecognized leadership unit.

Although it might *appear* that there is a single charismatic leader who determines the success of a company, if we look more closely, there is typically a core leadership team (in the true sociological sense) with defined but overlapping and complementary roles. Specifically, this team is actually performing the five key strategic leadership tasks, discussed above, as a collective unit rather than as a set of individuals. We refer to this true team of leaders as a "leadership molecule."[4] When we refer to a true leadership team, we do not mean a nominal team or a team in name only. Calling a group of people a "team" does not make them a team. We mean a team in the sense of relative equals in decision making, where rank and ego do not trump candid discussion of organizational issues, strategies, and problems. Such a team will have open debate, without hidden agendas, and challenge each other's assumptions and ideas, and it will think of itself as a team. Do such teams really exist? The answer is—occasionally.

We have observed such teams in business and have even helped some of them form. A great example, as discussed below, is the original senior leadership team at Starbucks in the early 1990s. Based on our research and experience in working with companies, we believe that as entrepreneurial organizations grow, they require a leadership molecule to perform the key functions of strategic leadership.

Accidental Discovery

Although most of the literature dealing with leadership focuses on the individual as a leader, there has been previous recognition of the notion that leadership can be exercised by a team or group rather than by an individual.[5] However, the notion of a leadership molecule, as defined below, has not been generally recognized.

Like the identification of the antibiotic properties of penicillin, the existence of the notion of a leadership molecule was an accidental discovery. It occurred as a by-product of organizational development work with several companies over many years. Specifically, Eric Flamholtz observed that a common aspect of a number of highly successful companies was the existence of a "core leadership team" (in the true sociological sense of a "traditioned" group) *with defined but overlapping and complementary roles*.

The initial instance of recognition was at Starbucks Coffee. The core senior leadership team, as explained further below, was comprised of three leaders who worked as a team and possessed complementary skills and overlapping but semi-distinct roles.[6]

Performing the Key Strategic Leadership Tasks as a Team

This leadership team at Starbucks was performing the five key strategic leadership tasks as a collective unit rather than as a set of individuals. Each member of the core senior leadership team at Starbucks (Howard Schultz, Howard Behar, and Orin Smith) had his own defined formal role. Schultz was CEO, Behar was head of retail operations, and Smith was the CFO. The formal roles were somewhat of a misnomer and only partially reflected (and partially obscured) the actual or real roles of each of these three individuals. Each member of the team was, in fact, *primarily (but not exclusively) responsible* for a strategic leadership function. Howard Schultz (the CEO) was primarily (but not exclusively) responsible for the vision and culture of Starbucks. Schultz was also involved to some extent with operations and systems at Starbucks. Howard Behar, SVP and head of retail operations was primarily responsible for retail operations (which, at the time of this observation in 1994, accounted for approximately 95% of Starbucks' revenues). However, Behar was also involved to some extent with creating the vision and culture of Starbucks as well as its systems. Finally, Smith, who was formally CFO, was involved primarily with the development of the systems required by Starbucks—not just financial systems, but information systems, planning systems, human resource management systems, and other systems as well. However, he too was involved in creating the vision and culture of Starbucks and to some extent with operations as well. All three were involved with innovation and change at Starbucks.

Taken together, Schultz, Behar, and Smith were functioning not as a set of discrete individuals preforming independent roles; they were functioning as a true team (not just a team in name only) performing a set of complementary but somewhat overlapping roles. They comprised what we have termed a leadership molecule.

The Catalyst for the Leadership Molecule Construct

During early 1994, when Starbucks was still a relatively small company, Eric Flamholtz was invited to coach the three senior leaders of Starbucks, consisting of Howard Schultz, Howard Behar, and Orin Smith. His initial assignment was to coach each of them individually and to work with them to iron out some conflict and differences that had emerged in the stress of building a company so rapidly. After this initial work, they became a very effective leadership team. Flamholtz began to view them as an ideal senior leadership team: a set of very talented individuals with complementary capabilities, working as a true team.

The specific catalyst for the notion of the leadership molecule was the observation that people inside of Starbucks referred to them as "H2O." This was a clever play on the initial letters of each individual's name: (H)oward Schultz, (H)oward Behar, and (O)rin Smith. Clearly people within Starbucks saw the three as a unit, and not just three guys running a company.

That moniker started Flamholtz thinking about other teams that he had observed in different companies: some with monikers such as "The Three Musketeers," "The Troika," The "Gang of Four," "Batman and Robin," and "The Ghost and the Darkness."[7] He realized that a nickname might be a "marker" or a signature for a true leadership team.

After the initial observation of this phenomenon, he began to investigate it more systematically. Based on an analysis of hundreds of companies, Flamholtz determined that where a "true team" existed, there was high performance and where it was lacking, performance tended to be low or even disastrous. This, in turn, led to what can be termed the Leadership Molecule Model and the Leadership Molecule Hypothesis.

Emergence and Development of a Leadership Molecule in Organizations

The leadership molecule tends to emerge as a function of the stage of development (growth) of a company. At the initial new venture stage, the leader is typically a one-man or -woman band that should be performing all of the required strategic leadership functions. This happens whether or not a single individual possesses all of the competencies to execute each of these leadership tasks.

As the organization grows, there is a need for managerial specialization and the development of a set of people to perform these functions rather than a single individual doing them all. Even when a single person possesses all of the capabilities to perform all of these leadership tasks, as an organization increases in size, it becomes more and more difficult to perform all functions.

As a result, a set of individuals tends to emerge to perform these tasks with one person typically focused on vision and culture, another on operations, a third on the development of systems, and the team as a whole working together to perform the task of change and innovation. If this set of individuals is not functioning as a team, then each person consists of an individual "atom." Sometimes the set of individuals morphs into a true team with overlapping and complementary responsibilities. Only when the set of individual atoms has transformed into a true team or "molecule" does the so-called leadership molecule exist.

Core Roles of the Leadership Molecule

As implied above, there are certain core roles comprising the leadership molecule. These roles are related to the performance of individual strategic leadership tasks or combinations of these tasks. As illustrated in the example of Starbucks presented above, there is a tendency for these core roles to combine certain strategic leadership tasks. In addition, more than one person can perform aspects of a given strategic leadership task. As a result, there is typically overlap between the people comprising the leadership molecule, as shown in Figure 12.3.

Vision and Culture Role. One classic core role is the person who combines the "vision" and "culture" tasks. This is most often (but not always) performed by the CEO of a company. Sometimes vision and culture are not performed by the same person. It depends upon their competencies and, to some extent, personality. Nevertheless, the classic role is for a combination of vision and culture to be performed by a CEO.

Operations Role. Another classic core role is "operations." This can be the role of a COO or another executive charged with overseeing day-to-day operations. For example, Howard Behar, who was responsible for the retail stores at Starbucks, was the member of the leadership team responsible for operations, even though he was never COO

Systems Role. The third classic core role is "systems." This involves responsibility for initiating the need for and overseeing the development of various operational and management systems, ranging from budgeting and planning systems to human resource management and logistics systems. This role might never even appear on an organizational chart, but it exists in the informal organization and in the leadership molecule. It is sometimes performed by a CFO, because that person tends to think in systems terms. It is also often performed by an SVP of HR, or sometimes others.

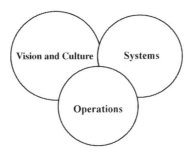

Figure 12.3   The Classic Form of the Leadership Molecule

It refers not necessarily to the designer of systems, but to the person responsible for the oversight of the development of systems.

Our prediction is that a more formal role for the systems leadership function will be emerging during the next few years. The occupant of this role will be someone with a strong technology background and capabilities. For example, in 2015, Starbucks announced that it had hired Kevin Johnson, a former chief executive at Juniper Networks with additional experience at Microsoft, as president.[8] Mr. Johnson was a member of the Board of Directors of Starbucks and had been engaged with the company's digital operations. In his role as president, he oversees digital operations as well as supervising information technology and supply chain operations. This fits Starbucks' view that the company must "shift to online purchasing for everything from food to clothing by finding new digital strategies to help consumers engage with the Starbucks brand and buy its products."

Innovation and Change Role. There does not tend to be a defined role for the innovation and change function of leadership; rather, this tends to be performed by the leadership molecule as a whole.

Structural Variations (Forms) of the Leadership Molecule

As in any molecule in nature, there are various structural forms that can occur in an organization. Although the most common structure is a set of three people comprising the leadership molecule, three is not a magic number. Sometimes it is a team of two, and occasionally a team of four.

Where the molecule consists of two people, this is sometimes referred to as "the Dynamic Duo," a term that owes its origin to the Batman and Robin myth. A good example of this is the duo of Bill Gates and Steve Ballmer of Microsoft. Another example of a duo is Sergey Brin and Larry Page, founders of Google.

Although it is theoretically possible for a leadership molecule to be comprised of five or possibly even more people, we have never observed this in practice. Most often, there is a core team of three people performing the five key strategic leadership tasks. For this reason, we refer to the three-person leadership molecule as the "classic" form or structure.

In the classic form, the first four strategic leadership tasks (vision, culture, operations, and systems) exist as an integrated unit performed by three people. The fifth strategic leadership task—innovation and change—is not shown (as is the case in the classic leadership molecule shown in Figure 12.3) because it is performed by the team as a whole and is not the primary focus of a single individual. The classic example of this form was the H2O molecule at Starbucks.

Another example of this three-person molecule was in operation at Google. Known as "the Troika" (a reference to the three-horse Russian sleigh), it consisted of founders Sergey Brin and Larry Page plus Eric Schmidt, who was hired to be CEO.

In contrast to the leadership molecule as shown in Figure 12.3, there are many times when there are three people who comprise a senior leadership "group" (but not a true team). This is shown schematically in Figure 12.4, where the three people comprise "three atoms in search of a molecule."

When the Three Atoms Are Not a "Molecule." When the three atoms do not come together as a molecule, there can be a significant impact on the organization's effectiveness, and organizational success can be suboptimal. The lack of a molecule can contribute to significant conflict—not

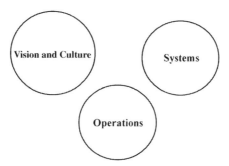

Figure 12.4   Three Leadership Atoms in Search of a Molecule

only among the people comprising the senior leadership team but also among people throughout the organization as a whole. As a result of the lack of alignment among the three large "organizational gorillas," people tend to be cautious. They do not want to cross swords or offend any of the senior leadership team, so they tend to keep quiet and proceed with caution. This obviously results in less innovation throughout the organization. It also tends to result in political behavior or "organizational tribes" (silos).

There also tends to be a culture of "you stay out of my territory, and I will stay out of yours." This leads to a lack of coordination and cooperation. It also leads to a lack of communication across the organization. People will resist change because of the danger of "crossfire" among the organizational gorillas. These symptoms are each problems in themselves. However, they are also symptoms of an underlying systemic problem—the lack of a cohesive leadership molecule.

We have observed several examples of this phenomenon in practice. In one instance, the chairman and CFO were aligned, and the CEO was the odd man out. He was eventually squeezed out of the organization. In another instance, the founder and CEO was isolated from his two most senior leaders, the COO and CFO. The latter were termed the "Ghost and the Darkness" by members of the organization, aptly named after the two man-eating lions of Tsavo, Kenya, that were celebrated in the film of the same name.[9]

A Complete Leadership Molecule

We believe that to be optimally effective, a leadership molecule must include people who perform all of the five key leadership tasks or functions. However, a molecule can exist where some but not all of the five key leadership task are performed. There can be a two-person unit that performs some, but not all of the key leadership tasks. For example, Apple Computer (now Apple) was founded by Steve Jobs and Steve Wozniak. Steve Jobs was the visionary and cultural leader, while Wozniak was the developer of the technology for the Apple Computer. He was neither an operations nor a systems person. As a result, Apple did not have a true or complete leadership molecule. This is termed an "incomplete molecule" and is not likely to be optimally effective. Similarly, at Ben and Jerry's (the ice cream company) both Ben and Jerry were entrepreneurial types who were visionaries and "product guys" and did not possess the other skills required to form a complete leadership molecule.

Design of a Leadership Molecule

What causes a "leadership molecule" to exist? Does it occur by accident, or can it be created by design? What happens to organizational success when a previously existing leadership molecule disintegrates?

A leadership molecule can occur as a natural by-product of day-to-day operations as well as by design. Managers understand that they should be a "team." As they work together, a true team can emerge. This means that the group thinks of itself as a team and that it has defined but overlapping roles corresponding to the five core roles of the leadership molecule.

Leadership molecules can also be created by design. This involves (1) defining the core roles (as described above), (2) selecting individuals to occupy or perform those roles, and (3) developing a true molecule. The first two are analytic steps. The third is a process of creating a true team from a collection of individuals. This was the process (described above) that was used at Starbucks.

Empirical Support for the Leadership Molecule Model

Recent empirical research has supported the existence of the leadership molecule and its positive impact on organizational performance.[10] Specifically, the purpose was to (1) test whether the five hypothesized strategic leadership tasks actually exist as independent variables or "leadership factors", and (2) the extent to which the presence or absence of a leadership molecule impacts organizational development and, in turn, performance.

The test was executed as part of an executive coaching program conducted for 40 very senior leaders of companies in China. All 40 participants were enrolled in the "CEO Leadership Program" at the Cheung Kong Graduate School of Business, Beijing and Shanghai, China. The intent of the program was to enhance the leadership skills of the participants.

Participants were asked to complete two surveys: (1) the Leadership Profile Survey and (2) the Organizational Effectiveness Survey. The Leadership Profile survey instrument was designed specifically for this project to assess each leader's perception of the *requirements* of their roles in terms of the five key strategic leadership tasks, as well as their perceived *capabilities* with respect to effectively performing these tasks. The Organizational Effectiveness Survey (discussed in Chapter 2) had previously been shown to have predictive validity as a leading indicator of financial performance.[11]

Using cluster analysis, the research confirmed the existence of these five strategic leadership tasks in managing entrepreneurial organizations. In addition, the research also confirmed the hypothesized relationship between the existence of a leadership molecule and organizational effectiveness. Specifically, a regression analysis indicated that there was a statistically significant relationship between the existence of the leadership molecule and the measures of organizational effectiveness. It was significant at the 0.001 level! Stated differently, this indicates that the existence of the leadership molecule is related to organizational effectiveness, which, in turn, is a driver of financial performance. There was also a significant negative relationship between the leadership molecule and the severity of growing pains in rapidly growing entrepreneurial businesses. Specifically, where a molecule existed growing pains were less severe than where a molecule did not exist.

The Leadership Molecule at Different Stages of Growth

Previous sections of this chapter presented the basic concept of the leadership molecule and identified the key strategic leadership tasks that need to be performed by members of the molecule. This section discusses how the leadership molecule can or should differ at each of the stages of organizational growth.

Stage I: New Venture

During the first stage of growth, there is not likely to be a leadership molecule. During this stage, a single strong leader tends to perform all five strategic leadership tasks by himself or herself, unless the firm is founded by more than one person. In circumstances where a company is founded by more than one person, there is sometimes a predetermined division of labor that approximates a leadership molecule. However, it also happens that when there are two (or even sometimes more) people involved, they will not necessarily comprise a true or "complete" leadership molecule, as cited in the examples of Apple and Ben and Jerry's described above.

Stage II: The Expansion Stage

As the organization evolves in the expansion stage, there still tends not to be a true leadership molecule. Companies in Stage II will not typically have the resources required to hire people with the differentiated skills required, and it will still tend to be managed as a one-person band. As the company grows in size, the need for a leadership molecule will increase. It is theoretically possible for a classic three-person molecule to exist at Stage II, but not likely. It is more likely that there will be a two-person molecule, with a CEO performing the core function of vision and culture management, and a partner performing operations. Systems will be basic and possibly shared by the leadership molecule duo, or possibly will be the handled by a financial person.

Stage III: The Professionalization Stage

By the time the organization reaches Stage III, the molecule is increasingly necessary, but possibly not in existence. At this point, the company will have the need and the resources to recruit and hire the people required to create a true leadership molecule. The people added should complement the skills and focus of the entrepreneurial founder. It should be noted that the need and the resources available to create the molecule will be less in the early phases of Stage III than in the later phases.

By mid-Stage III (or about $50 million in revenues), the organization is likely to have a COO focused on operations with the CEO focused on vision and culture. The third person in the molecule at this point can be either a CFO or an HR person. It should be noted that while the classic form of the molecule is a CEO focused on vision and culture, and a COO focused on operations, and someone else focused on systems, the functions can be rearranged differently.

Stage IV: The Consolidation Stage

By the time an organization reaches Stage IV, the leadership molecule ought to be in place. Most likely it will be a three-person molecule in the classic form. However, if the leadership molecule does not exist by Stage IV, the organization is not likely to be growing and developing optimally.

The existence of a molecule at Stage IV is one of the secrets to the success of high-performing entrepreneurial companies like Starbucks. In addition, our published empirical research has shown that there is a statistically significant relationship between the existence of a leadership molecule and the extent to which a company has developed the appropriate systems, processes, and so on to meet current and anticipated needs.[12]

By Stage IV, it is also possible to have a four-person leadership molecule. This is likely to be the classic three-person molecule plus a fourth person who performs special functions, such as acquisitions or special projects. This is where an organization might differentiate between the two versions of the molecule with nicknames such as "the Gang of Three" and "the Gang of Four."

Stage V: Diversification

By Stage V, a molecule should now exist at the corporate level, and be roughly similar to Stage IV. However, molecules should also be forming at the divisional levels, as well. It must be noted that occasionally (quite rarely) a molecule does not appear to exist at Stage V. If it does not exist, there are likely to be significant growing pains.

One area of the world where we have observed a lack of a leadership molecule at Stage V is Asia, and in particular China. Traditionally, China is a place where there is typically a strong individual (male or female) who is "emperor" of the business, surrounded by "helpers." Although there are some exceptions, there is typically one true decision maker, not a leadership group. Even in Japan, where there is often the surface appearance of group decision making, the reality is that of a "kabuki dance," an activity or event that is designed to create the appearance of a search for consensus when it is actually a ritualized "dance" of ultimate public submission to the will of the prevailing emperor.

Stage VI: Integration

By Stage VI, molecules are likely to exist at divisional as well as the corporate level. For example, at Berkshire Hathaway, there is a corporate molecule of Warren Buffett and Charles Munger. Where molecules do not exist at either the corporate or divisional levels, an organization is not likely to function optimally.

Stage VII: Decline and Revitalization

At Stage VII, it is doubtful that a single "heroic" leader might well be able to perform all of the strategic leadership functions required by revitalization. The reversal of decline will typically require a leadership team. One leader might be the "face" and "voice" of a team, but undoubtedly a team will be required. When Howard Schultz returned as CEO to Starbucks, he quickly put a team together. In a personal communication during his visit to UCLA to receive the John Wooden Global Leadership Award, he told Eric Flamholtz that he tried to hire Howard Behar and Orin Smith to come back to help him (thus recreating their leadership molecule); but they had retired and were not willing to return.

Implications of the Leadership Molecule for Building Successful Organizations

During the early stages of organizational growth, a single "heroic" leader may well be able to perform all of the strategic leadership tasks. However, as the company grows in size, the need for a leadership molecule will increase. Further, where this molecule has existed and then "disintegrates" (e.g., Starbucks), the company's fortunes are likely to decline, sometimes precipitously. The short-term decline at Starbucks during 2007 can be attributed to the disintegration of their original leadership molecule, consisting of Howard Schultz, Howard Behar, and Orin Smith.

The molecule model of leadership also has implications for executives, boards, and venture capitalists. The first is that executives who comprise a company's senior leadership need to ensure that they are individually and collectively performing the five key strategic leadership tasks. However, at present, people do not think in terms of this construct since it is not developed in the literature. A comprehensive search of the literature indicates that this concept does not exist and is novel.

Since boards, executives, venture capitalists, and others do not think about company leadership in the way we are suggesting here, the creation of a true leadership molecule occurs currently only by chance or accident alone. What is proposed here is that its creation must become a specific organizational objective. When Howard Schultz sought to replace himself and his core team at Starbucks, it is doubtful that he thought in terms of a leadership molecule. He hired Jim Donald, an experienced retail executive from Walmart, who was ultimately fired. The problem was as much Schultz's failure to recognize the need for a leadership molecule as it was a lack of competence by Donald.

Another implication for action is that it is not just a matter of putting together a set of ad hoc individuals to create the molecule; they need to be able to effectively combine—that is, work together—in a manner that supports organizational development. This typically will require some team building—either time for the molecule to gestate naturally or to accelerate its development through coaching and special team-building activities.

The concept of the leadership molecule suggests that boards that are responsible for selecting company CEOs need to focus on the entire executive team—working to ensure that the team possesses the core "atoms"—versus selecting a single individual. Similarly, venture capitalists need to build a top management team capable of successful scale-up of a new venture so that, for example, it becomes Starbucks rather than Coffee Bean and Tea Leaf or any other similar company.

The message can be applied in the real world because it provides a template for building a successful top management team. It identifies the competencies required and the need for the individuals to function as a true team rather than a collection of individuals.

Summary

This chapter has provided a framework for understanding and enhancing leadership effectiveness—to support effective day-to-day operations and to support the organization's long-term development. On a day-to-day basis, effective leadership involves choosing the "best style" (that is, one that fits the situation) and regularly (and effectively) performing five key tasks—setting, communicating, and monitoring performance against goals (goal emphasis); helping people work effectively together (interaction facilitation); ensuring that each direct report has what he or she needs to perform their work (work facilitation); providing effective feedback (supportive behavior); and developing the people on their teams (personnel development). Those at the most senior levels of the organization also need to perform the five tasks of strategic leadership—creating and communicating a vision, managing the organization's culture, overseeing operations, developing and managing organizational systems, and managing innovation and change. As organizations grow, these five key leadership tasks need to be performed by a leadership team, which, to function effectively, needs to become a true molecule.

The ultimate leadership challenge for an organization over its life cycle is to transition from a "lone wolf" leader into a true leadership team. The leadership "pack" (or leadership molecule) is stronger than any individual leader. This chapter deals with the concept of a leadership molecule, what it means, and how it can be developed. The existence of a leadership molecule in an organization is a hidden success factor and a valuable intangible asset.

Notes

1. This conceptualization is a slight modification of the four-factor theory of leadership proposed in David G. Bowers and Stanley E. Seashore, "Predicting Organizational Effectiveness with a Four-Factor Theory of Leadership," *Administrative Science Quarterly* 11, no. 2 (September 1966): 238–263. The four factors that Bowers and Seashore identified are goal emphasis, work facilitation, interaction facilitation, and support. In this chapter, we have subdivided the factor originally labeled "support" into two dimensions: supportive behavior and personnel development.

2. Eric Flamholtz and Yvonne Randle, *Corporate Culture: The Ultimate Strategic Asset* (Stanford, CA: Stanford University Press, 2011), 207.

3. Randall W. Forsyth, "A Bad Week for Hillary and Comcast," *Barron's*, April 27, 2015, 6.

4. The first reference to the notion of a leadership molecule was cited in Eric G. Flamholtz and Yvonne Randle, *Leading Strategic Change* (New York: Cambridge University Press, 2008), 60–62.

5. There have been a few prior studies dealing with the notion of shared leadership as an alternative to the conventional model of the single leader. See Craig L. Pearce and Jay A. Conger (editors), *Shared Leadership* (Thousand Oaks, CA: Sage Publications, 2003) for prior studies. For further discussion, see also David A. Heenan and Warren Bennis, *Co-Leaders* (New York: John Wiley & Sons, 1999).

6. The actual team consisted of Howard Schultz, CEO; Howard Behar, SVP retail operations; and Orin Smith, CFO.

7. The term "The Troika" was used at Google to refer to founders Sergey Brin, Larry Page, and Eric Schmidt, who was hired to be CEO.

8. Ilan Brat, "Starbucks Picks a President from Technology Industry," *The Wall Street Journal*, January 23, 2015, B5.

9. The 1996 film starring Michael Douglas and Val Kilmer released by Paramount Pictures, was titled "The Ghost and the Darkness," based upon the book by John Henry Patterson, *The Man-Eaters of Tsavo* (New York: Macmillan and Company, 1907). Colonel Patterson was a British military engineer engaged to build a bridge at Tsavo, Kenya.

10. Eric Flamholtz and Rangapriya Kannan-Narasimhan, "Examining the Leadership Molecule: An Empirical Study of Key Leadership Roles in Rapidly Growing Entrepreneurial Businesses," *International Review of Entrepreneurship* 11, no. 2 (2013): 1–22.

11. See Eric G. Flamholtz, "Towards an Integrative Theory of Organizational Success and Failure: Previous Research and Future Issues," *International Journal of Entrepreneurship Education* 1, no. 3 (2002–03): 297–319; and Eric Flamholtz, "Towards Using Organizational Measurements to Assess Corporate Performance," *Journal of Human Resource Costing and Accounting* 13, no. 2 (2009): 105–117.

12. Eric Flamholtz, "The Leadership Molecule Hypothesis: Implications for Entrepreneurial Organizations," *International Review of Entrepreneurship* 9, no. 3 (2011): 1–23.

CHAPTER 13

Building Sustainably Successful Organizations®

The Frameworks, Tools, and Methods in Action

As noted in the Preface, this book is the fifth edition of *Growing Pains*. Since its initial pub-lication in 1986 (under a different title), thousands of organizations around the world (both for-profit and nonprofit) have applied the managerial paradigms, methods, and related tools (intellectual content) that we present. Some of these companies have invited us to work with them to implement the intellectual content of this book. As a result, we have had the opportunity to obtain intimate knowledge about how our concepts, methods, and tools have and are being applied in practice. Some of the companies with which we have participated in such applications have already been cited throughout the book, including Starbucks, PowerBar, Simon Property Group, and Guangzhou Construction.

This chapter presents some additional examples of companies that have applied the intellectual content of previous editions of *Growing Pains*. These examples are organizations where either one or both of the authors have been personally involved in the application or where one of our affiliates has been involved.[1] As previously noted, the authors have a firm (founded in 1978) that applies our methodology throughout the world. We have also developed a network of global affiliates whom we have licensed, trained, and certified to deliver our methodology. Where the applications discussed were conducted by affiliates, this is noted.

Our primary purpose is to share insights with you that will help facilitate the application of the intellectual content presented in this book to your own organization. We will describe what was done and, to the extent possible, the results. We focus upon companies from Stages III to VI because that is primarily where the concepts, frameworks, methods, and tools have the greatest impact, and those companies have been our focus in our consulting applications. In these examples, we discuss (to the extent feasible) the issues faced at various stages of growth in each company's life cycle.

Organizational Development at American Century Investments

American Century Investments ("American Century") presents a comprehensive case study of a company that has used many of the frameworks, methods, and tools presented in this book to enhance its capabilities and continue its success.

Founded as Twentieth Century Investors in 1958, American Century is a highly successful, rapidly growing investment management company. American Century's founder, Jim Stowers, Jr., started his first fund in 1958 with $100,000 in assets and 24 shareholders.

By 1988, American Century had grown to more than $6 billion in assets under management. Because the firm charged a 1% management fee, its revenues were in the range of $60 million. The company had excellent people, products, and day-to-day operational systems. It also had a strong culture that emphasized "doing the right thing." However, the company lacked well-developed management systems. It did not have a formal strategic planning process. There was no budgeting process. In addition, although there were several individuals with strong managerial skills, there was no process for management development.

During 1988, Stowers and the senior management team recognized that the firm had outgrown its informal management processes, and they embarked on a process of making the transition to a professionally managed firm (that is, moving to Stage III). Eric Flamholtz was engaged as the consultant to facilitate the process of organizational development and help the firm (and its management team) make this transition.

The first step was the introduction of a strategic planning process. This process applied the concepts and methodology described in Chapter 6. It focused not only on the firm's competitive strategy, but on goals for the development of American Century's organizational infrastructure as well. In this sense, the planning process was designed to facilitate strategic organizational development—not simply traditional strategic planning.

At first, planning meetings were difficult. There were some contentious issues to be resolved (such as whether the firm's funds would continue their no-minimum-investment policy). In addition, there were problems in the decision-making and meeting-management processes of the firm. The senior management group was accustomed to meetings where virtually anything might be discussed: major issues, personnel problems, how much to spend on holiday decorations. In addition, these discussions tended not to remain focused.

The new strategic planning process focused on some of the core strategic planning issues discussed in Chapter 6 such as "What business are we in?" and "What do we want to become in the long term?" Planning was also done for specific objectives and goals in each area of the Pyramid of Organizational Development (markets, products, resources, operational systems, management systems, and culture) and financial results. In addition, the firm's management team met on a quarterly basis to review performance against goals and to refine the plan to better reflect changing market and organizational conditions.

Another aspect of the professionalization process was the introduction of a management development program. The objective of the program was to help managers develop the advanced management capabilities required to take the firm to the next level successfully. The management development program used at American Century is very similar to the approach described in Chapter 9.

Results

American Century's management team remained committed to the changes in the systems that they had begun making in 1988. By 1996, the results of their efforts were evident. The management team had improved their capabilities with respect to managing the much larger firm that American Century had become. Over this time, in fact, the company had grown to managing more than $50 billion in assets.

The ultimate test of a company is its ability to enhance shareholder value. In 1996, J. P. Morgan acquired a 45% interest in American Century for $800 million. This implied a market value of $2 billion for the firm. It was a testament to the progress made since the program began. Today, the company manages a family of mutual funds (both equity and fixed income), employs more than 2,000 people, and has more than $150 billion in assets under management.

Organizational Development at Infogix

This section presents a comprehensive case study of Infogix, a company that has used most, if not all of the tools and methods presented in this book to successfully manage organizational transitions while simultaneously defining a new market space. The firm was originally founded in 1982 as Unitech Systems, and was renamed Infogix in 2005 to represent its focus on what its founder, Madhavan Nayar termed "the information integrity space."

Infogix is a multinational data controls and analytics software (technology) firm that helps businesses manage, analyze, and monitor their data for business operations. The company is based in the United States with headquarters in Naperville, Illinois. Infogix primarily serves clients in the financial services, health care, property and casualty insurance, telecommunications, and retail industries. It began as a one-man consulting firm with a focus on automated data controls software. Madhavan Nayar, who received degrees from The Indian Institute of Technology and the Illinois Institute of Technology, pioneered the concept of "information integrity" software solutions at a time when few had realized the need for specifically designed systems that helped customer organizations ensure the validity and accuracy of information.

In 1982, Nayar developed his first software product in partnership with Blue Cross Blue Shield of Illinois. During the next two decades, the company successfully developed a number of other products through similar strategic customer partnerships. From its founding through 1992, the firm grew rapidly, reaching $12 million in revenue and a cumulative annual growth rate of 65% for the first 10 years.

During this period, the company evolved from a one-person consultancy to approximately 80 people, with a president, executive vice president and COO, and several vice presidents with directors, managers, and employees below them. Early in 1992, the company was reorganized into six operating groups, each headed by a group leader; the position of executive vice president and COO was eliminated. Throughout this stage, Unitech adopted a series of conventional business practices for a growing entrepreneurial company. This included the way the company was structured, as well as the way people were compensated.

Beginning in 1993, the company initiated a series of changes, many of which (viewed in retrospect) may have impeded its continued rapid growth but contributed to organizational learning. That year, the company decided to decentralize sales management by hiring area sales managers in North America and establishing a separate international sales group. By the end of 1993, however, no area sales managers had been hired, and there was no revenue growth. Also in 1993, the senior leaders of the company learned about the management philosophy of W. Edwards Deming and, after several months of study and deliberation, decided to adopt it. The decision was implemented by holding a weekend retreat for influential team members from different groups in the company and then a two-day off-site meeting for everyone.

The implications of the Deming philosophy were radical and extensive. The classic approach to performance management was abandoned. Specifically, quotas and other numerical objectives linked to incentives and compensation were discontinued. Formal performance evaluations and salary adjustments tied to performance evaluation were also eliminated. All processes within the company were to be mapped, defined, and improved. The reaction of most of the team members of the company was skeptical, if not overtly negative. Many of the star salespeople left the company, and over the next 18 months, almost 95% of the salesforce left the firm. Employee turnover exceeded 50% in 1994. An employee survey revealed that employee morale was far below industry average. In spite of these problems, by 1998, Unitech had grown to be a $20 million company, with offices in North America and Western Europe.

The Catalyst for Strategic Change

In March 1999, Nayar attended a Forbes Presidents' Conference, where he heard Eric Flamholtz make a presentation about building successful organizations. The approach made sense to Nayar, and in late 1999 he invited Flamholtz and his team (including Yvonne Randle) to work with the company and apply the framework and methodology described in this book.

Organizational Transformation at Infogix

The organizational development process began with a series of interviews with selected group and unit leaders during the summer of 1999 to provide the consulting team with an understanding of the company and its development issues. The next step was a strategic planning retreat, attended by all leaders in early December. The retreat was intended to introduce all of Unitech's leadership team to the Pyramid of Organizational Development framework described in Chapter 2 and take the company to the next level of planning capability.

Planning had always been a part of Unitech's culture. The company has always had a well-established strategic planning function, and the leaders of the operating groups have always prided themselves on their strategic capabilities. However, the growth and diversification experienced during the 1990s demanded a new scale of planning altogether. Management needed to address not only new industry segments and larger operating units but increased organizational complexity as well. The strong entrepreneurial spirit and autonomy that had long been part of Unitech's culture now presented a management challenge. Although at one time that spirit had helped to create a vibrant, nimble operating environment, it had also resulted in counterproductive organizational silos that resisted cooperation.

Strategic Planning to Support the Organization's Transformation

At the retreat, a management planning simulation revealed internal areas that needed to be strengthened. The group discovered that its current planning was too grandiose to be feasible and chose to adopt the approach to strategic planning described in Chapter 6 of this book. Unitech already had a formal strategy and planning process, but the objective of the new process was to improve the existing planning system and ensure that it became a way of life. The strategic planning process was intended as a tool for the alignment of the various units of the company.

Unitech also adopted the pyramid framework as the platform for the development of their strategic plan. This template was used to assess the strengths and areas for further development. Based on this analysis, it was clear that Unitech was relatively strong at the bottom four levels of the pyramid but needed further development at the top two levels, which include management systems and culture management. It also required some redefinition or fine-tuning of the business foundation to fit Nayar's vision.

Developing the New Business Foundation. The first step was to develop the new Unitech "business foundation"—a business definition, a strategic vision, and a core strategy. (At Infogix, the term *strategic vision* is used rather than the term *strategic mission*, as used in Chapter 6.) By the end of the initial planning workshop, the leadership team had defined their business as that of "helping Global 2000 organizations improve the quality of their information through information integrity systems." This meant that the organization was going to evolve from one that was currently focused on selected tools for automated balancing of accounts and statements to a total information integrity solutions business. This meant, in turn, that Unitech would create a new market space: the "information integrity space." An intermediate step was for Unitech to evolve from its current product portfolio to a business with automated controls, services, and processes for information integrity. This was to happen through three phases.

Once the new business definition and strategic vision for the organization had been established, there was a need to complete the plan to the level of developing goals and assigning priorities and roles.

Developing Priority Objectives. Although there can be many objectives in any strategic plan, a well-thought-out set of priority objectives (key objectives that receive the most management

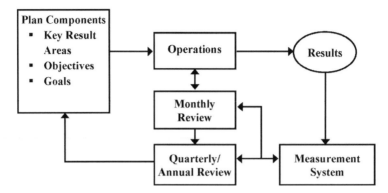

Figure 13.1   The Infogix Performance Optimization System

focus) is one of the secret ingredients that were important to make planning work at Infogix. These objectives are derived from the strategic vision and related key result areas.

Role of Performance Optimization in the Transformation Process

Another strategic innovation at Infogix (formerly Unitech Systems) was the creation of a unique "performance optimization system" (see Figure 13.1) that combined with the planning system to create an overall strategic management system. In brief, this system was introduced to strengthen the levels of accountability and enhance the execution of the strategic plan. *Performance optimization* is a term coined at Infogix to refer to an innovative alternative to the conventional notion of performance management, as discussed next.

The conventional model of performance management typically links the planning system and measurement of results with the evaluation and reward systems within the organization (see Chapter 8). One thing that is very different about the concept of performance optimization at Infogix, as compared with the conventional concept of performance management, is that it does *not* link performance directly to rewards. This is for philosophical reasons. Consistent with the Deming philosophy, Nayar believed strongly that rewards ought to be based on *company* rather than individual performance.

Use of Measurement in Planning and Performance Optimization

One of the key contributors to the ultimate success of Infogix's strategic innovation with planning and performance optimization was the development of detailed measurements for objectives. As a CPA once said, "What gets measured gets counted!" This means that the things that get measured are the ones that are most important in influencing people's behavior in organizations.

At Infogix, a great deal of time and care was put into the development of measurements of goals. In part, this is because Infogix is a highly analytical and process-oriented organization. The company takes great care to be precise with its use of terminology and the need for operational definitions. The net result was that Infogix created a detailed set of measurements for every objective and goal. These measurements are critical to making the plan operational and specific. They are a significant strength of its performance optimization system.

Results of the Transformation to Professional Management at Infogix

As a result of this organizational development process, a number of significant benefits (both tangible and intangible) were realized. First, there was an increased clarity and focus on the vision of the company that did not exist to the same extent in the past. One of the company's growing pains was that a relatively large number of people did not understand where the company was headed. However, people now understood that Infogix was in the information integrity business. This broader concept had replaced the more narrow focus on specific information integrity products, such as automated balancing and controls. People now also understood that its long-term vision was to help create and, ideally, to dominate the information integrity space. This provided a big-picture context for short-term decisions and actions.

Another benefit of the strategic planning and performance optimization process is greater focus on priority objectives. In a business, there are countless things to deal with; the Infogix strategic organizational development plan provided focus by clearly identifying the priority objectives.

A third benefit relates to the productivity and accountability of people. The specificity of the measurements increased the extent to which people were accountable for specific results rather than just vague responsibilities. The plan provided a tool to monitor overall performance of the company (as well as that of specific business units) on a systematic basis.

Longer-Term Results

What were the results of this organizational development process at Infogix? In brief, the enterprise value of the firm increased. Specifically, on June 1, 2012, Infogix announced that H.I.G. Capital, a global private equity firm, had "recapitalized" the business[2] and The Dow Jones *Private Equity and Venture Capital* reported that "H.I.G. Buys Infogix in $75M–$150M Deal."[3] In addition, on January 10, 2014, both Infogix and H.I.G. publicly announced a completed acquisition of Agilis International, Inc., a provider of predictive customer and operational analytics.

Organizational Development at Bell-Carter Foods

In 1993, Bell-Carter Foods, Inc. ("Bell-Carter") was experiencing a number of growing pains brought about by the company's own growth. After reading the 1990 edition of *Growing Pains*, Tim Carter, then CEO, contacted us for assistance in helping his company implement the processes and tools presented in this book—including leadership development (including coaching), strategic planning, performance management, and culture management—to support Bell-Carter's continued development.[4] As of 2015, these systems were still very much alive and being used by Tim T. Carter (Tim's son, who became CEO in 2012) and his executive team. This case describes the process that Bell-Carter used to put these systems in place and how they have been used to support and promote the company's transitions since 1993.

Company Background

What was to become Bell-Carter Foods, Inc. was founded as Bell-Carter Olive Company by brothers Arthur and Henry Bell in 1912. The company began as an olive grower, but in 1930 the firm began packing, distributing, and marketing their own olives under the Bell's brand. The olive market expanded throughout the 1950s and 1960s into grocery stores, delicatessens, and supermarkets.

In the mid-1960s, the third generation of the family joined the business with the entry of brothers Tim (in 1964) and Jud (in 1965) Carter. When Tim and Jud entered the company, sales were only $1 million, but the market was continuing to expand. The company continued with modest growth.

By the time Tim and Jud took over the day-to-day management of the company from their father in 1973 (with Tim becoming CEO and managing the sales and administrative side of the business and Jud becoming president and focusing on production and developing and maintaining grower relationships), the company's sales had grown to $6 million. It was at this time that the olive industry began to experience some problems, along with consolidation. In 1958, there were 27 U.S. olive companies, but by the early 1970s, only a few large players remained. Bell-Carter Olives made a critical decision at this time: to focus on private-label versus branded olives. The Carter brothers determined that the margins in branded olives were so thin that the best they could do was to break even. Private label held greater opportunities.

The company continued to grow on the strength of its dominance in the private-label market. In 1990, the company acquired the operating assets of Olives, Inc., and in 1992 the firm acquired Lindsay Olive Company, one of the most recognized brands of olives in the United States, when it came up for sale. At the time of the Lindsay acquisition, Bell-Carter's revenues were $53 million. One year later, they had grown to $85 million.

Recognizing the Need to Further Develop the Company's Infrastructure

The senior leadership team had been making significant progress in developing the day-to-day operating systems needed to support continued growth and had a strong functional culture. They recognized, however, that their management systems were significantly underdeveloped.

Our work with Bell-Carter began with a seminar that introduced the senior leadership team to the Pyramid of Organizational Development and growing pains. One output of this seminar was a decision to embark on a formal process of leadership development. A second was to further develop and enhance the effectiveness of the company's planning process. The leadership team also identified additional opportunities to enhance the company's effectiveness through management systems and culture, as described below.

Leadership Development

The first area of focus for Bell-Carter was leadership development—that is, on helping the managers and leaders at all levels develop the skills needed to make the transition from a "doer" to a manager/leader and to effectively execute their roles. This involved designing and delivering a four-day group-based leadership development program and providing one-on-one coaching.

Group-Based Leadership Development Program. Using the principles and approach described in Chapter 9, we designed and delivered a four-day leadership development program first to the members of the senior leadership team (including Tim and Jud) and next to several groups of middle managers and first-line supervisors. The program focused on the management role, time management, delegation, operational leadership effectiveness (described in Chapter 12), and decision making. It was conducted over a period of six months—with the first two days of the program being delivered back-to-back, the third day occurring approximately two months later, and the final day of the program occurring two months following day three. This schedule provided participants with the opportunity to apply concepts they were learning in the program and then report back on their progress. As a part of the program, each participant was asked to complete a series of four questionnaires designed to assess their effectiveness related to the three dimensions of management/leadership effectiveness, delegation, time management, and operational leadership effectiveness. By the end of 1994, all managers at all levels of Bell-Carter had completed this program.

In early 1995, Bell-Carter decided to implement a second phase of the program (for all those who had completed Phase I). This program consisted of two days of training, held approximately four months apart. The first day of this training focused on reinforcing the concepts presented during Phase I (through exercises and case studies) along with presenting tools and techniques for improving communication effectiveness. The second day of this program focused on control systems and corporate culture management (higher-level skills that Bell-Carter felt could be beneficial to all levels of management). Again, all three levels of management participated in the same program. They also continued to offer the original program to new managers who had joined the company or who had been promoted. These programs continued through 1997.

In 1997, it was decided that Bell-Carter would develop the capability to conduct what had now become its own management development program using internal trainers. Two internal trainers were selected and participated in a "train-the-trainer" program, conducted by Yvonne Randle. The company would now have the ability to continue providing (and adapting) the leadership development program to meet its needs.

One-on-One Coaching. In early 1994, Tim and Jud began an executive coaching program. The program was not started because of a crisis or because of problems between them or between them and their management team. Instead, the brothers believed that they could benefit personally from working with an adviser on specific development issues—personal and organizational—that they faced. This was very consistent with the family culture that, "We can always be better than we already are."

This program began with the coaching team (Yvonne Randle and Eric Flamholtz) soliciting feedback from Tim's and Jud's direct reports about what they could do to improve their effectiveness as the leaders of a company that would soon have revenues of $100 million. Those providing feedback were very candid (there was little fear of reprisals), with some people saying, "You can put my name on that if you want." It was clear that the partnership and trust that Tim and Jud had had between them throughout their lives had been embraced by those with whom they worked.

Using the information provided by the members of their team, Tim and Jud worked with their respective coaches to create their own personal development plans. These plans identified what each needed to focus on in the coaching process. In addition, each coaching session included not only one-on-one work but also a segment in which the two brothers worked together with their coaches on identifying and developing strategies for resolving organizational development issues (which they would then take back to the larger team). Over the next several years, other members of Bell-Carter's management team would participate in a similar coaching process.

Strategic Planning

Also in 1994, Bell-Carter initiated a strategic planning process using the approach described in Chapter 6. The strategic planning process focused on where the company was—one of four major competitors in the ripe black olive business—and where the company needed to be to continue its success into the future. In developing the strategic plan, Tim and Jud were just two of the company's 10-person planning team. Although the Carters might have operated under the principle that "all votes are equal but some are more equal than others," that is not how they approached most decisions. Instead, they worked as a part of the team to decide where the company would go and how it would get there.

There was, however, a key point in the first (1994) strategic planning retreat where Tim chose to use his extra vote (and for good reason). The team had decided that Bell-Carter should be in the business of "processing and selling ripe, green-olive, and olive-related products to our customers." After a half-day of debate, Tim arrived the next morning and said, in effect, "We can't do everything and be everything to everyone. We need to focus. I am recommending that we limit our business definition to ripe and green olives." The entire team was given the opportunity to challenge the concept, but in the end, they all agreed that this was the right way to go.

With the business concept finalized, the team worked together to establish the company's strategic mission, which included becoming (within three years) a $100 million company, becoming a leader in the ripe olive category, and establishing a presence in the green olive business. The team identified key ingredients to successfully achieving this mission and assigned responsibility for managing each to a team member. For example, the plant manager, working with Jud, was in charge of working toward becoming the "best cost producer." The vice president of sales and marketing was given responsibility for profitability—increasing sales and growing market share. The CFO was responsible for tracking financial performance. Each team member had a role, and the team trusted (much as Jud and Tim trusted each other) that the job would be done. All team members also knew, however, that they could go to anyone for help when needed.

The team established quarterly review meetings to discuss progress against the plan. Each team member was asked to report on the progress made against his or her goals. If problems were identified, the entire team provided help in solving them. The plan was *their* plan, not just Tim's and Jud's. There was no question among the team about who Bell-Carter was, where it was headed, how it was going to get there, and who was responsible for what. Unlike other companies, Tim, Jud, and their management team were on the same page, and when potential problems arose, the team worked them out together.

By 1999, Bell-Carter's strategic planning process also included departmental plans—which were structured in the same manner as the company's overall plan (that is, each clearly identified the department's business definition, strategic mission, objectives, and goals). The head of each department provided quarterly updates on the progress his or her team was making against goals as a part of the overall company strategic plan review.

Performance Management Systems

Bell-Carter established an annual strategic planning calendar that identified key dates in the plan review process. Approximately two weeks before each plan review meeting, goal owners were asked to submit written updates to Tim's executive assistant on progress being made against goals. She then recorded them in the status column of the company's corporate scorecard (which included objectives and related goals organized by key result area). This document was then used as the basis for discussion by the leadership team during the plan review meeting. Tim's assistant attended these meetings to record additional output and updates, and to prepare meeting minutes. Following the meeting, all team members received an updated written plan that could be used as their guidebook for the next quarter.

At the individual level, Bell-Carter designed and implemented (although the full implementation was not completed until much later) a performance management system based on individual key result areas. During the leadership development program, participants were introduced to the key result area–(KRA)-based role description methodology. One deliverable from this program, in fact, was the development of KRA-based role descriptions for all management and leadership positions. This methodology was then used to develop role descriptions for all positions at Bell-Carter.

Both the time utilization targets and specific, measurable, time-dated goals (which were linked to each position's key result areas) were used as the basis for evaluating individual performance. Each individual worked with his or her manager to create specific, measurable, time-dated goals for the key result areas in his or her position's role description, which in turn supported the achievement of the company's (or departments') annual goals. These goals were used as the basis for evaluating performance. The use of this process, which has been refined over the years, continues today. Bell-Carter, in fact, now uses a computer-based program—designed and managed by their head of IT—to support the implementation of this process.

Culture Management

Bell-Carter has always had a strong, functional culture that emphasizes teamwork (being part of the "family"), customer service, and fun. Although for many years Bell-Carter did not have a formal culture or values statement, everyone—those inside and those outside of the company—understood the culture. As part of their overall organizational development effort, Bell-Carter's senior leadership team decided in 1996 that it would be appropriate to assess the effectiveness of the company's culture and asked us to assist.

The culture assessment involved collecting information through one-on-one interviews with a representative sample of employees and through a workshop with the company's senior leadership team. A culture survey was also developed and administered to all Bell-Carter employees to collect their input on the extent to which people were embracing and behaving in ways consistent with the company's desired culture (as defined in the items included on the survey). Not surprisingly, the information collected suggested that the culture at Bell-Carter was, for the most part, positive and functional.

As positive as the results were, the leadership team identified some areas that could be focused upon for improvement. Specific objectives and goals were developed to address these areas and were included in the company's strategic plan (to support the key result area of culture management). In addition, a task force led by the company's CFO was formed to promote Bell-Carter's culture throughout the company. As one way of tracking process, the culture survey was readministered in 1998. Results suggested that progress had been made in addressing the issues identified.

As Tim and Jud were approaching retirement in 2005 and as they had been very much a part of the company's culture management process, the leadership team decided that it was time to try to document the company's values. During the company's 2006 strategic planning meeting, Tim and Jud were asked to define (on paper) the elements of the culture. Among other things, they identified the following:

- *"Work hard, but have fun."* Tim said that when he and Jud first joined the company, things were tough, and they both agreed that if they weren't having fun, they should find something else to do.
- *"B's or better."* Bell-Carter doesn't need everyone to be an "A" player. Tim and Jud jokingly said that they would have been gone a long time ago if this were the case. But Bell-Carter does need people who are "above average" and who are willing to work to improve.
- *Common sense and good judgment.* The implicit message in this statement was, "We trust you to base your decisions and actions on what will be best for you and the team."

Since Tim and Jud's official retirement, the formal statement of Bell-Carter's values has been somewhat refined, but the basic themes remain virtually unchanged. Culture management continues to be focused on as a key result area in the context of the company's strategic plan. Tim T. Carter (Tim's son), who became CEO of the company in 2012, and his leadership team are working to ensure that the company's culture continues to support Bell-Carter's success.

The Results

When the organizational development process began in 1993, Bell-Carter was, as noted above, one of four major competitors in the ripe black olive business. By 2000, there were only two ripe black olive companies remaining in the United States and Bell-Carter was one of these companies.

Bell-Carter achieved and then surpassed its 1997 target of $100 million in sales and has continued its success and growth. To support this growth, the company has continued using the systems that were first developed in 1994, refining them as needed to support current operations. Strategic plans are still developed and implemented using the approach described in Chapter 6. In 2012, the company revisited and updated senior leadership team role descriptions. A new director of organizational development (OD) was hired in 2013, and she participated in the train-the-trainer program with Yvonne Randle to understand the concepts and tools included in the original 1994 leadership development program. These concepts and tools were incorporated into "Bell-Carter University"—a leadership development program that was designed and delivered by the director of OD. The director of OD also focused on updating the role descriptions for all positions within the company. The senior leadership revisited and refined (slightly) the online individual performance management tool (as it had become somewhat complicated for managers to use). Finally, Tim T. and his team continue to focus on culture as a strategic asset.

SmileSaver

In the early 1990s, Eric Flamholtz and Yvonne Randle worked with Dr. Chris Kamen, DDS, and his leadership team to identify and address growing pains at SmileSaver[5]—a company he jointly owned (with a partner). Our work included helping Dr. Kamen, his partner, and his leadership team:

- Develop and implement an effective strategic plan and planning process
- Clearly define roles, responsibilities, and an overall structure that would support the achievement of the company's goals
- Enhance their skills and capabilities through leadership development and executive coaching

In the following discussion of the application of growing pains intellectual content, we describe how Dr. Kamen used the methodologies and tools to build SmileSaver into a successful business. The discussion is based upon an interview with Dr. Kamen, several years after work was completed. For the most part, it is stated in his own words.

SmileSaver as a New Venture

While he was still a student at USC's Dental School, it occurred to Chris Kamen that dental students received "essentially no business training to help us manage our practices. We did not have basic information about insurance companies and how to help people afford the dental work they needed."[6]

Chris began talking to dentists who were knowledgeable about these issues in 1976, while he was still two years away from graduation. While he had heard a little bit about insurance companies and HMOs, there was no formal education on these matters in school.

He discovered that most patients could not afford the dental care they needed and wanted. At that time, very few people had dental insurance, and those who did usually worked for very large companies. For people who worked in, or owned, small companies, there were no options.

Based upon this, he decided to start his own dental insurance business with a partner rather than practice dentistry per se. The company he created was called SmileSaver.

SmileSaver's Business Definition. SmileSaver's core business was providing patients to dentists who needed more patients and providing dental coverage to the public who were otherwise unable to get insurance coverage anywhere else. The company contracted with dentists to provide benefits to the patients and charged the patients an annual or monthly premium depending on their plan. Eventually SmileSaver added group coverage, which grew as well. It developed quality-assurance programs and protocols designed to protect the quality of care received by its members, including physical audits of the dental offices and patient records and also had a grievance committee of practicing dentists who would perform peer review if a patient had a grievance and would make a determination about a resolution.

The company began to grow. As Dr. Kamen stated: "Like most entrepreneurs, we thought we could learn and do anything. We felt 'All Knowing' and were quite pleased with ourselves for discovering this niche market that was doing so well."[7]

Growing Pains

As the company grew, it began to experience the classic problems entrepreneurs face when they are successful. As Dr. Kamen stated, "I was a dentist, and my partner was a lab tech. We could grow a company to a certain point because we were clever enough, but, at a certain level, being clever was just not enough. We did not know it at the time, but our company was showing the classic growing pains of a small entrepreneurial company that was trying to graduate to a professionally managed organization. Indeed we learned a lot and became quite skilled at what we did, and the company prospered. But at a certain point, the company began to outgrow us."[8]

Dr. Kamen and his partner were aware of problems developing within the operations of the company. They were aware that something was holding them back from getting to the next level. However, in his words:

> We were not experienced enough at the time to realize that what was holding us back was, in fact, us! We had the ability, but not the knowledge and experience. I learned about a seminar at the UCLA Anderson School of Management called "Growing Pains" by Dr. Eric Flamholtz and Dr. Yvonne Randle. I read the brochure; it outlined the tell-tale signs of "growing pains" a young company needs to recognize and resolve in order to progress to the next level. I realized our company had all the symptoms. I attended the course, read the *Growing Pains* book, and was convinced that Eric and Yvonne understood what it meant to be an entrepreneur. They knew the problems a growing company faces when it reaches critical mass, and what to do to grow the management team into professionals that can take the company to the next level.[9]

I convinced my partner to let me bring Management Systems into the company. After some discussion, he thankfully agreed to retain them, though I don't think he saw the need as clearly as I did at that time. We had many challenges we were facing when we brought Management Systems in. For example, we had the following issues:

1. My partner and I were young and inexperienced at that time and were really entrepreneurs, not professional managers.

2. The business was naively set up as a 50-50 partnership, which inevitably led to ego clashes and disagreements on virtually every issue. The more the company succeeded, the more acute these disagreements became, and "deadlock votes" on important issues became common.

3. Since we weren't professional managers, we only had a rudimentary organizational structure, and it was based more on our own impressions of what we were good at or maybe even just what we liked, and was not based on our actual talents or skills.

4. There were no written procedures for important procedures (no employee manual, no formal organization chart) and little operational coordination between departments within the company, leaving the company extremely "segmented."

5. Employees began to rally around their "boss," and so there became a "camp" for each partner. Employee morale was adversely affected by this.

There were other challenges but these were the most significant.

The SmileSaver Organizational Development Program

There were concrete steps taken and progress made in working with Management Systems. As Dr. Kamen explained:

> First, Eric and Yvonne explained what "growing pains" were. We learned that growing pains were a normal and predictable result of entrepreneurial growth, and that there were effective solutions that could be implemented.
>
> Second, they met individually with my partner and myself and were able to gain the full trust and commitment from each of us in order to have our full and complete cooperation. At this time, things had become so strained between me and my partner that we were barely speaking and we disagreed on almost every issue.
>
> This presented a significant challenge to Eric and Yvonne, but by gaining our trust completely, they were able to provide us with very blunt, very constructive, and much needed analysis of what the issues were in our relationship dynamic. They provided insight on our problems as partners, and what potential solutions could be explored. To their credit, they did not pull any punches and each of us had to hear about areas of our own performance where we were deficient. It is always tough to hear that you are actually the root of the problem in some instances. To our credit, we listened and accepted their comments with trust and admiration. We knew it was hard to hear, but we also knew they were there to help us in this process.
>
> Third, they interviewed the other managers and employees extensively. This resulted in a very accurate picture of what was happening within the organization. We saw what was working, what was not working, and what the most significant challenges were in the organization. We also had some offsite sessions with employees.[10]

An Organizational Development Road Map

Based upon our assessment of the situation at SmileSaver, we prepared a feedback report and a "road map" for the future development of the company. Dr. Kamen states: "In the end, Eric and Yvonne's analysis, looking back on it, was spot-on accurate, timely, and most importantly, provided a 'road map' to the future and a way out of what felt like our present day 'successful quagmire.'"[11]

Dr. Kamen also stated, "Eric, Yvonne, and their team rolled up their sleeves, and worked with us side-by-side to develop organization skills in all the managers. They interviewed everybody, including the two partners and suggested an organizational structure that raised some eyebrows, which was 'skill based' not 'ego based.' The new structure provided important insights into how we could organize responsibilities, reporting structures, and departments. It fostered a new team spirit, and helped enhance our personal skills as partners, and helped employees feel like they wanted to be on the 'company team' and do a good job. Before, employees felt they had to be on one of the partner's teams to feel 'safe.'"[12]

As a result of this organizational development initiative, the entire company was restructured based on talents, skills, and experience. Procedures and systems were put in place. Outside management talent was recruited and hired to broaden the experience of the management and marketing teams. A reporting structure was put in place that specifically dealt with the problem of employees trying to play one partner against the other to curry favor, and it was strictly followed. Marketing plans were developed, and budgets were sharpened and adhered to within the organization.

Most importantly, the two partners were allowed to manage the organizational areas best suited to their skill sets. They were required to relinquish other areas to the other partner if that partner was better able to perform in that capacity.

Results

Within a short period of time, employee morale improved, and the partners were able to work together. The company began to grow, and, just as important, SmileSaver had the operational structure and capacity to handle that growth. The company was humming.

Soon, a very large organization took notice of the growth, profits, and professional management style of the company, and they initiated a business partnership with SmileSaver. Over the next year, they observed how the company operated, and how SmileSaver continued to grow and succeed. As Dr. Kamen stated: "Using what we learned from Eric and Yvonne, we prospered and grew with control systems and planning. Operationally we had the structure and talent to professionally manage the growth we were experiencing. Eventually, this company, a subsidiary of one of the largest financial organizations in the world, acquired our company allowing my partner and I to retire at what was at that time, the very young age of 43."[13]

Organizational Development at Ballistic Cell

This case study of the application of our frameworks, methodologies, and tools is different from the others in this chapter in several important respects. First, it is of a company located in Bulgaria. Second, it is an example of organizational development work facilitated by our Affiliate, Ivailo Iliev, CEO of Forteam, in Bulgaria.[14] Third, it describes a work in progress.

Soon after graduating from his business administration bachelor's program, the founder of Ballistic Cell, Julian Petkov, founded a company with the ambition to create a successful business in the fast-growing industry of information technology. His strategy was to represent best-of-breed technological solutions in the Bulgarian market and develop additional competitive advantages through excellent business analysis, fast and effective integration of new solutions, and impeccable customer service. His initial strategy was to work with public and government organizations.

The analysis of the market in Bulgaria suggested that there was a significant opportunity for his potential clients to finance their technological improvements using available government funding and European Union structural funds. Petkov was quick to act on this opportunity, consulting with his clients on how to effectively obtain funding for their technological improvements. What he learned was integrated into Ballistic Cell's sales process and strategy.

In five years, the company became a leading provider for e-learning solutions and Enterprise Resource Planning (" ERP") systems for public and private universities in Bulgaria. Following his entrepreneurial spirit, Petkov quickly built on this success by expanding the business to other niches such as intelligent transportation systems, legal informational web-based services, contact and support centers, and software development.

By 2014, the company had 45 employees and approximately $8 million (U.S.) in annual turnover. The company had eight active profit centers, operating like separate businesses and at different levels of development. Petkov's desire to work with like-minded people led to him hiring young professionals as department managers. For many of them, their employment at Ballistic Cell was their first experience occupying a managerial position.

The Onset of Growing Pains at Ballistic Cell

By 2014, certain problems at Ballistic Cell were becoming evident to Petkov, and he began to feel that they might prevent him from achieving the growth he aspired to. That same year, his partner in e-learning platforms—a worldwide leader in the field—offered to represent Ballistic Cell in neighboring markets such as Romania and Poland. It was clear to Petkov that he had to drastically improve the operations in Bulgaria to be able to focus on developing a market in Romania and Poland, which were at least five times larger than in Bulgaria.

When Petkov approached Ivailo Iliev (Management Systems' affiliate in Bulgaria), the former shared the following concerns about how the business was operating:

- Nothing was getting done on time or within the budget, unless Petkov was personally involved in managing the task or project.
- Deadlines were often missed, not only internally, but also with clients.
- The company would pay a high salary to an employee who was believed to be a "qualified expert" only to find out in several months that he did not deliver what was expected and had to be fired. Then, in order to deliver the product on time, Petkov had to hire an external consultant to do the job, which resulted in increased expenses and decreased margins.
- All departments were operating as separate companies with little coordination between them; and, as a result, a great deal of time was being wasted. The company had to postpone new projects and initiatives, which resulted in missed business opportunities.
- The overall standard operating procedure in the company at that time was a continuous reactive approach of putting out fire after fire.

Designing the Organizational Development Plan

After an extended interview with Petkov, Ivailo Iliev proposed a solution, consisting of three steps:

1. Conducting an organizational diagnosis and preparing a plan for the strategic development of the organization.
2. Implementing a strategic planning process and creating a strategic plan.
3. Developing and implementing a customized performance management system.

The plan was for Ivailo to work with his U.S. colleagues to design and implement these systems.

Organizational Diagnosis. The organizational development intervention process started with administering Management Systems' Growing Pains Survey (see Chapter 5) and Organizational Effectiveness Survey (see Chapter 2).[15]

Results from the surveys were not surprising. Ballistic Cell was at the professionalization stage of organizational development (see Chapter 3) in terms of its size as measured in revenues. However, the company lacked nearly all the necessary infrastructure for this stage and was also struggling with some of its operational systems. Ballistic Cell had a high overall Growing Pains score (which of course is negative, as low scores on this survey are positive). In addition, five of the classic growing pains were in the red zone and five in the orange zone. The top five (ranked) growing pains (all in the red zone) were:

1. Many people are not aware of what others are doing.
2. There are too few "good" managers.
3. People are spending too much time "putting out fires."
4. People feel that there are not enough hours in the day.
5. People have a lack of understanding of where the company is headed.

The results of the Organizational Effectiveness Survey showed a serious need for improvement in operational and management systems. The discussion of the results with the management team identified the following most urgent organizational development areas:

- The company did not have clear organizational structure.
- Managers lacked many of the necessary skills to manage their departments and profit centers.
- No performance management system was in place.
- There was no systemized approach in recruiting, hiring, and induction of new personnel.
- Operational systems were missing or ineffective in most of the departments.
- No planning system was in place, and no follow-up was done on progress on the company goals.
- The values, which the founder and the first few people employed at Ballistic Cell developed and shared as a way of working, were not followed and demonstrated by the new hires, and this led to culture clashes between new and old hires.

Organizational Development Initiatives. The next step in the organizational development process was to conduct a two-day workshop to train the Ballistic Cell managers in the Pyramid of Organizational Development framework (see Chapter 2). During this workshop, results of the two surveys were presented, and initial steps were taken toward positive change.

As a result of this first workshop, the management team initiated several immediate changes. They established communication and coordination principles to follow within the organization and updated and officially announced an organizational structure, which accurately described the actual division of work and responsibilities in the company. An HR manager was appointed, and systems for recruitment and selection and employee induction were developed and put in place.

Strategic Planning Implementation. In the next phase of the intervention, a strategic plan for the company was developed, using the Management Systems' methodology (see Chapter 6). The management team defined the "business foundation" of the company, which was a key step toward working as part of one company, not eight different businesses. Based on the strategic plan, each department manager developed an operational plan for 2015.

Developing and Implementing Performance Management Systems. The third phase of the project (still in progress at the time this book was completed) was the creation of a performance management system with key result area–based role descriptions and a process of goal setting, monitoring, and evaluation (see Chapter 8).

Results

When interviewed about the effects and benefits of applying Management Systems' methodology of organizational development, company founder and CEO Julian Petkov identified the following results:

- Managers now are clear about where the company is going and what they need to achieve in order to contribute to our success. We all have a common understanding of the company strategy and competitive advantages, which focuses the work of the management team and makes decision making easier.

- Operational plans and delegated budgets for each of the departments save me time from department managers involving me in operational issues, which used to happen a lot in previous years.

- The new organizational structure and coordination and communication principles helped us increase our effectiveness in terms of faster decision making, being less reactive, and decreasing the frequency of crises.

- We will be able to quickly spot underperformance and take corrective measures, which will decrease the losses caused by expensive personnel not delivering the expected results on time.

Authors' Note

This case illustrates what we have observed in working with companies around the world. The methods and tools presented throughout this book have general applicability regardless of difference in countries and culture.

Organizational Development at GroundSwell

This section describes the application of the frameworks, methods, and tools presented throughout this book at GroundSwell Equity Resources, Inc. ("GroundSwell"). It is useful as a comprehensive, capstone example of application of most, if not all, of the content in this book in an actual organization.

This example of applications is different from the others described above in two respects: (1) it involves the application at a business partner of the authors, and (2) it is written in a very personal, candid way, and is full of realistic detail. As a result, we believe it will resonate and be meaningful to readers—especially CEOs.

About this Case Application

As described below in his own words, Bob Bennett, founder and CEO of GroundSwell, engaged the authors' firm, Management Systems, to work with two of his portfolio companies. The case below was written by Bob Bennett, and edited by the authors. It describes the arc of his activities and thinking, which led to a joint venture to apply the frameworks, methods, and tools presented throughout this book at GroundSwell (his own firm) as a precursor to their application in GroundSwell's portfolio companies as a private equity investor. Here is Bennett's story of the application in his own voice. It should be noted that in describing his experiences, he has disguised the names of people and companies to preserve their anonymity.

The Beginning Celebration

It was my first "acquisition closing dinner" as a freshly minted MBA at a private equity firm with one of the largest and most successful institutional investors in the United States. The dinner was in a private dining room of an exclusive, high-end steakhouse in Midtown New York City. Francis, head of our firm, welcomed the highly educated and esteemed individuals from our deal team to the closing dinner: members of a top-tier law firm, an accountant from a big four firm, as well as our other co-investors. I realized that each attendee had degrees and pedigrees most of us can only dream about, like a Harvard undergraduate, business and law degree all on one resume.

The Name of the Game: Close the Deal!

Once we were all seated, Francis rose from his seat and said, "Thanks, everyone, for coming tonight. After nearly six months of a true team effort, we finally closed 'Project Stepping Stone' this afternoon." After acknowledging a number of key individuals for their particular contributions to the close (including the heads of our strategy, legal, accounting, regulatory and environmental due diligence teams), he looked at our partner CEO, Courtney Smith, who would be running our newly acquired platform waste services company (known internally as "Garbage Company") starting the next morning, and toasted him on his role in closing this major investment for our firm. Then Francis took a very long pause, with a slightly sheepish grin on his face, and again raised his crystal champagne glass to Courtney and said: "Now let's hope the lights come on in the morning tomorrow and our trucks start!"

Everyone cheered, laughed, and congratulated Courtney and one another; but something just didn't feel quite right, at least for me, and I didn't then know why. Psychologists call the feeling "cognitive dissonance." It is generally a signal that is not to be ignored.

Initially, I thought Francis was just kidding about "let's hope the lights come on in the morning tomorrow and our trucks start"; but as both the dinner and as my career continued, I realized Francis wasn't kidding at all. Yes, he was joking about the lights and the trucks starting; but he wasn't kidding about actually executing on our strategy for Project Stepping Stone. Our strategy called for significant changes in nearly every part of the company, from sales to finance, and I truly wondered how it was all going to get done.

How were all of our strategic and financial plans that looked so compelling and "tight" on paper (when presented to our investment committee) going to actually get completed at Project Stepping Stone? None of the attendees at our dinner were actually going to spend much time at the company. Everyone was at least a few hours away by air from corporate headquarters of Garbage Company in St. Louis. Our co-investors were from Houston, our law firm had offices on Park Avenue in New York City, and our strategy firm was headquartered on Boylston Street in Boston—and we were in downtown San Diego. Also, I knew (from working on the deal) that Courtney Smith was never in the office. Initially when we started working on the investment, I used to call Courtney at the office and literally each time got his voice mail. This was before cell phones were ubiquitous. Courtney typically would call me back in a few minutes and patiently answer my list of diligence or strategy questions.

Closing But No "Clothes"

In the classic Hans Christian Andersen fairy tale, an Emperor purchases a new suit of clothes created by two weavers who tell him that "these clothes are invisible to those who are unfit for their positions, stupid, or incompetent." When the Emperor parades before his subjects in his new clothes, no one dares to say that he doesn't see any suit of clothes—until a child cries out: "But the emperor isn't wearing anything at all!" In short, from my perspective, the private dinner the night of my first closing was full of "emperors with no clothes." "Emperors," who if challenged on how to actually run a business, had limited or virtually no ability to do so! They had impeccable credentials and might be great at strategy, financial analysis, legal contracts, and/or have billions of dollars in their war chest bank accounts; but not one of the attendees knew *how to actually run a business.*

The stated intent of making a solid investment and executing on our strategic plan wasn't the primary objective—it was just closing the deal. Closing the deal meant there was a nice payday for everyone involved; regardless of whether anyone in the room had the actual knowledge or skill to successfully execute on our investment thesis. Also, if we had a nice exit five years later, that was great, too; but it wasn't the real focus. "Closing the deal" was the name of the game.

How did I know these emperors did not have the right stuff to run a business? They told me! After each of the Emperors had a few drinks, I asked them (either during dinner or after in the bar) if they had ever run a business or thought they could. None of them ever had; and after a couple of vodka tonics and glasses of wine, each individual confidentially acknowledged they probably could not do it at all, let alone do it well. I really couldn't believe what I was hearing over and over, but it had the ring of truth.

How did Courtney get to run our acquisition? Courtney had mastered "EBITDA speak," the arcane language, or jargon, of investment banking and private equity. If you knew this virtually secret language (as I discovered), and you had had a decent level of measurable financial success at an operating level that you could lay claim to, the typical private equity professional was your avid fan and potential partner. Francis in particular had been enamored with Courtney's EBITDA speak. If you didn't have facility with this arcane language, *no matter how successful you had been as a business operator*, it was nearly impossible to even get a second meeting with Francis. Courtney spoke "EBITDA speak" very well; but that was about it.

As I progressed in my career (from associate to vice president to starting my own firm), I found that the entire institutional private equity world was well ensconced with emperors with limited to no clothes. In fairness, some admitted they were "without clothes." When I pressed many of the successful operators I met, I determined most (if not all) had basically gotten lucky. They did not have a repeatable system to build a business. Typically, they had been fortunate enough to rise to a senior management position in a company in an industry that was growing rapidly at the time, and as the saying goes, a rising tide lifts all ships. When these same "Captains" encountered difficult times (either from a deteriorating economy or a new competitive entrant in their industry), more often than not, they foundered like a ship hitting a rocky shoal.

I was left with a nagging question: If the emperors actually knew how to actually run a business, could they be even *more successful*? If they could rationalize making investments in a company with a management team that they had fully vetted, and if they could also truly evaluate that team's execution of that plan and provide real assistance when needed, could they significantly increase the probability of a successful investment while dramatically decreasing the risk of failure? I refer to this anticipated differential conceptually as "incremental alpha." My belief is there isn't an institutional investor in the marketplace that would not be eager to find a repeatable source of alpha returns in their portfolio.

Dissonance: A Catalyst to Change

The next morning after the dinner, while shaving in a luxury Park Avenue hotel room, I was thinking about the execution of the plans of the deal we had closed. I personally had done most, if not all, of the financial analysis to acquire Project Stepping Stone, as well as being part of much of the legal and accounting due diligence and contract negotiations. I also played a role in determining Project Stepping Stone's strategy for the next five years. However, I had no clue if Garbage Company was going to have enough cash in the bank in the next days, weeks, or months to make payroll or, indeed, keep the lights on, or how we were actually going to execute on our strategy. I could model out our working capital needs for all those new hires in a detailed Excel spreadsheet that hummed the 100 iterations for each of my formulas delivering dramatically different financial results with the stroke of a computer F9 button, but I had no idea how to actually execute those differences in the real world.

That morning, I decided to learn to fully understand what makes businesses truly tick, how things really got done—independent of all the fancy strategy, PowerPoint presentations, and Excel spreadsheets that drove the investment of billions of dollars in private equity each year. So the search began for the answer to some fundamental but key questions: How do businesses really work and how are successful businesses built?

In Search of The Rosetta Stone of Business

I began a search for what might be termed "the Rosetta stone of business," the key to unlocking the secrets or lessons of how to make a business really work. However, as I dove into one article or book after another—all espousing a system or solution for business success—I realized that I wasn't finding anything close to a turnkey set of concepts or ideas that consistently could lead to repeated business success. There was no holistic, integrated language. I found terms and concepts that made sense and worked, but only in a limited context or situation. They were either too tactical or too strategic and visionary. The more I searched, the more I felt lost looking for a framework that connected conceptual strategy to operational execution.

Similarly, as I both read about and met successful investors and CEOs, I concluded that *not one* had a generic and repeatable system for business growth and success. Some CEOs certainly sounded like they had a repeatable process, but no one had formalized them into a repeatable set of concepts, terms, or systems. They each had their own story, their own cookbook, their own "system" of how to do it; but I just could not believe that the same system that worked for Walmart, McDonald's, Zappos, or Google would work generically for all companies. What I found was more of a "book of the month club" mentality. Each month or quarter or year, a new framework or method or tool that promised much and in most cases delivered something, but never as much as they promised or what the customer testimonials claimed. If you visit my office, you will see all the books and articles I have read cover-to-cover (at least twice) to ensure I was not missing a concept or nuance.

Eureka!: I Found Growing Pains

At last, Eureka! I came across an article written by Eric Flamholtz.[16] This article went on to discuss the nature of Flamholtz's holistic framework, how it had been validated through empirical research, and had been proven to work in actual organizational applications to contribute to financial success. Unlike the balanced scorecard, it was both strategic and operational.[17] It even called out operational targets and goals as an individual aspect of its model. As I read the article, I was impressed by the level of academic rigor and validation that had gone into developing the content. In simple language, Flamholtz effectively outlined his Pyramid of Organizational Development ("pyramid") in detail and then synthesized and summarized the entire article in one diagram. In that one pyramid he included all the strategic determinants of financial success a company needed to address, based on his extensive academic research. End of discussion.

He had created the big picture framework as well as the details of how to scale a business, in one diagram. I had found what I had been searching for over the last couple of years. I read the article, underlined it, took notes, went on line and found other articles and books Eric had published, and came across Eric's and Yvonne Randle's now classic book, *Growing Pains*. Needless to say, I bought *Growing Pains* from Amazon *for next day delivery*, which significantly added to the cost of the already quite expensive hardcopy book.

Upon receipt of *Growing Pains*, I read and I read and I read! The content was music to my ears. It was logical, and it had compelling case studies of real-life application of both success and failure. Within a couple weeks, I called Eric's company Management Systems (MS) and hired them to train my team. It was intended as a "pilot" engagement, like road-testing a car. I wanted to be sure it was the real deal before we started implementing their tools and frameworks in all of my portfolio companies. I certainly had drunk the Kool-Aid. As I was to learn over time, I was also giving myself the opportunity to truly look in the mirror and try to create sustainable success both personally and organizationally.

The next sections provide my observations on what I learned from the concepts, frameworks, and methods in this book as we applied them to GroundSwell's own business. I will also discuss the surprises encountered in learning to apply this set of ideas and tools.

Applying the Leadership Development Three-Factor Approach

We began the application of the concepts, frameworks, and methods in *Growing Pains* at GroundSwell with leadership development for our core team. My team was initially trained on the management and leadership development content.[18] I think of this content as the fundamental individual building blocks of managerial and leadership success. Without these basic skills, I would argue it is almost impossible for a management team to execute a strategic plan. Countless articles have been written about why strategic planning fails most of the time, and I would argue that if the team accountable for executing a given strategic plan doesn't have the critical core management and leadership skills described in *Growing Pains* (see Chapter 9), it is almost inevitable that the team will fail.

The three-factor approach described in Chapter 9 roughly corresponds to the skills an individual and/or management team collectively needs to successfully transition a company from an entrepreneurially managed business to a professionally managed firm. Just as there are six stages of organizational development above the base of a business foundation in the Pyramid of Organizational Development, there are five skill levels in the Pyramid of Management and Leadership Development above a base of a "role concept."

The Role Concept. As described in Chapter 9, role concept is about behavior, and a role description is a tool for influencing behavior. It's easy to mistake the foundational notion of a role concept as just another name for a job description; but that assumption is invalid. The efficiency and effectiveness of a job description pales in comparison to the notion of a role concept (operationalized in a key result area-based role description). Job descriptions typically have a list of all the activities the job requires as well as maybe who that hire will report to and sometimes the overarching goals for the position, but that is about it. The role description includes those details as well, but it is more clear and specific—which makes it both a powerful recruiting and hiring tool as well as an essential management tool.

In order to explain how we used this concept, I need to indicate how a role description differs from a typical job description. There are four fundamental differences. First, the role description has a clear individual mission statement that supports the overall mission of the company. An individual looking at a role description will know specifically how and why that role supports the overall mission of the company. Second, it has a clear definition of the level and detail of decision-making authority a specific role has. Not only does a role description define who the role reports to, it clearly defines the level and type of decisions that role is responsible for making.

Third, a role description has clear time allocation for each major goal, or key result area, that ties directly to the overall mission of the company as well as the individual mission of the role. For example, assume you are developing a role description for your sales team and have just installed Salesforce.com as a lead tracking system. A job description can mention using Salesforce.com to track leads, but it will not specify that only 5% of your team's time should be spent populating Salesforce. The role description gets into that level of detail. When we have applied this tool, I have found few if any surprises from new employees on issues like time utilization. On the contrary, I have made hiring errors because I was not clear up front in writing about how much of an individual's time was going to be spent where and on what task.

Finally, a role description is fundamentally different from a job description because it is the basis for the individual performance management system. In brief, in addition to identifying time utilizations for each key result area, SMART goals (see Chapter 6) are set for each key result area (in the context of the individual performance management system). An individual knows specifically up front what results are expected versus having just a list of activities they are supposed to participate in. For example, using only a job description, your new marketing hire won't know to allocate 90% of his or her time to purchasing Google AdWords and analyzing the results of those investments, nor would they know you are expecting 3,000 new leads at an average cost of $75 per lead and a conversion rate of 5.7%. They would with the KRA-based role descriptions and the SMART goals you created for them.

At GroundSwell, I have had great success using role descriptions as part of our annual strategic planning to fully engage each individual on my team in the strategic planning process. They can clearly see how the allocation of their time and expected results directly enables our strategic mission. The role description is the formal tool that enables buy-in by each individual at both a highly tactical and strategic level simultaneously. As mentioned above, it has also functioned as a powerful part of our recruiting process both at GroundSwell and in our portfolio companies. I have had many potential hires literally take themselves out of the running for a position when they saw the specific level of accountability they would be held to both from a time and results perspective. We are looking to hire and work with individuals that are empowered by (versus run from) that level of clarity.

Core Skills. The second part of the three-factor approach to management and leadership development includes a set of core skills (at the first level in the Pyramid of Management and Leadership Development) required to manage at any level, ranging from a first-line manager to a CEO. Obviously the specifics of a line manager's core decisions, delegation, or time management activities will vary drastically from a CEO's, but the same core fundamental skills are required in either case.

According to Eric's research, those core skills include delegation, SMART goals, operational leadership, decision making, and time management. Intellectually, this content was not a problem for my team. Nor has it been troublesome in our various portfolio companies. It is not particularly difficult to remember what a SMART goal stands for or what the four steps of delegation are (as defined in Management Systems' approach to delegation); however, I was genuinely shocked at how something so apparently simple in concept could actually be so difficult to execute. Even in a "safe" role-play scenario in a classroom environment in front of peers, the difficulty encountered was shocking. For example, as we each role-played the delegation process, I was amazed how hard it was to use the four steps effectively—even in a simple simulated task like planning the upcoming holiday party. Also, based on the candid feedback received during our delegation training, I realized those four seemingly simple steps were not as simple as they seemed. As simple as it sounds, just telling someone to do something more often doesn't work on even the most elementary goals. While I was often frustrated with my team, and sometimes thought they were incompetent, I thought maybe it was me and my skills deficiency (and not them) that was the root of the problem. Sure, I could model out the cash flows of a successful investment as well as put together a compelling PowerPoint outlining the strategic logic behind a successful investment; but it wasn't so easy to delegate that same financial analysis or PowerPoint presentation to someone else to do, and now I knew why.

As I learned, the more time I took up front in the delegation process, the more effective were my team members' results. It was actually somewhat magical for me at first. Now I almost always get what I want done when I delegate. Most (if not all) of the time when I don't get the result I expect, it's because I *didn't effectively follow the four-step process*. Realistically it required six months of consistent and conscious practice on my part to get to that level of proficiency.

Although I didn't know it at the time, based on Eric's experience, he estimates that only about 10% of the population is inherently good at managing others without some real formal training and even more practice. However, most if not all individuals can make significant improvements if they work to develop the core skills identified in *Growing Pains*. Perhaps that was why delegation was so difficult for me to master. Even though I had an undergraduate degree from Dartmouth and an MBA from UCLA's Anderson School, I wasn't part of the 10% of inherently good managers out there. However, in order to accomplish my personal and business goals, I realized I had to bite those kinds of bullets and learn to do well at what was not natural for me to do. I am sincerely glad I have done so.

After finally "mastering" delegation, we began our time management training! The first drill was to track our time for two weeks. How difficult could that be? We were given a simple spreadsheet that had us input the four to five key result areas we wanted to track (such as sales, strategy development, product development, etc.) and then track where we actually spent our time. First, it was much more difficult than I ever would have imagined to actually track the time I was spending on different activities. I found it necessary to record my time at least three times a day: once late morning, once around lunch or mid-afternoon, and once at the end of the day. If I missed even one of the three time-tracking recording periods, unless I had been on a call or in a meeting for the entire period, often I couldn't remember what I had spent my time on, even during the same day. Then, to try remembering what you did a day later or even two—it's almost impossible.

Once we completed this training, I made it a requirement internally for our people to track their time three times a day, unless they were traveling. This practice has paid huge dividends in a number of ways. Within a few weeks of tracking my time regularly, I realized I was often spending 35% or more of my time on purely administrative tasks: getting more ink for my printer, making travel plans, getting my mail. I didn't think I needed an assistant until I tracked my time. I have had an assistant ever since.

Now I regularly spend somewhere around 7–10% of my time doing purely administrative tasks. I still review payables and incoming state and federal tax filings, but that is about it. So at the end of the day, assuming a 50-hour week, I saved somewhere around 20% of my time. And imagine, my part-time assistant usually works around 10 hours a week, somewhere around two to three hours a day. That, in my opinion, is a lot of valuable time saved for anyone running a business.

More importantly, we started looking individually and collectively at where we were *investing* (spending) our time. Before I went through MS's time management training, I used to say, "Where do I spend my time?" Now, more often than not I say, "Where did I, or we, invest our time?" Particularly in light of building our pyramid, we started looking at our budgeted versus actual time spent on our key initiatives. As we tracked our time versus our pyramid key result areas such as products, resources, and operating systems, we found there was a direct correlation between how much time we invested in a key result area (as described in Chapter 6) and the SMART goals we accomplished (or didn't accomplish) in that particular area. It has become an incredibly powerful exercise. We do it quarterly, and it has helped us increase our success rate in completing our goals. Now we have fewer goals and accomplish more of them. We all used to have a large number of personal SMART goals for a month, quarter, or year, and we often didn't accomplish many of them. Now we have fewer and actually accomplish more.

Now when I meet with a management team at a company we are looking to invest in and I ask them to walk me through their top strategic goals for the year, I know we'll pass if they list more than 7 to 10 major goals. Once you fully understand time tracking (particularly at a team level), having a list of 30 strategic goals for a year just isn't realistic, at least for a team of three to five senior managers. I don't care how large the company is. You can and certainly will have more than 7 to 10 action items or tactical SMART goals to accomplish during any given period; but I am talking about strategic goals that take time to decide upon and usually require significant discussions with other parties internally and or externally to clearly define the goal.

Next, we were trained on SMART goals. This is also quite simple in concept—just a five-word acronym to recall. However, through role-playing, I realized I wasn't particularly good at actually creating good SMART goals. After about six months of practice, I realized that when I really followed the SMART process—particularly on key strategic goals such as setting up a new remote server to host our survey software—I miraculously started getting the results I wanted.

Applying Organizational and Management Surveys

Once I felt relatively proficient with the core management skills, we engaged Eric and Yvonne to coach and train us on a variety of other topics. We began by taking their three core surveys: the Growing Pains Survey ("GP"), presented in Chapter 5, the Organizational Effectiveness Survey ("OES") described in Chapter 2, and the Management Effectiveness Survey ("MES") described in Chapter 9. Even though we are a relatively small company, our survey results were crystal clear.

The surveys pointed out problems with great precision and clarity. For example, the MES score placed my capabilities lower than the position I actually held. I was scored as a "senior manager" when I was a "CEO." I had run one of our portfolio companies successfully, and I was on the board of others, which were all doing well, but my scores were lower than they were supposed to be. The same occurred with the rest of my team. Everybody was scored/placed a level or two below where they thought they should be and definitely lower relative to what their respective titles corresponded to. I had thought I was a good board member and investor, and I had a solid investment track record to support my opinion. Perhaps I was, but I could always be better both as a board member and in my ability to assess management teams for their potential to be a solid contributor to our investments. The MES survey told me exactly where I stood developmentally according to the three-factor approach to management and leadership development described in Chapter 9. I definitely knew where I stood now.

The same was true for my team and my company. We were basically a start-up with a new vision for private equity, and we definitely had some real holes in our strategy, as well as in the products, resources, and operating systems we would need to get us to where we wanted to go. All those issues showed up with incredible accuracy in Management Systems' OES survey. Yet no one from MS had ever interviewed anyone at GS! It was all done via the surveys. If you really want to know where you or your company stands on an absolute basis, you really owe it to yourself and company to take Management Systems' surveys.[19]

Assessing and Managing GroundSwell's Culture

I still remember the coaching session where Eric suggested that even though we were a small company, we should think about assessing our culture through his custom culture surveys. However, wasn't culture on the top of the pyramid and therefore only for really large companies? Yes, that is where you would focus your time when you're over $100 million in revenue, but his frameworks are integrated, interdependent, and holistic, so culture matters even for the small company. Even though, according to the stages of growth (described in Chapters 3 and 4) there is a time and place to focus on each aspect of the pyramid, you must know that all aspects are in play all the time, no matter what the size or stage of the company.

By this time I had learned to very much trust his recommendations. I also read Eric's published peer-reviewed empirical research on culture, noting that culture can contribute nearly 50% of a company's EBIT. Once I heard that, how could I not focus on culture?

As you know from reading Chapter 10, the overall concept of culture is comprised of three basic components: values, beliefs, and norms. Those are the basic building blocks of the *Growing Pains* culture framework. In addition, Eric has done cultural research and concluded there are five key *dimensions* of culture, which each have values, beliefs and norms.

As we worked through the culture management process described in Chapter 10, the results were impressive on a number of levels. So what specifically did the cultural surveys bring to my attention? We had scored poorly on our process orientation relative to our financial results management. Given my strategic choice to develop our infrastructure prior to scaling our business the last year, I had not been spending time comparing our company-level budget versus actual with the rest of my team, even though we had a budget for each project. Each individual managing a project knew the individual project budget but not the overall budget, and that lack of communication on my part showed up in our financial results management score on the Organizational Effectiveness Survey. It was reflected both on process orientation (a cultural dimension) and financial results management (an organizational development dimension). Based on that specific survey feedback, I immediately started sharing our entire budget with my team versus just the individual projects, and within a few weeks I saw significant positive change in our cultural survey results. I never would have thought such a slight change in my behavior could affect my team's perception of our culture so dramatically.

Applying the Strategic Planning Method

By now, we had been through management and leadership training. We had also taken all of the surveys and had been coached by Eric based on their results. He had kindly and candidly pointed out our opportunities for improvement both in our business foundation and our culture. So what was left for us in terms of Eric's content? The major remaining tools were strategic planning and performance management. We actually applied the methodology of the strategic planning process a bit out of sequence. Our first step was to reexamine and redefine our business foundation.

Assessing Our Business Foundation. One of the areas that Eric and Yvonne told us needed improvement was our business foundation. At the time I was quite reluctant to invest the time and money on our business definition for a number of reasons. I honestly thought we had our business foundation pretty much nailed. We had our mission and vision according to the balanced scorecard methodology—why we exist, as well as where we were going—but Eric prodded me to invest in his coaching on his business foundation concept, and I am very glad he did.

Fundamentally, we had missed a key concept. Who were we? When Eric asked us this question, I was amazed at the variety of answers in our small team. It led to the question, "Who *was* our real customer, and what exactly did we do create value for them?" I thought we would all have the same fundamental answer, but much to my surprise we did not. Some of us thought we are targeting rapidly growing gazelles, the top 1% of growth companies. Others thought the real opportunity was in helping the boiling frogs that had an entire host of issues, even though they weren't aware they were in hot water.

In the end, after literally six months of back and forth debate internally, and extensive discussions with Eric and Yvonne, we came to the agreement that we were open to assisting and investing in any profitable company truly looking to transition from an entrepreneurial business to a professionally managed company. We changed the business definition from the type of business quantified by revenue and/or financial success to an orientation toward change that would effectively pre-qualify businesses that would most likely benefit from all that we had learned from Eric.

Having been through Eric's business foundation process, I can tell you if you're not totally clear on all three aspects of your business foundation, it has an incredible ripple effect in literally everything you do—including what is on your business card, what type of content and word choices you use on your home page, and where you as a leader invest your time each day of each week. Your business foundation affects the norms that you implicitly demonstrate in your culture as well as how you respond to a competitive threat. If you're "just" in the railroad business, you don't see the growth of the airlines as a threat. If you're "just" in the private equity business, you might not consider a set of financially predictive surveys to be a potential due diligence tool because you don't survey businesses, you buy and invest in businesses. Or you might be open to the value of them as a relative and absolute measure of future financial success of a potential investment in a management team and company.

The results of the reassessment of our business foundation are shown below with our current business concept, strategic mission, and core strategy.

Business Definition: GroundSwell is the destination for entrepreneurial owner-managers transitioning their profitable $3–$30 million businesses to professionally managed, sustainably successful entrepreneurial companies. We support them by providing an integrated platform of necessary resources including capital.

Strategic Mission: We will be the partner of choice for owner-managers transitioning their entrepreneurial businesses to professionally managed, sustainably successful entrepreneurial companies. GroundSwell and its four product lines will be profitable independent of investment fund management fees.

Core Strategy: Create incremental alpha by providing a proprietary platform of predictive diagnostics, business scale-up training, hands-on support, and capital—all in one place.

Most strategic planning processes are focused primarily on a company's markets and products with little to no focus on infrastructure, or what is required to achieve the strategic plan. The planning process detailed in Chapter 6 deals with both aspects. We applied this process at GroundSwell.

After a detailed environmental scan of our target customers and competition, we spent the majority of our strategic planning time addressing what was necessary to build our infrastructure. This process requires you to have one or two priority objectives for each of those respective infrastructure areas. No other strategic planning process does that. In effect, it ensures that you are always investing in your infrastructure, the same variables that Eric has validated to lead to financial success. For us, the process forced us to look hard and long at where we were in building our infrastructure. I made the tough choice to focus on infrastructure over investing in new portfolio companies for a period of time given our business definition.

As we worked through the strategic planning process, I realized we needed our infrastructure to be in place before we sought to truly scale our business. We defined ourselves as the destination for owner-mangers looking to transition their profitable entrepreneurial businesses to professionally managed companies. As such, our destination had to be in place before our customers started to arrive. Much like a destination resort, I wanted my "guests" to be comfortable with all the amenities they needed for the duration of their stay. Given our emphasis on quarterly time tracking, I knew we couldn't successfully make both new investments while building out our infrastructure.

At the time we were doing this, I had a number of institutional investors who were prepared to invest in our first fund, but I made the choice not to raise that fund until our infrastructure development was complete. I drank the MS Kool-Aid and have (by design) overinvested in my infrastructure relative to my size. However, while I might have sacrificed the near-term management fees of a fund, I am confident I will provide my investors with alpha returns from their investments in GroundSwell. My vision is that each of our product lines embedded with Eric's content (our surveys, school, and consulting practice, as an integrated deal-sourcing platform) are changing the game in private equity by creating solid investments versus finding them.

Applying the Performance Management Methodology

A key part of the strategic planning process described in this book is the recommended quarterly management reviews of your strategic plan. Given the fact that the strategic planning process includes both product-line and division-level key objectives as well as individual key objectives and goals, this strategic planning process effectively embeds an opportunity for quarterly performance management reviews.

By integrating performance management into strategic planning, and by tying an individual's personal tactical SMART goals to long-term infrastructure-related key result areas, and then by integrating those two seemingly juxtaposed concepts into an individual's quarterly and annual performance reviews that are tied to individual compensation and rewards, this holistic performance management process gives a senior management team the ability to simultaneously look out a telescope and into a microscope in both their business and at their employees.

And therein is the real power of Eric's frameworks and methods. They are integrated and allow you to be visionary and tactical at the same time, both at the organizational and employee level. No other framework does that—not even close.

GroundSwell Summary

So now you have a detailed case study of my personal experience with applying the major concepts, frameworks, methods, and tools comprising *Growing Pains*. Hopefully you will realize, as I have, that Eric and Yvonne's content is like well-aged fine wine or a classic scotch, only getting better with time, as opposed to most (if not all) of the "book of the month" business content in the business marketplace today.

In my view, this content stands alone as the de facto gold standard for assessing and building sustainably successful organizations®. This content is both holistic and tactical, integrated yet independent. It's a set of frameworks and tools. It's a common language you can use to share both high-level strategy and tactical action items with others on your team. When someone says create a SMART goal, everyone can know exactly what that means. The same goes for a well-written and structured business foundation. You don't need to re-create the wheel each time you do something strategic or tactical. You already have the dictionary and the cookbook in one place. It allows you to simultaneously look out at your current business marketplace with the telescopic business foundation concept with a laser focus on the three fundamental "event horizon" questions you must answer for your business. Who are you? How are you different? And where are you going?

Simultaneously, you can peer through the cultural microscope. You can tactically splice the DNA of your corporate culture through custom surveys differentiating your ability to walk your talk according to your stated and desired deepest held beliefs, values, and what you think you do versus what the surveys can tell you that you actually do. And when you don't like what you hear in your cultural splicing, you can systematically eliminate the differences through a systematic and repeatable process.

At GroundSwell, we see this methodology as a vehicle to change the game of private equity investing. We are applying this methodology to create "incremental alpha"—higher returns and lower risk simultaneously. Incremental alpha refers to the differential value that a company creates vis-à-vis its competition.

Based on my experience, you don't need 20 years of training and practice to be proficient with this language and these methods. It will take you some time to truly master it, but as our experience has shown, both in our own business and in our portfolio companies, the impact of its application will occur relatively quickly for all who make a serious attempt to implement it.

Conclusion

This chapter has presented several comprehensive capstone case studies of companies that have used the concepts, frameworks, methods, and tools presented in this book to promote long-term organizational success. Our intent in this book has been to describe these concepts, frameworks, methods, and tools to assist the leaders of companies of all sizes in building sustainably successful organizations®. While the implementation of the systems described in this book requires time, perseverance, and a certain amount of patience, there will be an enormous return on this investment. It is an undertaking worth pursuing.

Notes

1. Our firm, Management Systems, has initiated a global affiliates program where we license, train, and certify other organizational development firms to deliver our methodologies and tools.
2. "H.I.G. Capital Completes Recapitalization of Infogix," *H.I.G. Capital*, June 4, 2012.
3. Michael Wursthorn, "H.I.G. Buys Infogix in $75M-$150M Deal," *Dow Jones Private Equity and Venture Capital*, June 1, 2012.
4. As Tim Carter stated to Eric Flamholtz in requesting that Yvonne Randle lead the engagement: "She is just as good as you are, but she costs less."
5. This case is based upon an interview with Dr. Chris Kamen, published in an article in *MS Perspectives and News* (the monthly newsletter published by Management Systems) September 2014.
6. Ibid.
7. Ibid.
8. Ibid.
9. Ibid.
10. Ibid.
11. Ibid.
12. Ibid.
13. Ibid.
14. Our Global Affiliates business was described in Chapter 4.
15. Management Systems' Survey of organizational Effectiveness (discussed in Chapter 2) is a proprietary instrument. For more information, see www.MGTsystems.com/Tools/Surveys.
16. Eric G. Flamholtz and Zeynpe Aksehirli, "Organizational Success and Failure: An Empirical Test of a Holistic Model," *European Management Journal* 18, no. 5 (2000): 488–498.
17. See R. S. Kaplan and D. P. Norton, "The Balanced Scorecard:—Measures that Drive Performance," *Harvard Business Review*, January-February 1992, 71–79. Also for a detailed discussion of the problems of the version of the balanced scorecard proposed by Kaplan and Norton, see Eric G. Flamholtz, "Putting Validity and Balance into the Balanced Scorecard," *Journal of Human Resource Costing and Accounting* (Autumn 2003): 15–26.
18. See Chapter 9 for a discussion of Management and Leadership Development.
19. These surveys are available commercially. You can find them all online line at www.groundswelldiagnostics.com.

ABOUT THE AUTHORS

Eric G. Flamholtz, PhD

Eric G. Flamholtz is Professor Emeritus of Management at the Anderson Graduate School of Management, University of California at Los Angeles, and president of Management Systems Consulting Corporation, which he founded in 1978.

Flamholtz received his PhD degree in 1969 from the University of Michigan, where he served on the staff of the Institute for Social Research under the direction of Rensis Likert. His doctoral dissertation, "The Theory and Measurement of an Individual's Value to an Organization," was co-winner of the McKinsey Foundation for Management Research Dissertation Award.

Flamholtz has also served on the faculties at Columbia University and the University of Michigan and has been a faculty fellow at Price Waterhouse & Co (now Pricewaterhouse Coopers).

He also served for eight years as a member of the Board of Directors of 99 Cents Only Stores ("NDN"), a NYSE company, where he was Chair of the Compensation and Strategic Planning Committees, before that company was taken private in a transaction in 2012.

He has broad interests in management and has done research on a variety of management topics, ranging from accounting and human resource management to organizational development and strategic planning. Dr. Flamholtz has conducted research projects for the National Science Foundation, the National Association of Accountants, and the U.S. Office of Naval Research.

The author of more than 100 articles and chapters on a variety of management topics, Flamholtz published *Human Resource Accounting: Advances in Concepts, Methods, and Applications* in 1985. He also published *The Inner Game of Management*, co-authored with Yvonne Randle, in 1987, *Effective Management Control: Theory and Practice* in 1996, and *Changing the Game: Organizational Transformations of the First, Second, and Third Kinds,* co-authored with Yvonne Randle, in 1998. He has also published *Corporate Culture: The Ultimate Strategic Asset,* in 2011, and will be publishing a book on successfully managing family businesses in 2016.

As a consultant, Flamholtz has extensive experience with firms ranging from entrepreneurships to members of the New York Stock Exchange and the Fortune 500. He has presented seminars and management development programs for organizations in Australia, Belgium, China, France, Germany, Greece, Kazakhstan, Mexico, the Philippines, Poland, Russia, Sweden, Singapore, and Vietnam, as well as throughout the United States.

In 2007, Eric received the "Distinguished PhD Alumni Award" form the Ross School of Business at the University of Michigan "in recognition of his contributions to and excellence in management and organization." In 2012, he was appointed Honorary Professor at the International Academy of Business, Kazakhstan. In 2014, Flamholtz was one of four people selected to receive a "Distinguished Alumni Award" from Washington University in St. Louis, where he received his MBA.

Yvonne Randle, PhD

Yvonne Randle is Executive Vice President of Management Systems. Over the past 30-plus years, Dr. Randle has helped the leaders of companies (ranging in size from small entrepreneurships to members of the Fortune 500) develop and implement effective strategic plans, create systems for managing their companies' cultures, design and deliver leadership development programs, create and manage effective organizational structures, and implement well-designed performance management systems. Dr. Randle serves as a lecturer at the Anderson School at UCLA.

Her clients have included Amgen, Baskin-Robbins, Bell-Carter Foods, EAS, Emergent BioSolutions, GOJO Industries, Grocery Outlet, Guggenheim Partners, Guilford Pharmaceuticals, Inova Health System, Le Pain Quotidien, LifeScan (a subsidiary of Johnson & Johnson), MannKind Corporation, Infogix, Melvin Simon & Associates (now Simon Property Group), Mövenpick (Switzerland), Navistar, PacifiCare, PowerBar, Princess Cruises, Robbins Brothers, Rose Hills, Pardee Homes (a Weyerhaeuser company), Southern California Edison, Techmer PM, Surgitek (subsidiary of Bristol Meyers), the Kusto Group (Kazakhstan), Tommy Bahama, and Vans.

Yvonne has worked with a number of nonprofit organizations during her tenure with Management Systems. Her nonprofit clients have included Head Start (where she is a nationally recognized resource), Crystal Stairs, Southern California Presbyterian Homes, the American Legion, Pasadena Unified School District, the National Association of Women Business Owners (at the local and national levels), the Los Angeles Junior Chamber of Commerce, Interfaith Family, the Los Angeles Education Foundation, Stanislaus County Child and Family Services Division, Cen-Clear Child Services, Encounter, Footsteps, and Delta Dental of Missouri. Dr. Randle has also presented seminars and workshops for organizations such as TRW, Intel, the American Legion, Hughes Electronics, NAWBO-LA, SHRM, and the *Forbes* Presidents Forum.

Dr. Randle is the co-author of *The Inner Game of Management*, *Changing the Game: Organizational Transformations of the First, Second, and Third Kinds*, *Leading Strategic Change*, and *Corporate Culture: The Ultimate Strategic Asset*. Her co-authored book on successfully managing family businesses will be published in 2016.

INDEX

Page references followed by *fig* indicate an illustrated figure; followed by *t* indicate a table; followed by *e* indicate an exhibit.

Printed and bound by CPI Group (UK) Ltd, Croydon, CR0 4YY

17/04/2025

14658880-0001